Barranco

This photo, taken on the occasion of the visit of the Premier George Price to Barranco in the 1950s, shows the cliff, church, the priest house, the Police Station, and the pier. *(photo courtesy St. Louis University Pope Pius XII Memorial Library)*

Charlotte Lorenzo is the Queen for the 10th Day of September in 1979, two years before Belize's independence, so the Britsh flag. To the left of her is Village Chairman Isobel (Beans) Nolberto. At the far left is Ruben Palacio. *(photo by Joseph O. Palacio)*

Reviews of *Garifuna Continuity in Land: Barranco Settlement and Land Use 1862 to 2000*

This fascinating study gives us more than its title suggests; it is at once a searing portrait of the birth and persistence, against all odds, of a particular Garifuna community; an account of the conflictive relations between that community and the state power, whether colonial or nationalist; and a story about the people who call themselves Garifuna. We learn how they were formed, developed, ravaged by war, forced into exile, and how they rose out of the ashes of military defeat and expulsion from their homeland to preserve themselves triumphantly as a nation across borders imposed by states born after they had settled the lands they delineate.

This is a very close and penetrating study of land tenure and use in and around the village of Barranco, told in such authoritative detail that the authors felt the need to warn more than once that this is not an official publication, making it clear that people seeking to establish claims will need to have recourse to the government's Lands Department. There are 60 tables, 54 figures and 79 pages of appendices, with so much information that one marvels at the amount of dedicated work it took to amass.

For its methodology and trenchant analysis, as well as for the differences displayed in relation to other such studies, this study will become a touchstone for similar studies not only in Belize but in other Caribbean and Third World countries.

—Assad Shoman
Prensa Latina, Havana, Cuba

The Barranco story shows the capacity of the Garinagu to organize themselves firstly and afterwards within the framework of British colonial legislation. With detail, and in almost fastidious manner, *Garifuna Continuity in Land* explores every nook and cranny of the numerous aspects in which land and land tenure are linked together in Barranco from 1860 to the current time period. The exhaustiveness allows the reader to shy away from generalizations and to follow unexplored pathways to explain apparent contradictions and place them as ethnographic discoveries. ... By putting together this book in its own style the authors have brought forward a new manner of writing history, for and on behalf of the Garinagu but more particularly for the Baranguna, while at the same time reaching a public that is interested, knowledgeable or not, academic or not. From such a perspective the book is generously didactic.

—Odile Hoffmann
Institut de Recherche pour le Développement, Université Paris Diderot, France

More Reviews of *Garifuna Continuity in Land: Barranco Settlement and Land Use 1862 to 2000*

The objectives and perspective of the authors are perfectly explained and assumed, and give the book its liberty and originality, as a mix between scientific and personal perspective, historical data and subjective engagement. The book is based both on a deep knowledge of everyday life in Barranco and an incredible recollection of archival documents. It is illustrated by a great number of superb black and white photographs, lots of maps, tables and figures to help the understanding and almost one hundred pages of appendix.

—Elisabeth Cunin
Guest Researcher, *Universidad de Quintana Roo, Chetumal, Mexico*
Institut de Recherche pour le Développement, Université Paris Diderot, France

Up to now we have approached Garifuna territoriality from a generic viewpoint that shows the significance of the localities occupied, the associated family lines, and their articulation with levels of spirituality, among main highlights. From this study by Palacio, Tuttle, and Lumb about land tenure in Barranco, the reader becomes exposed to how such mechanisms function as kinship forming a hinge for tenure and transmission. Furthermore, they use a longitudinal perspective that has never been attempted within the Caribbean in such detail, thereby bringing to light some primary distinctions about kinship."

—Alfonso Arrivillaga Cortes
University of San Carlos, Guatemala

The authors lay out to the reader how our ancestors, faced with the power of a colonial government that refused to recognize their collective rights to land, appeared to conform but managed to maintain an informal system that was consistent with their traditional values, values that were clearly grounded in their spirituality. Maybe a heightened awareness of our status as a cross border nation and this story of how our founding families and their children confronted the challenge of colonial heavy handedness will enable the present day leaders in the Labuga-Peini-Barangu triangle to derive a model of development that will enable us to assert ourselves, demand our space, survive and even thrive in this capitalistic globalized world while remaining true to our traditional values.

—E. Roy Cayetano, Baranguna

More Reviews of *Garifuna Continuity in Land: Barranco Settlement and Land Use 1862 to 2000*

The publication of *Garifuna Continuity in Land: Barranco Settlement and Land Use 1862 to 2000* marks 150 years since the establishment of Barranco Village by Santiago Avilez. What a remarkable way of re-visiting the achievements, struggles, successes, and failures of our Baranguna pioneers under British colonization and 30 years of Belizean independence. This book is highly informative, inspiring and thought-provoking, especially when one analyses, and then realizes where we came from, where we are today, and where we are headed. It is regrettable that we now have road access to our farms, but you can hardly find any farmers, especially young farmers, in Barranco. This book is very timely as it coincides with the 150th anniversary of the village in 2012. It is a must read for all Belizeans, especially Garinagu.

—Sebastian Cayetano, Baranguna
Luba Garifuna Museum

Where are we now in 2011? *Garifuna Continuity in Land* posits this question. I read with interest the efforts of Jose Maria Nunez in Punta Gorda and Macario Blas *et al* in Barranco to secure farm lands for their people. Whereas the leasing of land is a precarious situation, the Lands Department is amenable to land transfers to family and there seems to be significant land ownership by Barangunas around Barranco. Whereas the Toledo District has become the frontier of development in Belize, coupled with the fact that it is deemed to be rich in petroleum reserves, what will Barrangunas do with their land resources? As indicated, this book could serve as our springboard for this dialogue. I encourage every Barranguna to read *Garifuna Continuity in Land*–to know yourself and take your place!

—Evan Cayetano, Baranguna
Inter-American Development Bank

Garifuna Continuity in Land: Barranco Settlement and Land Use 1862 to 2000

Joseph O. Palacio, Carlson J. Tuttle, and Judith R. Lumb

Barranco
November 2011

Front Cover: The top aerial photo is of Barranco (*Courtesy of the Sarstoon Temash Insitute for Indigenous Management*). The bottom photo is of Charlotte Lorenzo as Queen for the 10th of September celebration; to the left of her is Village Chairman Isobel (Beans) Nolberto and on the far left is Ruben Palacio. (*Joseph O. Palacio*)

Back Cover: (*top*) Vickie Nolberto on Barranco pier in 1979; (*bottom left*) Rudy Valencio with a gibnut; (*bottom right*) Augustin Palacio and his wife, Simeona Mejia Palacio. (*all by Joseph O. Palacio*)

Cover design is by Judy Lumb. Unless otherwise indicated, all photos are by Judy Lumb.

Producciones de la Hamaca is dedicated to:
- Celebration and documentation of Belize's rich, diverse cultural heritage,
- Protection and sustainable use of Belize's remarkable natural resources,
- Inspired, creative expression of Belize's spiritual depth.

Contents

List of Tables

List of Figures

Acknowledgements

This book started in Barranco and has returned in finished form back to the village. At various points in its gestation several men, women, and children have given me much help. My natal family consisting of my late father Joseph P. Palacio, step mother Carlota Palacio, brother Theodore J. Palacio, and sister Olivia P. Palacio Avila always made sure that wherever in Belize we happened to be we were only in *Lisurnia* (a Garifuna word meaning "away from one's home community for a period of time") and would return home.

Planting the seeds that would slowly grow to become the book took place during my year's fieldwork in the village as a student at the University of California, Berkeley 1979-1980. Among the many persons who gave of their kindness were Eulalia Arana, Candido Arzu, Crispulo Chimilio, Diega Gabriel, Henry Loredo, Clarence and Dionicia Marin, Myrtle Palacio, Paul Palacio, and Cloutildo Zuniga. During my student years I received valuable advice from Burton Benedict, Nancie Gonzalez, Laura Nader, and Bill Shack.

My invaluable introduction to coastal Central America, the Central American territory of the Garifuna nation, came in 1982-1983 through the efforts of Alfonso Arrivillaga of Guatemala, Carmen Murillo of Costa Rica, David Smith of Panama, and Salvador Suazo of Honduras. As the content of the book gradually evolved from field data to nuggets of scientific information another set of persons gave of their kindness. They include Marti Arana, Peitra Arana, Ana Arzu, Marion Cayetano, Roy Cayetano, and Girvan Morgan. Finally, my co-authors, Judy and Carlson, deserve the highest praise for their selfless sharing. Mabuiga hun sungubai,

—Joseph O. Palacio
Benebu, Barranco

First I wish to thank the ancestors for passing on their wisdom and knowledge that has allowed me to become who I am. I am grateful to Vicki Nolberto for first introducing me to Barranco and sharing her love and enthusiasm for the village and setting my course; to my mother and father-in-law, Lucille Zuniga Valencio and Raymond Valencio for their patience and knowledge in answer the untold number of questions that I have asked them over the past 20-odd years; and to all the other Baranguna who have tolerated my numerous questions.

Thanks to the Chief Lands Officer for allowing me access to the land records in Punta Gorda and Belmopan which was very important in making this work possible; and to Miss Edwards, Mr. Vasquez and Mr. Villafranco of the Punta Gorda Lands Office for opening up the lands records to me and helping me find what I needed. For information on and the picture of Father Jean Genon and the parishes of Punta Gorda and Livingston thanks to D. Butaye, S.J. And Herman Cordemans, S.J. of

Library SJ in Heverlee-Leuven, Belgium and Brigitte Bosset of Archives BME in Brussels, Belgium. Thanks to Nancy Mertz of the Midwest Jesuit Archives in St. Louis, Missiouri, who helped me find material on the earlier church in Barranco and the many pictures pertaining to the village.

I am grateful to E. Roy Cayetano who copied the sacramental records of the Punta Gorda Parish and of Livingston, and made them available to me. These helped immensely in preparing the genealogical history of the members of the Barranco community. Dr. Pietra Arana introduced me to the Archives of Central American in Guatemala City and for her genealogical work which she shared so willing I am grateful. I thank Charles Gibson, Lizet Thompson, Marvin Pook and the rest of the staff at the Belize Archive and Records Service for their help and suggestions in my many visits there. And I am grateful to my two colleagues Dr. Joseph Palalcio and Judy Lumb whose different eyes have forced me to look at data differently and get more out of it. Lastly thanks to Ann Kieffer for her love, support, and encouragement.

—Carlson Tuttle

I, too, am grateful to the ancestors who have guided and supported me throughout the past 17 years since I first set foot in Barranco, and to all the Baranguna who have contributed so much to my life and to this project. Special thanks go out to Vickie Nolberto who brought me back to Barranco, took me in, and cared for me; to Naomi Colon and Lynn Zuniga who have fed me, both physically and spiritually; to Shorty Cayetano whose counsel and friendship has made my life richer and increased my understanding; and to Sebastian and Fabian Cayetano for their enthusiastic willingness to help in any way they can.

Thanks to the staff of the Lands Department for their help in accessing maps and for tolerating my presence among them as I traced Plan 541. Thanks to the staff at the Archives Department for their willing help with whatever materials I requested. I am grateful to Dr. David Miros of the Midwest Jesuit Archives for permission to reprint photos from that collection. We were privileged to receive very helpful, even enthusiatic, reviews of a preliminary copy of this book from Alfonso Arrivillaga Cortes, Evan Cayetano, E. Roy Cayetano, Sebastian Cayetano, Elisabeth Cunin, Odile Hoffmann, and Assad Shoman.

I am grateful to Shirley Young, who has provided a quiet, safe place for me to live and work these past 24 years, and to my family for their loving appreciation of my work. And, finally, I am eternally grateful to my two colleagues on this project, Dr. Joseph Palacio and Carlson Tuttle, for our productive collaboration, many, many hours over the past ten years, which has culminated in this book.

—Judith Rae Lumb
October 15, 2011

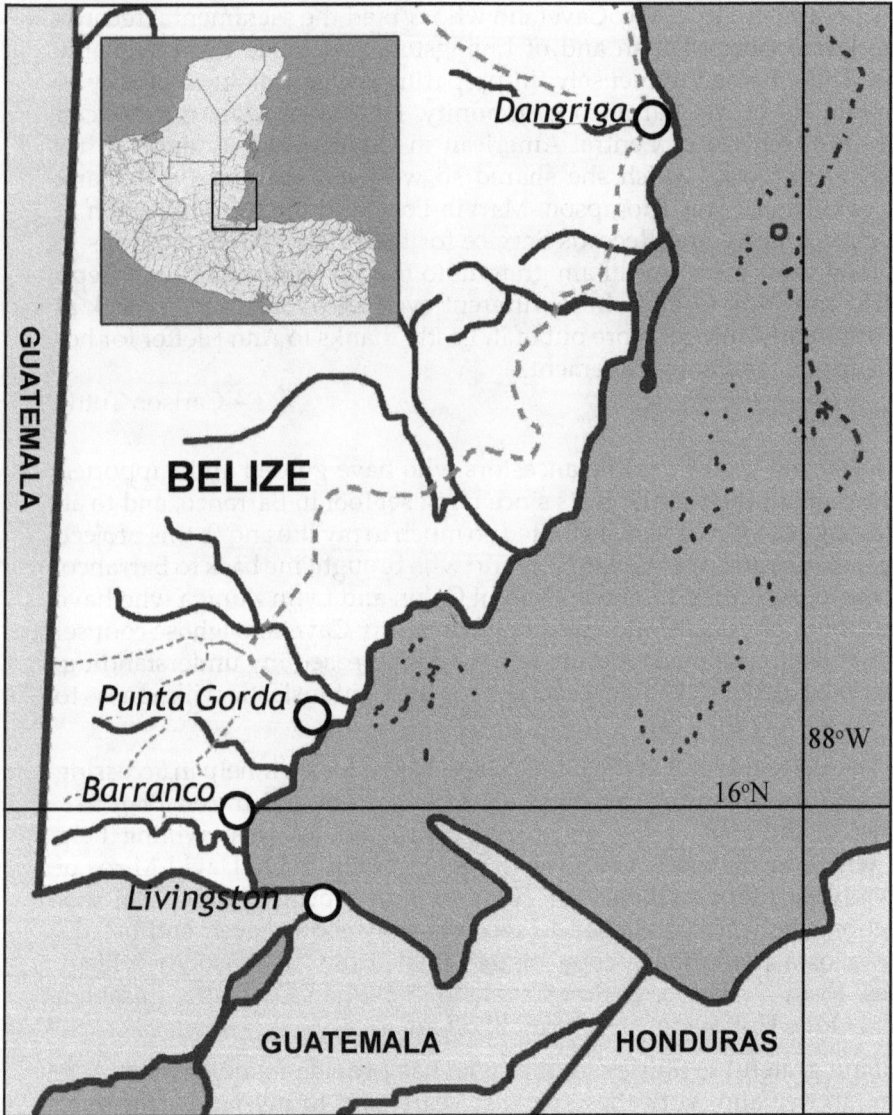

Figure 1.1. Map showing Barranco location in the region.

Chapter One
Introduction

This book is the result of a study of the ownership of land—both house lots and farmlands—in the village of Barranco in southern Belize. We looked at who owns land, how they got it, the use they made of it, and the importance of all of this in the economy and socio-culture of the village, in the context of both the informal system and the formal system as sanctified by colonial and postcolonial governance structures.

It is a collaborative effort among three persons that has been in various stages of implementation for the past thirty years. The one common link among them is unbending love for the village. This book has arisen from different ways of expressing this commitment.

Joseph Orlando Palacio is an anthropologist (Ph.D., University of California at Berkeley). He is deeply interested in the indigenous peoples found within the Central America-Caribbean region. Among the many topics he has investigated has been their livelihood patterns, focusing especially on how they have attempted to live their own lives, while being subjected to forces from the government often in collusion with the private sector and the church. Palacio started collecting genealogies in 1979 when he was doing his dissertation fieldwork in his own village of Barranco. The fact that he is a trained anthropologist and also Garifuna puts him in the unique position of both looking out from the inside and looking in as an academic researcher.

Dr. Palacio was joined in the very engaging task of collecting genealogies by **Carlson John Tuttle**, a North American who married a woman from the village and has lived in Barranco since 1986. Carlson Tuttle is trained in geography and history (B.A. University of Windsor, Windsor, Ontario). He is a craftsperson—basketry—and came to Barranco initially to teach crafts to the women of the village. His way of becoming part of the community was to do research about the Garifuna culture. As a result, he has amassed a comprehensive library of documents on Garifuna language and culture that contains most of the information available on Barranco. He started collecting data on lot ownership in the late 1980s partly out of his concern about the large number of unused, but surveyed, lots and farmlands and their impact on the future development of the village. He bought maps of the village from the Lands Department and saw that there were blanks that he wanted to fill in, so he contacted Dr. Joseph Palacio for help in getting access to the Lands Department records. He has spent many, many hours delving into the records to obtain much of the data upon which this study is based.

The current form of the book took shape when the third author joined the effort, **Judith Rae Lumb**. She is a North American who retired early due to illness from a career in cancer research and graduate education (Ph.D. in Medical Microbiology, Stanford University, Stanford, California) and came to live on Caye Caulker, Belize. She then began a new career in writing, editing, and publishing books and newsletters, mostly about Belize. The launching of a bilingual book in Garifuna and English led her to Barranco in 1994 and she has returned several times each year for various events and projects ever since. Barranco is her spiritual home, the site of a major healing and other inspiring experiences. She brought skills in computer graphics and mapping, together with editing, layout, and design. The stage was set to link the information from genealogies to where persons lived and farmed. Her invaluable work crowned this major effort of collaboration, something that would have been impossible for any one of us separately.

As an interdisciplinary effort this study results from methods derived from anthropology, geography, and history. But rather than a deductive approach this study uses an inductive approach that starts with the people and their community. Unlike an anthropological study that would make generalizations about the Garifuna culture from the study of one village, this study is designed to determine what is unique about Barranco.

As we planned our fieldwork in 2001, we informed appropriate authorities of our intentions and requested permission where necessary. We did so with the Village Council and then Chief Executive Officer in the Ministry of Rural Development, Roy Cayetano, who had oversight of village councils and is himself from Barranco. Both he and the Village Council agreed with our plans, adding that our research could help establish the historical limits of the village lands. We also got the blessing of the National Garifuna Council (NGC) of which the village community is a member.

There were some applied developmental concerns that guided our focus, including the need to establish the historical boundaries of village lands and plan for village development in support of the Village Council and related agencies, such as the Toledo Development Corporation and the Sarstoon Temash Institute for Indigenous Management (SATIIM), which manages the Sarstoon Temash National Park that adjoins the village. For the rest of the Toledo District and the entire nation, the study provides information useful for land policy formation.

Aim of the Study

The primary aim of this study is to do an historical overview of Barranco settlement through the ownership of house lots and farmlands. More particularly, it is to establish patterns of land tenure within the village and surrounding farmlands from 1892 to 2000.

The main focus of this study is on self-settlement by the Garifuna, a nation formed from the blending of African and Native American roots. Settlement occured despite opposition from the land settlement policies of British colonial authorities. The interplay between the formal government land systems and the informal systems of land tenure and use in village lots and farm parcels has affected, and continues to affect, land use and settlement. We document the land of the village of Barranco—its village lots and farmlands, both historically and today. By focusing on this continuity, this study can inspire others to be better able to respond to current problems.

Many aspects are investigated:

- informal versus formal systems,
- location of lots within the village,
- kinship groupings,
- generations of tenure within family groups,
- patterns of transmission of house lots and farmlands,
- whether lands are leased or purchased,
- gender of owners,
- location of farm plots, and
- continuity of occupation and land use for a century and a half.

This study does not consider specific agricultural production systems. We must caution that this book is not an official publication, merely a study of the records executed as accurately as possible, and only up to the year 2000. There are several sources of potential errors— errors in the original records, errors in copying the records, and errors in the construction of the tables for this book. For official up-to-date information on specific lots or farmlands, one must consult the Lands Department.

Sources of Information

We requested permission from the Commissioner of Lands to have access to the extensive records in Belmopan and the Punta Gorda Lands Offices. Table 1.1 lists the sources of information used in this study.

The primary data for this study comes from land transaction records in the Belize Archives and Land Departments, located in Belmopan and Punta Gorda.

Copies of maps were obtained from the Belize Archives and Lands Department, beginning with the first official plan of the village in 1892. Original maps had been drawn in ink and lease or grant information— location, size, and the name of the owner/lessee—was added in pencil on the maps.

Sacramental records of births, baptisms, and marriages were obtained from the office of Monsignor Gabriel Peñate, who heads the Izabal Vicariato in Puerto Barrios, Departmento de Izabal, Guatemala. These records began in 1843 with Santo Tomas, then expanded to include Livingston, and the rest of Izabal. Census records for 1821 in Trujillo, Honduras, also included information about people whose descendents resided in Barranco.

Barranco St. Joseph Roman Catholic Church is part of the Punta Gorda Parish, so sacramental records on baptism, confirmation, and marriage were obtained from the St. Peter Clavier Church in Punta Gorda. Church records start in 1860. Most of the early records were the original handwritten Latin and Spanish entries by the priests. The pages are very fragile, which discouraged any handling at all, but they have now been photographed.

Birth, marriage, and death records were available from the government registry in the Belize Archives Department in Belmopan. The government records start in 1885.

There is some compatibility between the church and government sources. The church baptism records also include birthdates, government records include birthdates, and both record marriages. We used both sets of data to compile as complete a record as possible of the residents of Barranco at various stages of their lives. This may not

Table 1.1. Sources of Information

Sources	Location of Data	Dates[a]
Oral Information[b]	Barranco and the Diaspora	1860 – present
Sacramental Records	Puerto Barrios R.C.C. Records[c]	1843 – 1940
Sacramental Records	Punta Gorda R.C.C. Records	1860 – 1930
Census Records	Trujillo, Honduras	1821
Government Vital Statistics	Belize Archives	1885 – 1930
St. Vincent Block List[d]	Punta Gorda	
Archival Records	Midwest Jesuit Archives	1860 – 2003
Archival Records	St. Johns College Collection in the St. Louis University Pope Pius XII Memorial Library[e]	1880 – 1939
Lot and Farmland Leases and Titles[f]	Belize Archives – Plan Books	1880 – 2000
Lot and Farmland Leases and Titles	Belize Archives – Official Gazette[g]	1880 – 1930
Lot and Farmland Leases and Titles	Lands Department in Belmopan	1880 – 2000
Colonial Government Minute Papers	Belize Archives	1885 – 1919
Probate and Court Records	Belize Archives	1885 – 2002
Maps containing tenureship records	Lands Department in Belmopan	1892 – 1970
Lot and Farmland Leases and Titles	Lands Office in Punta Gorda	1900 – 2000
Literature Research	Libraries	2000 – present
Community Consultations	Barranco and the Diaspora	2001 – present
Field Trips with elders – Temash River and farmlands	Barranco and environs	2002 – present

a) Dates covered indicate the records used for this study, not the extent of records available.

b) Land use and ownership, place names, genealogy, folklore, etc.

c) R.C.C. = Roman Catholic Church.

d) The St. Vincent Block is a 960-acre plot, also called "Cerro", which was purchased from funds raised by Jose Maria Nuñez among the Garifon of Punta Gorda for the use of the Garifuna people. A List of eligible people was compiled by going house to house and collecting genealogical information about each family.

e) The St. Johns College Collection is a collection of Jesuit records from Belize that were indexed in 1968 by Father Anthony Short. The records consist of nearly a complete collection of *The Angelus* and the *Historia Domis* (church diary) of the Punta Gorda Parish from 1915 – 1939.

f) Most of the recent Lands Department records were copied by Carlson Tuttle in November and December of 2000. Changes after that are not reflected here.

g) The official notices for the Government of Belize and its predecessors are published in the *Gazette*, initially called *Honduras Gazette* and now *The Gazette*.

reflect all the people, as we cannot vouch for the completeness of our sources.

At the Midwest Jesuit Archives and the Saint Louis University Pope Pius XII Memorial Library we have received full support to obtain information, which includes very helpful observations, documents, and published articles written by priests in the Belize Mission beginning in 1894. The topics included the performance of church duties, economics of life in the colony; and travelogue notes about hardships, the flora and fauna, and customs of the natives. The collections have photographs and some information about Garifuna, Q'ekchi', and Mopan languages.

We interviewed villagers and had one well attended open village meeting. The synergy within the group provided a depth of information not possible in one-on-one sessions. These oral sources added information about personalities and village idiosyncrasies that helped to clarify written archival information.

In addition to sources from archives and oral history, we took field trips with knowledgeable villagers to outlying farmlands on the Temash and Sarstoon Rivers, Boyo Creek, and Lidise. They were helpful in getting an holistic perspective on topography, drainage, specific land forms, and location of boundaries.

Some villagers showed us their "land papers", copies that had been in family possession for decades in some cases. They were official receipts for annual leases, copies of fiats, etc.

Methods of Analysis

The next challenge was to analyze the data, attempting as much as possible to reflect the people's perspective. To do this the three authors had many meetings to refine the synthesis and make recommendations for additional fine-tuning. Each time we raised new questions and then looked at the data in a different way, which again raised more questions that caused us to conduct more interviews and meetings with the villagers. It was an iterative process that ultimately built to this final document.

Genealogial data was entered into John Steed 's Brother's Keeper, a genealogy software programme, which allowed easy access for the social reconstruction of the village in 1892 and for kinship analysis in the transmission of village lots. We caution readers that, while we have used genealogical information to study land, this book is not a comprehensive genealogy for Barranco. More work is needed to produce a genealogy of Baranguna. For updated information, see Carlson Tuttle's Barranco genealogy website <mccourry.net/barranco>.

Land data from the Lands Department offices and the Belize Archives and Records Service were initially entered into spreadsheets to allow searches according to lot and parcel numbers, names of owners, dates of transactions, gender of owner, and whether the land was leased or purchased. Spreadsheets were used for analysis and to create graphics (*Appendix C*).

A database was created for further analysis of kinship relationships, the role of gender in land ownership, and the evolution of the village over its 150-year history. We used the filter and sort functions with queries for analysis of the database.

The information from transaction records was supplemented with that on maps housed in the Lands Office. The practice of the Lands Department was to create a large map with boundaries and parcel/lot numbers in ink as they existed at that time and then to enter future transactions in pencil on those same maps. Maps of village lots were drawn in 1892, 1928, and in the 1950s. A map was drawn in 1913 of the greater area, showing farmlands along the Temash River (Plan 541). In 1954 lands surrounding the village were regularized by surveyor Carl Gibson, who drew a map entitled "Lands Laid Out." Mr. Gibson was kind enough to offer his memories and insights of the process of creating that map.

We obtained copies of these maps in one of three forms: blueprints of the entire map, copies of the map in 8.5 x 14-inch sections, and, in the case of Plan 541, the map was traced on velum as no other means of copying was available. Each map was then scanned in sections, reconstructed in its entirety, and traced for digitization.

Parcel numbers were not included on the original Plan 541. For some parcels we found numbers assigned in the records, but for many there were no identifying numbers. In such cases we arbitrarily assigned numbers to identify each location. These are not official parcel numbers, but created only for our analytical purposes.

Terminology

The word, "Garifuna" is used in this book referring to anything pertaining to the Garifuna people, the language, culture, and the people. In the past the Garifuna were called "Carib" or "Black Carib" in the literature. These terms are no longer acceptable to Garifuna, but will be found in this book in quotations or names such as "Carib Reserve".

The Garifuna word *"Baranguna"* means "one who belongs to Barranco". While it usually refers to the people born in Barranco or whose parents were born in the village, it can also be used to refer to persons with a deep connection to the village.

Except in quotations, place names and spellings are those in current English usage. Barranco has been variously called, "Red Cliff", "Red Clif", "Redcliffe", "Red-Cliff", "Barranco Colorado", "Baranco" or "Barangu" (in Garifuna). The Catholic Church used the term "Red Clif" until 1886. The Colonial Education Department used "Red Cliff" and "Baranco" interchangeably until the 1930s. The Colonial Government used the spelling "Baranco" well into the 1930s.

Belize was called "British Honduras" until 1976, and Dangriga was called "Stann Creek Town". Quotations retain place names and other terms as in the original.

Because this book reflects very much the Baranguna idiomatic expression, we have chosen to use the word "whites" for European descendents and "blacks" for African descendents.

The word "Indian" is used for indigenous groups in Belize only in quotations or names such as "Indian Reserves". To avoid confusion we refer to those from India as "East Indian". The word "Maya" is a European designation for a number of indigenous peoples of Central America. Where possible we use the specific self-designation, such as Mopan, Q'eqchi', or Yucatec. In some cases it is convenient to refer to the other three indigenous cultures in Belize collectively as "Maya."

The word "Mestizo" is used in Belize to indicate people who have mixed heritage, Spanish and indigenous; but in other areas in Central America, "Mestizo" refers to a larger range of mixtures which would include blacks and whites.

The metric system is used where possible, although historical maps use the imperial system of inches, feet, yards, chains, and miles.

Glossary

We have used several Garifuna and Spanish words that do not translate into single English words, but require a longer explanation. They are used in the text in Italics and defined below. Garifuna spellings follow *The People's Garifuna Dictionary.* Stress is on the first syllable of two-syllable words and on the second syllable of longer words unless marked otherwise. As in the convention in Spanish, stress is on the second to last syllable unless otherwise marked. Land terms are also included.

ábunagutian: those who are building

adugahani: going to catch fish and other prerequisites for the dügü ceremony

agiwerihatian: those who are carving a dory

aguyemehani: contracting spousal relations, or marrying into a particular family

Barangu: Barranco.

Baranguna: person born in Barranco or otherwise acknowledged as having deep connections with the village community

degegua: divided into two parts

dabuyaba: the temple where dügü and related ceremonies are held.

dügü: a placation ceremony where food, drinks, and dances are offered to the spirits of ancestors

ebenenei: sponsor of a child at baptism or godfather/godmother

hamúa wafamilia: land that the family owns

iduheguaii: kinship

iduheñu karnal: close relations, used for relatives that may be as close as parents, offsprings, siblings, etc.

iduheñu diseguaña: relatives who are further away than *iduheñu karnal*

Lagueríba: Glover's Reef

ligaradana múa: official document assigning lot or farmland to a person

lumua Barangu: land located within the subregion of Barranco that has traditionally been used by the villagers

múñasu: refuge or shelter

Péine: Punta Gorda

Péinina: a person from Punta Gorda

-rugu: suffix meaning "within"

tabureme muna: owner of the house, a woman

tábuti muna: head of the house, a man

úbiabaraii: an area, usually a beachhead that a person has frequented and gradually takes over as one's own.

Yurumein: St. Vincent

Spanish

hacendados: an institution during the Spanish colonial period. After the conquistadores had reduced the population, they would divide the areas into large farming holdings to further reduce the Indians while Christianizing them. The Indians were virtual slaves.

latifundistas: large land owner

Creole

Pañatón: Spanish Town

Land Terms

Location Ticket: a system of purchasing farmland on Crown land paying a set amount annually over a given time with title given after certification by Lands Department official

Lease: a system of paying to the government a certain amount annually for the use of a lot

Grant: paying the full amount that the government is charging for a piece of Crown land with title granted when the full amount is paid

Name Variations

One problem that arose in this study was the variation in spelling of names of villagers. The administrators wrote what they heard, rather than correct spellings. For example, Simon Mejia was listed as "Simon Miguel" and "Simon Magill"; Pio Nolberto was listed as "Peon Alberto". Paulino might be given as "Lino". The Spanish letter "V" is often written as "B", Viviana is listed as "Bibiana".

There was confusion between masculine and feminine names such as Francisca and Francisco. There was also confusion in the order of names arising from moving from the Spanish-speaking countries where naming differed from British customs. In the case of Francisco Nolberto, Francisco also appeared as a last name among the recently arrived Garifuna from St. Vincent. In such cases, we did not know whether one was a first name or both were last names, the first for the father and the second for the mother. In some cases Francisco became Fernandez. There were persons with the Fernandez last name in Jonathan Point.

In confirmation records, if the priests included a last name, it could have been the nickname or the full first name of the father. Examples include the listing of Casimira "Leandro," "Leandro" being the abbreviation for Alejandro (Nicholas), who was Casimira's father. So, her full name, not included in the list, was Casimira Nicholas.

Similarly, Macario Nolberto was listed as Macario Francisco, Francisco being a substitute for Nolberto because it was his father's first name. His sponsor was Alejandro Casimiro. Alejandro Casimiro was actually Alexander Nicholas but using another last name, probably from his mother.

Determining to whom the written information was referring came from triangulation after observing many examples. Oral history from informants was also helpful. Names are corrected to the modern spellings of those names to the best of our ability. Sometimes it was the nicknames that resolved the identity of the person. Appendix A is a list of the spellings that we used, the misspellings, and other names for the same person in the records.

Overview of the Book

Chapter 1 introduces the initiation, evolution, and aims of the study; sources of information, methods of analysis; and provides an overview of the book.

Chapter 2 brings the Baranguna from St. Vincent to Central America and Belize, losing and acquiring land along the way.

Chapter 3 describes the founding of Barranco, topography of the location, the journey required to get there, and the families who arrived and established the village.

Chapter 4 starts the narrative on land ownership in the village with the 1892 survey and map by colonial authorities. Combining the 1892 map information with genealogical data allows a social reconstruction of Barranco at that time.

Chapter 5 continues the story with the efforts by Baranguna to transmit ownership to lots from 1892 to 2000. In doing so they used both the formal governmental system as well as their customary rights to ownership.

Chapter 6 extends the discussion on ownership to farmlands. The patterns of ownership follow villagers as they move from one farmland area to another within the extended village sub-region, or *lumua Barangu*.

Chapter 7 describes the role that land plays in the socio-cultural value system of Baranguna.

Chapter 8 summarizes the conclusions of the study, describes developments since 2000, and discusses future prospects.

Because the intention of this book is to be accessible to the general reader, as well as useful to academic social scientists, endnotes are used for more technical discussions. Endnotes are numbered consecutively in the text throughout the book, but with the chapter numbers indicated in the endnote section. For example, the first endnote in chapter 3 is marked "57" in the text, but appears as "3-57" in the Endnotes.

Endnote references are to the author and year. The Bibliography contains the full citations for references cited in the text, as well as others that provide relevant general information.

Appendices contain detailed tables of data on genealogy and land transactions. To avoid confusion between the tables in the text and the tables in the appendix, each chapter has an Appendix labeled with a letter: A, B, etc. and contains Tables that are referenced in that chapter. For example, the first Table in the text of Chapter 3 is Table 3.1, and the first Table in Appendix C is Table C.3.1.

Chapter Two
Garifuna Nation Exiled from St. Vincent and Reconstituted in Central America

What do we mean by the "Garifuna nation"? A nation is a people who share a language, culture, and history. While the earth has 193 states, there may be as many as 5,000 nations. "Rarely do state and nation coincide… some 73% of the world's states are multinational."[1] Furthermore, as in the case of Garifuna, several nations are found across borders. Indigenous peoples have used the term "nation" extensively to demonstrate a sense of cultural integrity as against being reduced to an ethnic group, which is an arbitrary subset within a state.[2] It is within this meaning that we use the term "nation" to describe the Garifuna in this volume. Other synonyms include people, peoplehood, or nationhood.

The visceral assertion of nationhood takes place during periods of crisis when a group is threatened. The Spanish officer in charge of Trujillo includes the following entry in his diary, a statement uttered in English by a leader of the arriving Garifuna, "I do not command in the name of anyone. I am not English, nor French, nor Spanish, nor do I care to be any of these. I am a Carib, a Carib subordinate to no one. I do not care to be more or to have more than I have."[3]

From 1622 to 1796 the Garifuna nation underwent a series of displacements within St. Vincent. They waged a war in retaliation for British invasion of their lands and then participated in a second war against the British that the French instigated. They were finally banished to Balliceaux in October of 1796, and then exiled in March of 1797, arriving in April, 1797, to the coast of Honduras in Central America.[4]

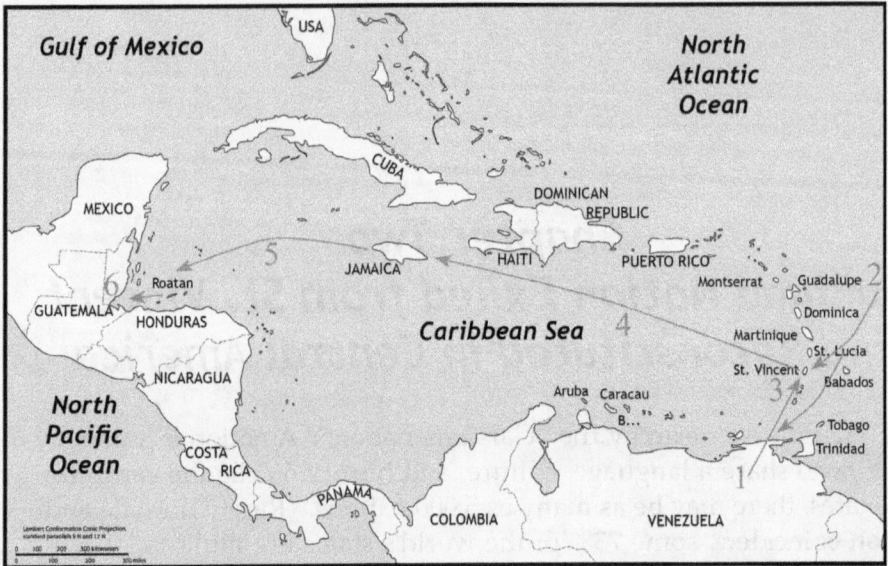

Figure 2.1. The Garifuna Journey

1) Arawak and then Carib people migrate north through the islands from the Orinoco River area.
2) Africans escape slave ships and join the Arawak-Carib forming the Garifuna culture.
3) Following their defeat in the Second Carib War on St. Vincent, approximately 5,000 Garifuna are marooned on Balliceaux.
4) Six months later the surviving 2,600 Garifuna are boarded ships that went first to Jamaica for resupply.
5) Survivors of the voyage are exiled to the island of Roatan.
6) Garifuna settle the western Caribbean coast of Belize, Guatemala, Honduras, and Nicaragua.

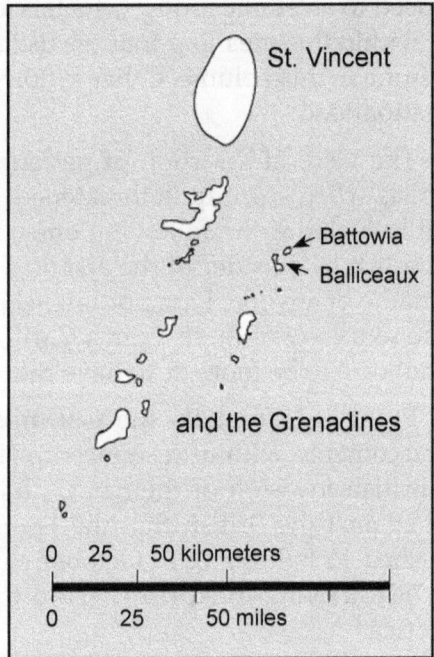

This chapter begins by telling that story of conflict, loss, and genocide. It goes on to address the questions of nation-building. How did the Garifuna survive such a tremendous loss? What did they bring along to help them re-constitute their nationhood after arrival in Central America.[5] What reception did the Garifuna receive in Central America? What combined forces rendered the Garifuna landless first in Hispanic Central America and subsequently in Belize? How and where were communities formed in Belize?

The Garifuna Nation Exiled from St. Vincent

The rivalry between indigenous peoples and Europeans was played out intensively within the larger Circum-Caribbean region. In the Eastern Caribbean, centred around the island of St. Vincent, the players included the Caribs, the British, and the French.

For 130 years after Columbus arrived, the Eastern Caribbean subregion from Antigua to Trinidad had remained under extended Carib domain, where men traded, raided, and occasionally waged full-blown wars at will. One of the most densely populated and heavily wooded of the islands, St. Vincent remained a primary axis of Carib control.

St. Vincent, together with Dominica, was declared "neutral territory" through the Treaty of Aix-la-Chappelle in 1748. Neutrality meant that both islands would remain beyond French and British domain and left under the control of the Caribs. But this only lasted for 15 years, because the Treaty of Paris in 1763 that ended the "Seven Years War" between Britain and a French-Spanish coalition gave St. Vincent to the British.

When the British formally took full control over St. Vincent in 1763, the French settlers already there were allowed to stay if they swore allegience to Britain. The British effort to survey the island met with stiff rebuttal as their teams wandered into Carib areas, notwithstanding orders from London "not to molest them in their possessions nor to attempt any survey of their country without previous word from home."[6]

The French maintained peaceful co-existence with the Caribs, but the British came to St. Vincent with a deep prejudice and outright hostility because of previous military engagements in other parts of the Eastern Caribbean. At first there were a few skirmishes, leading to open warfare in 1772, called the "First Carib War." That war ended

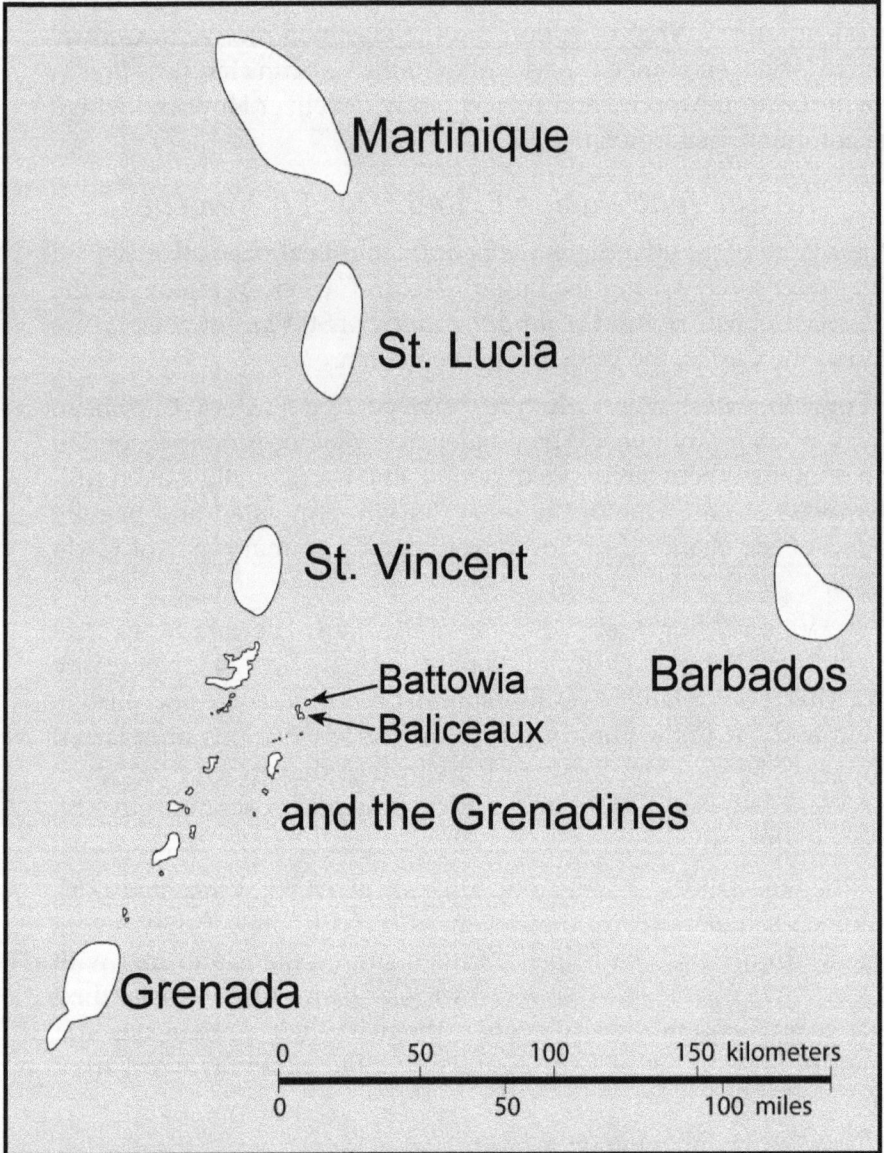

Figure 2.2. Map of St. Vincent (*Yurumein*) and the Grenadines in relation to the other islands, including Baliceaux

in 1773 when the Carib leaders signed a treaty confirming that they retained their right to exist as an independent nation, but they ceded some of their lands to the British, leaving themselves only the northern third of the island.[7]

At the same time the so-called "American colonies" were in the midst of rebellion against the British. The two rebellions were connected in the eyes of the British public and there was considerable sympathy generated for the Carib cause, which brought discord within sections of the British colonial administration.[8]

When France declared war on Britain in 1779, the French and the Caribs took the opportunity to wrench St. Vincent out of British control. With the help of French troops from Martinique, they held St. Vincent for the next four years, until in 1783 Britain again took full control of St. Vincent.

Second Carib War Leads to Balliceaux

The Second Carib War started in March, 1795, and ended in October, 1796. The French who were settled on St. Vincent were allowed to remain, again if they swore allegiance to the British crown, but the Caribs were required to surrender completely. The British confined 4,338 Carib survivors on the small island of Balliceaux for eight months prior to loading them unto 11 ships for their journey to Roatan, Honduras. The transport of survivors to Balliceaux took place between July, 1796 and February, 1797.[9]

To Garifuna Balliceaux was a humiliation. They had seen many of their close relatives killed and at the end of the war, they witnessed the destruction of their personal belongings, houses, farms, dories, and food supply.[10] Already emaciated, they were further ravaged by an epidemic that killed more of them while at Balliceaux. For the survivors, the final embarkation was no doubt full of much sadness. They were leaving their island home of Yurumein (the Garifuna name for St. Vincent), where they had formed as a people and had full autonomy over themselves and their lands. Garifuna painter Pen Cayetano has rendered the embarkation in a tear-jerking scene depicted in Figure 2.3. Balliceaux is also memorialized in the hymn, "Luagu ubouhu Balliceaux" (On the Island of Balliceaux), which is sung often in Barranco and other Garifuna village churches. Balliceaux was a transition between the ending of St. Vincent and a new beginning in Central America.

Figure 2.3. Artist Pen Cayetano has imagined the scene as Garifuna are loaded unto ships after being marooned on Baliceaux for six months.

Luagu Ubouhu Balliceaux
by Sebastian Cayetano and Dale Guzman

Luagu ubouhu Balliceaux,
Ñei wañura,
Ñei wayahuaha
Ladüga súfuri (*bian weyasu*)

On the island of Balliceaux
That is where we sat
That is where we cried
Because of suffering (*sing twice*)

Aba hachagaruniwa Ingüleisi
Luagu Balliceaux
Lun hagumuchaguágüdüniwa.
Ida luba gi wadaunrüni wagarawoun
Lidan fulasu lira?

The English threw us
on the island of Balliceaux
To make sure that they could destroy us
completely; How can we beat our drums
In that place?

Dimurei le lídangien wayuma,
Luma saminaü le tídagien wanigi,
Gadünama la ligibugien bagu
Wawagurügü

This word is from our mouth
This thought comes from our heart
Please find this worthy of your sight
For our sake.

The Tool-Kit of Nation-Building

What did the Garifuna bring along as part of their cultural baggage that helped in their self-restitution as a people? Were they going to be a nation-in-exile to disappear into extinction or would the nation survive? If they were to survive, what form would their survival take? Would they be subsumed into the Mestizo amalgam where their skin colour would be lightened through the intermixture, even as culturally they lose their Garifunaness? These questions become less abstract if we picture infant Juan Pedro Cayetano, who was born 1804 in the Trujillo area to two of the newly arriving couples from St. Vincent.[11] What future did they envisage for him? We will meet Juan Pedro Cayetano as he matures at various stages in this volume.

The discussion on what socio-cultural traits the Garifuna brought along from St. Vincent has been done within the larger debate on the relative strength of their Amerindian versus their African origins.[12] Always open to challenges on the socio-cultural evolution of its informants, the field of anthropology has responded with two approaches to the profound paradigm changes that the Garifuna have undergone. In the first approach, the Garifuna are a newly formed ethnic group under the direction of colonial Spain, in Nancie Gonzalez's terminology, a "neoteric society". Gonzalez's theme of ethnogenesis in her volume *Sojourners of the Caribbean* elaborates on the process of this formation.[13]

The second approach looks more at how the Garifuna attempted to re-constitute their nationhood to survive, not as an ethnic fragment within their new host society, but as a nation on their own terms with rights to land, their body-politic, spirituality, and whether they should articulate or not within the nation-state.

To a great extent the two approaches are the products of the larger thinking in Western anthropology on how small societies become incorporated into nation-states. The spotlight on ethnicity during the immediate post-WWII era was a welcome reprieve to the hideous experiences of the mass slaughter of millions because of racial origin a few years earlier. The contribution of anthropology to the new era of peaceful co-existence of the races was to accept ethnicity as a welcome change in subject matter to race and to ground it in intense micro-level study in such areas as ethnogenesis or the beginning of groups finding themselves within new nation-states,[14] the boundary-maintenance mechanisms that such groups put in place,[15] and comparative diagnostics of cultural traits across ethnic groups.[16]

In the 1980s and 1990s the people who had been classified as "ethnics" started mobilizing to define themselves as they wanted and not as the states and its teams of social scientists had done since the 1950s. Becoming leaders in this new thinking were indigenous peoples, who used 1992, the quincentenary of Columbus landfall, to argue that they had been in the Americas before the white man came, continued being here five hundred years afterwards, and would like their descendants to remain as distinct peoples that do not need the states or its social scientists to define them.

Within the Caribbean the Garifuna offered to provide leadership to the newly formed Caribbean Organization of Indigenous Peoples (COIP), which was founded in 1989.[17] In Honduras since the 1990s, the Garifuna have mobilized politically to wrest from the state internationally accepted conventions, primarily on land claims as indigenous people.[18]

How did the Garifuna demonstrate their dedication to re-constituting their nationhood? What did they bring along from St. Vincent to contribute to their nation building in Central America? The inventory within their tool kit for survival falls under social structure, extra-domestic economy, and a spirit or worldview of nationhood. Under social structure falls the abiding strength of women within the domestic socio-economy. Under extra-domestic economy falls the predominant role of men in seafaring and wage labour, which in turn became the basis of their coastal settlement pattern in Central America. Under the worldview of nationhood falls their spirituality in which the spirits of their ancestors contribute to a cosmology that links the earth and afterlife. All of these form the cultural capital springboard the Garifuna inherited from St. Vincent and have used extensively in Central America.

The dedication to re-constitute themselves in Central America contrasts with the resignation that the authorities enforced on their brothers and sisters and their immediate descendants who remained in St. Vincent. In a 1902 petition to the St. Vincent colonial government they wrote, "We are the descendants of the Caribs of this island who remained faithful to their allegiance when the rest of their fellow countrymen rose in rebellion in 1795 against British Arms, and after the war the Imperial Government settled our forefathers on a grant of land at Morne Ronde which we were to possess without individual freehold rights and to work as a community. Since that time we have always been devoted subjects of the Crown."[19] This petition was an abbreviated political manifesto arguing that the British had broken an agreement that they had made with the remaining Caribs for land

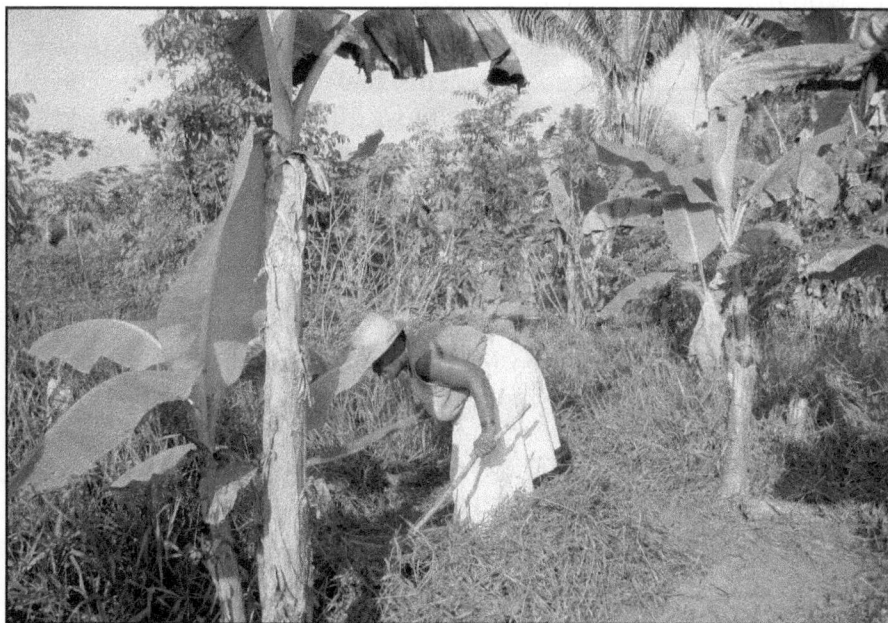

Figure 2.4. Garifuna woman (Baranguna Paula Nolberto) cultivating food crops

Figure 2.5. Garifuna fisherman (Baranguna Derrick Zuniga) throwing a net to catch bait

settlement in exchange for not engaging in war against them like the others, who had been pressed into exile.

Such a political component of nationhood to negotiate land ownership with mutually agreed benefits had been well defined in St. Vincent. On the other hand, it was most difficult to regenerate in Central America, where the Garifuna were consistently being denied that they are a people with rights to their own land and to negotiate with the authorities about their well-being. The authorities in charge of the political economy kept mounting obstacles against them. From their very landing in Roatan the parents of Juan Pedro Cayetano confronted these obstacles. They and Juan Pedro Cayetano, together with his peers and their descendants, have lived trying to overcome them wherever they have found themselves in Central America.

Garifuna Arrival in Central America: Confronting the Obstacles

Having been dumped by the British on enemy territory, the Garifuna had no choice but to take control over their lot. Their initial response was not to take full control of Roatan as their new homeland, contrary to British expectations, but to go to Trujillo on the mainland, taking their destiny in the direction of Central America. On May 19, 1797, a little more than one month after their arrival on Roatan, they formally surrendered to the Spanish authorities and implored them to take them away from Roatan to Trujillo.

Gonzalez's rich description captures the gist of the conundrum and the vacuum surrounding them. "Had the Black Caribs stayed in Roatan, they would have been limited to desultory subsistence agriculture in an inhospitable environment. Breaking into smaller traditional residential groups would not have improved their lot much, for they would have had little to live on, no houses, and no jobs. ... When they arrived in Trujillo the *Comandante* of the military post noted with surprise and pleasure that most of the men and many of the boys had some familiarity with their [weapons] use. They were immediately absorbed into the local militia, thus assuring their people's survival over the short term at least."[20]

Together with military skills they brought along a loose political grouping of captains who took limited authority over the new subregions that they formed along the coast. The 1821 census gives a comparative overview of the persistence of Garifuna cultural traits in the Trujillo area as against those among another group of African-descendants, Haitian immigrants. Taken as the last colonial census in that part of Central America before independence, the count was comprehensive in its coverage of Trujillo and several adjoining communities. The total population was 3,575 subdivided into seven ethnic groups—black French (*negros franceses*), black English (*negros ingleses*), Garifuna, mulatos, Spaniards, brown-skinned persons (*morenos*), and native American (*indígena*). The Garifuna numbered 64% of the total population.[21]

Coming twenty-four years after their first arrival in Roatan, this count showed their first large-scale dispersal in the adjoining part of the mainland. Payne makes a comparison between the Garifuna and the men and women that Spaniards brought from Haiti to do manual labour in civil and military works on the port of Trujillo. They lived closer to the central portion of the Spanish-dominated town centre than the Garifuna, who were widespread. Another difference is that they were Catholic, while slightly more than half of the Garifuna were Catholic, with 48% being unbaptized. Furthermore, several still retained their own Garifuna non-Hispanicized names, some of which are shown in Table 2.1. On the basis of these perdurable traits Payne makes the argument that the Garifuna displayed greater traditional folk characteristics that were in practice even two decades after leaving St. Vincent.

Table 2.1. Randomly Selected Non-Hispanicized Garifuna Names In the Trujillo Area 1821[21]

Name	Gender	Age	Religion	Community
Caraiyamu	Female	7	Unbaptized	Limonal
Barabenu	Male	4	Unbaptized	Limonal
Urinamu	Male	2	Unbaptized	Limonal
Acambe	Female	52	Unbaptized	Limonal
Guayarano	Male	15	Unbaptized	Limonal
Yacatay	Male	8	Unbaptized	Limonal
Macuma	Female	22	Unbaptized	Limonal
Ymaruyatare	Female	34	Unbaptized	Limonal
Mamimana	Female	6	Unbaptized	Limonal
Cayamu	Female	62	Unbaptized	Limonal

Within the larger political economy of the 1800s, the whole of Central America went through very difficult times.[22] The political struggles for independence from Spain were violent. After independence, factionalism continued with periodic violent outbursts for the rest of the century. Concurrently, there were efforts to consolidate mercantilism in both Belize and the rest of Central America through monopolizing land ownership in the hands of *latifundistas*. In turn, this led to landlessness for the masses, a deliberate ploy by the political authorities to increase the numbers forced to become wage labourers.[23]

The Garifuna did not fit the image of the immigrant preferred to generate economic development. Instead, colonies of Europeans from Belgium, Scotland, Italy, and England were attracted with subsidized travel and initial settlement expenses.[24] Similarly, in Belize during the latter half of the 1800s hundreds of U.S. ex-confederates were invited by the colonial government to settle and jump start agriculture in the Toledo District, among other parts of the country.[25] Because the lands allocated to the US ex-confederates threatened the Punta Gorda Carib Reserve already allocated to the Garifuna, they threatened to leave the colony and go back to Honduras, according to a 1868 letter that Father Jean Genon wrote on their behalf to the Lieutenant Governor (*Fig. 3.8, p. 53*).

With the rise of borders across the newly independent Central American states, there were also increased opportunities for the smuggling of goods and people, an activity for which the Garifuna have received much blame. Attributing such culpability, however, overlooks the fact that traveling in small sailing boats, together with the complement of boat building and navigation skills, had long been the tour de force of the Garifuna, among other coastal dwellers. Indeed, the capability to move at will from any part of the coast to any other had been the primary reprieve to the Garifuna to escape their recurring hardships. A man by himself, or with his family and other relatives, could leave one place looking for *múñasu* (a refuge) at another. Alternatively, he could start an *úbiabaraü* while escaping from a location. An *úbiabaraü* could be abandoned after serving as campsite, or it could grow gradually to become a full fledged village community. The usefulness of boating skills, as a safety valve to escape and look for better options for survival, also contributed to the spread of the Garifuna nation within what gradually became their larger territory along the Caribbean coast of Central America.

From St. Vincent the Garifuna also brought their cuisine and agricultural systems with their gender-based division of labour, among other traits. The significant economic unit in St. Vincent was the extended family, which could be a settlement of up to 30 to 100 persons. Extended families or clans, had their own territory bounded by rivers.[26]

The daily working of the household was the domain of women, but there was a gender-based division of labour. The women dominated in the cultivation of food crops in small gardens adjoining the residence. The men, on the other hand, dedicated much time to raiding and trading, as well as fishing and hunting. These observations on gender roles and the importance of the extended family within domestic organization are still found today in Garifuna villages. They provide the social structure that still guides behaviour in the use of house lots and farmlands.

Several additional nodes of cultural continuity crossed the Caribbean with the arriving Garifuna men, women, and children. They include cross-cousin marriage, the significance of the extended family, and the communal use of land. These traits greatly facilitated their adjustment to their new environment while promoting their self-restitution as a people.

Arrival in Belize

The initial travels of the Garifuna from the north coast of what is now Honduras to Belize would have been part of their wider speculation for better living conditions, including looking for wage labour. On the other hand, the colonial authorities in Belize were aware of the reputation of the Garifuna as treacherous and unworthy from the British experiences with them in St. Vincent. Having initially allowed 150 men to work on logging operations in the Dangriga area in 1802, five years after the arrival at Roatan, the British lifted the ban against hiring them after 1827, when loggers cried for more workers and the Garifuna had already earned a reputation of being among the best available.[27]

In 1833 Methodists missionaries estimated that Dangriga had a population of 500.[28] Crossing the Gulf of Honduras on their way to Belize would have been a traumatic experience, especially during earlier decades of the 1800s before their sailors would have acquired familiarity with reef patches, atolls, cayes, and the coastline. Informants, who did the crossing in the mid-1900s, described the waves as high as the roof of a house. They added that from the small dories luggage and even babies could be easily swept away in the occasional swells; the worse that happened was to capsize and lose lives.

Sailors told us there were traditionally two pathways to reach Belize from Honduras by dory. The first route came from the earliest settlements near Trujillo going northwest towards Glovers Reef, *Laqueríba* in Garifuna, and then toward the mainland to arrive in the general location of Dangriga (*NW Route in Figure 2.6*).

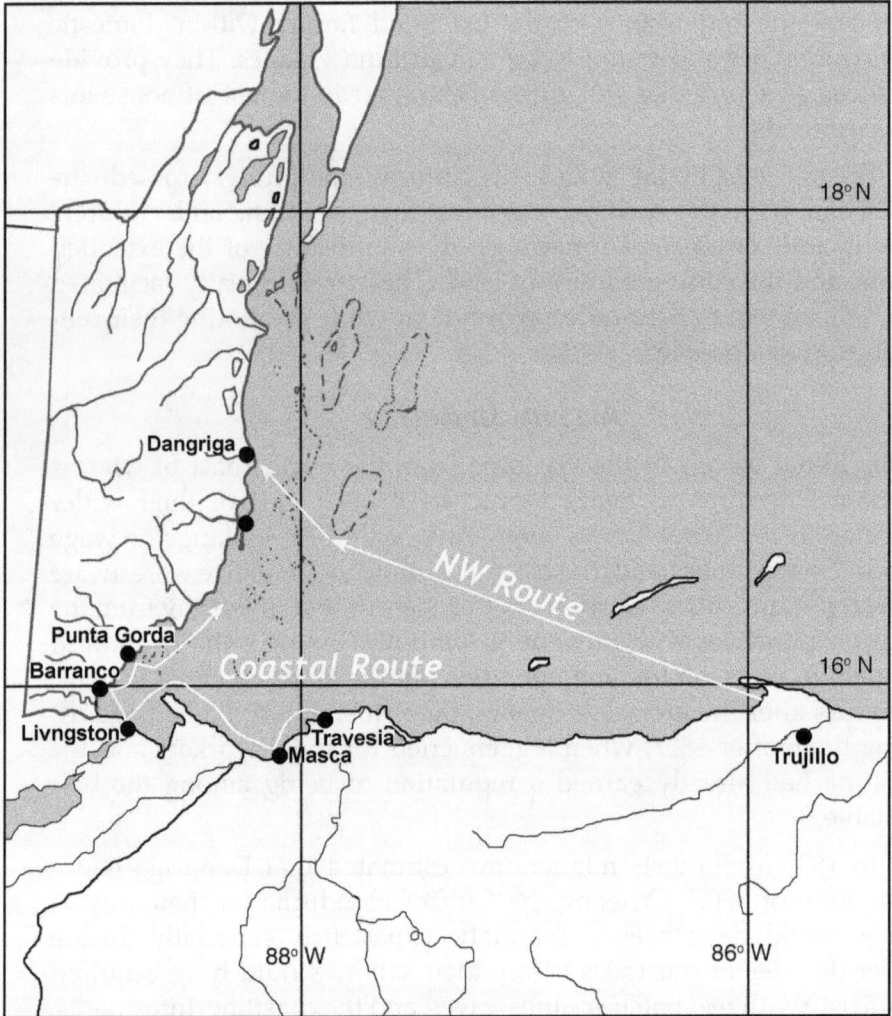

Figure 2.6. Map showing two routes that Garifuna used in crossing to Belize from Honduras

The other route hugged the coast, stopping off at several villages along the way. It was used later as the communities of Masca and Travesia were developed along the coast of Honduras. This route would have made a stop at Livingston, Guatemala, before proceeding to Barranco, Punta Gorda, and further north (*Coastal Route in Figure 2.6*).

Land Tenure in Belize

Having undertaken the difficult sea voyage from Honduras to Belize, what awaited the exhausted men, women, and children? A brief history of the settlement of Belize is shown in Table 2.2. For the greater part of almost a hundred years from 1765 to 1854 the loose governance structure was dominated by a few white men, who also were the principal landowners.[29] There was absolutely no decisive role to be played by the Garifuna in the economic and political life of the colony.

Prior to emancipation in 1838, land was free. White settlers merely had to stake a claim. But in 1837, in anticipation of emancipation, that policy was changed and a high price of one pound per acre was set, effectively preventing the freed slaves and other marginalized people like the Garifuna from purchasing land. This was a conscious, deliberate effort to maintain a labour force to work in the timber camps.

The 1855 Laws in Force Act granted title to those already occupying land, but Garifuna and Maya were specifically exempted so they could not own land. All land that was not then occupied was declared Crown land, which was mostly south of the Sibun as land in the north was almost all in private hands.

"Clearly a double standard was operative in the Settlement: while members of the dominant class who occupied land were considered to be 'locators' and were subsequently confirmed in their possession, members of the 'free coloured and black' population who acted in the same manner were discriminated against by being considered as squatters who could be dispossessed."[31]

In 1857 the colonial officials ruled that the Garifuna should pay annual rent on house lots, which they and their ancestors had occupied, but it was not enforced until 1879 when the Garifuna in Dangriga were creating "serious disturbances; ... [they] "do not know why they are to pay rent as Stann Creek is their place, that long ago the land was given to them and they settled the place."[32]

Table 2.2 Settlement of Belize: Treaties, Arrivals and the Expansion of Logging Operations

At the time of the entrance of the British into the Central American area that is now Belize, there were three groups of indigenous Maya who inhabited the area:

1) Yucatec were, and still are, in northern Belize.
2) Itza were in western Belize, centered around Tipu (now Flores, Peten, Guatemala).
3) Manche Chol were in the Maya Mountains of southern Belize.

After the Maya, the next settlers were British buccaneers, also called the "baymen." There are no written records establishing the time of the first British settlement in Belize, but it could be around the time that Britain obtained Jamaica by conquest in 1655. The Treaty of Madrid in 1670 committed the British to abandon piracy on the high seas, so the buccaneers turned to logwood, which was abundant along the rivers of Belize. The entire area of Central America was claimed by Spain, but the English negotiated with Spain for logging rights and proceeded to settle Belize. When the logwood prices dropped the buccaneers turned to mahogany. This history is well documented[30] and summarized in the timeline below.

Year	Treaty	Activity/Arrival	Boundary/Location
1670	Treaty of Madrid	No more piracy	High Seas
1762	Treaty of Paris	Logwood only	No set boundaries
1783	Treaty of Versailles	Logwood only	Rio Hondo to Belize River
1786	Convention of London	Logwood and mahogany, no plantations	Rio Hondo to Sibun River
1799		Mahogany logging	Reached Deep River
1802		Garifuna settle coastal plain	South of the Sibun River
1814		Mahogany logging	Reached Moho River
1825		Mahogany logging	Reached Sarstoon River
1859	Treaty between Great Britain and Guatemala	Current boundaries established	Rio Hondo to Sarstoon River
1880s		Mopan settle Maya Mountains	San Antonio, Toledo District
1880s		Q'eqchi' settle southwest Toledo	San Pedro, Sarstoon, Toledo District

The 1872 Crown Lands Ordinance and the subsequent regulations established the Indian and Carib Reserves, along with rules for operation and the prohibition against either group holding title to land; however, no Reserves were declared and the law was repealed in 1879 after the disturbances in Dangriga. The Crown Lands Ordinance of 1886 restored the authority to create Indian or Carib Reserves. Carib Reserves were designated for Stann Creek and Punta Gorda, and rules published in 1890. The consent of the District Magistrate was required before a house could be built on a lot and rents were to be paid yearly. Leases were subject to additional conditions: good behavior, keeping the lot clean, and the performance of work up to 12 days per year. Fortunately the latter was never enforced.[33]

The obstacles toward poorer people owning land were finally lifted by law in 1883 to encourage divestment away from timber into agriculture. By lowering the price of grant land and making purchases easier, the government was able to inject some life into the southern part of the country for a cross-section of the population.[34]

Toledo District: Boom and Bust

In his historic overview of the economic development (or lack of it) in the Toledo District, Wilk suggests that the Toledo District is a classic case of the boom-and-bust cycle where capitalist ventures come, exploit the area, and then leave nothing behind except the workers who were attracted by the jobs offered.[36]

A typical example is the Young, Toledo and Company, which owned one million acres in southern Belize. Felipe Toledo was a Central American who lived in Belize in the mid-nineteenth century. During the Caste War in the Yucatan he got concessions to log mahogany from either the Maya or the government, depending upon who was in control of the territory at the time.[37]

Following their defeat in the U.S. Civil War, Confederates came to Belize looking for land where they could continue their pre-war lifestyle. By then Young, Toledo and Company was in financial difficulty and selling land at bargain prices. The Confederates bought land and settled at Cattle Landing, the settlement being called "Toledo" after the previous owners, a name which was later applied to the entire District.[38]

Large areas of land in the Southern District were purchased by a German named Bernard Cramer, who lived in Surrey, England, and controlled his investments in Central America and the Yucatan from there. Cramer brought Q'eqchi' laborers to Belize for his rubber and nutmeg production. They settled in the upper reaches of the Sarstoon River near the current village of Dolores.[39] The Catholic Church ministered to the Q'eqchi', which attempted to stabilize the population. The priests came through Barranco and took along Garifuna as boat captains and translators, so the Garifuna were part of the stabilization force.

By 1861 the Garifuna had survived genocide in St. Vincent, Balliceaux, and also during their initial stay in Roatan. They had formed their own communities from Belize to Nicaragua, a distance of 1500 kilometers. Their survival as a nation came from deliberately separating themselves within enclaves where they grew their own food and governed themselves through extended kinship networks, while paying respect to the state authorities from whom they needed wage labour. From their social conditions in Belize we spotlight three examples of their projections to continue defining themselves taking advantage of whatever opportunities were available. The first example is a review of the 1861 census, which shows them concentrating along the southern coast of Belize, while going on migratory wage labour to other parts of the colony. The second is a microscopic view of their life within their village community of Barranco, using the 1891 census figures. The third is their move toward the early celebration of Garifuna Settlement Day in the 1940s as rallying point for self-consciousness and community self-help.

1861 Census

Coming a year before colonial status, and before the establishment of Barranco, the 1861 census was the first to record the Garifuna as they were becoming Her Majesty's colonial subjects. In addition to the usual census data on numbers of inhabitants, age, gender, household membership, occupation, education and so on, the 1861 census gave information on the racial groups in the colony and their intermixture.[40]

The result was a list of forty categories of these racial intermixtures, which undoubtedly taxed the patience of the enumerators. For us, the additional information gives an interesting spotlight on the Garifuna as participants within the intermixture being identified at that time in the population. Unfortunately, we do not have an explanation of the categories and their breakdown, leaving the reader only an inkling from the suggestive terms used, such as "Indian and Carib" and "Carib and Indian".

Table 2.3. Ratio of Mixed to Nonmixed Individuals for Major Racial Groups In Belize, 1861[41]

Ethnic Category	Total	No of Mixed Individuals	Number of Nonmixed Individuals	Ratio of mixed to nonmixed
Indian	13,527	8,852	4,675	1.89
Spanish	9,707	7,994	1,713	4.66
African	7,513	4,985	2,528	1.97
White	5,784	4,683	1,101	4.25
Black Carib	2,385	560	1,825	0.30
Total	38,196	27,074	11,842	2.29

The total population was 38,529 and the Garifuna numbered 2,385 or 6%. The five main racial groups in descending order of plurality are listed in Table 2.3. They were Indian, Spanish, African, European, and Black Carib. Mixing took place extensively across races with the least involving the Garifuna. Those mixing the most were the Spanish followed by Europeans, Africans, and Garifuna.

The Garifuna were found throughout the country, with the largest proportion being in Dangriga, followed by Commerce Bight, with Rio Grande trailing behind, as shown in Table 2.4. With the exception of Belize Town, Corozal, Dangriga, and Punta Gorda, the communities listed in this table were the locations of mahogany works along main rivers. Garifuna men would have been working at these locations, being absent from their home towns in the south.

Table 2.4 Proportion of Garifuna in Some Communities in Belize

Community	Total Population	Garifuna	%
Rio Hondo	2,883	55	2
Corozal, Blue Creek, New River	10,664	14	0.1
Northern River	761	27	4
Belize Town	5,067	104	2
Sibun	492	9	2
Manatee	204	3	1
Mullins River	226	3	1
Dangriga	1,113	1,022	92
Commerce Bight	375	204	54
Rio Grande	438	135	36
Punta Gorda	306	56	18

While the 1861 census already pinpoints the concentration of the Garifuna in the south (*Table 2.4*), it is worthy to note that at least one community traditionally regarded as mainly Garifuna was not so in 1861. Only 18% of the 306 people in Punta Gorda were Garifuna. Even Rio Grande, which probably was located closer to the Seven Hills Estate, had twice as many Garifuna as Punta Gorda. One reason for this small proportion is that there was a high rate of mixture by the Garifuna in Punta Gorda, mainly with Indians, leaving a small number of nonmixed Garifuna. The breakdown of races and their intermixture in some communities in the south appears in Table 2.5.

Table 2.5. Proportion of Races in Select Communities in Southern Belize, 1861 Census

Community	Total Pop	Races	
Punta Gorda		Indian[a] and Carib	105
	291	Carib and Indian	106
		Indian and Spanish	17
		Spanish and Indian	7
		Garifuna	56
Commerce Bight	388	African	36
		Anglo-African	35
		Anglo-Indian	25
		Spanish	66
		Garifuna	204
Mullins River	226	Africo-English	104
		Africo-Spanish	46
		Spanish-Indian	41
		Garifuna	3
Manatee	204	African	108
		Anglo-African	27
		Garifuna	3
Rio Grande	438	Spanish	128
		Anglo-African	69

Table 2.5. Proportion of Races in Select Communities in Southern Belize, 1861 Census (*cont'd*)

Community	Total Pop	Races	
		Carib-Indian	106
		Garifuna	135
Sibun River	477	African	222
		Anglo-African	202
		Indian-Spanish	44
		Garifuna	9

ª "Indian" might include both Maya and Miskito.

As the Garifuna moved further away from the south, they mixed more with other groups, as shown in Table 2.6. The concentration of the Garifuna south of the Sibun, removed from the more populated parts of the country, is a primary reason. On going to other parts for wage labour, Garifuna men mixed with others.

Table 2.6. Distribution of Mixed and Nonmixed Garifuna

District	Mixed		Nonmixed	
	No	%	No	%
Southern	223	40	1,426	78
Northern	191	34	298	16
Central	146	26	101	6
Total	560	100	1,825	100

1891 Census

After 1861 British Honduras carried out censuses every ten years. Between 1871 and 1891 the population in the Southern District of Belize nearly doubled,[35] as people from the rest of the country, as well as Central America, moved southward to take advantage of the banana boom. As we shall see in the next chapter, this caused a major boost to the population of Barranco. Mullins River and Monkey River showed the greatest increase as small farmers took advantage of the lower price for land and the boom in banana sales.[42] Boats picked up the fruit along the coast from Honduras, travelling north in British Honduras, before proceeding to New Orleans and other ports in the United States. The 1891 census indicates the relative conditions of Baranguna within the larger subregion of the south.

Table 2.7. 1891 Population and Housing

Community	Under 15			Over 15			Totals			Houses	Avg**
	M	F	T	M	F	T	M	F	T		
Red Cliff	43	50	93	59	73	132	102	123	225	59	3.83
Monkey River	121	117	238	236	167	403	357	284	641	149	4.30
PG, Ct, BV*	97	109	206	132	181	313	229	290	519	133	3.90
Sarstoon	66	54	120	60	74	134	126	128	254	31	8.19
Temash	1	1	2	7	2	9	8	3	11	6	1.83
Rio Grande	23	16	39	74	39	113	97	55	152	73	2.08
Toledo Settle	90	47	137	203	119	322	293	166	459	110	4.17

*Punta Gorda, Cattle Landing, and Buena Vista **Average per household

The seven communities within our focus include, from north to south, Monkey River, Rio Grande, Punta Gorda-Cattle Landing-Buena Vista, Red Cliff (the name at that time for Barranco), Temash, and Sarstoon (*Table 2.7*). The three largest in population were Monkey River (641), Punta Gorda-Cattle Landing-Buena Vista (519), and Toledo Settlement (459). With a population of 225, Barranco was fifth in size among the seven communities. There were 59 houses in the village with an average occupation of slightly fewer than four persons.

There are some leads on the socioeconomy of the subregion forthcoming from the breakdown in age and gender (*Table 2.7*). From the male/female demography there are three patterns that are discernible about the relative need for men to leave their home communities to look for wage labour. Three communities had a greater proportion of men than women—Monkey River, Rio Grande, and Toledo Settlement. These communities attracted more men than those available locally for temporary wage labour.

One community showed the reverse, a larger proportion of resident women than men. This was the Punta Gorda-Cattle Landing-Buena Vista area from where men travelled away for temporary wage labour. The third pattern shows a relatively equal proportion of men and women. Two examples are Sarstoon and Barranco. The indications are that men were working within their own communities or a short distance away.

Sarstoon refers to the Q'eqchi' community of San Pedro, whom Cramer had resettled from neighbouring Guatemala. At that time Barranco men might have had less need to travel away for wage labour, as they were most probably preoccupied with fishing and farming for subsistence and surplus cash sales. Cal's analysis of the periodic shifts from being peasants and proletariats for Maya in their rural communities in northern Belize is quite appropriate for what was taking place among the Garifuna in southern Belize in the late 19th century. They were dependent for whatever wage labour opportunities could be afforded them; but should this not be available they could remain as peasants relying more on their subsistence food production and minimal surplus sale. Survival meant being able to move between these two economic systems.[42]

Table 2.8. Country of Birth

Community	British Honduras			Central America			Other		
	M	F	T	M	F	T	M	F	T
Red Cliff	72	77	149	29	46	75	1		1
Monkey River	183	185	368	137	88	225	11 "other British Possessions", maybe Jamaica		
PG, Ct, BV*	157	225	382	58	59	117	2 England 4 USA		
Toledo Settlement	102	49	151	74	44	118	25 USA	22 USA	47 USA
Sarstoon	9	12	21	117	116	233			
San Antonio	46	54	100	168	179	347			
Rio Grande	44	26	70	40	24	64			

*Punta Gorda, Cattle Landing, and Buena Vista

The topic of country of birth is covered in Table 2.8. Large proportions of persons in all of the communities were born in Central America, with the largest in Sarstoon and San Antonio, being newly arriving Q'eqchi' and Mopan respectively. In the other communities the arrivals would have been Mestizos, Creole, and Garifuna originating in Honduras and Guatemala. There were a few persons in Monkey River originating from "other British Possessions", probably Jamaica. In Punta Gorda two persons came from England and four from the United States of America. In the Toledo Settlement 25 men and 22 women from the United States were ex-Confederates. In the case of Barranco, as many as 75, or one-third, were born in Central America. The ease of cross-border movement, which marked the first arrival of the Garifuna people to Belize in the early part of the 19th century, continued up to the last decade in the century. Later we will observe that as the Garifuna moved to settle Barranco, Mestizos also came to do likewise.

Table 2.9. Male Occupations

Community	Occupations				
	Carpenter	Tailor	Planter (large scale)	Farm Servants &Labourer	Fisherman
Barranco	5	2	0	15	1
Monkey River	3		6	72	
Punta Gorda	8	7		24	3
Toledo Settlement	1		18	181	
Temash			1	3	1
Rio Grande				14	
Moho River				3	
Cayes					21

Information on male occupation comes from Table 2.9. The three categories of employment that are revealing are farm servants and labourers, artisanal trades, and planter. There were seven men doing artisanal trades, such as carpentry and tailoring in Barranco, indicating that there were men trained in these skills and that there was enough cash flow to keep them employed. Because of the opportunities available to work at farms there were several men who gave "farm servants and labourers" as their main employment. At a frequency of 15, it was the largest source of employment in Barranco. In comparison the Toledo Settlement, the location of the ex-Confederate community owning large farms, listed 181 men as "farm servants and labourers" and Monkey River, well known for having several banana farms, had 72. The 15 who listed it in Barranco could have gotten work on one of several Cramer estates along the Moho, Temash, or Sarstoon Rivers, as well as at the Toledo Settlement.

Table 2.10. Land Ownership

Community	Less than 10 acres	Between 10 & 640 Acres	More than 640 acres (1sq. mi.)
Barranco	0	0	0
Monkey River	17	11	1
Toledo Settlement	14	1	1
Punta Gorda	1	9	1
Sarstoon			1
Punta Negra	5	1	
Punta Icacos, New Haven	6	2	
Deep River	4		2
Middle River, Golden Stream, Seven Hills	2		3

Land tenure receives some spotlight in Table 2.10. We assume that ownership in this table refers to grant lands as against leasehold. If such is the case, Barranco had no land ownership. In the chapter on farmlands we will show that applications for land grants for Baranguna started in 1891. In retrospect this census information confirms that whatever lands they were using to grow their own food in 1891 was Crown land.[43] Furthermore, they might have been using it for generations under customary tenure, although legally they were accused of being squatters, as we shall see later in discussing farmland ownership. Monkey River, Toledo Settlement, Punta Negra, and Punta Icacos (New Haven) had several smaller plots of less than ten acres, while Monkey River and Punta Gorda had plots between ten acres and 1 square mile. Finally, there were also several communities having lands measured in square miles.

Table 2.11. Literacy

Community	Can Read			Can write Name	
	Yes	No		Yes	No
Barranco	37	188		30	195
Monkey River	134	507		123	518
Toledo Settlement	114	345		101	358
Punta Gorda	124	395		112	407
San Antonio	2	446		2	446
Sarstoon	1	253		1	253

There is some information on literacy in Table 2.11. The figures reflect an abysmally low level of literacy in all of the communities. Although the Methodists had been teaching primary school from the first quarter of the century in Dangriga,[43] further south there was barely any impact on literacy. The census figures show that only 16% of the village population could read and only 13% could write their name. The caveat here is that in calculating the percentage even school age children and younger were included. From other sources we know that there was a church-supported private school in the village from 1885 and a Garifuna teacher, Mr. Arzu, taught there in 1892.[44]

T. V. Ramos—The Twentieth Century Ideology of
Garifuna Nationhood

The information that we have presented on the census has been official information from written sources. There are rare efforts to have the Garifuna be the subjects of their own story. The transcription of oral history filtered from the great-great-granddaughter of Joseph Chatoyer's daughter Gulisi has been an unusual effort in capturing impressions of their life in St. Vincent as well as after their initial settlement in Dangriga and New Town.[45]

It is within this regard that we highlight the stellar contribution of T.V. Ramos during his lifespan in Dangriga from 1923 to 1955. He was the first to articulate an ideology of Garifuna nationhood in Belize as a community activist and avid writer. His take-off point was the need to restore to the Garifuna their humanity after generations of abuse in Central America, about which he knew a great deal, both from what he had heard and his own experiences having been born and raised in Honduras.

Thomas Vincent Ramos was born in 1887 near Puerto Cortez, Honduras. In 1923 he came to Dangriga where, along with his wife, he built a family of more than ten children. He instilled among his children a strong sense of dedication to the family, community, the Methodist Church, and the larger society. Through his involvement in sports, he also encouraged among his children a sense of fair play and discipline in dealing with others. These are some of the social values he brought to his neigbourhood community in Dangriga. He believed in belonging to groups and became a leader in several. He joined the Carib International Burial Fund Society in 1926, two years after founding the Carib Development Society.[46]

Ramos' aim in participating in these groups was to preach self-help for the Garifuna people through more productive agriculture and small scale cottage industry in food processing and preservation. He received much encouragement from the United Negro International Association (UNIA) branch in Belize, which preached the same message for black people in the United States, Caribbean, and Central America—to work themselves out of the poverty in their communities. To better broadcast his message Ramos used his other skills as writer, intellectual leader, Methodist elder, and inspirational speaker. He was a correspondent for the Belize City-based newspaper, the *Belize Independent*. In 1943 he wrote a booklet entitled *Carib History* and he wrote poetry and songs and countless letters broadcasting his message.

By the early 1940s Ramos was ready to undertake what would become his immortal legacy to the Garifuna cause, getting the colonial government to legally declare November 19th as a public and bank holiday, first in the Stann Creek District, later in the Toledo District, and finally the momentum had been set for the rest of the country. The achievement transcended the psychological and cultural dimension of having the Garifuna pull themselves up by their bootstraps. With the help of his friends and supporters, Ramos succeeded in convincing the British governor to so honour the Garifuna people that their arrival in Belize would be commemorated by the whole country. A people who had been among the most discriminated had shown that they could reach the highest level in political authority to accede to their request.

In lobbying for support in his campaign for the formalization of Settlement Day, Ramos received endorsement from the Carib International Society (CIS) and the Carib Development Society (CDS), two cultural organizations that worked in all Garifuna communities, including those in the diaspora in Guatemala and Honduras.

A.C. Francisco, Secretary, Carib Development Society, wrote, "In reference to your letter of the 17th instant, re-establishment of Disembarkartion Day (previous name for Settlement Day) Celebrations. I am directed by my society as well as by the Carib International Society to suggest the formation of a Committee whereby a proper understanding of the celebrations can be effected. As this is something new to our people, I further suggest that instructions of some sort be given to them." (Stann Creek, 24 Sept. 1941)[47]

Profilio Marin wrote "I have read with careful attention some brief correspondence in the BELIZE INDEPENDENT between yourself and the two societies, viz., the Carib Development and International, respectively, relative to a "Carib Disembarkation Day Celebration" (earlier name for Settlement Day) to be observed on the 19th Nov. 1941, and, I suppose on subsequent years thereafter.

"In my humble opinion, a move of this nature is very much of commendation and serious consideration by the people, but particularly by the heads of the societies; as a step like this should be to revive and foster a spirit of patriotism among the people and an everlasting TRIBUTE (sic) to our forefathers which is so highly necessary, and I would further assert had been long overdue through some neglect on the part of some disloyal members of the race.

"As a proud member of this much neglected and backward race (sorry to say) and as one who is honestly wishing to see it emerge into a respondent betterment in every respect, I would here suggest that you and the members of the suggested committee get together and make some arrangement whereby the people, ESPECIALLY THE YOUTH (sic), be properly informed and impressed about the history of our race ... Yours for the betterment of the race." (Puerto Barrios, Nov. 8th, 1941)[48]

Ramos' success has to be seen within the limitations of what he perceived was attainable. It was a major step toward the upliftment of an oppressed people within a multiethnic colonial society. Later in the 1940s and 1950s there took place throughout the country the nationalist movement leading toward political independence. Ramos died in 1955, but his message of self-worth, strong discipline, hard work, and resourcefulness resounded with what would also be needed from all Belizeans to prepare themselves for independence. Notwithstanding the concise vision left behind by Ramos, since the beginning of the nationalist movement there has been relatively little direction by the Garifuna toward their own nationhood, i.e. access to their own lands, their body-politic, and a worldview of themselves as a people, who have defied genocide. Their ancestors created indelible marks of their nationhood that need to be reviewed and appreciated.[49]

Garifuna Settlement Day was first celebrated in Dangriga in 1941 and then in the Stann Creek and Toledo Districts in 1943, finally becoming a national holiday in 1977.[50]

The Garifuna, Indigenous Peoples/Afro-descendants, and Land Tenure

In the 1990s several Latin American states passed laws for the first time granting to indigenous and Afro-descendant peoples equal access to development, including the rights to reclaim ancestral lands.[51] In Central America, Nicaragua was the first to pass laws under its proclamation of autonomy in 1987 to Garifuna among others living in the country's Caribbean coast. The law received further support in 2003.[52] The 1995 and 1996 Peace Accord in Guatemala, designed to put an end to that country's decades of civil unrest, gave the indigenous Maya, Xinca, and Garifuna rights to reclaim ancestral lands. Rey has investigated how the Garifuna in Livingston have put in motion their own claims.[53] Anderson has noted, however, that among the countries, Honduras has most sharply outlined equal rights for indigenous and Afro-descendant peoples.[54]

Figure 2.7. Re-enactment of the arrival of the Garifuna to Belize in celebration of the 19th of November in Barranco in 1979
(photo by Joseph O. Palacio)

Figure 2.8. 19th of November celebration, procession to the church in Barranco in 2004

The overt actions that these states and their citizens have taken on land tenure for the traditionally dispossessed indigenous and Afro-descendants contrasts with the relative lack of activity by the states in the Anglophone Caribbean and the limited political mobilization undertaken by the people themselves. Indeed, there is difficulty among the citizens of these countries to come to terms with the facts that there are indigenous peoples in their midst and there is a need to right centuries old injustices, which have been defined by such multilateral agencies as the Organization of American States and the United Nations.[55]

In Belize the Maya have won cases about their land claims at the regional Inter-American Court of Human Rights as well as the Supreme Court. However, the government has shown reluctance to follow through with the decisions. The Garifuna have not followed the litigation procedures of the Maya against the government, although Noe asserts in a preliminary study that "there is a strong legal argument that the Garifuna do possess some form of land rights which are entitled to protection under domestic and international law."[56] Furthermore, this study shows that Baranguna were practicing customary rights to both residential space and farmlands preceding the presence of the British in that part of southern Belize. Because the governor did not know on what lands the village was located, he dispatched surveyors to the area to investigate whether it was on Crown land, a Carib Reserve, or private lands, more than two generations after the village started (*see Chapter 6, p. 156 and Appendix D, p. 271*).

Summary and Conclusion

As a community, Barranco is the result of the settlement efforts of a handful of men and women, who were among the first and second generation descendants of the almost 2000 Garifuna who were exiled by the British from St. Vincent. Their basic survival for the first few months and, indeed, for the rest of their time in Central America has relied on what they brought along from St. Vincent and adapted to what was made available to them by the Spanish and British colonial authorities. At the core were the strength of their matrilocal extended family, the capability of men to wield arms and find wage labour either close by or much further away, and their dedication to the spirits of their ancestors to provide guidance. These building blocks rested on Garifuna nationhood, the collective spirit of being one people, who could overcome all obstacles. It was not in the strategic interest of leaders in the political economy to have black people reclaim their nationhood. Rather, they should remain powerless ethnic minorities fit only for cheap wage labour to be squatters on public lands. The basis of this dialectic between the people and the state, and its perdurability for two hundred years are the primary topics for this chapter.

The information includes figures from the 1861 census in Belize that show that the Garifuna had settled into their enclave communities along the southern coast of Belize, from where the men went on stints of wage labour to other parts of the country. The 1891 census spotlights the village of Barranco, where both men and women worked farmlands, although they had not yet received land titles. Thomas Vincent Ramos articulated a 20th century ideology of Garifuna nationhood to counter what he saw as the continued discrimination against his people. His stellar achievement was to have the colonial governor acknowledge November 19th as public and bank holiday. To Ramos and his supporters this was the ultimate vindication of full acceptance into colonial society.

But full acceptance into society did not necessarily come with land rights. Since the 1990s Latin American states have begun recognizing the rights of indigenous nations. The Maya in Belize have won several cases, but the Garifuna have not taken the route of litigation. While the political and juridical dimensions of land claims grab media headlines, there still remains the need to investigate the background topics of public administration of land tenure. Our approach started with the painstaking task of identifying who owned what lots and farmlands from the time of the first land surveys and following through with the succession in ownership of each one up to 2000. We injected social and cultural life into this data by examining overlaps among kinship, gender, and cultural identity. After much analysis, what emerged were distinctive patterns in community organization and nationhood based on land tenure.

In providing a social and cultural context of the Garifuna nation, this chapter has opened the panorama for small groups of men and women to partake in several land transactions as we shall see in the rest of this volume. The topic of the next chapter is the small group who joined efforts to lay the foundation for the village of Barranco.

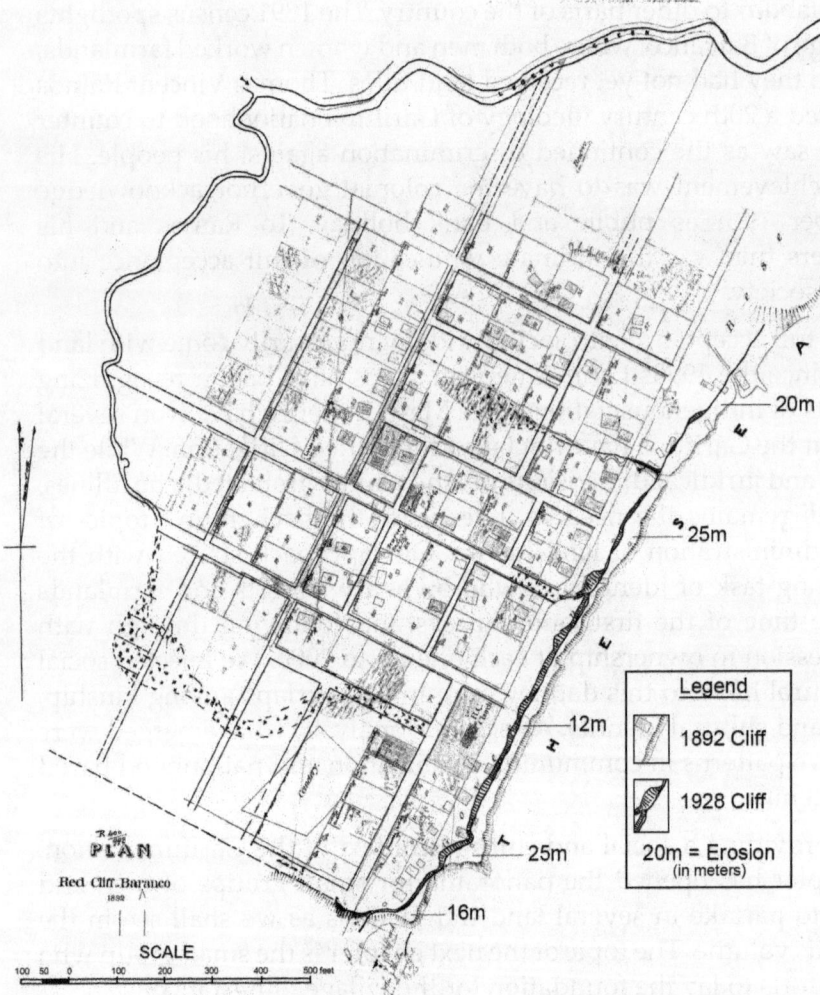

Figure 3.1. 1928 map of Barranco superimposed over the 1892 map showing the erosion of the cliff.

Chapter Three
The Founding of Barranco

As one travels along the southern Belizean coast in the Gulf of Honduras, one passes mile after mile of wet, lowland mangroves. After rounding Mother Bush Point, the high bank of Barranco with its towering, luscious green trees comes into view. Early settlers must have been attracted to this beautiful site, an obvious place to stop to spend the night for anyone traveling on the sea. Indeed, in a visit to Barranco in 1896, the Governor, His Excellency Sir Alfred Moloney commented on the "prettily and healthily situated Baranco Colorado or Red Cliff."[57]

As immortalized in its name, Red Cliff (*Baranco Colorado* in Spanish, and currently spelled "Barranco"), the most striking feature of Barranco is the fifteen-foot cliff at the seaside. In earlier times the cliff appeared red because the underlying red soil was visible from the sea. In its natural state, the waves of the sea lapping at the base undercut the high cliff, leaving a shear red face. After a century and a half of human habitation, the cliff is no longer shear, but somewhat rounded at the top, allowing the growth of vegetation on the edge. Thus, the cliff is no longer red, but green with vegetation. One area has been bull-dozed to allow access; another has become less steep with use. A comparison of the maps of 1892 and 1928 indicate considerable erosion of the cliff, ranging from 12 to 25 meters over that 36-year period, up to the size of one lot (*Fig. 3.1*).

A beach of brown sand supports vegetation, mostly natural elephant grass and planted coconut trees. Barranco is surrounded by water—the sea, Legegu Creek and its tributaries. The high cliff of most of the village drains toward the west and north into two swampy areas and Legegu Creek that empties into the sea north of the village. The cliff of the northern "Louba" area is somewhat lower and two creeks drain from there directly into the sea south of the mouth of Legegu Creek. The northernmost does not have a name and the second one is *Magüsineru* Creek.

45

An aerial view of Barranco in 2008 shows that the village is carved into a lush rainforest that supports many fruit trees, game animals, black howler monkeys, and many of Belize's 550 species of birds (*Fig. 3.2*).

Settlement of Barranco

The men and women who first settled the village of Barranco were the first and second generation to be born to the 1797 exiles arriving in Central America. Having heard from their parents about the violence in St. Vincent, the epidemics in the holding camp at Balliceaux, and further depravations on the trans-Caribbean crossing from St. Vincent to Roatan, they found themselves undergoing their own unwelcome adjustments to living under Spanish colonial rule, marked by forced labour in the militias, in food production, and in manning forts along the coast and main rivers. They must have heard about new lands further east (along the Miskito Coast) and west (in the area of Belize) beyond the Spanish domain, where they could find *muñasu* (safe haven in Garifuna) for self-settlement, where the whites had minimal presence and control.

Figure 3.2. Aerial view of Barranco looking south
(photo courtesy SATIIM)

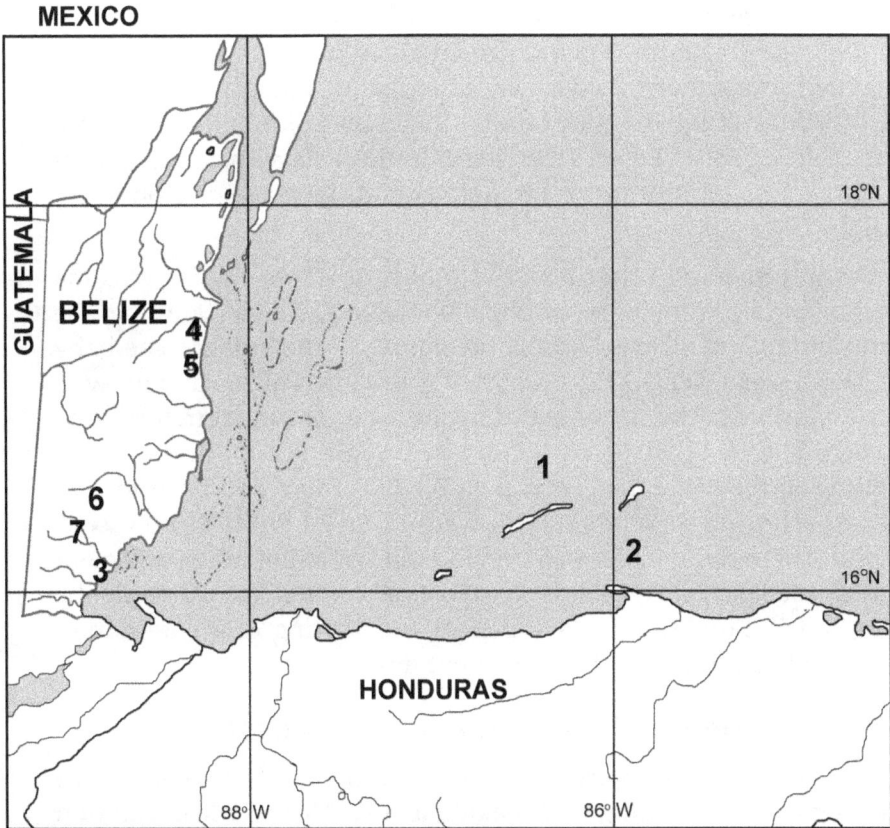

Figure 3.3. Baranguna came from several communities—from the east and from the north—

Legend

1—Roatan, Honduras

2—Trujillo, Honduras

3—Livingston, Guatemala

4—Dangriga, Belize

5—Jonathan Point, Belize

6—Punta Gorda, Belize

7—Barranco, Belize

The search for refuge continued even after the explorers were in British territory for they could have been given employment in logging camps, where conditions were slave-like; or they might have found areas to settle only to be driven away by landowners. Oral tradition tells of earlier generations being driven away from lands where they had settled in southern Belize. The founders of Barranco came from as far north as Dangriga, stopping at Jonathan Point and later Punta Gorda, before proceeding further south to the village location. Others came from the community of Livingston and the coast of Honduras. (*Fig. 3.3*)

The intertwining of written and oral history has had a welcome impact on public knowledge among the villagers, which states that the birth of the first child marked the beginning of the village. The baby was Maria Loreta Palacio, the daughter of Teodoro Palacio and his wife Tomasa Martinez. The name and date are recorded in church records (*Appendix Table B3.1*). This date, however, might not mark the actual beginning of the settlement. It is possible that there had been infants born earlier in the settlement, who were taken to Punta Gorda to be baptized. There could have been previous efforts to initiate a settlement that did not last. Nevertheless, as the first written record from the village, Maria Loreta's birth symbolizes the starting of a community that has had continuity up to the present time.

Founding Families: *Aguiwerehatian*

In describing Baranguna, those who belong to Barranco, we use the analogy of the two stages of making a dory. Nearly a lost tradition now, Garifuna were well known across coastal Central America for making dories.[58] A dory is carved from a single tree trunk by carvers, *agiwerihatian* in Garifuna, which necessarily happens where the tree falls (*Fig. 3.4*). The second stage is building a useful dory from the carved tree trunk. We are using the term *ábunagutian*, meaning "builders" for the second stage of the building of the community. (*Fig. 3.5*).

The *agiwerihatian* are analogous to the families who first came to live in Barranco. The qualities that are comparable to beginning a settlement include starting a major project, which could last more than a year; doing hard and relentless work; maintaining a vision of the end product; and engaging in group work at given phases. There are distinct roles for several persons in both dory carving as well as starting a settlement from scratch. We should insert one *caveat* about the analogy not being fully complete. Traditionally women were not allowed near the dory being carved. On the other hand, the task of building a settlement cannot be done without men and women

Figure 3.4. Representing the *agiwerihatian*, Raymond Valencio is shown carving a dory from the fallen tree in 1979
(photo by Joseph O. Palacio)

Figure 3.5. Representing the *ábunagutian*, Clotildo Zuniga is shown finishing (building) a dory, also in 1979
(photo by Joseph O. Palacio)

displaying the degree of tenacity and inter-group reliance fundamental to dory carving.

To describe the founding families, the *aguiwerehatíñe,* we integrated information from several sources. We took every opportunity to avail ourselves of the oral information in the commnity. The list prepared for the St. Vincent Block, the land purchased by and for the community of Punta Gorda, included genealogies that extended to Barranco. To a great extent we used the genealogical information found in church records written by the priests officiating at the ceremonies, both from Puerto Barrios, Guatemala, and Punta Gorda, Belize. The records from Puerto Barrios include events in Santo Tomas, Livingston and other areas in Departmento de Izabal, Guatemala. The records from Punta Gorda include events in Barranco and other places in the Toledo and Stann Creek Districts of Belize.

Father Jean Genon

Fr. Jean Genon (*Fig. 3.7*) began recording sacramental events in Santo Tomas, Guatemala, in 1843 when he baptized two sons of Juan Pedro Cayetano, Ignacio Cipriano by Maria Cardemi and Luis Tomas Leopoldo Cayetano by Maria Celestina. Fr. Genon gradually concentrated his efforts in Livingston. While there, he adopted a comprehensive vision for the Garifuna, whom he saw as one people occupying the coastal strip from Belize to the Miskito Coast. Furthermore, he was convinced that their religious needs should be serviced from one central location.

Figure 3.6. Barranco Village in 1910 *(photo courtesy Midwest Jesuit Archives)*

Figure 3.7. Father Jean Genon, S.J. (*photo courtesy Library S.J. in Heverlee-Leuven, Belgium*)

During that time he was also visiting Punta Gorda and his records there begin in 1859. The periodic expulsions of the Jesuits from Guatemala no doubt influenced Genon to move from Livingston to Punta Gorda, from where his records started in 1859. Using his own trustworthy dory, from Punta Gorda he ministered to Belizean communities from Barranco to Dangriga.[59]

Father Jean Genon wrote two letters of protest to the Lieutenant Governor on behalf of his Punta Gorda parishioners. His concern was the sale of large blocks of land to the ex-U.S. Confederates, which would leave the longer settled Garifuna with insufficient lands for their homes and farms, and confined within a limited area between Orange Point and Joe Taylor Creek. If this injustice persisted, the Garifuna told Genon, they would return to Central America, where they could get more lands without paying the rent of $3.00 being levied on them for house lots and farmlands. Given the minimal concerns in writing by the Garifuna about their own welfare at that time, the second Genon letter is so significant for being one of the earliest archival records on their confinement in land tenure that we reproduce it here (*Fig. 3.8*).[60]

In Punta Gorda Fr. Jean Genon made most of the entries between 1860 and 1872, when he was transferred to Dangriga. Between 1872 and 1882 no priest was resident in Punta Gorda, leaving gaps in the records that were periodically filled by visiting priests. After 1882 priests resident in Punta Gorda also ministered to the parishioners of Barranco and other villages.

Deciphering the Records

One had to become accustomed to the individual styles of the writers to eventually decipher names. There was no doubt a church rule specifying that all females being baptized be given the first name Maria, seen in the designated names. But there was also the problem of the writer entering what he heard, which might not have been what he was being told.

July 20, 1868

Lt. Governor

I wrote on a former occasion to your Excellency on the 14th of March last on the subject of the Charaibs of the coast of Guatemala and then of Punta Gorda, pressing that they could be assured and informed in the making of their plantations by reason of the sale of certain lands. I am ... after receiving your Excellency's answer to my letter from Belize dated March 23 ...

I was at Belize towards the end of April. I then sent to the Colonial Secretary a note which made him acquainted with two pieces of information which claimed that Punta Gorda is the property of the Crown. The first of these pieces of information was that given five years ago by Surveyor Mr. Faber. He told me that Punta Gorda had been reserved from the sale of that district [portion] of land. The second is that of Mr. Toledo himself who one day said to me that Punta Gorda might not have as much ground as I said but that he was able to know exactly how much on consulting his title deeds.

However that may be, here is what can be alleged before all the world here –

1. They have traced a line that leaves the village of Punta Gorda outside that which the Americans are now occupying but that this line at 900 yards from the sea near Chotela and 700 yards at Arinchwaga Orange Point only leaves room for the village and a very little farmland although their plantations are beyond and already partly ruined. Only a few families are able to live here now.

2. They tell me also that each family has to pay $3.00 of which one is for the home and two for the milpa or field. How is it possible to make them pay for the lands which are not left to them?

In making your Excellency acquainted with these facts, I satisfy as much my inclinations and my feeling of pity and sympathy for these poor Charaibs as the fulfillment of the request which they have made of me to make known the state to which they are reduced.

The infallible consequence of this state will be to cause a noticeable quantity of the inhabitants of this village to disappear, because [above all] beside they are able to have in Central America a house and plantation at will without paying anything. It will be hard without doubt to lose their homes but notwithstanding they will be forced to abandon them if this Evil be without remedy.

Signed J. Genon

Figure 3.8. Letter from Fr. Jean Genon to the Lt. Governor.

As we gleaned the information from these records, the question arose, "Who is Baranguna?" Even today many people consider Barranco home though they have never lived there. In this study, we include life events—birth, baptism, marriage, or death—that happened in Barranco, as well as persons involved in events elsewhere who appear in the records for Barranco or owned lots in Barranco.

Family structure among the Garifuna does not follow the nuclear family, but rather an extended family pattern, which is reflected in our approach to this study. For the Garifuna, the family extends both vertically through ancestors and descendents, and horizontally among siblings, aunts, uncles, and cousins, even distant cousins. It was difficult to take this kind of deep view because one needs a large amount of information available at any one time. Through the generations there are similar names, so it was sometimes difficult to identify a particular person.

Individually each of these sources of information was somewhat limited, but the triangulation among them provided a wealth of cross-fertilization, allowing us to describe the founding families and those who joined them in Barranco.

On the basis of this integrated information we find several child-bearing families living in Barranco in the 1860s. In the following sections we describe these families using the surnames that appear in the records: Avilez, Castillo, Cayetano, Garcia, Jimenez, Marin, Nolberto, Nicholas, Palacio, and Paulino. Although the surnames are those of the males, we mean no disrespect for the females. We are aware, of course, that there might have been other adults in the settlement. Our emphasis has been on women and men who contributed to the growth of the community and settlement by having children. All families are distinguished not only by their early arrival but also by their progeny, who continued the labour of pioneering.

Desideria—Palacio—Avilez [61]

The man given the distinguished reputation of identifying the Barranco location is Santiago Avilez, who first used it as a fishing/turtle camp and then brought his wife, Desideria and her two adult sons to join him as the first settlers in Barranco.

Desideria is known by several names: Martina Francisca Desideria, Desideria Alvarez, Desideria Lambey, Francisca Isideria, Francisca Desideria, Quiteria, and Maga Gidei. We will refer to her as Desideria. She had four children, three by her previous husband Francisco Palacio—Teodoro, Anastacio, and Iginia. The fourth child is a son

Figure 3.9. Descendants of Desideria

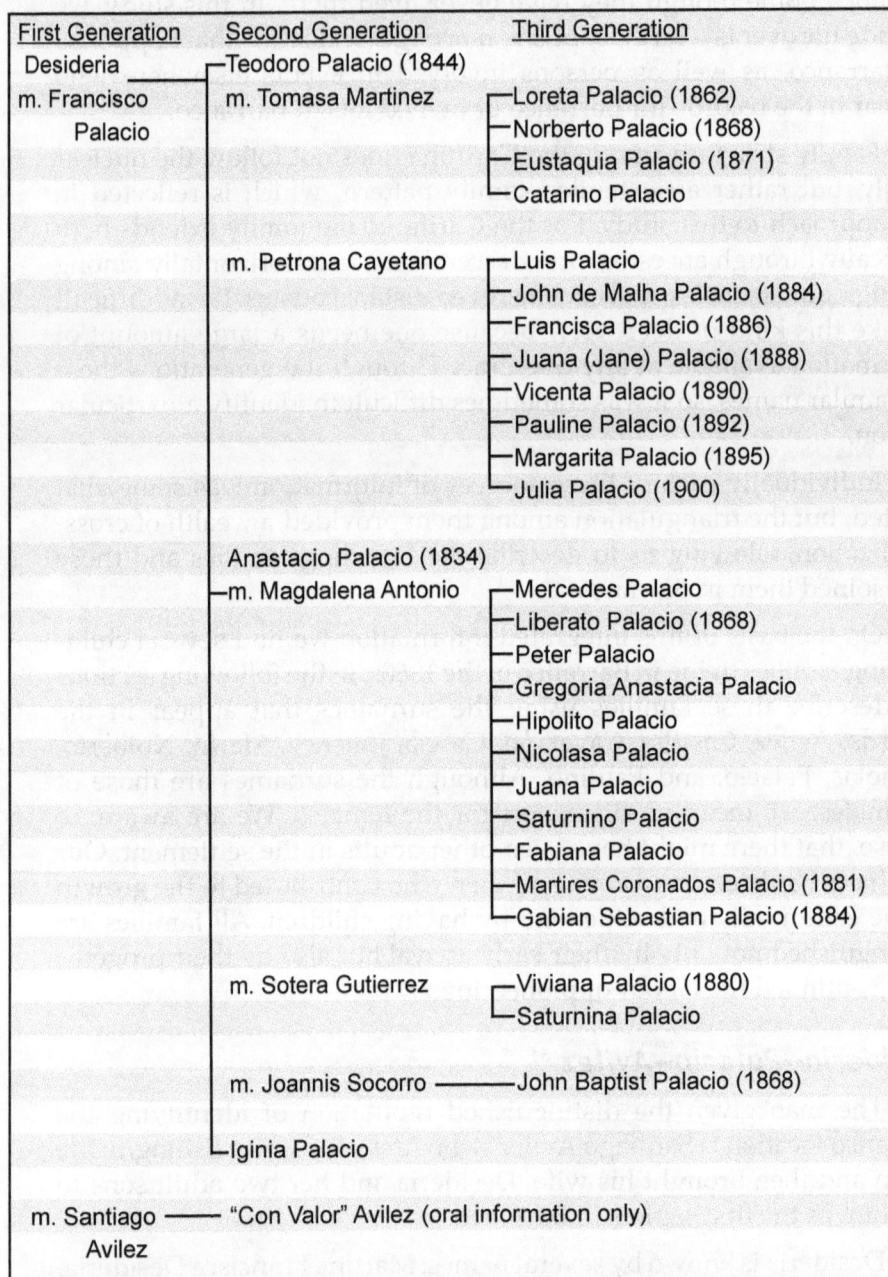

First Generation	Second Generation	Third Generation
Desideria	┌Teodoro Palacio (1844)	
m. Francisco	m. Tomasa Martinez	┌Loreta Palacio (1862)
Palacio		├Norberto Palacio (1868)
		├Eustaquia Palacio (1871)
		└Catarino Palacio
	m. Petrona Cayetano	┌Luis Palacio
		├John de Malha Palacio (1884)
		├Francisca Palacio (1886)
		├Juana (Jane) Palacio (1888)
		├Vicenta Palacio (1890)
		├Pauline Palacio (1892)
		├Margarita Palacio (1895)
		└Julia Palacio (1900)
	Anastacio Palacio (1834)	
	├m. Magdalena Antonio	┌Mercedes Palacio
		├Liberato Palacio (1868)
		├Peter Palacio
		├Gregoria Anastacia Palacio
		├Hipolito Palacio
		├Nicolasa Palacio
		├Juana Palacio
		├Saturnino Palacio
		├Fabiana Palacio
		├Martires Coronados Palacio (1881)
		└Gabian Sebastian Palacio (1884)
	m. Sotera Gutierrez	┌Viviana Palacio (1880)
		└Saturnina Palacio
	m. Joannis Socorro ─────	John Baptist Palacio (1868)
	└Iginia Palacio	
m. Santiago ─────	"Con Valor" Avilez (oral information only)	
Avilez		

m. means "married," but throughout this volume we use that to mean a relationship resulted in children, not necessarily that they went through a ceremony.
The years in parentheses are approximate birth dates. Some were calculated from the age given in death records which are approximate. Birthdates found in baptismal records are more accurate.

whose nickname was "Con Valor." We have no genealogical records of him, only oral history (*Figure 3.9*).

Desideria was in Dangriga when she gave birth to Teodoro Palacio in 1844. We do not know how long she spent in Dangriga but we know that Santiago also made trips to Dangriga from the area of Trujillo to visit with relatives, so that is probably where they met.

Santiago was born around 1804, just seven years after the Garifuna were exiled from St. Vincent. He might have come to Belize during the first phase of Garifuna arrivals between 1802 and 1832. He is said to have originated in the community of Griga (Santa Fe) located 16 kilometres west of Trujillo. In Honduras he had a daughter, whose son became the father of Felicita Francisco, who was the fifth generation great-granddaughter of Gulisi, the daughter of Joseph Chatoyer.[62]

It is said that Santiago came from Punta Gorda to set his turtle nets using the distinctive red clay ridge as his marker. While setting his nets, Santiago ventured onto the beach and climbed on top of the cliff at *Magüsinero* Creek. Along with a few fellow fishermen he came more often and set up temporary camps to stay for longer periods. He found out that not only was the sea bountiful, the land was also fertile, as he planted food crops to sustain him for the short periods. To help him maintain his camp he brought along his wife Desideria with her two sons, Teodoro and Anastacio. Gradually Santiago and Desideria invited others to settle, building their own camps that became homesteads. The community of Barranco was on its way toward fruition.[63]

Santiago was a restless explorer. He pioneered a part of Punta Gorda before proceeding to the fishing campsite that was to become Barranco. He pioneered a farmland site called Cowshade on the Guatemalan side of the Sarstoon River. Santiago had children by four women in Honduras, Punta Gorda, and Livingston. One of his sons, John Justo (Bangi) Avilez, worked with him at Cowshade and moved to Barranco in 1906 where he was a shopkeeper.

Santiago died in Barranco in September 1894 at the age of 90 and Desideria died also in the village at the age of 98 in December 1907. While we cannot be certain about the ages attributed at that time, indications are that both Santiago and Desideria were among the first Garifuna to be born in Central America around 1804 and 1809 respectively.

The first recorded birth in Barranco was in December of 1862— Mariai Loreta, the daughter of Teodoro Palacio and Maria Tomasa Martinez. From his death record we have calculated that Teodoro Palacio was born around 1844. With Tomasa, he had three other children, Norberto born in 1868, Eustaquia born in 1871, and Catarino.

Paul Palacio and **Clarence Marin**
Paul Palacio is the grandson of Ignacia Arana and Norberto Palacio,
Auralia Chilmilio and Santiago Martinez. Clarence Marin is the grandson of
Mercedes Palacio and Celestino Paulino

Gregorio Ruben Palacio

Alvin Loredo

Gregorio Ruben Palacio is the grandson of Magdelana Cesario and
Anastacio Palacio, Mauricia Cayetano and Claro Zuniga. Alvin Loredo is the
great-grandson of Gregoria Palacio and Eulalio Loredo

After Tomasa died, Teodoro married Petrona Cayetano in 1880 and together they had nine children born from 1882 to 1900 (*Fig. 3.9*).

Desideria's son Anastacio Palacio, better known as "Baibai", is a good example of a pioneer maintaining relationships in different communities. He maintained a union with Sotera Gutierrez from Livingston, while having a wife in Jonathan Point, Magdalena Cesario.

We have no information to indicate when Anastacio married Magdalena Cesario, who either came along with him from Dangriga or met him in Jonathan Point. Together they had 11 children. Liberato was born in 1868, but does not appear in church records for Barranco, so we assume that he was born elsewhere. Oral tradition says that Mercedes and Gregoria were born in Jonathan Point. For over twenty years Magdalena had children by Anastacio.

Anastacio had children with Sotera and Magdalena, both before coming to Barranco, as well as after he had settled them in two separate households in the settlement. We know they were having children contemporaneously because Sotera had Viviana Palacio on the 14th of July, 1880, and on the 2nd of December, 1881, Magdalena had Martires Coronados Palacio.

Cayetano—Paulino

We have already met Juan Pedro Cayetano as a child of parents newly arriving from St. Vincent and as a 17-year-old living in the area of Trujillo in 1821 with a spouse named Maria Dorotea.[64] That means he was born around 1804, the same as Santiago Avilez.

Twenty-two years later he had two sons who were baptized by Father Genon in 1843 in Santo Tomas, Guatemala. Juan Pedro and Maria Celestina had several other children baptized in Santo Tomas and then in Livingston. For decades Juan Pedro's name appears in records in Livingston along with Maria Celestina, so it is likely that he lived in Livingston rather than in Barranco. The name of Juan Pedro appears only once in the records for Barranco as witness for the marriage of his granddaughter Victoriana Cayetano, daughter of Anacleto Cayetano, in 1877.

One of Juan Pedro and Maria Celestina's daughters, Vivciona Cayetano, married Sebastian Sanchez in Livingston and moved to Barranco before their first child, Francisco Xavier Sanchez, was born in 1865. They had five more children, most of whom were born in Barranco.

Figure 3.10. Baranguna descendents of Juan Pedro Cayetano and Nicolasa Moralez and their spouses

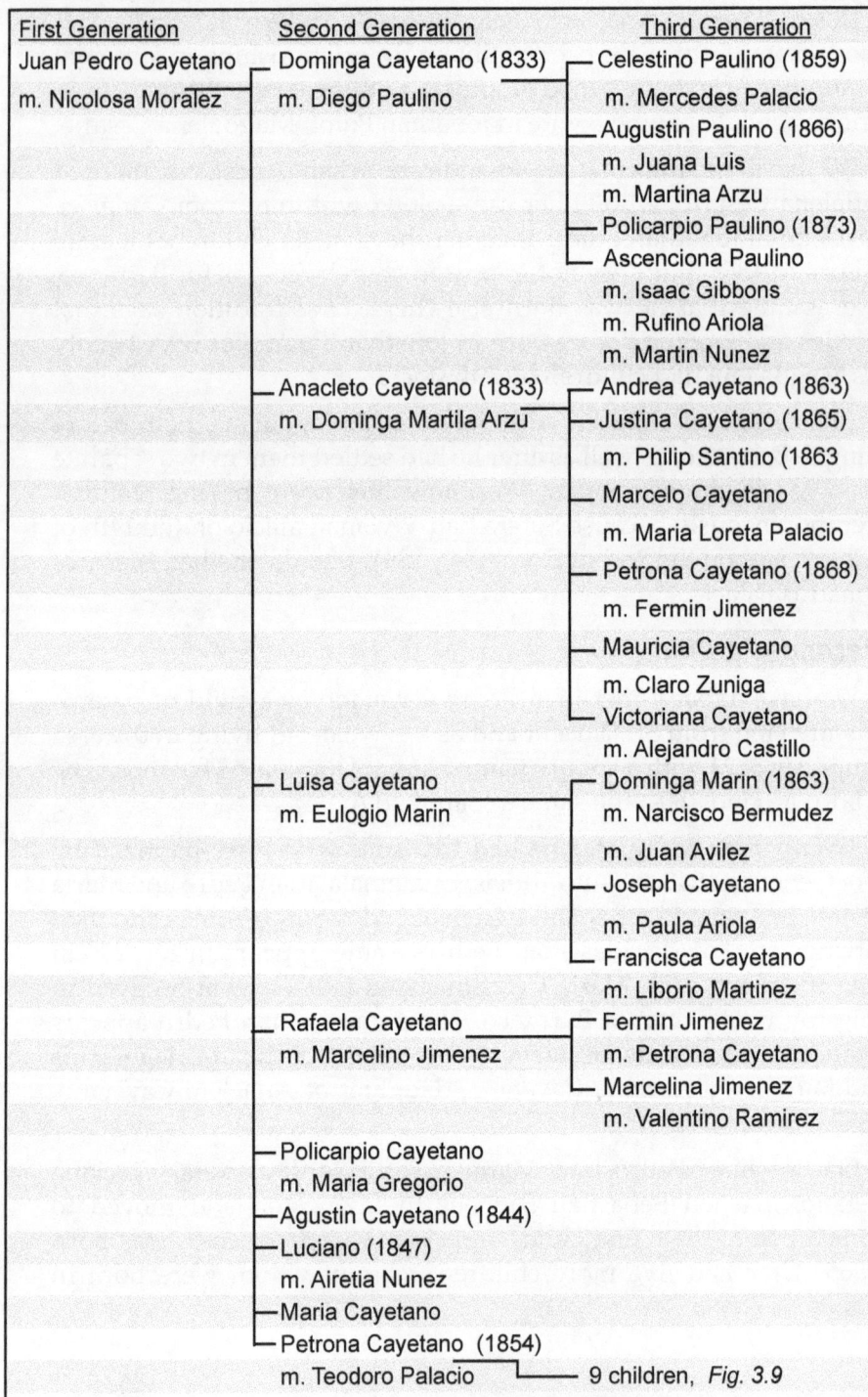

First Generation	Second Generation	Third Generation
Juan Pedro Cayetano	Dominga Cayetano (1833)	Celestino Paulino (1859)
m. Nicolosa Moralez	m. Diego Paulino	m. Mercedes Palacio
		Augustin Paulino (1866)
		m. Juana Luis
		m. Martina Arzu
		Policarpio Paulino (1873)
		Ascenciona Paulino
		m. Isaac Gibbons
		m. Rufino Ariola
		m. Martin Nunez
	Anacleto Cayetano (1833)	Andrea Cayetano (1863)
	m. Dominga Martila Arzu	Justina Cayetano (1865)
		m. Philip Santino (1863
		Marcelo Cayetano
		m. Maria Loreta Palacio
		Petrona Cayetano (1868)
		m. Fermin Jimenez
		Mauricia Cayetano
		m. Claro Zuniga
		Victoriana Cayetano
		m. Alejandro Castillo
	Luisa Cayetano	Dominga Marin (1863)
	m. Eulogio Marin	m. Narcisco Bermudez
		m. Juan Avilez
		Joseph Cayetano
		m. Paula Ariola
		Francisca Cayetano
		m. Liborio Martinez
	Rafaela Cayetano	Fermin Jimenez
	m. Marcelino Jimenez	m. Petrona Cayetano
		Marcelina Jimenez
		m. Valentino Ramirez
	Policarpio Cayetano	
	m. Maria Gregorio	
	Agustin Cayetano (1844)	
	Luciano (1847)	
	m. Airetia Nunez	
	Maria Cayetano	
	Petrona Cayetano (1854)	
	m. Teodoro Palacio	9 children, *Fig. 3.9*

We know that Juan Pedro Cayetano also had nine children with Nicolasa Moralez, six of whom moved along with her to Barranco. Oral tradition says that Nicolasa's mother, Tomasa Avila, lived in Livingston, so it is likely that Nicolasa lived there before moving to Barranco. The first mention of Nicolasa in the records was her confirmation in Barranco in 1866, along with her son Anacleto, and her daughter Dominga. Dominga and Anacleto were born around 1833, so they were of child-bearing age when they moved to Barranco in the 1860s. The adult children of Juan Pedro Cayetano and Nicolasa Moralez contributed greatly to the growth of Barranco. Of the six who moved to Barranco, five had children there (*Fig. 3.10*).

Dominga (Waganga) Cayetano was born around 1833 and her husband Diego Paulino was born around 1827. Together they had four children. From the age given in death records we have calculated that Celestino was born around 1859 and Augustin around 1863, but the records do not show where Celestino, Augustin, or Ascensiona were born. Policarpio was born in Barranco in 1873. At the same time Diego Paulino was also having children with Maria Victoria Gamboa, two of whom were born in Barranco, Eustachio Paulino born in 1863,Delfinia Paulino in 1865, and Josefa Paulino in 1868.

Another child of Juan Pedro and Nicolasa, Anacleto Cayetano, was born around 1833 and married Dominga Martila Arzu of Punta Gorda. Their oldest child, Victoriana, was baptized in Punta Gorda in 1860, but at least two of their other children were born and baptized in Barranco, Andrea in 1863 and Justina in 1865.

Females predominated among the Cayetanos and other families who were among the first to move to Barranco, so one might say that the women settled Barranco and afterwards husbands joined them. However, since a woman takes a man's name, it is not so obvious in the records when a man brings a woman from the outside because no new name appears. For example, one of the few Cayetano men, Anacleto Cayetano married Dominga Martila Arzu, but that did not bring the Arzu name into the Barrano records. However, Barranco women are very much aware of their maiden name, as against their acquired married name.

E. Roy Cayetano

Melvinia Martinez (Granda Me)

Eldrid Roy Cayetano is the great-grandson of Paula Ariola and Joseph Cayetano, Mercedes Palacio and Celestino Paulino. Melvinia Martinez is the granddaughter of Ascenciona Paulino and Martin Nuñez, Regina Virgen Luis and Pedro Martinez

Naomi Colon

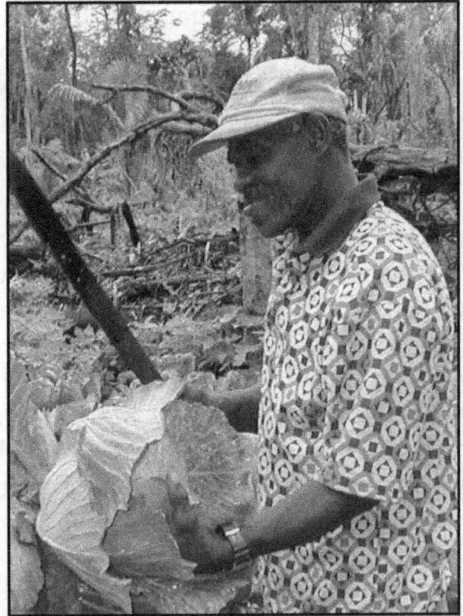

Nathaniel (Shorty) Cayetano

Naomi Colon is the great-granddaughter of Francisca Cayetano and Liborio Martinez, Dominga Cayetano and Diego Paulino. Nathaniel Cayetano is the great-grandson of Maria Loreta Palacio and Marcelo Cayetano, Andrea Nicholas and Simon Mejia.

Nolberto—Nicholas

The Nolberto and Nicholas families share several traits as pioneers. Having arrived from the Trujillo area, both probably came through Dangriga, stopping in Jonathan Point, and proceeding to Punta Gorda before ending up in Barranco. According to oral tradition, the two families were closely related and the men spent much time away from the settlement.

The first mention of Alexander Nicholas in the records for Barranco was in 1864 at the baptism of his daughter Alejandra. Alexander was a witness for the confirmation of Macario, son of Francisco Nolberto and Serapia, in 1880. Alexander's daughter Casimira also got confirmed in 1880. Figure 3.11 shows Alexander Nicholas and Eugenia Delavez's five children and 20 grandchildren, who are part of the growth of Barranco.

Serapia, the wife of Francisco Nolberto, was referred by different names: Serapia Alvarez, Serapia de Jesus, Serapia de Jesus Nolberto, Serapia Teus, Serapia Flores, Serafina Garcia, Serapia Nolberto, and Josefa Secundino.

Serapia appeared often in church records, mainly as witness for baptisms, confirmation, and marriages, first appearing at the baptism of her daughter Cristina in 1861 in Punta Gorda. Figure 3.12 shows the nine children, who were born to Francisco Nolberto and Serapia in the 1860s and 1870s. Their 29 grandchildren also contributed to the growth of Barranco.

There are marriage ties between the Nolberto and Nicholas families. Francisco and Serapia's son Pio married Casimira Nicholas, daughter of Alexander and Eugenia, and their son Leoncio's second wife was Alberta Nolberto.

Serapia died in 1910 at the age of 85 according to the registry information, so she was born around 1825. Eugenia died at the age of 64 in 1904, so she was born around 1840. According to a note at the marriage of his son Sotero, by 1897 Alexander had already died.

Figure 3.11. Alexander Nicholas and Eugenia, their children with spouses

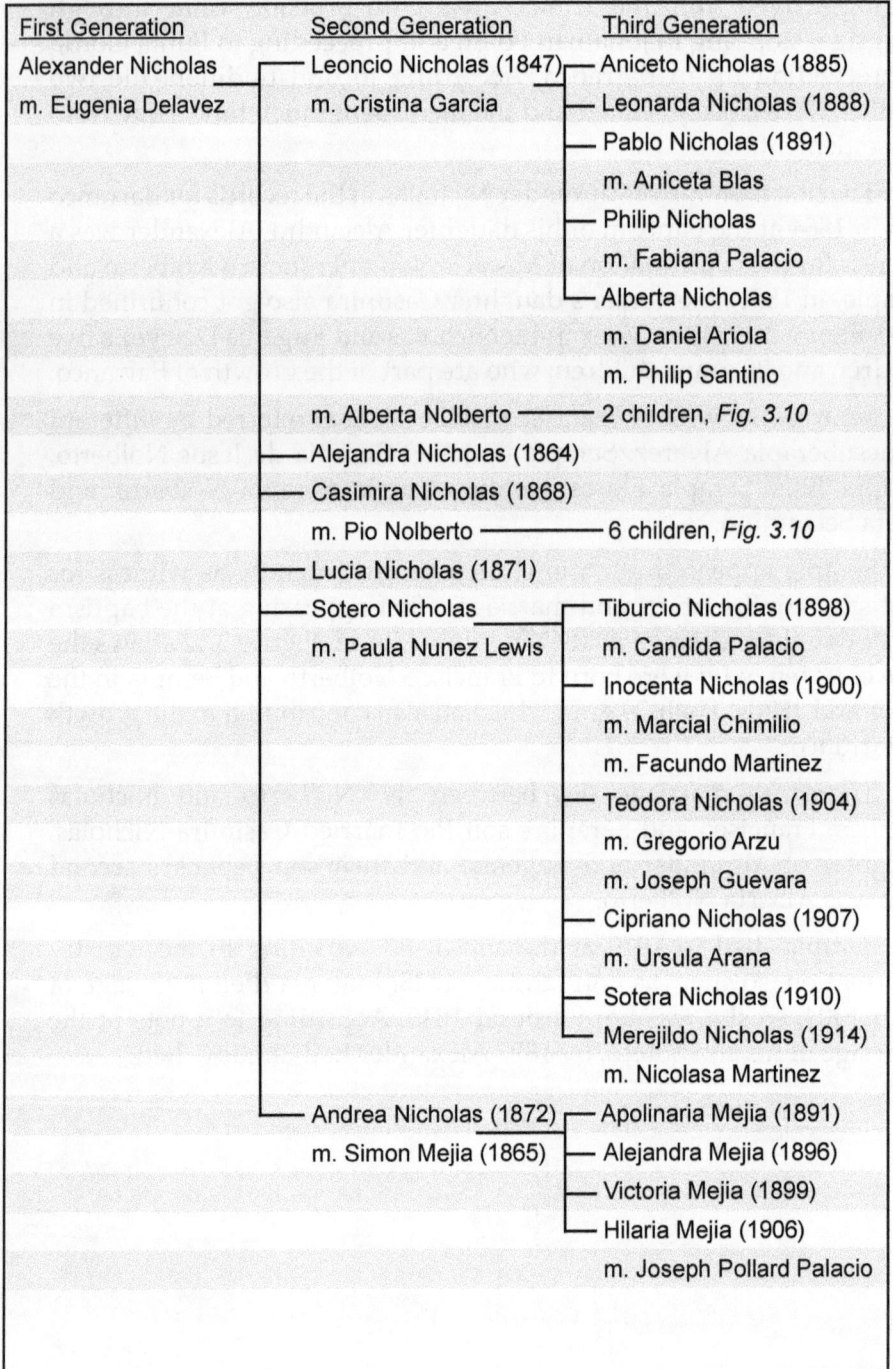

First Generation	Second Generation	Third Generation
Alexander Nicholas	Leoncio Nicholas (1847)	Aniceto Nicholas (1885)
m. Eugenia Delavez	m. Cristina Garcia	Leonarda Nicholas (1888)
		Pablo Nicholas (1891)
		m. Aniceta Blas
		Philip Nicholas
		m. Fabiana Palacio
		Alberta Nicholas
		m. Daniel Ariola
		m. Philip Santino
	m. Alberta Nolberto	2 children, *Fig. 3.10*
	Alejandra Nicholas (1864)	
	Casimira Nicholas (1868)	
	m. Pio Nolberto	6 children, *Fig. 3.10*
	Lucia Nicholas (1871)	
	Sotero Nicholas	Tiburcio Nicholas (1898)
	m. Paula Nunez Lewis	m. Candida Palacio
		Inocenta Nicholas (1900)
		m. Marcial Chimilio
		m. Facundo Martinez
		Teodora Nicholas (1904)
		m. Gregorio Arzu
		m. Joseph Guevara
		Cipriano Nicholas (1907)
		m. Ursula Arana
		Sotera Nicholas (1910)
		Merejildo Nicholas (1914)
		m. Nicolasa Martinez
	Andrea Nicholas (1872)	Apolinaria Mejia (1891)
	m. Simon Mejia (1865)	Alejandra Mejia (1896)
		Victoria Mejia (1899)
		Hilaria Mejia (1906)
		m. Joseph Pollard Palacio

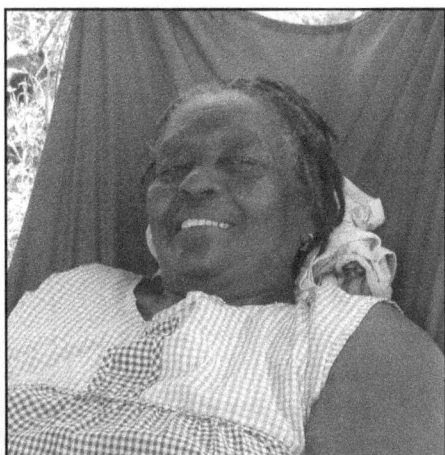

Lucille (Chilagu) Valencio

Angelina (Angie) Nicholas

Lucille Zuniga Valencio is the granddaughter of Casimira Nicholas and Pio Nolberto, Mauricia Cayetano and Claro Zuniga. Angelina Alvarez Nicholas is the granddaughter of Simon Mejia and Nicolasa Palacio.

Olivia Palacio Avila

Delaine Nicholas Ogaldez

Olivia Palacio Avila is the granddaughter of Andrea Nicholas and Simon Mejia, Ignacia Arana and Nolberto Palacio. Erlinda Delain Nicholas Ogaldez is great-granddaughter of Paula Nuñez Lewis and Sotero Nicholas

Figure 3.12. Francisco Nolberto and Serapia, their children and grandchildren

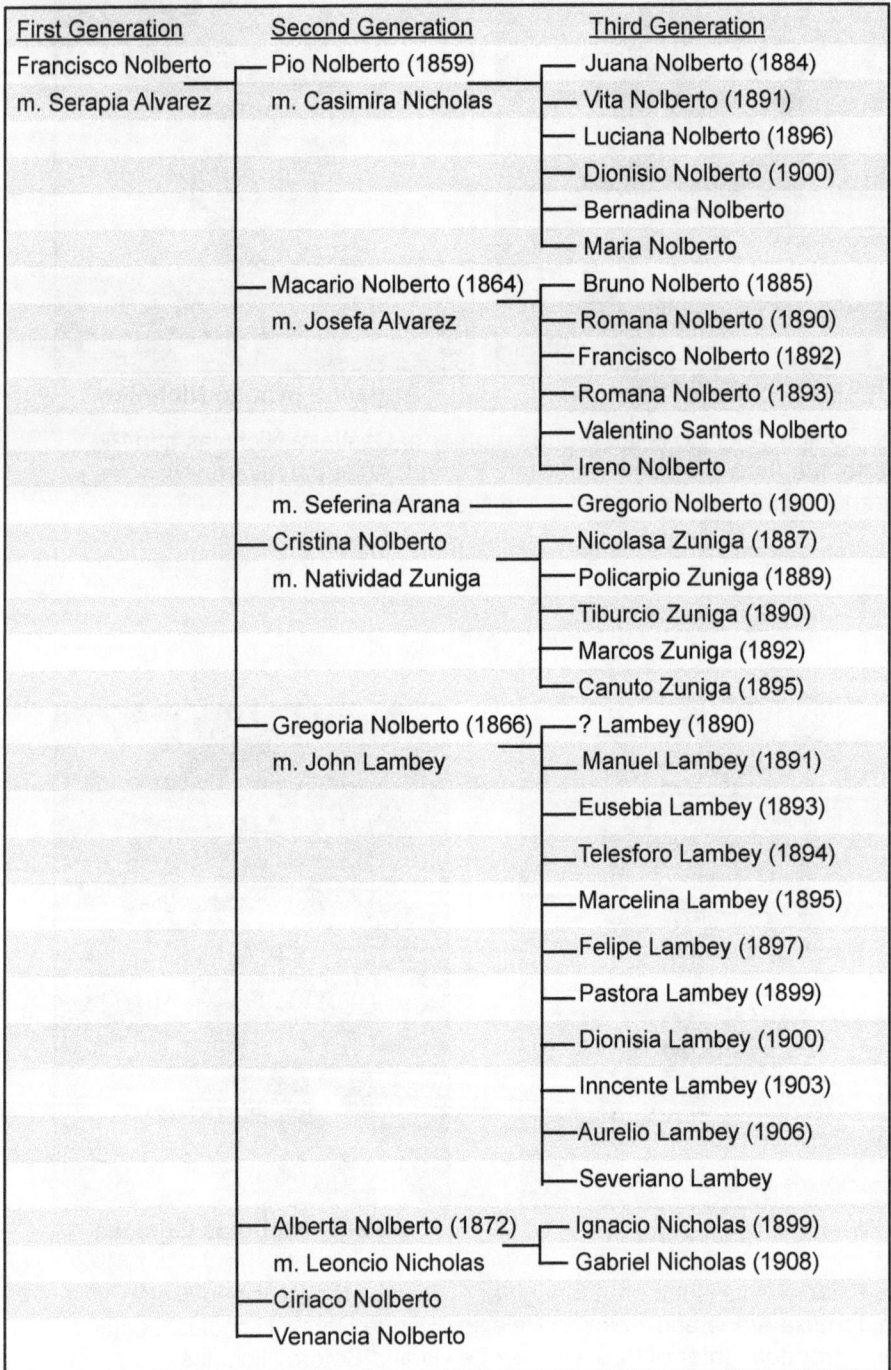

First Generation	Second Generation	Third Generation
Francisco Nolberto	Pio Nolberto (1859)	Juana Nolberto (1884)
m. Serapia Alvarez	m. Casimira Nicholas	Vita Nolberto (1891)
		Luciana Nolberto (1896)
		Dionisio Nolberto (1900)
		Bernadina Nolberto
		Maria Nolberto
	Macario Nolberto (1864)	Bruno Nolberto (1885)
	m. Josefa Alvarez	Romana Nolberto (1890)
		Francisco Nolberto (1892)
		Romana Nolberto (1893)
		Valentino Santos Nolberto
		Ireno Nolberto
	m. Seferina Arana	Gregorio Nolberto (1900)
	Cristina Nolberto	Nicolasa Zuniga (1887)
	m. Natividad Zuniga	Policarpio Zuniga (1889)
		Tiburcio Zuniga (1890)
		Marcos Zuniga (1892)
		Canuto Zuniga (1895)
	Gregoria Nolberto (1866)	? Lambey (1890)
	m. John Lambey	Manuel Lambey (1891)
		Eusebia Lambey (1893)
		Telesforo Lambey (1894)
		Marcelina Lambey (1895)
		Felipe Lambey (1897)
		Pastora Lambey (1899)
		Dionisia Lambey (1900)
		Inncente Lambey (1903)
		Aurelio Lambey (1906)
		Severiano Lambey
	Alberta Nolberto (1872)	Ignacio Nicholas (1899)
	m. Leoncio Nicholas	Gabriel Nicholas (1908)
	Ciriaco Nolberto	
	Venancia Nolberto	

Anacleta Nolberto Loredo

Clotido Zuniga

Anacleta Nolberto Loredo is the granddaughter of Casimira Nicholas and Pio Nolberto, great-granddaughter of Vivciona Cayetano and Sebastian Sanchez. Clotido Zuniga is grandson of Cristina Nolberto and Natividad Zuniga, Carmen Garcia and Victoriano Castillo.

Lorenzo (Thunder**) Nolberto**
(*photo by Joseph O. Palacio*)

Adriana Casimira

Lorenzo Nolberto is the grandson of Josefa Alvarez and Macario Nolberto. Adriana Casimira is the granddaughter of Bernadina Nolberto and Pablo Casimiro.

Garcia—Castillo

By 1870 Apolinario Garcia and his wife Marcelina Martinez, like Santiago Avilez, had come from Jonathan Point to Barranco. Marcelina may have been related to Tomasa Martinez, who came as a pioneer along with her husband Teodoro Palacio, son of Desideria. The earliest mention of them in Barranco was the birth of their son Jose Apolinario in 1870. They had seven children, including four daughters (*Fig. 3.13*).

In another instance of siblings marrying siblings, Felipa Garcia married Luis Palacio while her sister Nicanora Garcia married his brother, John Palacio. Nicanora left no offspring, but left a legacy of songs and stories (*Chapter 7*).

As their children became of child-bearing age, some attracted spouses from other communities. On getting married some left the village to start their families, making the fledgling Barranco a sending community even as it attracted younger men and women. Anacleto Garcia married Martina Arzu in Punta Gorda. Juliana married Pantaleon Avila and had six children with him, two of whom were born in Barranco before the family moved to Punta Gorda.

There are several connections between the Garcia family and the Castillo family. Carmen married Victoriano Castillo from Livingston. In 1871 Augustin Castillo was born in Barranco to Simona Garcia and Rafael Castillo from Dangriga. Furthermore, Victoriana Cayetano married Alejandro Castillo in 1877, the son of Jose Castillo and Santiaga Avila from Dangriga. We found no direct connection in the records, but perhaps Barranco provided an opportunity for convergence of these extended families from Dangriga in the north and Livingston in the south.

Figure 3.13. Apolinario Garcia and Marcelina Martinez, their children and grandchildren

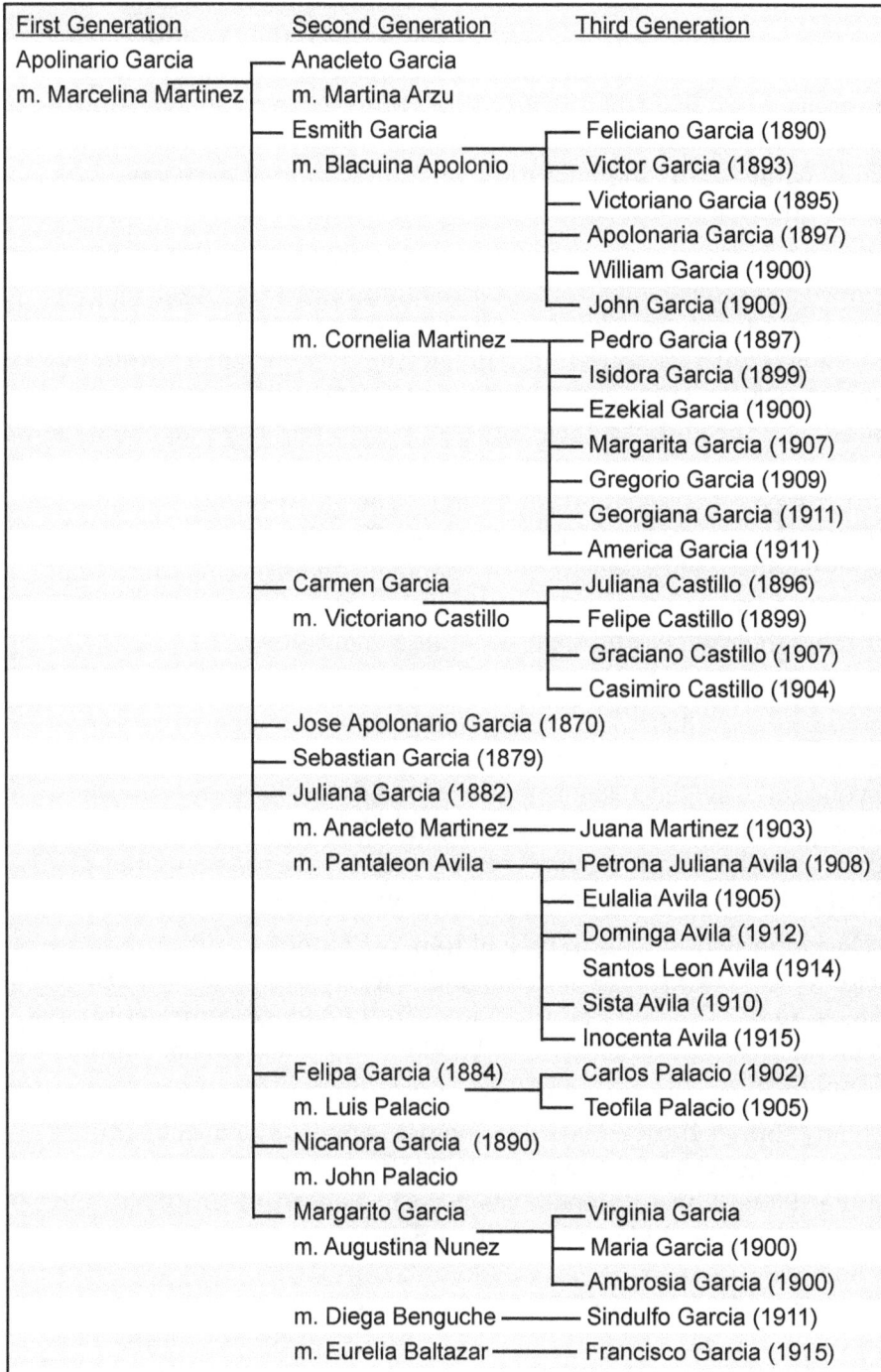

First Generation	Second Generation	Third Generation
Apolinario Garcia	Anacleto Garcia	
m. Marcelina Martinez	m. Martina Arzu	
	Esmith Garcia	Feliciano Garcia (1890)
	m. Blacuina Apolonio	Victor Garcia (1893)
		Victoriano Garcia (1895)
		Apolonaria Garcia (1897)
		William Garcia (1900)
		John Garcia (1900)
	m. Cornelia Martinez	Pedro Garcia (1897)
		Isidora Garcia (1899)
		Ezekial Garcia (1900)
		Margarita Garcia (1907)
		Gregorio Garcia (1909)
		Georgiana Garcia (1911)
		America Garcia (1911)
	Carmen Garcia	Juliana Castillo (1896)
	m. Victoriano Castillo	Felipe Castillo (1899)
		Graciano Castillo (1907)
		Casimiro Castillo (1904)
	Jose Apolonario Garcia (1870)	
	Sebastian Garcia (1879)	
	Juliana Garcia (1882)	
	m. Anacleto Martinez	Juana Martinez (1903)
	m. Pantaleon Avila	Petrona Juliana Avila (1908)
		Eulalia Avila (1905)
		Dominga Avila (1912)
		Santos Leon Avila (1914)
		Sista Avila (1910)
		Inocenta Avila (1915)
	Felipa Garcia (1884)	Carlos Palacio (1902)
	m. Luis Palacio	Teofila Palacio (1905)
	Nicanora Garcia (1890)	
	m. John Palacio	
	Margarito Garcia	Virginia Garcia
	m. Augustina Nunez	Maria Garcia (1900)
		Ambrosia Garcia (1900)
	m. Diega Benguche	Sindulfo Garcia (1911)
	m. Eurelia Baltazar	Francisco Garcia (1915)

Growth of Barranco: *Ábunagutian*

The vision that the *agiwerihatian* (carvers) had for Barranco was to lay the foundation of a Garifuna community that would benefit from the two worlds they knew—the indigenous as well as western civilization. They wanted to lead a life without the excessive control they had experienced at the hands of the Spanish and British colonial masters, while still being able to engage in economic exchange with them for goods and services.

The initial carving had to be followed by the next group of workers, whom we call *ábunagutian* (builders), continuing the Garifuna analogy we had started with *agiwerihatian*. We trace who they were and the ties they retained with the founding families living in Barranco within the period of 1860 to 1891. Fortunately, some members of the founding families lived through the 1860 and 1891 period and beyond, enabling them to assist their children and grandchildren with the challenges of constructing a settlement and community. The line running through all of these achievements was kinship that we have been able to reconstruct through the life cycle events of birth, baptism, confirmation, marriage, and death. As men and women celebrated these rituals, they were also celebrating themselves and their unfolding community.

In addition to the increases in their own families, which were extensive in the 1860s and 1870s, the pioneer families were joined by several others, mostly by Barranco women attracting husbands. The younger Cayetano daughters continued the Barranco tradition of bringing men into the village. Rafaela Cayetano married Fermin Jimenez and their son married her brother Anacleto's daughter the younger Petrona Cayetano, in a cross cousin marrage (*p. 79*).

Desideria's grandchildren, children of Teodoro and Anastacio Palacio, were growing to adulthood and starting their own families by the 1890s. Other Garifuna family names in the village community by 1892 include Avila, Arana, Ariola, Lambey, Martinez, Mejia, Santino, and Zuniga.

Many Spanish non-Garifuna names appeared in the church records. One quarter of those confirmed in Barranco in 1880 were non-Garifuna. Florentina Cardenas was born to Leocardio Cardenas and Luisa Rodriguez in 1870, and Martina Sanchez, daughter of Petrona Andrade and Tomas Sanchez, was baptized in Barranco in 1871. The family names of Andrade, Cardenas, Rodriguez, and Sanchez continue to appear in the Barranco genealogical records for the rest of the 19th Century. Oral history describes Pañatón in the southeastern area of Barranco as a Spanish settlement (*see map of area Figure 4.11, p. 100*)

The period 1860 to 1891 saw the growth of Barranco from a temporary fishing camp site to a village community with scores of residents. The first information about its size in the 19th Century is in a letter from Father di Pietro in 1880, "Near Punta Gorda, about nine miles south, there is another Catholic village, Red-Cliff, of two hundred inhabitants, with small chapel and small hut for the priest."[65] In the 1891 census Barranco had a population of 225.

During that period the village experienced the least amount of intervention from outside sources in its entire existence. Loggers came to buy provisions and offered wage labour stints to the men.[81] More substantial cash inflow came during the later years of the 1880s when villagers sold bananas to boats passing from Guatemala on their way to the Stann Creek area. All of these interventions, however, were seasonal and did not come with the kind of direct imposition that the colonial government subsequently made, as in the subdivision and allocation of ownership to lots and farmlands. Within this relatively open environment, both Garifuna and non-Garifuna men and women came, several passing through, but many stopping and taking up residence in the village.

The possibility of non-whites forming a non-authorized community along the coast and near the estuaries of three main river waterways, then constituting the primary setting for economic exploitation through timber and estate agriculture, contradicts the impressions of unrelenting colonial vigilance on the socioeconomy.[66] Such intransigence has been identified much earlier among the Maya during the pre-British era in western Belize.[67] Apart from highlighting the over-extension of colonial authority in southern Belize in the latter years of the 19th century, there is another way to account for this anomaly. It is the desire of preliterate peoples to use their indigenous culture traits to form their own settlements.

While kinship was the primary medium of recruiting new members into the community, ethnicity became the source of social and cultural differences between the larger Garifuna population and non-Garifuna men and women, who also became members of the community or remained in adjacent communities, frequently coming to use the church and other village services. We describe who these people were and the interactions they formed with the Garifuna majority. We analyse how the villagers used kinship and ethnicity as methods in building a settlement from the beginning through the use of blood relations (consanguineal) and marriage relations (affinal).

Life Cycle Events

Baptism is the formal acceptance into the body of the Roman Catholic Church, normally administered to an infant in the presence of the immediate family members and a sponsor. Usually referred to as *ebenenei* (godfather or godmother in Garifuna), the *ebenenei* is to assist the parents in the spiritual well-being of the new entrant into the Church. Among the Garifuna, the *ebenenei* is usually a very close relative who is selected to validate kinship ties rather than fulfill the spiritual role stipulated by the church. By and large, the ties among the adults—parents and godparents—remain stronger than between the godchild and godparent. To the godchild the godparent is neither parent nor surrogate. Should the child need help unavailable from the parent, he/she would sooner look to a blood relative, who just may happen to be his godparent.[68]

As a ritual, confirmation re-affirms church membership within a complement of specific rights and obligations. Youth around the ages of ten to fourteen receive the sacrament, also in the presence of a sponsor. Among the Garifuna this ceremony had far less significance compared to baptism. They participate to satisfy their church obligations, which would have had minimal currency within the social life of Barranco.[69]

Figure 3.14. Pastores at Christmas 1941

On this photo at the Midwest Jesuit Archives is this caption. "My church and house in Barranco. The house was built in 1901. Last month during a good blow, I thought house and pastor would be up on the church roof in the morning. The children are not a First Communion class but the Pastores at Christmas time." Father Marion Ganey was the priest in Punta Gorda in 1942. (*photo courtesy Midwest Jesuit Archives*)

On the other hand, the sacrament of marriage received much communal support during that time. Living in sin (not in wedlock) and indulging in idolatry (native spirituality) were two evils against which the church preached relentlessly. Apparently, they achieved some success in increasing the rate of marriage by the 1880s. In going through the records of persons from birth onwards, we have observed a high rate of marriage taking place between 1860 and 1891 compared to the limited proportion in current times.[70]

Birth and Baptism: Linkages to Founding Families

According to our records there were 80 Garifuna infants born and/or baptized in Barranco from 1860 to 1891. We have placed all their names in the Appendix (*Table B3.1*) in chronological order. This list is incomplete because of the gap between 1872 and 1882 when there were no resident priests in Punta Gorda.

All except 11 of the Garifuna infants had linkages to the founding families (86%). Table 3.2 summarizes these linkages. The two ancestors, who had the largest number of direct ties with those baptized, were Juan Pedro Cayetano and Nicolasa Moralez. The actual founder of the location, Santiago Avilez, had only one descendant born in Barranco, while his wife's Palacio progeny remained firmly rooted during the first three decades of the settlement. It is interesting to note that both Nicolasa and Desideria had greater presence in the village, which would have given them more lasting influence in their interactions with their progeny than their husbands. The impact of matrilocality on settlement pioneering comes through clearly

Table 3.1. Summary of Linkages to Founding Families: Baptism and Birth

Baptism and Birth		
Cayetano	27	35%
Desideria	15	19%
Nolberto	13	19%
Nicholas	8	10%
Garcia	5	8%
Avilez	1	1%
Total	69	

We could find no link to the founding families for the three Gamboa children. Juan Garcia's father is Timoteo Garcia, who was confirmed in Barranco in 1880. He may be related to Apolinario Garcia, but we could not confirm this.

Three of the Garifuna infants born in Barranco were linked through a step-daughter relationship. Santita (1880), Felicita (1886), and Stanislao Reyes (1889) were all born to Martin Reyes and Luisa Ventrana Roches, the daughter of Sotera Gutierrez through her previous marriage with Venancio Roches. Gutierrez had several children by Anastacio Palacio, so these three were step-grandchildren to Desideria. They are counted in Table 3.1 as linked to Desideria. This is not inconsistent with Garifuna culture, for there is no word for "step-daughter" or "step-son" in Garifuna, only "daughter" and "son". Besides, the relations between step parents and step children should be identical to those between parents and their offsprings.

By the 1880s, as the next generation appeared, some persons showed linkages to more than one of the founding families. One example is Francisca Palacio, who was born in 1886 to Teodoro Palacio and Petrona Cayetano. Teodoro's direct ties are to Desideria, while Petrona's are to Juan Pedro Cayetano and his wife Nicolasa Moralez. These are indications that not only were the pioneers partners in overcoming the challenges of starting a new community, they were also galvanizing the ties among themselves through the marriage of their sons and daughters.

Confirmation

We have records of three confirmation ceremonies during Barranco's first thirty years. At the first one on the 29th of November, 1866, several adults were confirmed. Anacleto Cayetano was the first confirmed with Santiago Avilez acting as his godfather. Having just been confirmed, Anacleto acted as godfather to others being confirmed that day.

Of these ten participants, five were related to the Cayetanos and two to Desideria (*Table 3.2*). We don't know if Santiaga Nolberto is related to Francisco Nolberto and Serapia, who were only beginning to have children in 1866, so none would have been old enough to be confirmed. There was only one non-Garifuna, Maria Victoria Peña.[71]

Table 3.2. Barranco Confirmation Class of 1866

Name	Linkage to Funding Families	Age
Anacleto Cayetano	son of Juan Pedro Cayetano	36
Martila Arzu	wife of Anacleto Cayetano	30
Iginia Palacio	daughter of Desideria	
Dominga Cayetano	daughter of Juan Pedro Cayetano	33
Nicolasa Moralez	wife of Juan Pedro Cayetano	
Santiaga Nolberto	relationship to Nolbertos unknown	29
Anastacio Palacio	son of Desideria & Francisco Palacio	32
Diego Paulino	husband of Dominga Cayetano	39
Maria Concepcion Avila	Garifuna, mother of Nicolasa Moralez	
Maria Victoria Peña	non-Garifuna	

Figure 3.15. Barranco's confirmation class of 1979
(*from left* unknown girl, Lisette Arnold, Urban Avila, Nigel Underwoood, unknown girl, Xavier Sandoval, Glen Avila, unknown boy, Elida Palacio (*tall girl in the back*), Aurily Alvarez, Lilette Aranda, Glen Underwood, Sharon Nunez, Nelson Nunez, unknown girl, unknown girl, and Edith Sanchez. *(photo by Joseph O. Palacio)*

Table 3.3. Barranco Confirmation Class of 1880

Name	Founder Relationship	Age
Petrona Cayetano	grand-daughter of Juan Pedro Cayetano	15
Anacleto Garcia	son of Apolinario Garcia	
Maximiliano Garcia	son of Apolinario Garcia	10
Rafael Garcia	Garcia relationship unknown	
Timoteo Garcia	Garcia relationship unknown	
Rosa Mistica Lambey	sister-in-law to Ascenciona Paulino	
Macario Nolberto	son of Francisco Nolberto	16
Casimira Nicholas	daughter of Alexander Nicholas	12
Gregoria Nolberto	daughter of Francisco Nolberto	14
Ciriaco Nolberto	son of Francisco Nolberto	
Liberato Palacio	grandson of Desideria	12
Gregoria Palacio	grandaughter of Desideria	
Norberto Palacio	grandson of Desideria	12
Fernando Paulino	Paulino relationship unknown	12
Florencia Zuniga	Zuniga relationship unknown	
Faustina Francisco	Garifuna, no known link	
Thomas Francisco	Garifuna, no known link	
Juan Miguel Luis	Garifuna, no known link	
Vicenta Luis	Garifuna, no known link	
Secundino Sabio	Garifuna, no known link	
Francisca Albina	non-Garifuna	
Justa Andrade	non-Garifuna	
Marcelo Andrade	non-Garifuna	
Nasario Andrade	non-Garifuna	
Jose Santos Cardenas	non-Garifuna	
Julian Cardenas	non-Garifuna	
Juana Isidoro	non-Garifuna	
Juana Maria Paula	non-Garifuna	
Hilario Romano	non-Garifuna	
Juan Pablo Sanchez	non-Garifuna	
Martina Sanchez	non-Garifuna	

By the next confirmation in 1880, the candidates were at the age range when that sacrament is normally administered (*Table 3.3*). Those for whom we knew birthdates were between 10 and 16 years old. There were 31 participants, 20 being Garifuna and 11 non-Garifuna. Of the Garifuna participants, half (10) had known ties with the founding families, which is a smaller proportion than the previous confirmation and what we have already seen with baptisms and birth.

Some Baranguna were confirmed in Punta Gorda. Mauricia Cayetano was born and married in Barranco, but confirmed in the 1880 class in Punta Gorda. Josefa Paulino, although she was born and married in Barranco, was confirmed in the 1881 class in Punta Gorda.

Table 3.4. Barranco Confirmation Class of 1887

Name	Founder Relationship	Age
Vincenta Castillo	Mother Simona Garcia, **Father Rafael Garcia**	9
Carmen Garcia	daughter of Apolinario and Marcelina Garcia	
Margarito Garcia	son of Apolinario and Marcelina Garcia	
Teodora Garcia	Garcia relationship unknown	
Florencia Lambey	daughter of Rosa Mistica Lambey	
Cornelia Martinez	Martinez relationship unknown	
Andrea Nicholas	daughter of Alejandro Nicholas & Nicolasa	15
Alberta Nolberto	daughter of Francisco Nolberto & Serapia	15
Celestina Nolberto	Nolberto relationship unknown	
Venancia Nolberto	daughter of Francisco Nolberto & Serapia	
Aloysius Palacio	Palacio relationship unknown	
Eustaquia Palacio	granddaughter of Desideria	16
Nicolasa Palacio	granddaughter of Desideria	17
Bonifacia Paulino	Paulino relationship unknown	
Hilario Sanchez	grandson of Juan Pedro Cayetano	9
Ursula Andrade	non-Garifuna	
Paula Duarte	non-Garifuna	
Rafaela Juliana	non-Garifuna	
Valentino Linares	non-Garifuna	
Nolberta Peña	non-Garifuna	

Seven years later in 1887 about one-third of the Garifuna candidates had links to the founding families (*Table 3.4*), and one-quarter were non-Garifuna. Table 3.5 summarizes the linkages to founding families among confirmation candidates.

Table 3.5. Summary of Linkages to Founding Families in Confirmation Classes

Founding Family	1866	1880	1887
Cayetano	5	1	1
Desideria	2	3	2
Nolberto	0	3	1
Nicholas	0	1	1
Garcia	0	2	1
Garifuna, no link	2	10	8
Non-Garifuna	1	11	5
Total	10	31	19

Marriages among Garifuna

There were 36 marriages in Barranco or of Barranco residents in the first thirty years. Of these, 28 were Garifuna and eight non-Garifuna, but the latter occured only in the last 12 years, 1880–1892. The Garifuna marriages are listed in Appendix B (*Table B3.2*). Seven showed no linkages with the founding families. The linkages of the other 21 are summarized in Table 3.6. Ten of the grooms and 14 of the brides had direct links. The Cayetanos had the most links, four among the grooms and seven among the brides. The other families each had a few, except the Garcias. Being the youngest of the founding families, the Garcia children were not yet of marrying age during this period. Though his progeny were not seen often in the other events we studied, Santiago Avilez had two sons and one daughter who were married in Barranco. The sons were Ambrocio Avilez (Sabigi) who married Justa Apolonio and Justo James Avilez (Bangi) who married Cornelia Luis; the daughter was Gregoria Avilez who married Martin Garcia.

Table 3.6. Frequency of Linkages to Founding Families: Marriage

Grooms		Brides	
Cayetano	4	Cayetano	7
Avilez	2	Palacio	3
Palacio	2	Nicholas	2
Nicholas	1	Nolberto	1
Nolberto	1	Avilez	1
Total	10		14

During the first three decades of Barranco one did not select one's spouse. Rather he/she was prescribed by cultural norms. Kinship rules established who in the community were potential spouses as against those with whom one should retain friendly, non-spousal relations. The result was that the community ensured its own continuity, which was essential for community start-ups like Barranco. We have examples of this prescription for marriage partners, which declined in frequency after the 1900s.

Two rules of marriage are demonstrated in the following examples—cross-cousin and sibling exchange. A cross-cousin marriage was common practice in Garifuna culture. Cross cousins are the children of a brother and a sister, as opposed to parallel cousins who are children of brothers or children of sisters. For example, Anacleto Cayetano and Rafaela Cayetano are brother and sister. Anacleto's daughter Petrona married Rafaela's son Fermin Jimenez (*Fig. 3.16*).

Figure 3.16. Cross cousin marriage

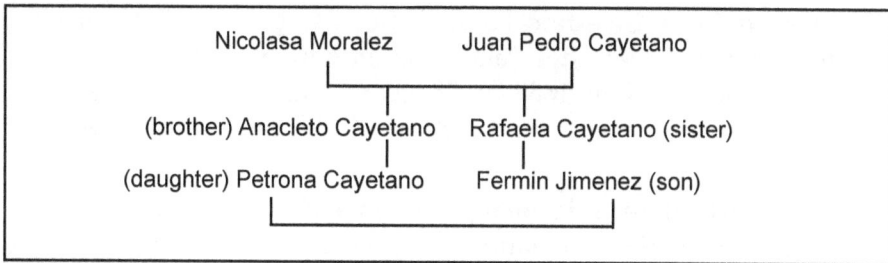

Figure 3.17. Brother-sister marriage exchange

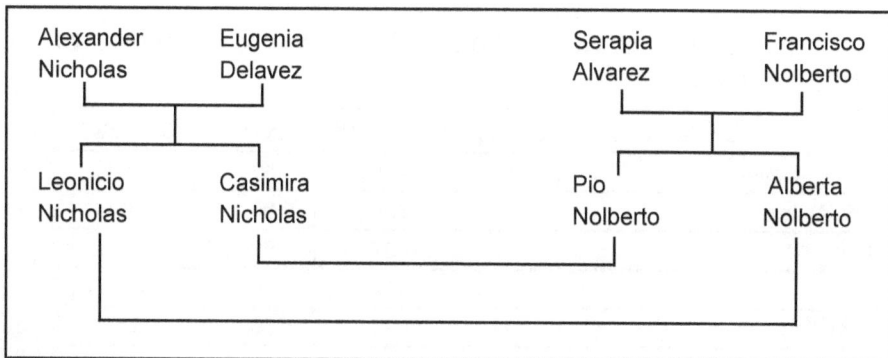

Sibling exchange is when two siblings marry two siblings from another family. An example is Leoncio Nicholas marrying Alberta Nolberto while Leoncio's sister Casamira married Alberta's brother Pio (*Fig. 3.17*).

While the examples so far have been about men and women entering into marital ties taking place within the settlement, they were also doing so across communities using the same kinship prescriptions. Both the Cayetanos and Paulinos had relatives living in Punta Gorda and continued the practice of marrying into each other's families.

Death Records

The government began registering deaths in 1885, so records were limited to the last few years of the period 1862–1891. There were sixteen deaths reported, nine Garifuna and seven non-Garifuna, showing the highest proportion of non-Garifuna people for any event. Few of the death records included next of kin, so we were not able to connect them with a particular family. Examples are Timotea Sanchez and Jose Teodoro Garcia. Both last names were well represented in the village and indicate probable ties, but we have not been able to determine them. Timotea was one day old, while Jose Teodoro Garcia was 27 years old.

The only two we were able to identify as linked to the founding families were in-laws. Celestino Paulino died at age 28 in 1887, the year after he married Mercedes Palacio, granddaughter of Desideria. Narciso Bermudez died in 1888 at 38 years old, eight years after marrying Dominga Marin, granddaughter of Nicolasa Moralez and Juan Pedro Cayetano.

Because the death records often provide the person's age at death, they were useful for the calculation of approximate birth years for members of the founding families. The age was given by the person reporting the death, so it may not be as reliable as when we have the birth record (*Fig. 3.7*).

Table 3.7. Calculation of Approximate Birth Years for Members of Founding Families

Name	Death Year[a]	Age	Birth Year
Juan Pedro Cayetano	1821[b]	17	1803
Santiago Avilez	1894	90	1804
Desideria	1907	98	1809
Serapia	1910	85	1825
Diego Paulino	1896	69	1827
Dominga Cayetano	1930	97	1833
Anacleto Cayetano	1901	68	1833
Anastacio Palacio	1924	90	1834
Martila Arzu	1904	68	1836
Clara Martinez	1906	70	1836
Sotera Gutierrez	1919	79	1840
Santiaga Nolberto	1871[c]	29	1842
Teodoro Palacio	1909	65	1844
Leoncio Nicholas	1921	74	1847

Name	Death Year[a]	Age	Birth Year
Narcisco Bermudez	1888	38	1850
Jose Teodoro Garcia	1889	37	1852
Petrona Cayetano	1908	54	1854
Rufino Ariola	1888[c]	33	1855
Marcelo Cayetano	1907	52	1855
Cristina Garcia	1893	35	1858
Celestino Paulino	1887	28	1859
Pio Nolberto	1921	62	1859
Philip Santino	1908[c]	45	1863
Petrona Cayetano	1880[c]	20	1860
Simon Mejia	1923	58	1865
Augustin Paulino	1931	65	1866

[a]Some entries were calculated from age given for the record at other life cycle events.
[b]Birth Year was calculated from age at Trujillo, Honduras, 1821 census.
[c]Birth Year was calculated from age at marriage.

Summary of Garifuna Participation in Life Cycle Events

The data from all these life cycle events is summarized in Table 3.8. The number of participants in each event is listed, as well as the number and percent of the Garifuna people having direct links to the pioneers. We include the non-Garifuna participants in the last column.

Table 3.8. Participants in Events 1860-1891

Event	Garifuna			Non-Garifuna
	No.	with links	% with links	
Birth/Baptism	80	69	86%	17
Confirmation				
1866	9	7	78%	1
1880	20	10	50%	7
1887	15	7	46%	5
Marriage	31	25	80%	7
Grooms	31	9	29%	7
Brides	31	17	54%	7
Death	10	2	20%	7
Total	168	120	72%	45

The families who carved out the settlement of Barranco were few, and through the life cycle events of birth, baptism, confirmation, marriage, and death, they reinforced kinship obligations among themselves and their first and second generation descendants. Quite in contrast to a suspicion that the Garifuna culture encircled the residents within a block of conformity, there was in fact much flexibility. Some of the sons and daughters of the pioneers went back to the communities from which the family had come, while their siblings stayed in Barranco. Similarly, other men and women, with only weak kin ties, if any, came and settled.

Inter-community Relationships

Baranguna have strong ties to the two closest communities of Punta Gorda and Livingston, making a somewhat fluid population. Many infants born in Barranco were baptized in Punta Gorda months later or as early as the next day. One family demonstrates the extent of inter-community relationships. Vivciona Cayetano married Sebastian Sanchez in Livingston the 24th of February, 1865. Their first son, Francisco Xavier Sanchez, was born in Barranco on the 6th of December, 1865, and baptized in Punta Gorda on the 3rd of January, 1866. Their daughter Eleuteria Cayetano was born in Barranco April 18th, 1868, baptized in Livingston May 30th, 1868, married January 12th, 1888, in Punta Gorda, and died in Barranco February 4th, 1927. This pattern is repeated often among many families.

Non-Garifuna Population

We noted the names of non-Garifuna persons in the church records. Most of the names were Hispanic like the names of the majority Garifuna population, but we were able to isolate which were Garifuna; and concluded that the non-Garifuna were Mestizos. If either spouse or parent was Garifuna, we have classified the event as involving Garifuna. Some of these names, such as Enriquez, Fuentes, Luis, Martinez, and Sanchez, are found in both the Garifuna and Mestizo communities. For example, Vivciona Cayetano married Sebastian Sanchez, a Garifuna, but Tomas Sanchez who married Petrona Andrade was probably not Garifuna, so their marriage was classified as non-Garifuna. Where we could not show a Garifuna linkage, we have classifed the event as non-Garifuna.[72]

The Mestizos came from the Caribbean coastal areas of Honduras and Guatemala, often from the same general sub-regions as the Garifuna. Some lived in Barranco while others lived in smaller settlements along the coast or the banks of the three rivers—Moho, Temash, and Sarstoon—that drain the village subregion. Wherever they lived, they participated in life cycle events taking place in the settlement. Table 3.9 is a list of these names in baptism, birth, marriage, and death events for the 1860-1891 period.

Table 3.9. Non-Garifuna Participation in Life Cycle Events

Year	Name	Parents
Birth		
1863-09-27	Damiana Feliz	Joseph & Maria Feliz
1869-10	Maria Feliz	(adult baptism)
1870-02-23	Florentina Cardenas	Leocardio Cardenas & Luisa Rodriguez
1871-01-20	Martina Sanchez	Tomas Sanchez & Petrona Andrade
1871-09-20	Eustaquia Diaz	Mateo Diaz & Higinia Acquirres
1872-05-08	Salome Gomez	Augustin Gomez & Stanisla Cardenas
1878-07-18	Sinforoso Vairez	Serapio Vairez & Francisca Peña
1879-06-26	Elizabeth Cardenas	Leocardio Cardenas & Petrona Andrade
1881-02-21	Arcadia Grianez	Florencio Grianez & Marta Alvarez
1885-10-24	Marian la Cruz	Dorotea Sala
1887-04-04	Isidora Vermosa	Jose & Dominga Vermosa
1887-02-02	Ignacio Baycina	Maria Baycina
1888-10	Syrian Hemmans	James Hemmans & Jane Harris
1889-03-02	Benicia Ortega	Cristino Ortega and Maxima Andrade
1889-05-25	Augustina Vairez	Serapio & Juana Vairez
1890-10-25	Crispin Caliz	Eligio Caliz & Maria Salas
1890-12-28	Esteban Martinez	Jose Luis Martinez (G) & Alejandra Vairez
Marriage		
1879-02-07	Jose Leon Mendoza & Toribia Peña	
1879-02	Sebastian Hernandez & Nieves Rodriguez	
1879-06-26	Leocardio Cardenas & Petrona Andrade	Bernardo Andrade & Mercedes Romero
1882-05-24	Serapio Vairez & Francisca Peña	Andres Vairez & Luciano Enriquez
1883-06-15	Benito Pineda & Georgia Mendoza	Apolonio Pineda & Juana Gertrudes Pineda Jose Leon Mendoza & Toribia Peña
1885-04-20	Julian Cardenas & Justa Andrade	Bernardo Andrade & Mercedes Romero
1887-12-09	Jose Isaac Zelaya & Ursula Andrade	Andalesio Zelaya
Death		
1888-03	Benito Calvera	No known relative; died at 38 years
1888	Manuel Romero	No relative; died at 36 years
1888-12-03	Mercedes Romero	wife of Bernardo Andrade, died at 36 years
1888-05-10	Tomas Vairez	No known relative; died at 65 years
1889-12-13	Margarito Andrade	No known relative; died at 60 years
1889-06-09	Augustino Vairez	No relative; died at 5 months
1890-02-07	Eusebio Vairez	No relative; died at 6 months

Andrade was the most frequently mentioned non-Garifuna family name. Two Andrades died in the late 1880s, one was Margarito, who died at the age of 60 and the other Mercedes Romero, who was the wife of Bernardo Andrade. The following Andrades were of child-bearing age—Petrona, Justa, Maxima, Ursula, and Teodoro. Two younger and pre-child bearing men, who were confirmed in 1880, were Nasario and Marcelo. The Andrades married into families with surnames Alvarez, Cardenas, Castro, Fuentes, Lambey, Lozano, Mejia, Ortega, Romero, Sanchez, and Zelaya.

Figure 3.18 is a kinship chart showing the proliferation of these surnames among the descendants of Bernardo Andrade. Participating in so many life cycle ceremonies in Barranco for at least three generations indicates that the Andrades had established permanent ties within the community.

The second most commonly occuring family name was Vairez in several variations—Bairez, Baires, Berez, Bayrez, Vera, and Viera. The Vairezes displayed a similarly prolonged relationship with the settlement as the Andrades. The first appearance of the Vairez name is in 1878 when Serapio Vairez had a son Sinforoso with Francisca Peña in Barranco. Serapio had a daughter Augustina by his wife Juana in 1889. There were two Vairez deaths registered. Augustino died at five months of age and Tomas at the age of 65 in 1888. We have no information on their linkages to the other Vairez families.

Figure 3.18. Children of Bernardo Andrade and Mercedes Romero

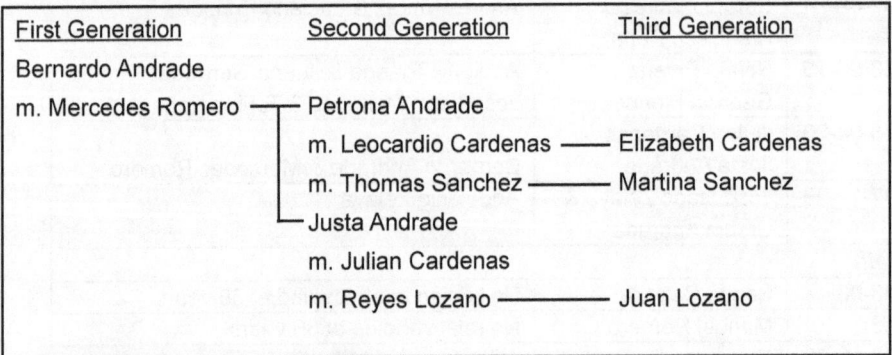

First Generation	Second Generation	Third Generation
Bernardo Andrade		
m. Mercedes Romero	Petrona Andrade	
	m. Leocardio Cardenas	Elizabeth Cardenas
	m. Thomas Sanchez	Martina Sanchez
	Justa Andrade	
	m. Julian Cardenas	
	m. Reyes Lozano	Juan Lozano

The name Cardenas (also appearing as Casanez) was mentioned in four events. Other names included Romero, Peña (also appearing as Paria), Mendoza, and Gomez. Apart from Andrade, Vairez, and Cardenas, the other surnames appeared only once or twice. It is possible that they were not permanent residents of Barranco or might have lived there for short periods without a succession of life cycle events. Among the non-Garifuna families, James A. Hemmans and Mary Jane Harris registered their daughter Syrian Elizabeth born in 1888. They were the only non-Garifuna family with a non-Hispanic surname.

Inter-Ethnic Relationships

Although the Mestizos and Garifuna were living within a small community, there were minimal interethnic unions among them. There was only one mixed marriage of a Mestizo male with a Garifuna woman, namely Jose Andrade who married Juliana Fuentes (*Appendix B 3.2*). The indications are that there were a few interethnic informal unions between Mestizo and Garifuna. Mestizo Teodoro Andrade had two children with Garifuna women, daughter Benita Andrade with Alejandra Alvarez in 1888 and son Canuto Andrade with Maria Lambey in 1894. Garifuna Simon Mejia had daughter Paula Mejia in 1894 with Micaela Andrade.

Table 3.10 summarizes the non-Garifuna participants in life-cycle events in Barranco. The death records were only for the last few of Barranco's first thirty years, so the higher proportion of non-Garifuna deaths reflects the composition of the village in the late 1880s.

Table 3.10. Summary of Non-Garifuna Participants in Events

Name	Total	Non-Garifuna	% of Total
Birth / Baptism	97	17	16%
1866 Confirmation	10	1	10%
1880 Confirmation	31	5	16%
1887 Confirmation	19	6	32%
Marriage	38	7	21%
Death	16	7	44%

Summary and Conclusions

F inding the initial location of Barranco might have been a
serendipitous act taken by a few explorers looking for a new *úbiabaraü*
(homeland) to escape harassment by Central American authorities. The
gradual growth from a fishing camp to a village community thirty
years afterwards, however, was the result of deliberate actions taken
by ever increasing groups of men and women within varying degrees
of kinship. Firstly, the location on top of a promontory was high, well
drained, and circumscribed by sea and land teeming with ample
natural resources. Secondly, there were no whites to drive them away
as they claimed their residential space, started building their houses,
and cleared the bush for their farms. Thirdly, it was a short distance
away from neigbouring communities, appropriate for trading and
learning about job availability.

This chapter has detailed how five founding family groups gave
birth, gave away their sons and daughters in marriage, and some saw
their grandchildren go through the next wave of life cycle events from
1861 to 1891.

Kinship through prescribed marriage patterns was a primary
method of drawing new community members through cross-cousin
marriage, the exchange in marriage of brothers and sisters between two
families, and the union of siblings with siblings of another family. The
result was the repeated crossover of consanguineal with affinal kinship;
or that men and women became husbands and wives, while still being
closely related by blood.

Joining the Garifuna as settlers were Mestizos who were looking
for better economic opportunities through agriculture and wage labour.
Like the majority Garifuna, Mestizos came after the middle of the 1800s
and by 1891 numbered almost 20% of the village population. Mestizos
engaged in life cycle events, such as baptism, confirmation and
marriage. A small community of 225 at 1891, Barranco was stratified by
ethnicity with a limited amount of inter-ethnic relations.

Having described how Barranco started and given a profile
of overlapping relationships within its population, we go to the next
chapter to describe how colonial surveyors drew their first gridlines
in the village and how the accompanying household survey they did
clarifies the settlement pattern in the village.

Chapter Four
The 1892 Village Lot Survey

Although the Garifuna had settled Barranco by the 1860s, in 1892 British authorities attempted to extinguish their customary rights to their own house lots and imposed legal ownership according to colonial law. One way of describing this exercise is "the appropriation of land of myth by land of law".[73] The stroke of the surveyor's pen firstly dispossessed many a person of his/her lot, then officially re-allocated the same lot to him/her; or, in some cases completely deprived him/her by giving the lot to others. This chapter analyzes the building of a community, where its members had to come to terms with the colonial rule of settlement. The village still exists in the early years of the twenty-first century, a monument to the persistence of the pioneers and their descendants, notwithstanding impositions by colonial authorities.

Presence of Surveyors

The exercise of the colonial government to overlay on existing communities its regimen of cadastral survey was not unique to Barranco. To exert control over land and people, the colonial government sent surveyors to regularize the residential use of land in villages in other areas of the colony.

When the Garifuna community of Dangriga was regularized by colonial authorities in 1887, Jesuit Brother Reynolds wrote "They [Dr. Jerningham, the Colonial Secretary and the Governor's private secretary, and the Surveyor General have] been spending two days with us. They have come to try and rearrange the houses, which are so irregular that no street in a right line can be found. By pulling some of these down and putting others back, they hope to make it more European like."[74]

Benque Viejo del Carmen and San Jose Succotz had been regularized in 1880 to attract people as labour for a nearby coffee plantation. The surveyors were instructed to avoid interference with existing houses or lots.[69]

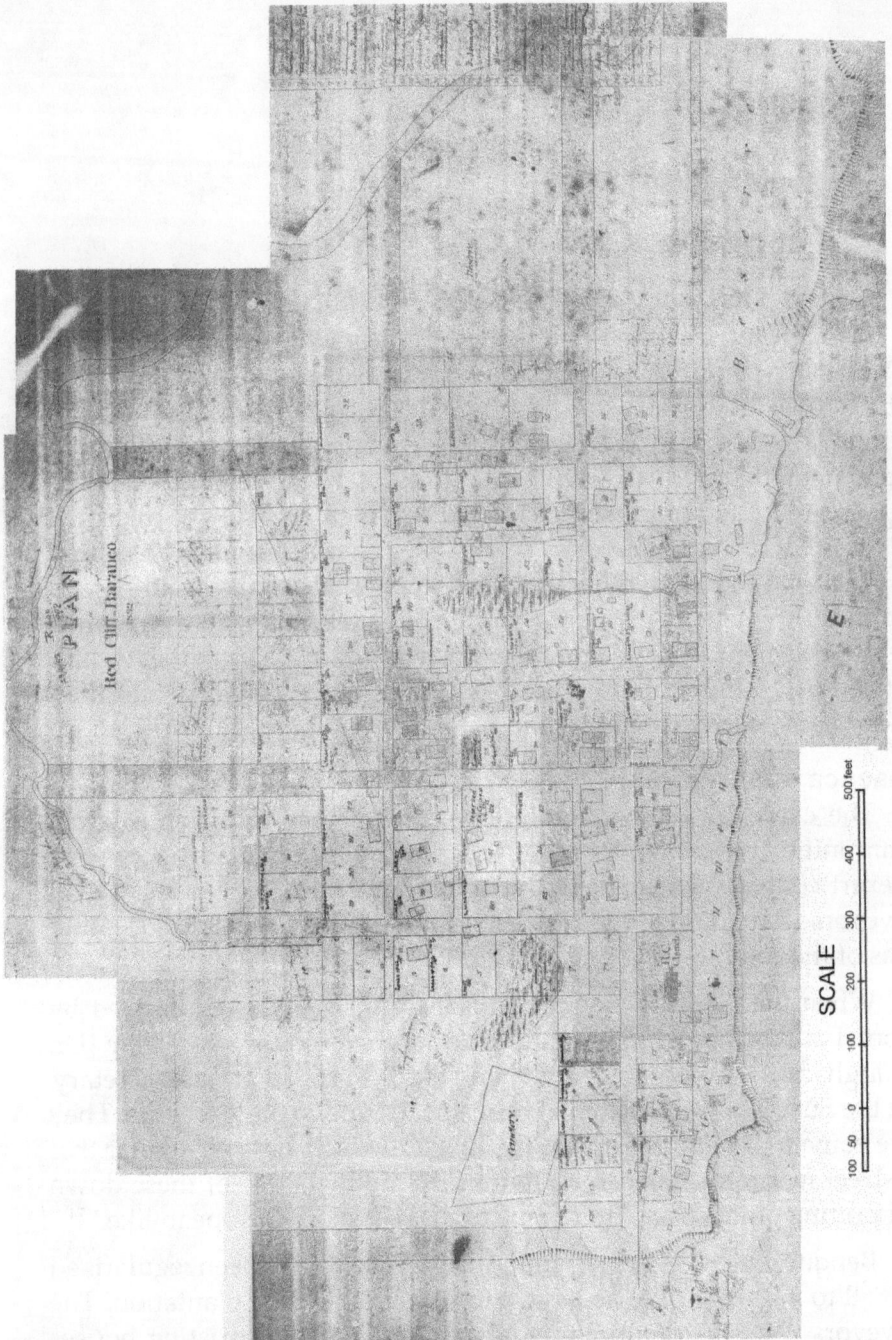

Figure 4.1. The 1892 Barranco map
It was reconstructed from scanned pieces of a blueprint copy of the original that is in the Belize Archives.

A similar survey was done in San Antonio, Cayo District, in 1913, but the community did not engage with that governmental invasion of their lives. Twelve of the families left right away; few of those who stayed applied for leases; and those who did get leases stopped paying rent so that within a few years no one was paying rent.[75]

In 1892, the surveyors were sent to Seine Bight, Monkey River and Barranco, which is the subject of this chapter. The people of Barranco already had some limited interactions with colonial authorities. The alcaldes were recognized and their names were published in the *Honduras Gazette* beginning in 1887. In 1892 the alcalde was Augustin (Big Ease) Paulino. The villagers' first prolonged exposure to colonial authorities, however, would have been the tour of duty by the surveyors. In order to conduct a complete survey, the officers must have spent several months in the village.

There had been a similar intrusion of land surveyors into Garifuna lands in St. Vincent in 1763, 129 years earlier, which had instigated the insurrection leading to the First Carib War and eventually their slaughter and exile to Roatan, Honduras, in 1797. The spirits of their ancestors were no doubt hovering close to their Barranco descendants as they decided what to do with a renewed offensive on their land rights again by the British and their agents.

Before the land survey could be completed, a survey of households was done. Identifying the head of each household was one of the tasks that brought out cultural differences between the surveyors and the Garifuna community. For the surveyors being the head of the household meant owning a dwelling and retaining primary control over household affairs as one's private domain. For the Garifuna, on the other hand, being head of household means exercising domestic responsibilities as a member of a larger family group. Sharing residential space with extended family is a kinship obligation. Ultimately being assigned the title of household head became an exercise less reflective of Garifuna cultural norms and more a need to fill in blanks on the surveyors' prescribed list.

1892 Map of Barranco

The 1892 map for Barranco is available in the Belize Archives and Records Services in Belmopan. The passage of 119 years has taken its toll as the map is faded and delicate. The map shown in Figure 1 is a digital version that was reconstructed from a blueprint by scanning 8.5 x 11 pieces and reassembling them (*Fig. 4.1*).

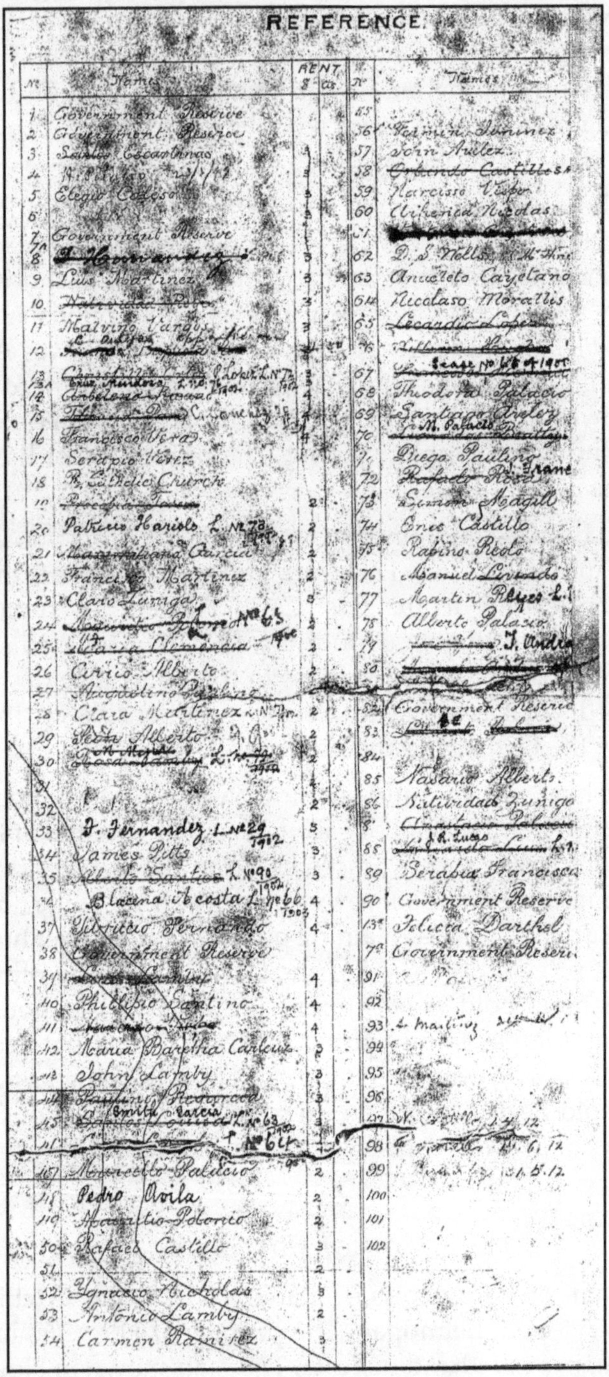

REFERENCE

No.	Names	RENT $	cts	No.	Names
1	Government Reserve			55	
2	Government Reserve			56	Fermin Jiminez
3	Santos Escarlinas			57	John Avilez
4	[illegible] 29/1/[illegible]	3		58	~~Orlando Castillo~~
5	Elegio Calesó	3		59	Narcisso Vesper
6		3		60	Atiberica Nicolas
7	Government Reserve			61	[illegible]
8	~~F. Hernandez~~	3		62	D. S. Wells, [illegible]
9	Luis Martinez	3		63	Anacleto Cayetano
10	~~[illegible]~~	3		64	Nicolaso Morallis
11	Malvino Vargas	3		65	~~Lecardio Lopez~~
12	C. Avilez [illegible] ~~[illegible]~~			66	~~William [illegible]~~
13	~~[illegible]~~ J. Lopez L. No. 7 1902	3		67	Lease No. 65 of 1905
13A	Cruz Mendoza L. No. 76 1902				
14	~~Crbelona Rosado~~	4		68	Theodora Palacio
15	~~[illegible]~~ C. Lorenzo 76	4		69	Santiago Avilez
16	Francisco Vera	4		70	M. Palacio ~~[illegible] Beattay~~
17	Serapio Perez			71	Diego Paulino
18	R. Catholic Church			72	~~Rafaelo Rosa~~ [illegible] Franc
19	~~Procopio Teron~~	2		73	Simon Magill
20	Patricio Hariolo L. No. 78	2		74	Enes Castillo
21	~~Maximiliana~~ Garcia	2		75	Rabino Reolo
22	Francisco Martinez	2		76	Manuel Livrado
23	Claro Zuniga	3		77	Martin Reyes L. [illegible]
24	~~Macario [illegible]~~ L. No. 65	2		78	Alberto Palasco
25	~~Maria Clemencia~~ 1900	2		79	~~[illegible]~~ J. Andrio
26	Cirrio Alberto	2		80	~~[illegible]~~
27	~~Agustino Paulino~~			81	~~[illegible]~~
28	Clara Martinez L. No. 7	2		82	Government Reserve
29	~~Seda~~ Alberto	2		83	~~[illegible]~~
30	~~[illegible]~~ L. No. [illegible] 1900	2		84	
31		4		85	Nasario Alberto.
32		2		86	Natividad Zunigo
33	F. Fernandez L. No. 29 1912	3		87	~~[illegible] Palacio~~
34	James Pitts	3		88	J. R. Lucas ~~[illegible]~~ L. [illegible]
35	~~Alberto Santiago~~ L. No. 90 1902	3		89	Serabia Francisca
36	Blacina Acosta L. No. 66 1903	4		90	Government Reserve
37	Tilvricio Fernando	4		13	Felicia Darthel
38	Government Reserve			7	Government Reserve
39	~~[illegible]~~	4		91	
40	Phillipio Santino	4		92	
41	~~[illegible]~~	4		93	A. Martinez [illegible]
42	Maria Barthia Carlews	3		94	
43	John Lamby	3		95	
44	~~Paulino Rodriguez~~	3		96	
45	Emilia Garcia ~~[illegible]~~ L. No. 63 1902	3		97	N. Castillo 1. 4. 12
46	~~[illegible]~~ L. No. 64			98	[illegible] 1. 6. 12
47	~~Marcello Palacio~~	2		99	[illegible] 1. 5. 12
48	Pedro Avila	2		100	
49	~~Mauritio Polonio~~	2		101	
50	Rafael Castillo	3		102	
51		2			
52	Ygnacio Nicholas	3			
53	Antonio Lamby	2			
54	Carmen Ramirez	3			

Figure 4.2. List of lot allocations on the right of the 1892 map

Table 4.1 Names listed on the 1892 Map

Lot #	Name listed[76]	Lot #	Name listed
1	Government Reserve	45	Louisa Santos
2	Government Reserve	46	Jane Lambey
3	Santos Cardenas	47	Martires Coronados Palacio
4	none listed	48	Pedro Avila
5	Luis Castillo	49	Mauricio Polonio
6	none listed	50	Rafael Castillo
7	Government Reserve	51	none listed
7A	Government Reserve	52	Leoncio Nicholas
8	Dolores Hernandez	53	Antonio Lambey
9	Luis Martinez	54	Carmen Ramirez
10	Natividad Reyes	55	none listed
11	Malvino Vargas	56	Fermin Jimenez
12	Juano Bropliola Teo	57	John Avilez
13	Christillo Ortez	58	Orlando Castillo
13A	Felicia Diaz	59	Narciso Paulino
14	Antonio Requeña	60	Eugenia Nicholas
15	Toliarosa Peña	61	Victoriana Cayetano
16	Francisco Vairez	62	D.S. Wells
17	Serapio Vairez	63	Anacleto Cayetano
18	R. Catholic Church	64	Nicolaso Moralez
19	Procopio Torres	65	Leocardio Lopez
20	Patricio Ariola	66	William Haughn
21	Maximiliano Garcia	67	Francisco
22	Francisco Martinez	68	Teodoro Palacio
23	Claro Zuniga	69	Santiago Avilez
24	Mauricio Polonio	70	Leonidas Beatty
25	Maria Clemencia	71	Diego Paulino
26	Ciriaco Nolberto	72	Rosa Mistica Lambey
27	Augustin Paulino	73	Simon Mejia
28	Clara Martinez	74	Eric Castillo
29	Pio Nolberto	75	Rufino Ariola
30	Rosa Mistica Lambey	76	Manuel Lorenzo
31	none listed	77	Martin Reyes
32	none listed	78	Norberto Palacio
33	Francisco Fernandez	79	Joe Young
34	James Pitts	80	Marcelo Cayetano
35	Alberto Santos	81	Marcelo Cayetano
36	Blacina Acosta	82	Government Reserve
37	Tiburcio Fernandez	83	Liberato Palacio
38	Government Reserve	84	none listed
39	Luis Lambey	85	Macario Nolberto
40	Philip Santino	86	Natividad Zuniga
41	Ambrocio Avilez	87	Anasticio Palacio
42	Maria Baltazar Castillo	88	Eduardo Luis
43	John Lambey	89	Serapia Nolberto
44	Apolonio Garcia	90	Government Reserve

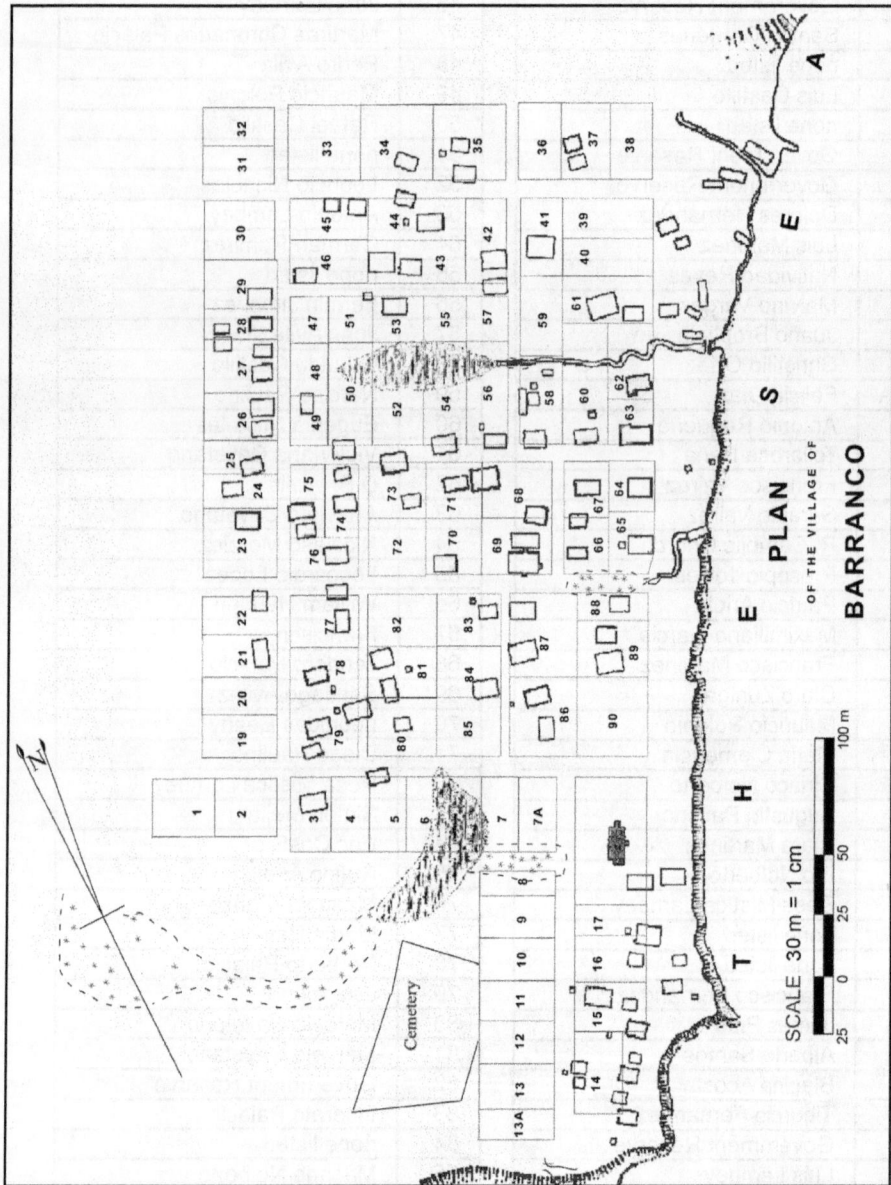

Figure 4.3. 1892 map partially re-drawn showing lot numbers

On the right side of the 1892 map is a list of the lot numbers with names, presumably the head of the corresponding household (*Fig. 4.2*). The crossing out and re-writing of additional names while deleting others have made it difficult to decipher the names that appeared initially. Fortunately, we were able to amplify on the computer monitor the digitized copy and to consult with each other to arrive at a consensus on particularly questionable cases. Even then we had to concede that the name of the household head for a few lots was illegible, among the 78 with deciphered names.

The surveyors arrived at a list of 92 lots numbered from lots 1 to 90, plus 7A and 13A. A re-drawn map appears in Figure 4.3 showing lot numbers and the names to which the lots were allocated are in Table 4.2. From this total the surveyors identified seven lots as Government Reserve (1, 2, 7, 7A, 38, 82, and 90) and lot 18 for the Roman Catholic Church, which left 84 for private residence. All but six lots (6, 31, 32, 51, 52, and 84) had names listed, leaving 78 names on the map. Under demand for lots in the village, these six were also occupied later.

Many of the names were misspelled by the colonial officer whose hand-writing appears on the map. In addition, there are some name conventions within Garifuna customs. For example, Narciso Obispo is really Narciso Paulino. We have corrected the British misspellings in the records we present, but we provide a listing of these corrections in Appendix A.

There were five persons who were heads of two households. These four men and one woman were most probably not living in two households. A more plausible explanation was that they were allowing close relatives to reside in the other dwelling. The fact that two of the heads had their names on adjoining lots would have made the overlap easier for them. Two of these men, Marcelo Cayetano and Macario Nolberto, had several sisters with whom they might share space.

These examples show two principles that undergird lot ownership at that time in Barranco. One was private ownership in terms of men and women having their own lots. The other was that private ownership operated in tandem with kinship or larger family obligations. While the surveyors would have reacted to the above examples of domestic practices as idiosyncrasies, the ethnographer sees them as providing interesting historical backdrops to data and analysis that social scientists have covered extensively on Caribbean societies through such topics as matrifocality, consanguineality, patronymic nomenclature, and—particularly in the case of Barranco—how men married Barranco women and came to settle in the village, a form of uxorilocal residence, as known in the anthropological literature.

Felicia Diaz, a five-year old girl, was listed as the allocated owner of lot 13A. She was born in 1887 to Martin Diaz and Clemencia Lorenzo. Perhaps her parents asked that the lot be placed in her name, or the designation meant an older relative after whom she had been named, but does not appear in our genealogical records.

Before the Gridlines

As the features they used to identify the lots, the houses received considerable attention from the surveyors in doing their map. They indicated the main structures in each lot. In order to reconstruct who was living in Barranco in 1892 and where they lived, we have removed the lot boundaries, leaving only the settlement pattern before the Colonial authorities came to systematize Barranco (*Fig. 4.4*).

There were 86 major structures indicated, not counting the small ones probably used for storage, outhouse, fowl coop, or pig pen. Some of the larger structures were undoubtedly kitchens, especially when there are two of these close together. If some of the structures were kitchens, this is consistent with the census data of 1891 that indicates 59 houses in Barranco. At that time the average number of persons per household was 3.83 with a total population of 225. Persons who were under 15 years of age numbered 93 (41%) and 55 percent of the adults were female.

The sketches drawn on lots in Figure 4.4 show approximate sizes of the structures. The largest and only public building was the church, while the largest private dwelling was on lot 69 belonging to the pioneer of Barranco, Santiago Avilez. Structures in the remaining lots were more or less of the same dimension.

Almost all of the houses had an east-west elongated orientation no doubt for ventilation coming mainly from the northeast trade winds. The alignment of the houses in Barranco was carried over to the orientation of the lots themselves.[77]

Applying the Grid Lines

The major task for the surveyors was to draw the first ever official plan of the village (*Fig. 4.3*). The map appears as if the British tried to accommodate what was on the ground. The village sits atop a roughly rectangular promontory reaching a dimension of about 800 meters long and 400 meters wide. While the location has slight inundations in some spots, the most noticeable obstacles to building houses were two marshy spots—one near the centre of the village and the other in the mid southern portion—both of which are shown in Figures 4.3 and 4.4. There is a belief about spirits that live in bodies of fresh water

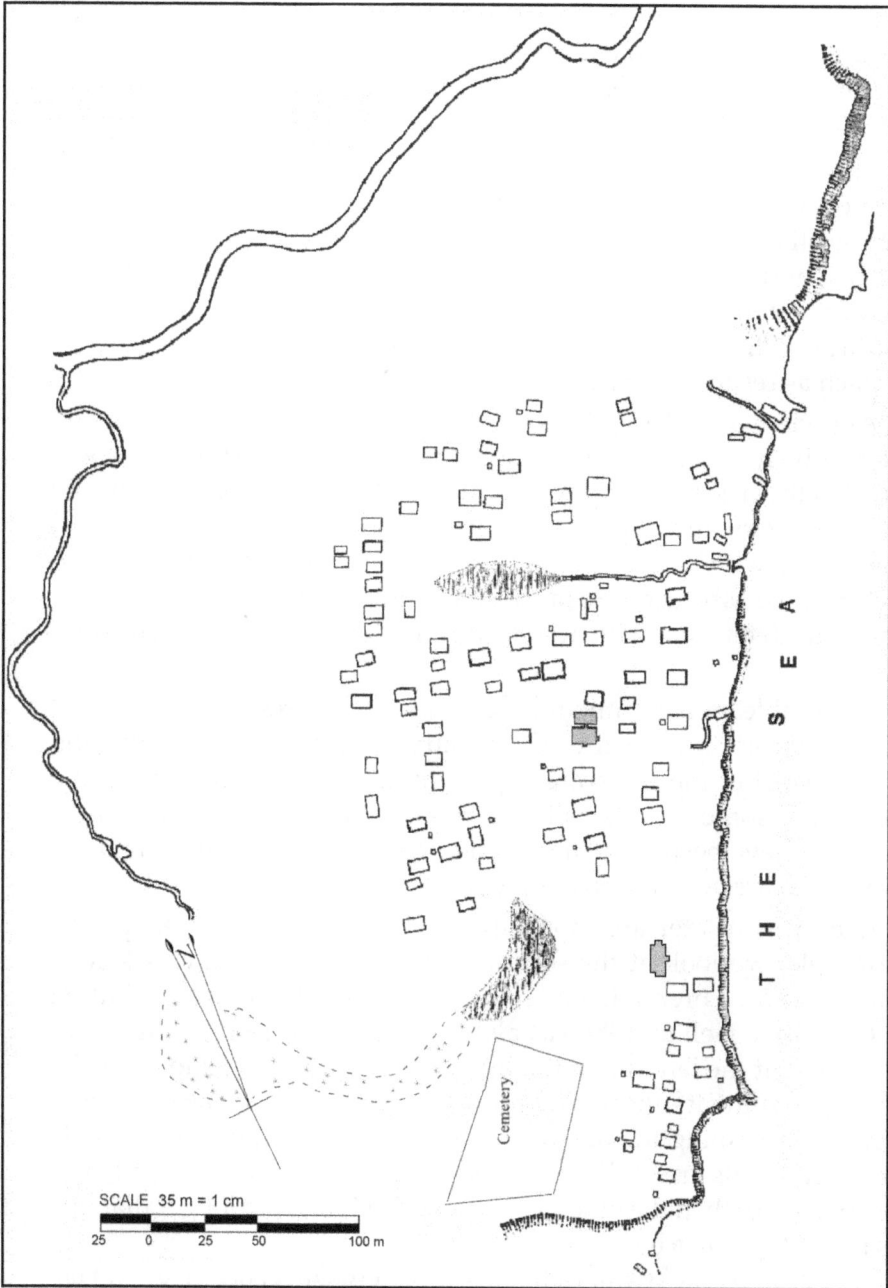

Figure 4.4. 1892 map with lot boundaries and roads removed.
The church (south) and Santiago Avilez's house are highlighted in grey.

and can be malevolent. Understandably, houses were not built in such swampy areas, although those areas served to drain the entire village. For example, lots 50, 51, 52, 54, 55, 56, 57 are all around one of the low areas, but where there are houses, they are removed from the swamp.

There are fourteen structures by the beach at the top of the cliff with no lot demarcation, although they did not differ in floor plan from the others in the village. They are in two outlying areas, six in the northeast and eight in the southeast. The surveyors declared the top edge of the cliff a Government Reserve, which included the fourteen structures. Belizean law still regards a distance of 22 meters wide on the beach as reserved for public use.

Applying a grid required considerable juggling. The surveyors were relatively successful in that only five structures were in the newly aligned pathways. But they are next to lots 50, 52, 53, 57, and 77, none of which had a structure within the indicated area, so we have associated those houses with the owners of those lots. Where some lots have two structures, we assumed one of those was a kitchen. In all cases it was possible to determine which buildings are associated with which lot numbers.

To be able to accommodate so many structures within the grid while leaving space for pathways, the surveyors ended up with varying lot sizes. Most of the lots were approximately 50 x 100 feet, but some were larger, some were smaller, and some were shaped differently. There may have been some negotiation between the residents and the surveyors to arrive at the sizes of lots.

Lots drawn later are more uniform in both size and shape. As an example, we look at the section of the village that covers lots 77 to 90 (*Fig. 4.5*). Three lots have no structures, 82, 85 and 90, but 82 was the public well and 90 was also a government reserve. In earlier years it was at the landing of the main pier, clearly a good location for official government offices. The rest of the lots have one or two major structures, assuming the one overlapping 79 and 80 goes with lot 80. Most of these lots are of different sizes. The center column, 78, 81, and 84 are narrower than the others. The top row (77-79) are longer than the ones in the two rows below.

Lots 77 to 90 are of different sizes, except the two largest, 87 and 90. The variation in sizes is shown in Figure 4.5 and Table 4.2. In contrast, the freedom from having to work around existing houses is shown clearly in the additional two rows laid as an extension anticipating future growth in the village, lots 91 to 114 (*Fig. 4.6*). Not only are these lots of equal size, the main street is also wider than the pathways in the older part of the village.

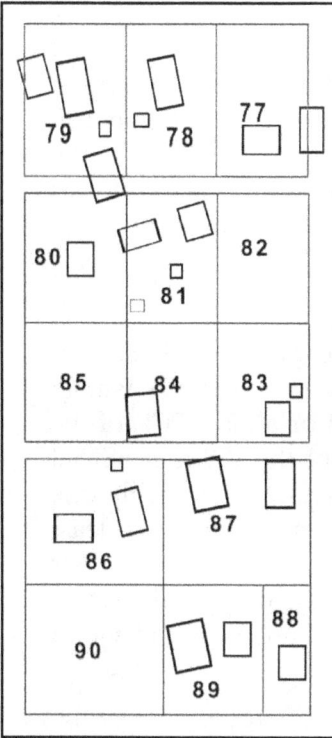

Lot#	sq. meter	% of lot 90
77	437	77%
78	420	74%
79	490	87%
80	416	74%
81	357	63%
82	371	66%
83	338	60%
84	325	58%
85	379	67%
86	565	100%
87	580	103%
88	163	29%
89	401	71%
90	565	100%

Figure 4.5. (*left*) Map of **Lots 77–90**

Table 4.2. (*right*) **Variation in lot sizes**

Excluding the beach reserve area, the surveyors demarcated 92 lots as shown in Table 4.1. There were seven lots declared reserve, one for the Roman Catholic Church and 6 for the government. Two reserve lots, numbers 90 and 38, are strategically located near the extremes of the first row and could be used as security outposts. Indeed, lot number 90 is currently the location of the Police Station. A total of 78 lots were set aside for residential use.

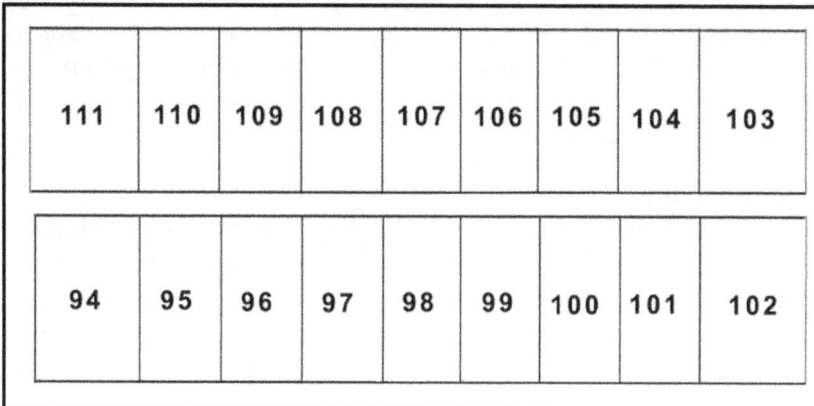

Figure 4.6. (*right*) **Village expansion area (Lots 94–111)**

Church

From the discussion of church sacraments in the last chapter, it is clear that the church had a pivotal role within the community. It would seem, however, that it was built after the initial settlement of the Garifuna heartland, as space was identified closer to the Pañaton section in the southern part of the village. Similarly the cemetery was located a short distance southwest of the church. Several churches have been built over the past century and a half (*Fig. 4.7-4.10*).

Gender Considerations

The name that the British obtained as the owner or lessee for the 1892 map may have been somewhat arbitrary—whoever was in the village at the time, perhaps. As many as 14 or almost 20% of the 78 occupied lots had women as heads, and 21 of the 138 first official lessees. They could have been heads in their own right, probably due to the permanent or temporary absence of men. Furthermore, at least three of these women used their maiden surnames even though their husbands were still living. The indication is that they could retain headship on behalf of their own family group and not as part of a joint conjugal property.

In Garifuna culture traditionally the woman is the owner of the house, tabureme muna in Garifuna, although the man is the head of the house, tábuti muna. In these culturally specific gender roles, the woman manages the household and the male is the final arbitrar of decisions, especially in regard to finances.

Barranco's pioneering families had more daughters than sons, so men came, married, and settled in the village to take advantage of this gender disparity, as well as the economic opportunities that Barranco offered. Lots 54 and 56 are examples of men coming to Barranco, getting married and settling there. Lot 54 was assigned to Carmen Ramirez, who married Eustaquia Palacio in 1889. Lot 56 was assigned to Fermin Jimenez, who married Petrona Cayetano in 1887. Fermin Jimenez's sister, Marcelina, married Valentino Ramirez, possibly related to Carmen, also from Livingston.

Ethnic Distribution

The surveyors might have reacted in surprise to the heightened degree of ethnic stratification found in such a small population within an equally small space. Chroniclers often remarked about the multiplicity of races in coastal villages in southern Belize during the 19th century, but we continue the analysis of this actual configuration that we started in the last chapter.[79] Using our familiarity with Garifuna first and last names, which are repetitive within the wide inventory

Figure 4.7. Barranco church with three steeple
The Barranco church had three steeples before the hurricane of 1945. This photo was taken on the occasion of the delivery of the new organ. (*photo courtesy Midwest Jesuit Archives*)

Figure 4.8 Barranco church with one steeple
This church is the same as the one above, but when repaired after serious damage from the 1945 hurricane two of the steeples were not replaced. (*photo courtesy Midwest Jesuit Archives*)

Figure 4.9. New Barranco church, built in 2004

Figure 4.10. Inside the new Barranco church.

of Spanish names, we arrived at a breakdown among the household heads as shown in Table 4.3.

Table 4.3. Ethnicity in the 1892 List

Ethnicity	No	%
Creole	5	6%
Mestizo	7	9%
Garifuna	65	84%
Total	78	100%

The Garifuna were clearly the majority, making up 84% of the household heads of Barranco. The Mestizo were a distant second at 9% and the Creole were the least at 6%. The distinction between the two groups was accentuated by the lighter skin colour of the Mestizo, reflecting their Hispanic and Maya heritage. Socioeconomically, both the Mestizo and Garifuna were dependent on the British for lands and jobs and had left their deprived state in their home countries in Central America searching for better opportunities in the British colony.

The Creole are the result of the physical and cultural intermixture between the British and their former African slaves. They came from further north in the colony, unlike the Garifuna and Mestizo, who came from south of the border. From their affiliation with the British in other parts of the country, the Creole were attracted to managerial and clerical tasks within the Barranco subregion, which was dominated by B. Cramer & Co. Their small proportion among the ethnic groups in the village reflects the distance they had to cover to reach the village and that their presence was underwritten by logging and plantation enterprises. By and large they were transient residents or speculators in contrast to the more permanent Mestizo and Garifuna settlers.

The central area of the village was occupied by the pioneering Garifuna families. By 1892 the pioneering families had been joined by several others, with the surnames Avila, Arana, Ariola, Blas, Lambey, Martinez, Mejia, Santino, and Zuniga. This central area is the highest land in the village, and has been occupied continuously from the beginning to the present day (*Fig. 4.11*).

The ethnic breakdown within Barranco revealed a greater concentration of the Mestizos in the southeast area of the village, in the part of the village still called *Pañatón* which means "Spanish town" in Creole (*Table 4.4*).

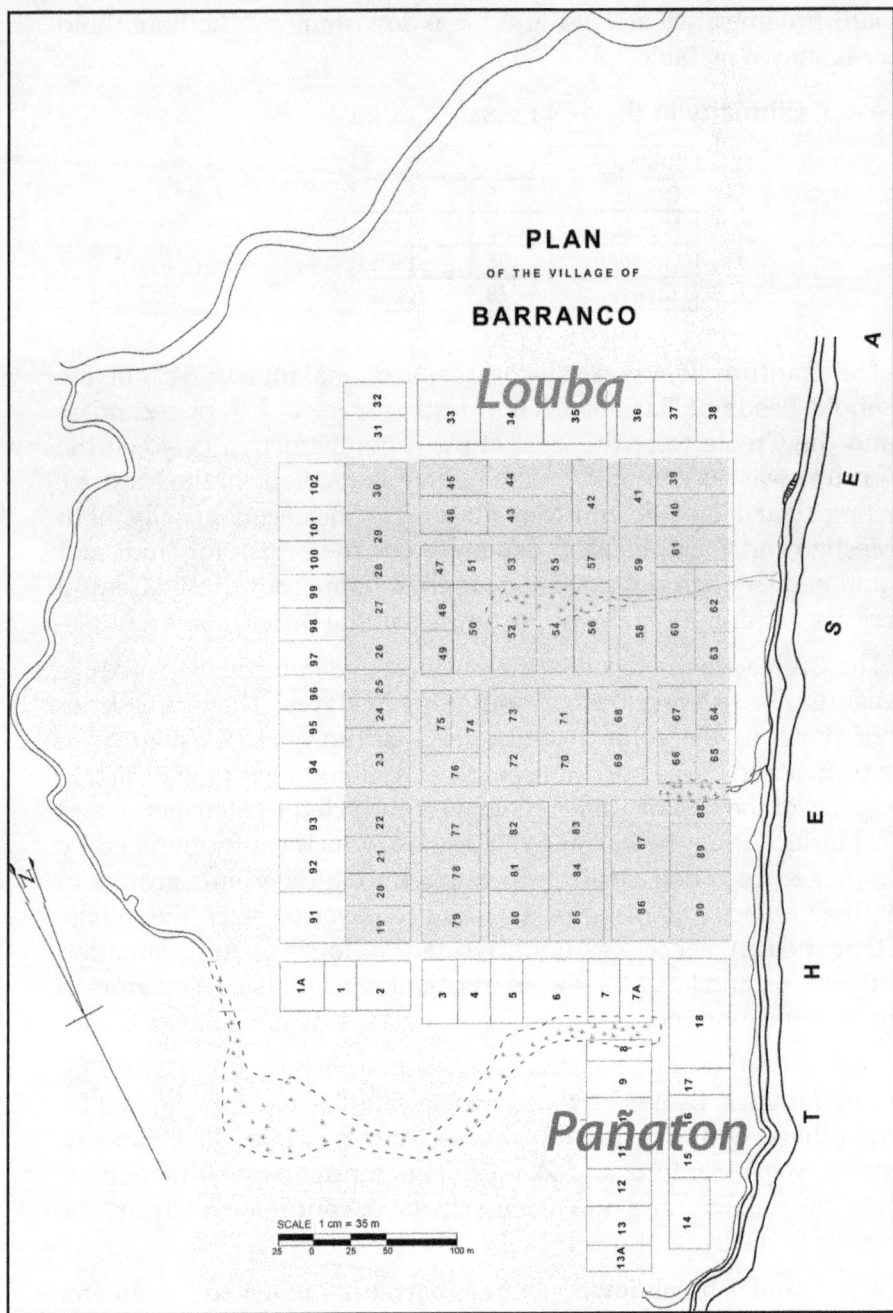

Figure 4.11. The sub-divisions of Barranco

Table 4.4. Inter-ethnicity in Pañatón from the 1892 List

Lot #	Name	Ethnicity
Pañatón		
3	Santos Cardenas	Mestizo
4	Serapio Vairez	Mestizo
5	Leoncio Nicholas	Garifuna
8	Dolores Hernandez	Mestizo
9	Luis Martinez	Garifuna
10	Natividad Reyes	Mestizo
11	Malvino Vargas	Mestizo
12	Juan Bautista Teo	Garifuna
13	Cristino Ortiz	Garifuna
13a	Felicita Diaz	Garifuna
14	Antonio Requena	Mestizo
15	Tiburcio Ponce	Mestizo
16	Francisco Vairez	Mestizo
17	Serapio Vairez	Mestizo

Residential Patterns

Four patterns result from the entrée of household heads into the community, which have implications for the stratification of residence by ethnicity as well as for the importance of gender relations. This originates from the Garifuna meaning of *iduheguaü*, blood and other kinds of social relations, which define the nature of social structure in a village community. Others were there for neither of these reasons and are categorized as having "**no-relation**s" within the community.

1) The "**consanguineal**" pattern is a blood relationship among those who were in Barranco because their parents were there, possibly going back more generations.

2) The "**affinal**" pattern refers to those who came to select a mate and settle. "*Aguyemehani*" means to take a spouse, found mostly among men establishing family ties with women in the village and becoming members of the community.

3) The "**no relation–Mestizo**" pattern shows a lack of permanence. The same person who was listed on the 1892 map generally did not apply for a lease, although in some cases it was another Mestizo name that got the first lease.

4) The "**no relation–Creole**" pattern shows the Creole purchasing freehold lots already assigned to Garifuna and displacing them.

No Relation—Creole

On the 1892 map, the originally assigned name for lot 56 was Fermin Jimenez, but the first to get a lease was Eugenio Kuylen, who appeared repeatedly in the records as a godfather in San Pedro Sarstoon, so he was probably an agent of Bernard Cramer.

Along the cliff of the village are five lots (61-65) that were purchased by wealthy, non-resident entrepreneurs in 1894, soon after the lots were designated, long before the Garifuna began applying for official leases in 1900. These were the only grants in Barranco at that time, a very different pattern from the lots assigned to Mestizos that eventually ended up in Garifuna hands.

The originally assigned owner of Lot 61 was crossed out and the name William H. Arnold written over it, so we could not decipher the original name. This lot remained in William Arnold's name as late as 2000. He lived on Dean Street in Belize City. When he died in 1948, his probate papers did not list the lot in Barranco among his properties.

Lots 62, 63, and 64 were granted to D. S. Wells, even though lots 63 and 64 were originally assigned to Baranguna on the 1892 map—Anacleto Cayetano and his mother Nicolasa Moralez. D.S. Wells worked for wealthy landowner Bernard Cramer as his representative in southern Belize. He also had lots in Monkey River and Punta Gorda and a shop in Punta Gorda. His name appears in the *Honduras Gazette* applying to cut timber and dig minerals in southern Belize. Cramer was listed on lot number 64, but it was soon transferred to D.S. Wells. However, when Herman Cramer, son of Bernard Cramer, died in 1947, lot 64 was listed among his properties in the probate. It was valued at $30 and was to be sold with the proceeds going to his daughter.

Lot 65 was granted to C. Melhado, also in 1894. Melhado worked for Cramer as his representative in Belize City and northern areas of Belize. We have no information on James Pitts (Lot 34) or Leonidas Beatty (Lot 67).

Table 4.5. Creoles with no relation to the Garifuna community

Lot #	Name	Ethnicity
34	James Pitts	Creole
56	Eugenio Kuylen	Creole
61	William Arnold	Creole
62	D.S. Wells	Creole
63	D.S. Wells	Creole
64	D.S. Wells	Creole
65	C. Melhado	Creole
67	Leonidas Beatty	Creole

No Relation–Mestizo

Eight structures were located close together near the cliff in the southeast area of the village known as *Pañatón*. No lots were associated with those structures, but eight lots were assigned west of that area with no houses on them. These lots (4, 6, 9 – 13, 13A) were assigned to people with non-Garifuna, Spanish names. Most of these persons listed on the 1892 map did not apply for an official lease for their lot. Either a different Mestizo or a Garifuna was the first to apply for these lots. By 1920 these lots were all owned by Garifuna.

Table 4.6. Mestizos with no relation to the Garifuna community

Lot #	Name	Comment
3	Santos Cardenas	Mestizo
8	Dolores Hernandez	Mestizo
15	Tolariosa Peña	Mestizo
	C. Sanchez	Mestizo
	Dolores Rodas	Mestizo
16	Francisco Vairez	Mestizo
	Nicolasa Vairez	Mestizo
19	Procopio Torres	Mestizo
36	Blacuina Acosta	Mestizo
79	Teodoro Andrade	Mestizo (long time resident)

Affinal

Affinal relationships are notoriously complicated. A woman, either on her own or through her family, may have a lot that she may transfer to her husband. In the case of multiple wives, each may have a lot of her own with the husband with his own or sharing with one of his wives. In the following examples, the affinal relations most often applies to men coming from outside the community in search of wives and through them receiving lots.

Anastacio Palacio (Baibai) was a character—a swash-buckler who wore an earring. He was married to Magdalena, with whom he had eleven children. Sotera Gutierrez also had two children during the same time period. It was Sotera who got the official lease for Lot 87 that was originally assigned to Anastacio Palacio. Martin Reyes, who married Luisa Roches, Sotera Gutierrez' daughter with Venancio Roches, was assigned Lot 77. Both Magdalena and Sotera contributed in different ways to the development of the village, notwithstanding the legality or illegality of the union. A daughter of Anastacio and Sotera, Viviana, got married to Pedro Avila (lot 48), who originated in Punta Gorda.

Francisco Martinez (Lot 22) came to Barranco because of his wife, Anacleta Avilez. Her brother Juan was married to Dominga Cayetano, daughter of Luisa Cayetano, who was the daughter of Juan Pedro Cayetano.

Juan Lambey (Lots 43 and 46) married Gregoria Nolberto, the daughter of Francisco Nolberto, one of the pioneers. His brother, Antonio (Lot 53), moved to Barranco as well. Lot 46 is listed as belonging to Jane Lambey, but there is no Jane Lambey in the genealogical records, so it is suggested that it is actually John (Juan). Lot 39 was assigned to Luis Lambey, also not found in the records.

Diego Paulino came from Punta Gorda and married the first Dominga (Waganga) Cayetano. Their son Augustin, also known as "Big Ease," got Lot 27 and the next lot (28) went to Clara Martinez, who also came from Punta Gorda and was the mother of his wife Juana Luis.

Two Zuniga men came from outside and married daughters of pioneers. Natividad Zuniga (Lot 86) was married to Cristina Nolberto. Claro Zuniga (Lot 25) came from Livingston and married Mauricia Cayetano, daughter of Anacleto Cayetano. Their son, Viviano, obtained a lease for Lot 41 in 1914.

Consanguineal

By 1892 those in the first generation born in Barranco in the 1860s were grown and having children of their own, sometimes while their parents were still child-bearing. By this time there were two generations of the pioneer families heading households and other families had joined them.

Table 4.7. Affinal (*aguyemehani*) relations between household head and the community

Lot #	Name	Comment
22	Francisco Martinez	Wife: Anacleta Avilez
23	Claro Zuniga	Wife: Mauricia Cayetano
33	Francisco Fernando	Wife: Maria Lambey/Nolberto
40	Felipe Santino	Wife: Justina Cayetano/Morales
43	John Lambey	Wife: Gregoria Nolberto/Avarez
48	Pedro Avila	Wife: Viviana Palacio/Gutierrez
65	Leocardio Lopez	Wife: Anacleta Garcia/Martinez
73	Simon Mejia	Wife: Andrea Nicholas/Delavez
75	Rufino Ariola	Wife: Ascenciona Cayetano/Morales
77	Martin Reyes	Wife: daughter of Sotera Gutierrez
54	Carmen Ramirez	Wife: Eustaquia Palacio/Martinez

Desideria's two sons, Teodoro and Anastacio Palacio both had several children who, by 1892, were grown and having children of their own. There were seven lots assigned to members of these two generations and two others had received official leases by 1900. Anastacio, Teodoro, Mercedes, Liberato, Hipolito, Catarino, Marcelo, Norberto, and Saturino all got lots in their own names. The only one of them who was female is Mercedes, but Gregoria's husband Eulalio Loredo got a lot, as did Viviana's husband Pedro Avila. Nine others did not get lots: Peter, Nicolasa, Juana, John, Paulina, Vicenta, and Luis, all of whom had probably migrated away. Luis Palacio was a bugler in the Guatemalan army and lived in Guatemala for many years.

The Nicholas family also had two generations born in Barranco by 1892 who were assigned lots. Also Lot 88 may possibly have been originally settled by the Nicholas family. The original assignment is listed as Leonardo Luis. That name does not appear in genealogical records, but it is probably Eduardo Luis, who was married to Rosa Lambey, who had her own Lot 30 at the back of the village closer to the younger Nolbertos. Their daughter, Paula Luis, was married to Sotero Nicholas in 1897. Alexander Nicholas is an example of a pillar of the community who had no lot assigned to him or his wife, but he may have died by 1892. We know he was no longer living in 1897 when his son Sotero was married. However, Lot 60 was assigned to their daughter Andrea and their sons Sotero and Leoncio leased lots 58 and 73.

The Cayetano family did not fare as well. Anacleto, son of pioneer Juan Pedro Cayetano, was the original designee for lot 63, but that was purchased by D. S. Wells. It was the next generation, Anacleto's son Marcelo Cayetano, who got lots 80 and 81.

Ciriaco and Pio Nolberto, who got lots 26 and 29, were the sons of Francisco Nolberto and his wife Serapia. Pio's wife is Casimira Nicholas, daughter of Alexander Nicholas.

The non-assignment of a lot to Alexander Nicholas may also indicate that he was absent from the settlement most of the time, something repeated in oral tradition. There is little evidence in the genealogical records that Juan Pedro Cayetano actually lived in Barranco. The only reference to him being as a sponsor at his granddaughter's wedding. The corresponding importance of their spouses—Eugenia Delavez and Nicolasa Moralez—in building the new community becomes more noticeable.

Table 4.8 Consanguineal relations between household head and the Garifuna community

Lot #	Name	Comments
3	Catarino Palacio	Son of earlier settler family: Palacio/ Martinez
20	Patricio Ariola	Son of earlier settler Rufino Ariola
21	Maximiliano (Smith or Esmith) Garcia	Son of earlier settler family: Garcia/ Martinez
24	Mauricio Polonio (Apolonio)	Son of earlier settler family
26	Ciriaco Nolberto	Son of earlier settler family: Nolberto/ Alvarez
27	Augustin Paulino	Son of earlier settler family: Paulino/ Cayetano
28	Clara Martinez	Earlier self-settler thru daughter's husband Augustin Paulino Sr.
29	Pio Nolberto	Son of earlier settler family: Nolberto/ Alvarez
41	Ambrosio Avilez	Son of earlier settler: Avilez
44	Sebastian Garcia	Son of earlier self-settlers: Garcia/ Martinez
47	Martires Coronados Palacio	Son of earlier self-settlers: Palacio/ Cesario
52	Ignacio Nicholas	Son of earlier settlers
53	Antonio Lambey	Probably brought by his children
56	Fermin Jimenez	Son of earlier settlers Jimenez/ Cayetano
57	John Avilez	Son of earlier settler family
58	Sotero Nicholas	Son of earlier settler family: Nicholas/ Delavez
63	Anacleto Cayetano	Early self-settler with his mother Nicolasa Moralez
68	Teodoro Palacio	Early self-settler with mother and step-father
69	Santiago Avilez	Early settler, died 1894
71	Diego Paulino	Early settler, died 1896
74	Inez Castillo	Son of early settlers: Castillo/Garcia
78	Norberto Palacio	Son of early settler family: Palacio/ Martinez
79	Teodoro Palacio	Early settler, died 1909
80, 81	Marcelo Cayetano	Son of earlier settler family: Cayetano/Arzu
83	Liberato Palacio	Son of early settler family: Palacio/ Antonio
84, 85	Macario Nolberto	Son of early settler family: Nolberto/ Alvarez
89	Serapia Nolberto	Early settler with husband Francisco Nolberto, died 1910

Family Clusters

The previous discussion on the sociocultural context of residential use is an extrapolation from the 1892 list of lot owners drafted, not by social scientists, but by colonial surveyors. However, they have provided analytic leads to the norms that determine Garifuna behaviour toward their lot allocation. We have seen that there was a belief in communal rights to land by the family group, although each family maintained its own house(s), which subsequently became separated into lots after the survey. A microscopic spotlight on title holding by women shows that they could own lots in their own name, even though they might have been married and not yet widowed. Significance of titleship more at the family level and not the individual's came from the fact that children could be given titles to lots. Finally, there is information showing that non-Garifuna were able to participate in the customary rights prevailing in Barranco. Others were allowed space, notably Mestizo, although there was deliberate stratification separating the predominantly Garifuna section from others. All of these norms add a small but significant addition to our understanding of Garifuna indigeneity in terms of communal residential use of space. Recently, Forte used the term "indigeneity" to analyse the perduration of cultural identity over time among the Caribs of Trinidad. Here we are carrying his thrust to the pre-colonial and customary use of residential space by another indigenous people within the Caribbean.[78]

We defined a family cluster as three or more lots that were contiguous whose owners shared close blood or affinal ties. We noted that the clusters were not separated by symmetrical sides; rather the community knew where they were bounded. Besides, it was difficult to know where one cluster begins and another ends because of the overlapping ties among the villagers. Their significance was that persons had physical space that was available to him or her, whether it is a newborn or an adult arriving for the first time. The community was able to accommodate everyone through the norms of kinship, thereby consolidating the basis of Garifuna traditional rights to the ownership and use of residential space. The clusters are shown on Figure 4.12 with the indicated letter labeling the cluster.

Palacio Cluster (P)

The most extensive spatial cluster includes Desideria in Lot 69, her two sons, Teodoro Palacio in Lots 68 and 79, and Anastacio Palacio in lot 87. Living north of Teodoro in Lot 78 was his son Nolberto Palacio. East of Teodoro in two Lots, 80 and 81, was his grandson (his daughter Loreta's son) Marcelo Cayetano. In Lot 83, west of Anastacio was his son, Liberato Palacio.

Cayetano Cluster (C)

The cluster of Lots 61, 63, and 64 had as leader another pioneer, Nicolasa Moralez, wife of Juan Pedro Cayetano. She lived in lot 64. Next to her in lot 63 was her son Anacleto and two lots east was lot 61, where her daughter Victoriana Cayetano lived. All of these lots were granted to outsiders, Creole entrepreneurs, so this cluster ceased to exist after 1894. One wonders what happened, how they were informed, where they moved, and whether they were compensated.

Nolberto Cluster (N)

A third group includes Serapia Nolberto in Lot 89, her daughter Cristina Nolberto who married Natividad Zuniga in Lot 86; and her son Macario, who occupied two Lots, 84 and 85. There is a second Nolberto cluster that includes Paulinos in Lots 26, 27, 28, and 29.

Nicholas (E)

We will label the Nicholas cluster "E" for Eugenia Nicholas, the matriarch of this family, who lived in Lot 60. Her son Sotero Nicholas got the first lease for Lot 58.

Lambey (L)

There is also another large cluster at the outer edge of the heartland, where the Lambeys and Nolbertos overlap in Lots 30, 33, 43, and 53. Both are related through marriage.

Mestizo Clusters (S)

The other form of clustering has to do with the predominance of the non-Garifuna in the periphery of the village. We label Mestizo clusters as "S" for Spanish. The southeast Pañatón area initially included mainly Mestizos.

Public Well (W)

The public well is centrally located for everyone's use.

Church (X)

The church cluster includes the church and the priest house.

Outer Edges of the Central Heartland

By 1892, thirty years had passed since the pioneers founded the village and succeeding generations had established families. The newcomers and younger generations settled on the edges of the heartland, making the previous clustering less distinct. Because they were related to each other in several ways the distinctiveness of former

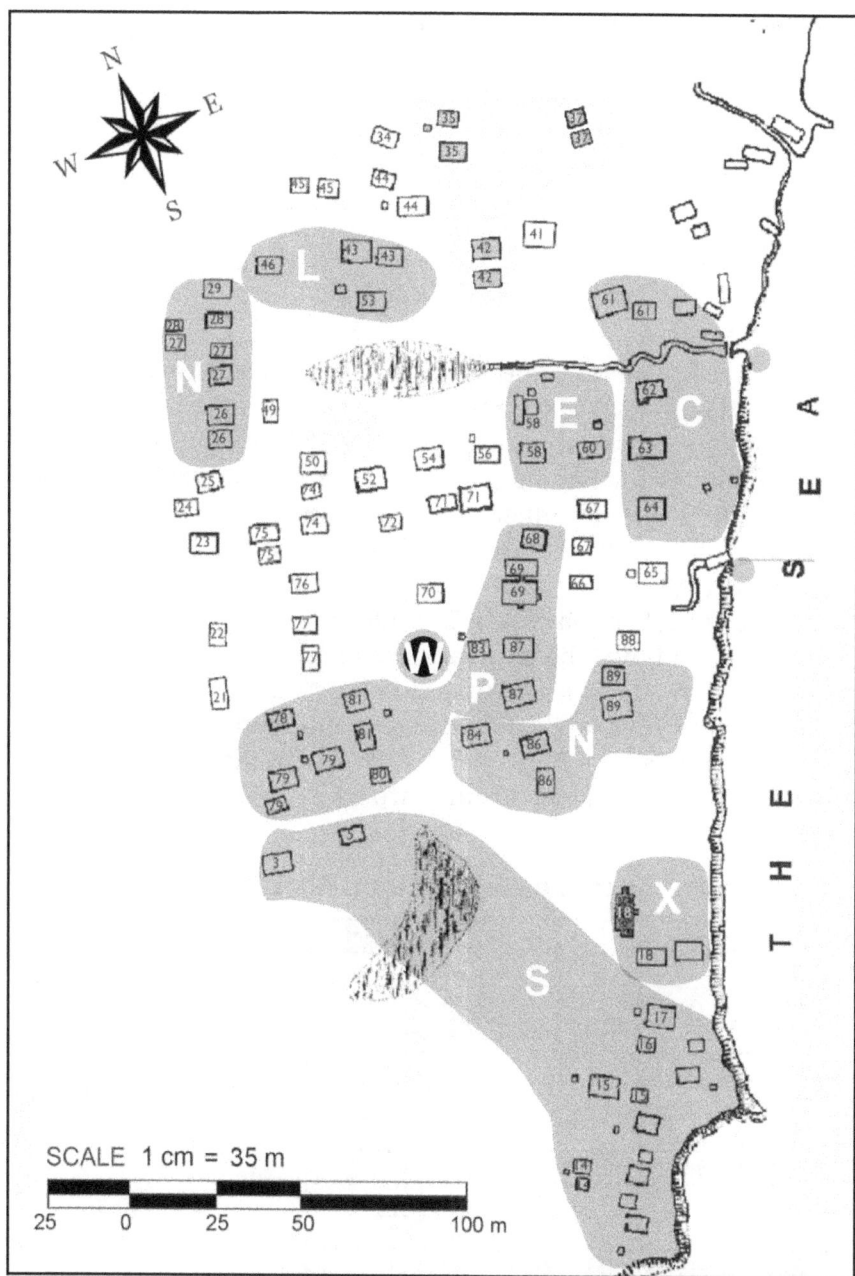

Figure 4.12. Family and other clusters in Barranco in 1892

N = Nolberto, L = Lambey, S = Mestizo, E = Nicholas, C = Cayetano,
    W = public well, P = Palacio, X = Church

clusters could no longer be identified. However, closely related persons live next to each other, as in Lots 27 and 28 for Augustin Paulino, Sr and his wife's mother Clara Martinez; Lot 47 for Viviana Palacio (the lot is in her husband, Peter Avila's name) and Lot 48 for her brother Martires Coronados Palacio. The pattern also extends to the non-Garifuna Vairezes with Serapio in Lot 17, while his daughter Alejandra lived in Lot 9 that faces Lot 17.

Post-Survey Period

While the lots were demarcated in 1892, official leases were not issued for Baranguna until several years later. However, five lots were purchased by businessmen associated with Cramer in 1894 and 1896 and four leases were approved in 1896 for non-Garifuna. The first four leases for Baranguna were approved in 1898. A large number of applications were filed in April of 1899, but none of these were approved until 1900 when 37 leases were approved with 24 more leases being issued over the next three years. By 1922, 84 leases had been approved for lots in Barranco, 33 under the same name as listed on the 1892 map and the others under different names. A few of those originally listed got official leases for a different lot, so there was some re-shuffling. A few died within that time frame and others got lots through their spouses. The time period over which the first leases for lots in Barranso were obtained is summarized in Table 4.9. Most were given in 1900 and 1902.

Table 4.9. Time Period for Lease and Grant Allocations

Time Period	#	Lease/Grant
1894	5	Grants
1896	3	Leases
1898	4	Leases
1899	1	Lease
1900	35	Leases
1901-1902	18	Leases
1903-1906	8	Leases
1907-1922	10	Leases
Total Grants	5	Grants
Total Leases	79	Leases

The relative order in which the ground survey seemed to have taken place belies the depth of the social transformation that it generated in Barranco through the new administrative alignment of lot space from communal to exclusively private ownership and the tendency of the colonial government to give land rights to persons as it saw fit, even to non-villagers.

To acquire legal possession of their lots the *de facto* owners had to first submit applications for leases. There were prescribed forms that had to be filled and taken to the administration centre in the Toledo District, Punta Gorda, for onward submission to the Governor's office in Belize City. The Governor-in-Council (i.e. with his top advisors) ultimately approved the application. After three publications in the *Honduras Gazette*, the government news journal, the applicant formally received his lease papers, or as called in Garifuna *"ligaradana múa"*. Between 1894 and 1922, there were 84 leases issued for the original 90 lots, 78 of which were originally assigned and six additional lots that had not been assigned on the 1892 map.

Ownership could be either grant title or lease. The former was an outright purchase and the latter was renting with an option to buy over a period of time. Almost all of the villagers went for the second option because of the more favourable payment terms. There were only five grants, issued in 1894, all to non-Garifuna men.

There were 45 lots out of the original 78 that changed hands between the pre-survey and post-survey periods, between *de facto* and *de jure* ownership. By a cursory review of the surnames, we can conclude that many of these exchanges took place between family members or other close relatives. The most dramatic effect was the transfer of five lots from Garifuna to Creole owners. Indications are that they were not by any means friendly exchanges for they were grants that new owners received in 1894, even before the *de facto* owners applied for them. The new owners must have learned about their availability through their government connections and circumvented the previous owners to acquire them. Because they were seaside lots, their logistical value to the new Creole owners was allowed to supersede the traditional rights of the Garifuna. The new owners were associates of Cramer and may have needed direct access to the beach for the transportation of their goods. The structures by the beach near these lots differ in floor plan from conventional residences and could have been for temporary storage.

Table 4.10. Inter-ethnic changes in lot ownership between the 1892 survey and first lease

Lot #	Original List	First Lease	Year
3	Santos Cardenas (M)[a]	Catarino Palacio (G)	1900
4	Hipolito Palacio (G)	Serapio Vairez (M)	1896
11	Malvino Vargas (G)	Natividad Reyes (M)	1900
15	Teodoro Pena (M)	Cayetano Sanchez (G)	1901
17	Serapio Vairez (M)	Luciano Arzu (G)	1913

56	Fermin Jimenez (G)	Eugenio Kuylen (C)	1896
61	Victoriana Cayetano (G)	W.H. Arnold (C)	1894
63	Anacleto Cayetano (G)	D.S. Wells (C)	1894
64	Nicolasa Moralez (G)	D.S. Wells (C)	1894
65	Leocardio Lopez (G)	C. Melhado (C)	1894
67	? Francisco (G)	Leonidas Beatty (C)	1896
70	Leonidas Beatty (C)	Mercelita Palacio (G)	1902
79	Teodoro Palacio (G)	Teodoro Andrade (M)	1902

[a] C = Creole, G = Garifuna, M = Mestizo

Another significant sociocultural transformation in the village ethnicity was the takeover of four lots by the Garifuna from Mestizo owners in *Pañatón*. The result was that what had been an almost exclusively Mestizo section of the community was now being taken over by the majority Garifuna population. There was, however, a marked difference from the takeover by the Creole of Garifuna lots insofar as there was government abetment forthcoming to the Garifuna. The Mestizo were no doubt leaving Barranco on finding better opportunities elsewhere, very much like Garifuna men and women, who relocated with many not returning.

Having discussed the changes taking place among residents, we should also focus on the responsibility of the government as the primary initiator of the transformation. A good question to ask is whether the villagers received monetary compensation for their dispossession of property. Those eligible would include the owners of the three houses that were placed in the pathways by the survey gridlines and the fourteen along the beach reserve. By extension those who forcefully lost their properties to newcomers would also be eligible.

Brother Reynolds commented on the important issue of compensation to the church from the 1877 lot regularization in Dangriga, "Of course compensation will have to be made, and we too shall, for what is taken from us, have a site given for another school at another end of town."[80] The Garifuna in Barranco could not share Brother Reynolds' exuberant confidence on compensation. Besides, even if they were compensated for their houses, there was the more significant matter of getting money to pay for the application fee and the newly imposed annual rent.[81]

Summary and Conclusion

Laying survey lines within an existing community and pinpointing some *a priori* principles of Garifuna customary practices in their use of residential space are two main topics covered in this chapter.

The twofold task for the surveyors was to draw an overall plan consistent with the conventions on what space should be used as residential within a community and laying gridlines for lots and streets. There were fourteen buildings located along the seacoast of the village. The surveyors did not include these in the village grid and instead designated that area to be a "Government Reserve" in keeping with the regulation still upheld in Belize to leave a 22-meter stretch by the beach for use by all residents and visitors.

The surveyors displayed a spirit of accommodation in drawing their straight lines around houses, resulting in only eight being cut through by the lines that left parts of houses in the newly designed streets. There would seem to have been another accommodation striking at the tenet of Garifuna spirituality. One spot almost at the heart of the village is swampy and would have been wet most of the year. Because the Garifuna believe that such bodies of water harbor evil spirits, they avoid building too close to them. A closer look on the plan shows that on the south side of the swamp the lots are elongated no doubt to allow the owners to build as far away from the swamp as possible and closer to the street. The north-south elongation of these lots continued further east following the course of the stream toward the sea.

By 1922, the last year in the regularization of lot ownership in Barranco, the colonial government had become responsible for the allocation of lot ownership and there had been some change in the demographic profile of lot owners. Although they had maintained customary rights to their lots, there was an exit of Mestizo from the village around the end of the 19th Century. They did not have the dedication springing from kinship and ethnicity, better said, "nationhood," that kept the Garifuna tied to the village up to this time. The year 1892 was a primary watershed in creating the present-day community of Barranco, where indigeneity remains a main focus of sociocultural identity.

We have shown how government surveyors succeeded in imposing the colonial government's gridlines within an existing settlement; what changes that imposition wrought in the community; and how three ethnic groups were living under the control of a colonial power. The chapter started with an indigenous people living independently on their lands and ends with their response to dis-possession and re-possession. The spatial clustering analysis leads to another major task of this work, the transmission of lots over time that is discussed in the next chapter. Again, the predominance of kinship is noticeable.

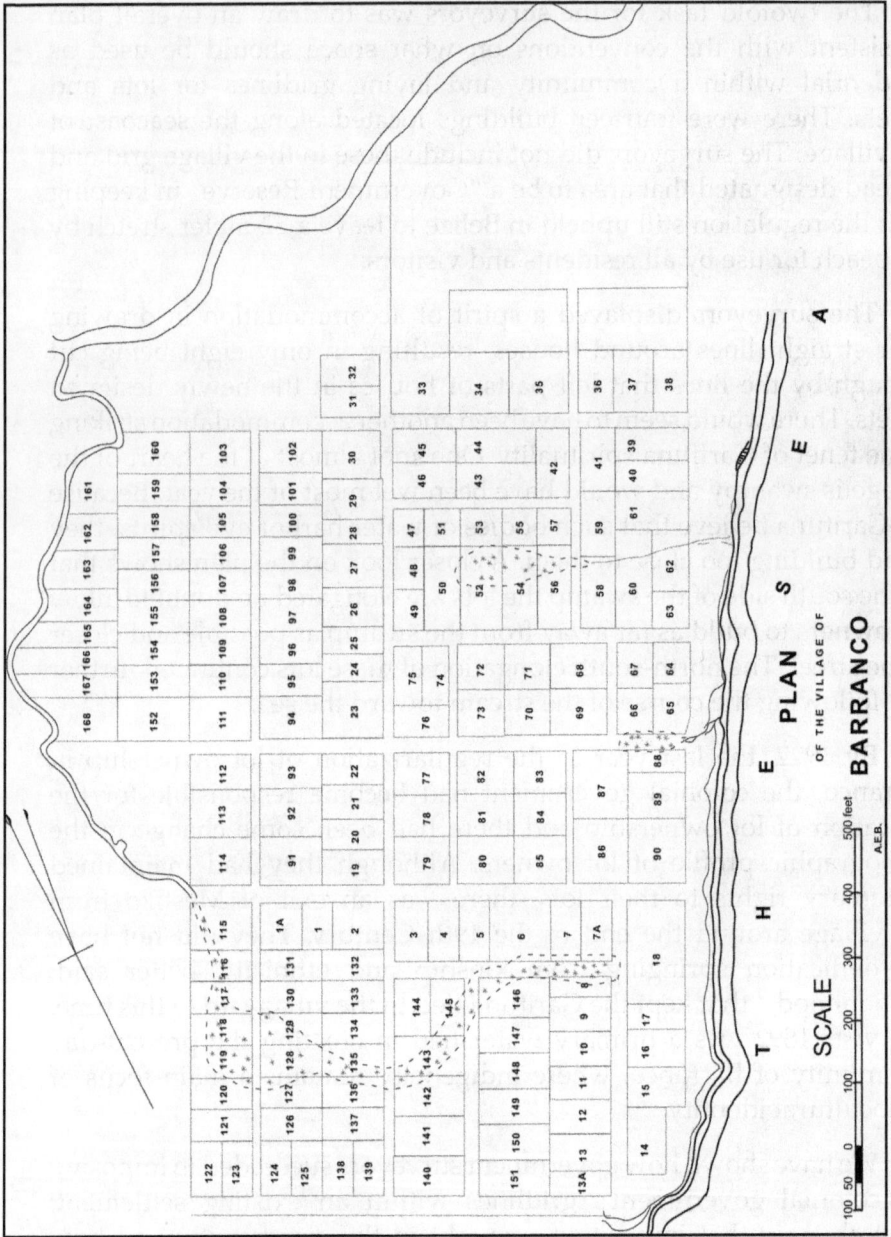

Figure 5.1. Barranco village lots

Chapter Five
House Lot Succession 1893-2000

In the previous chapter we analysed the question of first rights as the 1892 house lot survey introduced to Barranco the official colonial system of house lot tenure. We now examine the succession of these rights from one generation to the next from 1893 to 2000 (*Fig. 5.1*). We start by comparing the settlement patterns of the Garifuna with those in the Caribbean region. We then review the colonial lot administration system and the village community response. And, finally, we analyze the role of kinship and gender in lot ownership succession. Together all of these demonstrate that customary lot tenure is fully institutionalized within the village culture and that it has co-existed with the formal land administration system with minimal hostility.

The history of residential land tenure for the Garifuna in Belize sprang from men, women, and children arriving from Honduras and self-settling on vacant land. The vast majority became leasehold renters on public lands. The abundance of land in Belize relative to the Caribbean islands meant that there was less need for one's progeny to be confined within a given small space. Within their extended family system the Garifuna could move from one area to another, even across countries, whenever they saw better opportunities.

As among rural Caribbean folk, kinship is important as a medium for land rights among the Garifuna. But for the Garifuna, kinship is a network of relatives spread geographically, even in other countries. Kinship and migration became safety nets that facilitated the extensive use of land among the Garifuna. One primary value on ownership that the Garifuna share with their counterparts in the region is that a person has a right to residential space through his or her family or otherwise, including squatting on vacant land.

Settlement Patterns in the Caribbean

Because most of the studies on rural land tenure within this region have been done in the rural English-speaking Caribbean, we contrast briefly the backdrop of land ownership between there and Belize. Rural land tenure by peasants in Jamaica, for example, historically took place on leftovers that plantation owners had monopolized.[82] With an additional burden of thousands of peasants hungry for land, there was a bare minimum available. Whatever parcels the former slaves received at emancipation had the symbolic value of being the sanctuary for themselves and their descendants, forever secure from the confines of the plantation. Having paid for their plot as freehold, they designated it family land to remain inalienable and indivisible from generation to generation. In Barbados the "seed to seed" progeny are the equivalent of a corporate group with no one being able to act as the trustee.[83]

The house lot has received minimal attention among the students of land tenure within the larger English-speaking Caribbean. The main focus has been on the homestead, a combination of indoor space for residence and adjoining outdoors for intensive farming. The homestead is referred to as "house plot", "residence site", "yard", among other words in the vernacular. The term "house lot" is usually limited for the unit of domestic space found in towns, where, as in Barranco, it is demarcated by certified surveyors and isolated as a stand-alone unit according to national laws.

Because of the primacy of continuing blood ties being interwoven into land rights, the study of homestead succession is built into the larger topic of kinship obligations, a major topic of scholarly concern within the Caribbean. The daily livelihood of the family takes place within the confines of the homestead. There they produce to sell at the town or regional market using store-bought inputs within the prototypical peasant small-scale production system found throughout the rural Caribbean. The day-to-day economic function of the homestead, however, dwarfs its symbolic value as the unit of land that ancestors received at emancipation, forever separating their domestic sanctuary from the slave quarters of the plantation. Attaining freedom became concretized in the freehold possession of the homestead together with the right to pass it from one generation to the next.[84]

With only a few deviations, most of the studies previously mentioned have been done within periods of a few months using information collected from informants. The thrust, therefore, is to describe inheritance within the short period of study. From these examples ethnographers have assumed what customary practices had been over time. In contrast, this study covers the entire history of the village of Barranco, a period of 150 years.

Two longitudinal studies provide an extensive time-frame comparable to that in our study of lot succession. In Carriacou, Grenada, rural folk obtained freehold titles to their homesteads but transmitted them partly through non-legal customary practices based on traditional patrilineages.[85] On the other hand, in Trelawny, Jamaica, bilateral (through one's mother and father) family ties were used for land transmission. Bilateral kin ties have been found to predominate throughout the Caribbean.[86]

The deliberate passing of land through bilateral kin ties, from one generation to the next, has been also applied to the Garifuna in Livingston, Guatemala, in a seminal 1958 study by Nancie Gonzalez. She concluded "All children regardless of sex or birth order, inherit equally from both parents, although favouritism, the child's behavior and certain other factors may affect the actual distribution of property. ... [I]nheritable property includes money, residence sites in town, buildings, tools, and in some cases, cultivable land".[87]

The description of the Garifuna as "property-controlling descent groups" is not supported by our data on lot and farmland tenure in Barranco. Firstly, there have been hardly any opportunities available to consolidate farmland ownership over time whether in the hands of individuals or family groups, a point that will become clearer in our discussion of farmlands in chapter 6. In the following discussion on house lot tenure we will see that family groups perpetuate ownership notwithstanding formal government restrictions. If there are "property-controlling descent groups", as implied by Helm and Loveland, they are so informally and by default from the lack of imposition of government restrictions on leasehold. Secondly, the individualization of land tenure by the imposition of the British colonial system eliminated any possibility of families controlling land tenure over a period of time.

Overview of House Lot Ownership

At first glance the visitor might conclude that lot shortage is not a problem in Barranco, as there seems to be more unoccupied than occupied lots. However, a discussion with villagers would reveal that all lots, including the unoccupied ones, are owned. The enigma of ownership in such a contradictory situation immediately presents itself as a challenging social science topic. Some of the initial results of our study add to the enigma. Out of the total number of 394 lot transactions from 1893 to 2000, 79% took place in a little more than half of the village. The additional lots surveyed in the 1928-1929 period have been minimally used since the 1950s. The contradiction between availability and lack of use has a long history. By the 1930s the village had expanded to its current size of approximately 12 square kilometers. The average year for all the transactions in our sample stretching from 1893 to 2000 was 1938. A time dimension, therefore, needs to be added to the pressing questions of who owns which lots, how ownership is transmitted, what changes have taken place over time, and what is the significance of ownership within the cultural values of the community.

Formal/Non-formal Interplay in Lot Tenure

The discussion in this chapter adds to the continuing dialogue on the duality between the formal/legal and non-formal/non-legal systems of tenure found in rural communities across the Caribbean subregion. According to the Caribbean Land Policy Network Report, one of the "critical issues" that underlie policy, administration, and management of land in the English Caribbean is that "unofficial land tenure systems are as significant as the legal land tenure system."[88] The duality between the formal/legal and non-formal/non-legal systems of tenure found in rural communities across the Caribbean subregion has been much repeated in several studies.[89]

From the villagers' perspective the survey of lots is a primary function of the government. In many cases, however, the survey was not carried out to delineate lots for first occupancy but to demarcate what was already occupied, thereby legally validating *a priori* possession. The first survey in the village in 1892 was a playing out of this process, where the surveyors demarcated lots on lands that were already owned by the villagers (*Chapter 4*). After the 1892 survey, the villagers continued moving into new areas before they were surveyed, so the surveyors were forced to play catch-up. For example, for some new lots issued between 1909 and 1914 there was the notation in the official record "lot had no number when applied for" showing that persons were applying before the government had given the appropriate survey number. There is the distinct possibility that those lots were already occupied by the applicants.

While the colonial government forced families into individualized lots in the 1892 survey, they did not break the successive transmission of rights into a pattern that was not traditional, although the documents indicated that the government assumed for itself full legal rights to do so. Almost all of the lots in the village are characterized by the government as leased public lands, where ostensibly, not only the ownership but the timing of ownership has remained the prerogative of the government, and such is stated in all lease approval documents. Instead, the community has arrogated these prerogatives onto itself by maintaining and redefining the customary to fit into the individualization that the colonial authorities wanted. In effect the people lost space in the clustering, but began building property over time, so the lots remain in the family in perpetuity.

Family Lot Cluster

The villagers used the traditional system of having family groups live in clusters, as we described in Chapter 4. This practice continued after the 1892 surveyed lots had been exhausted and before the next survey was in 1928. To show the community's success at maintaining traditional kinship ties in ownership, we look at the Palacio cluster. Lots 120 to 123, 142 to 145 and 147 to 149 were added in the 1920s and 1930s to lots 2,3, 4 and 5, which they already owned, forming a rectangular block extending southward into what was then unsurveyed residential lands (*Fig. 5.2.*). Of these fifteen Palacio lots, in 2000 all but one remained in the names of descendents or wives of the original Garifuna owners (*Table 5.1*).

Table 5.1. Palacio Lot Cluster

Lot #	Original Name	Owner as of 2000	Relationship
2	Henry Loredo	Henry Loredo	Self
3	Catarino Palacio	Augustin Palacio	Nephew
4	Hipolito Palacio	Ruben Palacio	Son
5	Philip Nicholas	Martin Nicholas	Grandson
120	Bonifacio Ramirez	out of Palacio family	—
121	Joe Palacio	Felipa Palacio	Wife of Uncle
122	Felipa Palacio (Eulalia Arana)	Jose Velasquez	Husband of Eulalia
123	Patrocina Arzu	Eulalia Arana	First Cousin
142	Patrocina Arzu	Candido Arzu	Son
143	Patrocina Arzu	Candido Arzu	Son
144	Bonifacio Ramirez	Gumercinda Palacio	Second Cousin
147	Benigno Avila	Theodore J. Palacio	Second Cousin, once removed
148	Benigno Avila	Norberto Arzu	Second Cousin, twice removed
149	Benigno Avila	Hazel Arzu	Second Cousin, twice removed

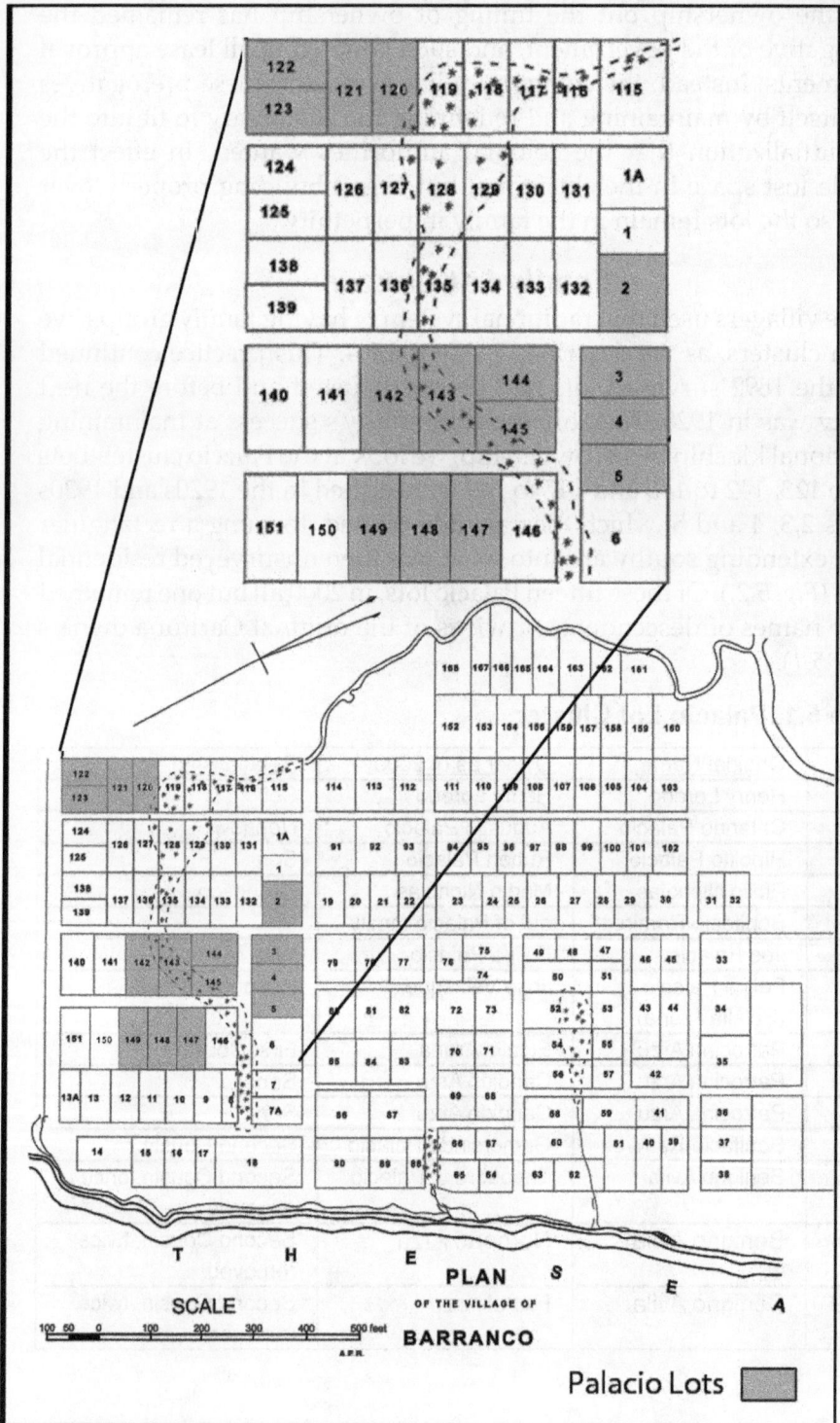

Figure 5.2. Palacio lots in Barranco

Figure 5.3. Augustin Palacio (Lot 3) and his wife, Simeona Mejia Palacio, in 1979 *(photo by Joseph O. Palacio)*

Formal Process for Leasing Lots

The procedures to apply for lots have remained virtually the same since Baranguna first applied for lots after the 1892 survey. Briefly, one fills out an application form to lease a lot, should one not be able to purchase it outright. Because purchasing has meant coming up with cash beyond the means of most villagers, they have taken the lease option. An example of the processing of a lease renewal application by colonial authorities is shown in Minute Paper 2965/13 (*Table 5.2*)

On approval, the government sends a formal document to the applicant giving the permission to rent the lot, usually for a maximum period of twenty years. Subsequently, one has the obligation to pay the rent. During the first round of lease approvals after the 1892 survey, the period was for ten years and the annual payment was $0.25. Since the 1920s the lease period was extended to twenty years.

The lease approval document is known in Garifuna as *"ligaradana múa"*. A loose translation is the "paper of the earth", an idiomatic expression for entitlement to own land from the Garifuna perspective.[91] This document is highly protected among family memorabilia. Paying one's lot rent is a duty that most villagers perform every year to safeguard remaining in possession of their lot. Figure 5.3 shows a copy of a lease approval document.[92]

Possessing a *ligaradana múa* has been a symbol of reaching adult maturity in the village, something that one, whether male or female, should have before starting a family. Older folks speak proudly of the time when they got their first lease as a major milestone in their life. Even after thirty and more years they still remember the date and the name of the officer who gave it to them, information that we have been able to corroborate from the official records. Most people remember their lot numbers. Mention of kinship, a topic always present in village talk, is always intertwined with which lot a person was born in and where he lived for most of his life. From such discussions we have learned that far more persons have lived in lots than those mentioned in official records.

Following from the *ligaradana múa* folk belief there is the further belief that on the death of the leaseholder, tenure automatically reverts to whom the deceased person or one or more close relatives might have chosen. Actually the law has always maintained that at death the lease expires and the onus is on the government to accept applications from any member of the public. But the prevailing practice by government officers is to follow the family decision on whom should become the successor.

Table 5.2. Minute Paper 2965/13[90]

Date	Action
18-8-1913	Surveyor General (S.G) rceives letter from Philip Nicholas requesting lease renewal for Lot 5.
18-9-1913	S..G. recommends renewal beginning 1 July 1914 for five years to the Colonial Secretary (Col. Sec.).
22-9-1913	Acting Col. Sec. approves and directs the District Commissioner of the Toledo District (D.C.) to delver a letter herewith to the applicant.
1-12-1913	D.C. informs that he has noted the renewal in the rent roll.
25-2-1914	S.G. submits the fiat to the Col. Sec. for signature.

Lessee Obligations

The obligations of the lessee toward the government as owner of the lot are spelled out in the lease document. Figure 5.4 shows a lease document from 1929. Since it was for a house lot, the words "per acre" after the price were crossed out. The terms and conditions were as published in the *Honduras Gazette*, which is also shown in Figure 5.4. They include paying the rent on time and not allowing others to use the lot, otherwise the lease could be revoked.

Notwithstanding the government conditions, lessees have allowed others to live in their lots. Such uses are not included in our database for they were not recorded within the official records. Only the names of persons who were given leases according to government records were listed in the database.

Freehold Grant

The final step toward acquiring full ownership may come years after receiving leasehold rights, when the lessee arranges to have the lot surveyed and pays the appropriate purchase price to the government. He then receives a deed with an official map of the lot. There is no word in Garifuna for "deed"or "title," so the villagers sometimes use the English word "title". Because most villagers never reach the point of fully purchasing their lot, the lease approval *ligaradana múa* is the document with which they are most familiar.

Lot Succession

On the death of a lessee, legally the lease reverts to the government, or to use the term in land administration language, it "expires". Expiration in village custom, however, does not mean that ownership reverts to the government. The deceased person might have already selected who should inherit the lot. If not, it goes to a relative according

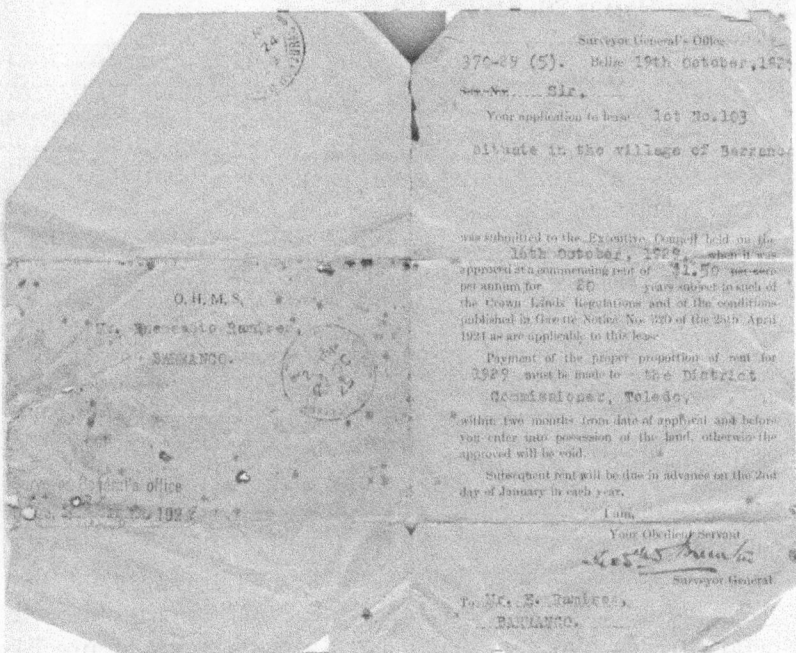

No. 320   SURVEYOR GENERAL'S OFFICE,
Belize, 28 April 1924.

Terms and Conditions of Leases of Crown Land.

IT is hereby notified for general information that all future leases of Crown Lands will be subject to such of the following conditions as are applicable to each lease, and to any further conditions which may be imposed in any particular case:—

1. Leases will be granted under the authority of Chapter 174 of the Consolidated Laws (Revised Edition), and subject to all powers, provisos and clauses therein contained which are applicable.

2. Precious metals, ores, gems, jewels, coal, petroleum oil and other bituminous minerals, timber and dyewood are strictly reserved and do not pass under this demise. and remove any of the above is reserved to His Majesty, his heirs or successors.

3. (a.) Non-payment of rent at specified time;

  (b.) Any dispositions or transfer or parting with the possession of the whole or any part of the land without written permission;

  (c.) Non-observance of or non-compliance with any of the conditions herein contained or referred to;

  (d.) Neglecting to keep the survey lines defining the land open and clear of bush;

  (e.) Neglecting to cultivate the land to the satisfaction of the Government's agricultural adviser;

shall in every instance authorize the Governor of the Colony by notice in the Government Gazette to declare this lease forfeited, and thereupon the same shall cease and become null and void, to all intents and purposes, and the land may be entered upon by or on behalf of His Majesty, his heirs or successors by any person duly authorized so to do, and possession thereof may be resumed as the property of His Majesty, his heirs and successors, and in such case the lessee shall have no claim to compensation for any improvement or outlay.

4. The lessee shall be taken to covenant, promise and agree with and to His Majesty, his heirs and successors well and truly to pay during the continuance of this lease the rent reserved, in yearly payments, in advance, unto the Treasurer for the time being.

5. The word lessee shall be read to include and be applicable to the lessee as well as the executors, administrators, and allowed assigns of such lessee as fully to all intents and purposes as if they had in every instance been specially mentioned.

6. The Government reserves the right to revise the rent at the end of any period of five years from the date of the commencement of the lease, but no increase of rent is to exceed five per centum of the unimproved rental value of the land as valued by the Surveyor General.

Gazette Notice No 133 of the 1st March 1922, is hereby annulled.

By Order.
FRED. W. BRUNTON,
Surveyor General.

M. P. 1150-24.

Figure 5.4. Lease approval and Conditions[93]

to a pattern that will be revealed further below in our spotlight on the actual transactions we recorded. What is important for our discussion at this point is that the government has allowed tradition to dictate lot transmission when the lessee dies. A potentially thorny problem in intestacy, which is prevalent in the village, becomes side-stepped by government into the arms of family members. Whoever takes over the lot of a deceased person can go to the government to apply for a new lease. In most cases the succession is agreed among immediate family members.

In discussing lot succession with a retired lands officer, his nonchalant reply was, "it is part of natural law that the family determines who should retain possession in the case of intestacy." He went further and gave an example where he was pro-active in intruding into a possible transmission because he detected blatant injustice. A person coveted a lot so much that he knew when the lease would expire. Stealthily, he submitted an application for that lot to the Lands Office. As officer, my informant became concerned and brought the matter to the attention of the owner, who immediately paid for an extension. He added that it was policy that in such cases he was to ask the owner whether he wanted an extension before proceeding with an application from another. According to him, not all lands officers would have taken it as a responsibility to intervene in such a case.

Intruding at such an interpersonal level gives added work to the lands administrator, who has not only house lots but also farmlands on lease under his responsibility for small villages like Barranco as well as for whole districts. At the district level he has to perform tasks in the field, such as overseeing boundary alignments in disputes among neighbours. In the office he oversees the payment of leases and advises on matters, such as lease application, approval, and extensions. This description is for the current time period, when there has been some streamlining of the bureaucracy. Earlier, during most of the 1900s, it was more haphazard with persons not trained in public lands administration being at the frontline, such as the District Commissioner or his chief clerk. For Barranco, rent payments have to be made in Punta Gorda.

Freehold, namely the outright purchase of lots, means the lot file would no longer remain within the land administration system as public property. Up to the year 2000, only 35 out of the 177 lots had reached the final stage of deed purchase. Five were purchased by non-villagers and another five are owned by the Roman Catholic Church, leaving 25 in the hands of Baranguna. Only three of these lots have proceeded from the first buyer to being re-sold to another. In short, market trading in house lots, which has overtaken other Garifuna villages in southern Belize, has not yet reached Barranco. On the other hand, lots have remained at the stage of leasehold with transmission taking place, not as closed cash-exchange, but in open-ended social relations where kinship plays a primary intermediary role.

Intercommunity Movements

The following information about early lot owners indicates inter-community movements, a pattern that no doubt existed in the earlier selection of settlements. There were two examples of lot transfers in the late 1890s that clarify very close linkages with communities at the polar ends of the Garifuna domain—Punta Gorda in Belize, and Trujillo in Honduras.

In 1899 Dominga Paulino received Lot 71, which had been in the name of her husband Diego Paulino, who died in 1896. Both Diego and Dominga came to the village from Punta Gorda from as early as 1866. Several of their offsprings, however, returned to live permanently in Punta Gorda, forming a linkage of close kinfolk between the two neigbouring communities. This lot is an interesting case of transmission through female descendents to which we will return.

Francisco Arzu came from Livingston and married Patrocina Palacio. In 1917 Francisco received lot 3 from from his uncle-in-law Patrocina's father's brother Catarino Palacio. Francisco Arzu had a brother or close relative, Luciano Arzu, who also came from Livingston around the same time and married Patrocina's older sister Eulogia. Lot 3 passed from Francisco Arzu back to the Palacios, to his brother-in-law, Augustin Palacio (Fig. 5.3).

In 1899 Andrea Nicholas transferred the lease to Lot 60 to her husband Simon Mejia, who, according to oral history, had come from Trujillo to Barranco via Punta Gorda and got married to Andrea in 1896. Simon Mejia's arrival in Barranco was most probably in search of his relatives, which included finding a potential spouse. Lot 60 passed on to Simon's son-in-law Pascasio Cayetano, and from him to Pascasio's daughter Sarah Palacio, and then became the site for the Marcelo Cayetano Dabuyaba Complex (Fig. 5.5).

These few examples indicate the intense nature of inter-community relations that influenced the settlement of Barranco, cementing the bond of circulatory migration that gained strength in subsequent generations as men and women moved freely in search of better livelihood. The unfolding picture of settlement—integrated into kinship, marriage, and other interpersonal ties—becomes clear as the fundamental right of the Garifuna to call Barranco their home.

Figure 5.5. Marcelo Cayetano Dabuyaba Complex on Lots 60 and 58 first built in 1996.

Family Surnames in Barranco

So far we have spoken of the community as the backbone of customary practices in lot tenure. But we need to answer the question of who made up the community in Barranco throughout the 1900s. We found that up to 1919 as many as one out of every three persons (37%) involved in lot transactions was non-Garifuna, mainly Mestizos, who had lived in the village with their own families from its early inception. The recurring family names were Andrade, Cardenas, Reyes, and Vaires. Their permanent outflow from Barranco became noticeable by 1909 when 22% of all donors were non-Garifuna but only 9% were recipients of lots. After the 1920s barely a handful of non-Garifuna were transmitting lots, which included both Mestizos and Creoles without the family support that earlier Mestizos had. The patterns of transactions that we are describing in this study are, therefore, overwhelmingly Garifuna.

We were able to isolate what Garifuna surnames were most frequently occurring in our database. The five most numerous in declining order were Palacio, Martinez, Arzu, Zuniga, and Nicholas. The ten most common names are shown in Table 5.3. These frequencies were taken from the global sample. We decided to go a little further and review the frequency of occurrence by decade from 1893 to 1999.

As expected the surnames in Table 5.3 were generally more common but they did not predominate markedly in each decade. The conclusion forthcoming is that in each decade there were several surnames, many barely recurring; or that many persons, mainly Garifuna, have come to the village engaged in a transaction or two and then left, indicating a continuous turnover within the village population.

Table 5.3. Frequency of Family Names in Lot Succession Records

Name	Frequency
Palacio	66
Martinez	54
Arzu	33
Zuniga	31
Nicholas	27
Nolberto	25
Paulino	23
Cayetano	22
Ariola	21
Castillo	21
Avilez	17

In lot ownership the villagers accepted people who came, stayed for a relatively short period and left. Those with the high frequencies in Table 5.3 have given the community some continuity over time. But equally important has been the co-incidence of customs on lot tenure that Garifuna people from other communities brought and contributed during their sojourn within the village, among them being non-British Honduran citizens. From our reading of the records and overall awareness of village wisdom, there was less concern with nationality than with whether newcomers abide by customary practices, including those of land tenure.

Analysis of Lot Succession

There are three attributes of lot possession that initiate the analysis of kinship relations:

1) Holding of leases in succession by different persons,
2) Kinship relations between two consecutive lessees, and
3) Selectivity, how a person becomes selected as inheritor of a lot.

Over the period of a little more than one hundred years since the first survey of lots in 1892, a few lots have had only two leaseholders, where the norm is four and more. For example, lot 4 has been held by Hipolito Palacio and his son Ruben Palacio. We have used the terms lot "donor" and "recipient" loosely in describing the various narratives about lot exchange. In fact, there was no actual giving and receiving. Hipolito got his lease in 1900 and it remained in his name, even after his death in the 1950s, until 1964 when Ruben applied and got it in his own name. Hipolito and Ruben got their own *ligaradana múa* for the same lot, but at different times. Ruben's 1964 lease acceptance did not mean that he started to live in the lot at that time. He had been living there all along with his father and assumed his responsibility as owner after his father's death. This observation goes for all leases indicating that there were no donations from a previous owner to another and that actual residence in a lot does not coincide with the beginning or ending of one's leasehold.

Database Analysis

As the wealth of the gradually accumulating field data dawned on us, we developed methods for electronic input to facilitate retrieval and analysis. The raw data was put into a spreadsheet that included all the records on each lot in the village: lot number, owner, map location, whether the lot is lease or grant, and the associated information on dates of approval, cancellation, etc. The complete spreadsheet representing the data we compiled is in Appendix C (*Table C5.1*), which shows the comprehensive nature of the details collected and digitized.

Using Joseph Steed's Brother's Keeper genealogical application we determined the relationship, if any, between the donor and recipient in each lot transaction. Those results are in Appendix C (*Table C5.2*).

We used a database to analyze the data in that spreadsheet, making a record for each transaction where a donor "passed" a lot to a recipient. There were 394 records and 13 fields in our database. We group the fields under five categories, each subdivided into specific fields as shown in Table 5.4, complete with frequencies and the number of lot successions that fall into each category.

Not all transactions were included in the database. There were three where lots were given to parents and two to a group. We excluded them for differing from the normal pattern in the village, where parents gave to children, generally persons who were younger, or to individuals.

Generally lots were not in joint ownership. There was only one lot owned jointly by an American and his Garifuna wife. For convenience we included only the name and other information of the husband.

Table 5.4. Database Analysis of Lot Transmissions

Category	Sub-category	Field	Freq*
1. Case Specific	1.1 Lot Number		
	1.2 Date		
	1.3 Local Area	1.3.1 First Set (lots 1-89)	271
		1.3.2 Second Set (lots 91-114)	66
		1.3.3 Third Set (lots 115–167)	57
2. Characteristics of Donor and Recipient	2.1 Name		
	2.2 Gender	2.2.1 Men Donors	283
		2,2.2 Female Donors	111
		2.2.3 Male Recipients	245
		2.2.4 Female Recipients	149
3. Awareness of kinship relation		3.1 Don't know (DK)	69
		3.2 No Relation	48
		3.3 No Specific Relation	93
		3.4 Relation	184
4. Consanguineal Relations	4.1 Relations	4.1.Father	59
		4.1.2 Mother	56
		4.1.3 Sibling	8
	4.2 Descent	4.2.1 Lineal	76
		4.2.2 Non-lineal	39
	4.3 Distance	4.3.1 One (CD1)	72
		4.3.2 Two (CD2)	13
		4.3.3. Three (CD3)	31
5. Affinal Relations	5.1 Gender	5.1.1 Male 5.1.2 Female	29
			32
	5.2 Distance	5.2.1 One (AD1)	24
		5.2.2 Two (AD2)	26
		5.2.3 Three (AD3)	11

*Freq = frequency

Date

There were 19 transactions where dates were unknown to us and remained undated in the database. The dated transactions started in 1893 and ended in 1999. The date was when the official lease went into effect, which was part of the lease number, or the year of the lease application.

Local Area

Local areas were assigned based on the chronological allocation of lot numbers. The first set was lot numbers 1 to 90 assigned during the first survey done in 1892. The second set was lot numbers 91 to 114 that were assigned after the 1892 survey, but added to the 1892 map. The third set, lot numbers 115 to 167 were added after the 1928 survey.

Awareness of Kinship Relation

Identifying the kinship relations between succeeding lessees depended on knowing the depth and breadth of blood and affinal ties among the villagers and their relatives in neigbouring communities. Because the kinship relation between the donor and recipient was crucial to our study, we relied on our genealogical record. The database included four possible answers to the question of relations:

1) relations (184),
2) no specific relations (93),
3) no relations (48), and
4) don't know (69).

The 184 transactions in the catgory "relations" where we knew there was definitely a relationship accounted for only 47% of the sample. In addition, there were 93 cases where we suspected that there could be some type of relationship. For example, the two persons might have had the same surname but we could not identify how they were related. Preferring to err on the side of caution we called such cases "no specific relation". There were 48 cases where we were certain that there was "no relation". In 69 cases we "don't know" whether there was any kinship tie between the donor and recipient.

Consanguineal Relations

The large category of "relations" is subdivided into blood or "consanguineal" and in-law or "affinal" relations. Furthermore, the consanguineal are broken into sibling exchange (8), father's link (59), and mother's link (56). The almost equal proportion between relations through the father's and mother's link substantiates the findings in kinship studies within the Caribbean about the significance of bilateral ties, or of being able to inherit property equally from one's father or mother.

No Relation

Examples of lot succession with no relation are Lots 63 and 64, which were listed on the 1892 map for Baranguna Anacleto Cayetano and Nicolasa Moralez. The lots were purchased in 1894 by D. S. Wells, a Creole businessman who was an associate of *latifundista* Cramer. The lots were then transferred to Eusebio Polonio, also a businessman with interests in Punta Gorda. We are certain there was no relation except for business associations among these owners. Eusebio's grandson Bartolo Polonio (*right*) now lives in Lot 64.

Bartolo Polonio

Aparicio Marin

Consanguineal Relations

Gabriel Velasquez was the first to apply for Lot 24. He was the second husband of Mercedes Palacio. Velasquez gave the lot to his step-granddaughter, Emelda Marin, who passed it on to her brother, Clarence Marin (*p. 57*) in a sibling exchange. Aparicio Marin (*left*) was the husband of Brigida Paulino, son-in-law of Mercedes Palacio and Gabriel Velasquez, and father of Emelda and Clarence Marin. This photo was on Aparicio Marin's immigration paper for Guatemala when he went to work for United Fruit in 1928.
(*photo courtesy of Pietra Arana*)

No Specific Relation

Lots 27 and 28 are interesting cases because both involve transfers where we think there may be a relationship, but cannot verify it. Lot 28 was initially listed for Clara Martinez on the 1892 map, but Josefa Amaya applied for the first lease in 1913. She is Josefa Paulino under a married name. But in 1920 Lot 28 went to Albina Martinez, for whom we have no information, except that she may be related to Clara Martinez. Thirty years later, in 1950, a group representing the Carib Development Society leased Lot 28. The group included one R. Martinez, another Martinez for which we found "no specific relation". This group built a Community Centre in 1960 (*below*). Today the SATIIM Resource Centre is on Lot 28.

Barranco Community Centre built on Lot 28 in 1960
(photo by Joseph O. Palacio in 1979)

Affinal Relations

Together with non-lineal consanguineal ties, affinal ties are normally not included in the study of inheritance within the Caribbean. We found 61 cases where succession came through affinal ties, which are half those going through consanguineal ties. A further look at affinal ties revealed that they can go either through male or female intermediaries.

Affinal Relations

Elorine Nuñez

Anastacio Palacio was the listed as the owner of Lot 87 on the 1892 map. Sotera Gutierrez, who had several children with Anastacio, got the first lease for the lot in 1902. But after 11 years, he took it back and then it went to his grandson-in-law, Evaristo Nuñez in 1960, 36 years after Anastacio's death. So, the lot went through three affinal transfers—from Anastacio to Sotera, back to Anastacio, and then to his grandson-in-law. The person who was an intermediary for the third exchange was Evaristo's wife, Alexine Loredo. Her mother was Gregoria Palacio Loredo, Anastacio's daughter with his wife, Magdalena Cesario. Today Elorine Nuñez (*left*), daughter of Alexine and Evaristo lives in Lot 87.

Degree of Distance in Relations

With such a wide range of consanguineal relations, we had to fit them into the pattern of selection on a case by case basis. Earlier we argued that our use of the terminology of "donor" and "recipient", does not signify purposeful acts; rather it was to facilitate the flow of the narrative. We did not interview actual donors and recipients to arrive at these patterns. Rather, they are a distillation from what was in the government records on the registration of lot lease holding. They, therefore, are a reflection of cultural practices that pinpoint norms of behaviour within a community that have persisted for three and more generations. As we have done in other cases of cultural norms in this study, we refer to the Garifuna language to help with an explanation. There is a distinction in the language of consanguineal kin into *iduhenyu karnal* and *iduhenyu diseguaña*. The former refers to relatives who are close, using the Spanish word *carnal* (meaning "carnal" in English) to underline affinity to the body itself. This group of relatives includes mother, father, sister, brother, etc. *Iduhenyu diseguaña*, on the other hand, refers to relatives who are further away. There is no definitive

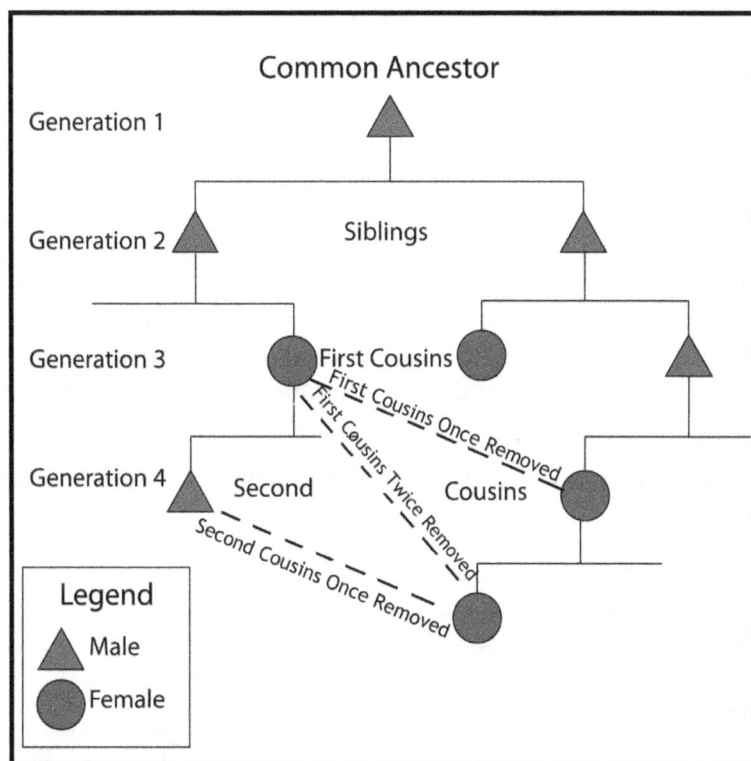

Figure 5.6 Kinship Chart

line separating one group from the other, each person having his/her own preference, depending upon the occasion.

In determining the patterns of succession using consanguineal ties we use the Garifuna distinction of kinfolk into *iduhenyu carnal* and *iduhenyu diseguaña* as our basis for classifying degrees of distance among consanguineal kin. CD is abbreviation for Consanguineal Distance and the numbers 1 to 3 signify degrees of distance. CD1 refers to offsprings and first cousins; CD2 to nieces and nephews, and CD3 to a wide range from grandchildren to second cousin twice removed (*Figure 5.6*).

Where the Garifuna have been flexible in their distinction between *iduheñu karnal* and *diseguaña*, we were firm in our categories to facilitate measuring for analysis. In Garifuna there is no distinction for affinal relations as we have outlined for *iduheñu karnal* and *iduhenyu diseguaña* in consanguineal relations. But we used a pattern similar to that in consanguineal relations of calculating distance into three categories as AD1, AD2, and AD3. The results are seen in the frequencies for each category with men and women as donors and recipients in Appendix C (*Tables C5.3-5.7*) and summarized in Tables 5.5 and 5.6.

Bilateral Kinship

The scrutiny that we have been able to apply to lot successions allows us to investigate the appropriateness of applying the anthropological term "bilateral kinship" to the situation in Barranco. Bilateral kinship provides a framework for the exchange of a lot from either one's father or mother. Table 5.5 shows that consanguineal relationship between the donor and recipient may derive through siblingship or through ties from one's father or mother. The frequencies for sibling are the least at eight while fathers (59) supersede mothers (56) by only three. These numbers confirm that under the immediate family subgroup of the consanguineal bond, bilateral ties are almost equally split between one's father and mother.

Table 5.5. Consanguineal and Affinal Relations Underlying Lot Transactions

Consanguineal Relations				
	Immediate Family			
		Lot Donor	Frequency	%
		Sibling	8	6
		Mother	56	46
		Father	59	48
		Total	123	100
	Other Relationship			
		Non-Lineal	39	34
		Lineal	76	66
		Total	115	100
Affinal Relations				
		Female	32	63
		Male	29	47
		Total	61	100

Having deducted the eight cases under sibling transmission, we differentiated whether the descent falls under lineal or non-lineal linkages. Lineal ties flow through the direct lines of one's grandfather, to father and to oneself. Descent can be *degegua* (literally divided into two parts), a close English translation would be "bifurcated". In anthropology the term is "collateral kin" or "non-lineal descent", which is traced from one's relative who is not a direct ancestor, such as one's grand-uncle, to one's uncle, to oneself. In our database lineal descent (76) occurs slightly more than twice the non-lineal (39). The distinction between the two is especially important in bringing forward the significance of cousins, whose role in lot succession we will discuss further below.[94]

In addition to blood or consanguineal ties, Barranco donors also use in-law or affinal ties to determine to whom to give a lot. As shown in Table 5.6, there are twice as many consanguineal transactions (123) as affinal (61). Slightly more affinal transactions derive from female donors (32) than male donors (29). Thus, we show that in Barranco the pattern is not simple bilateral kinship as has been found throughout the Anglophone Caribbean. In this study we add sibling exchange as another type of consanguineal relations and affinal exchange, which is a non-consanguineal basis for lot inheritance. Thus, it is more complex as donors transmit lots to a wide range of relatives, both consanguineal and affinal

Gender and Kinship

In order to determine the extent to which women participated in the lot transactions, we looked at transactions from the gender of the donor and recipient. Men are involved in more lot transmissions than women. Out of a total of 184 transmissions where there was a known relationship, 125 (68%) were initiated by men and 59 (32%) by women.

Within the gender role in the village, men are seen as the ones who should provide access to house lots. However, before the 1892 survey, access to lots was handled by the extended family. Under that regime women could be assigned lots for their family within the family cluster, but after the colonial authorities brought individualization to the village, the male became responsible to find a lot for his family.

Within this role specificity it is not surprising that men transmit to their sons (33) in far greater proportion than to their daughters (8), as seen in Table 5.7, which show transmission by men and women through both consanguineal and affinal kinship bonds. Even in the category of more distantly related kin, men transmit almost equally to men and women. With women on the receiving end, men give almost half of all their transmissions to their wives. In the remaining affinal cases, however, men give more to men than women.

While men show a disproportionate preference for male recipients in transmitting to consanguineal relations, women are more even in their gender preferencs, transmitting in 13 cases to their daughters and 10 to their sons. Among the remaining consanguineal relations, however, women show greater preference for women (16) as against men (6).

There are fewer instances of women transmitting to affinal relations. While their total consanguineal transactions are 47, their affinal are only 10. They do participate, however, as intermediaries in the male affinal relations. In almost half of all the male affinal ties, the

Table 5.6. Gender in Transmission of Lots

Donor	Recipient	Frequency	Percentage
Male	Male	67	54%
Male	Female	58	46%
Total Male Donors		125	100%
Female	Female	33	56%
Female	Male	26	44%
Total Female Donors		59	100%
Total Transactions		**184**	

Matrilineal Succession

When analyzing global patterns derived from frequencies, it is important to bring forward examples that go against the generalized cases and demonstrate what may be unusual, especially in an almost unbroken series of successions. Lot 71 is such an example showing succession through a line of women descendants.

The head of household listed on the 1892 map was Diego Paulino, but he died in 1896 before Baranguna began applying for leases, so his wife Dominga Cayetano Paulino applied for Lot 71. As shown below, the succession of Lot 71 was through females, with one exception. For two years it was in the name of Bertram Enriquez, an outsider. When the descendants of Dominga Cayetano Paulino discovered this apparent aberration, they quickly got the lot back into the female family line. Petrona Casimiro is the married name of Petrona Ariola.

Matrilineal Succession in Lot 71

Year	Donor	Recipient	Relationship
1899	Dominga Paulino	—	Self
1927	Dominga Paulino	Ascenciona Ariola	Daughter
1927	Ascenciona Ariola	Virginia Diego	Granddaughter
—	Virginia Diego	Petrona Ariola	Daughter
—	Petrona Ariola	Virginia Diego	Mother
1977	Virginia Diego	Bertram Enriquez	—
1979	Bertram Enriquez	Petrona Casimiro	—

influences of their spouses come when lots are transferred to brothers-in-law, wife's sister-in-law, niece-in-law, and so on. In short, women are more dedicated to their consanguines, where they show equal preference to both men and women. On the other hand, men transmit in all consanguineal and affinal categories and show more preference to men than women.

Social Value System

Ultimately, lot transmissions are interpersonal transactions that become easier to understand within the social value system of the community. The fact is that there is a finite number of lots within the village for the hundreds of people born since 1893. Fortunately, there has been heavy outmigration leaving fewer men and women to vie for the relatively small numbers that are available. To maximize access, there is a range of options that remain for one to acquire possession of a lot, whether on his/her own or through a spouse.

But how does the community react to the unequal supply and demand for lots? The village norm, which is a moral obligation sanctioned by public opinion, is that men make allocation for their sons and wives to inherit the family lot and that mothers do so for their daughters and sons. This statement summarizes what we see in CD1 and AD1 transactions where men and women are donors and recipients in Table 5.7. If men are not passing lots to their sons and wives and women are not passing to their daughters and sons, they commit a grave offense in the ever-roving discriminating public eye of the village. This is the highest level of the social value system having to do with the obligations in the community toward the transmission of lots.

Because the second level of the social value system, as seen in CD2, CD3, AD2, and AD3 transmissions, is not based on direct obligations, the sanctions are more tolerable. Furthermore, the transactions take place among a far wider assortment of relatives, which might be either consanguineal or affinal—nephew-in-law or second cousin twice removed, for example.

At the third level there is a deliberate intention to take advantage of a lot exchange for personal gain, as the following example elaborates.[95] One example of third level lot transactions underlines a deeper meaning in the never-ending web of interfamily relations. The names have been changed to maintain anonymity. The lot was registered in the name of Diego Bernardez. Eight years afterwards Josefa Castillo acquired possession of it only to lose it back to Diego a few years afterwards. The dealings around this lot actually were part of a larger web of spousal

Table 5.7. Examples of Donors and Recipients in Consanguineal Lot Transmissions

Donor	Male Recipient		Female Recipient	
Consanguineal Relations				
Male Donors				
CD1	Son	33	Daughter	8
	1st Cousin	2	1st Cousin	2
CD2	Nephew	5		
CD3	2nd Cousin	5		
	1st Cousin, 1R*	2		
	Grandson	3		
	2nd Cousin, 2R*			1
Female Donors				
CD1	Son	10	Daughter	13
	1st Cousin	2	1st Cousin	2
CD3			Granddaughter	4
			1st Cousin, 1R*	2
	2nd Cousin	1		
Affinal Relations				
Male Donors				
AD1			Wife	33
AD2	Brother-in-law	6		
	Son-in-law	4		
AD3	1st Cousin-in-law	2		1
	2nd Cousin-in-law			2
Female Donors				
AD1	Husband	2		
AD2	Son-in-law	3		
	Niece-in-law			1
	2nd Cousin-in-law			1
	Father of Co-spouse	1		

*1R = once removed; 2R = twice removed.

jealousy. Diego Bernardez's daughter and Josefa were co-spouses of Alfonso Martinez. Josefa succeeded in taking the lot from Bernardez as an attack on his daughter, who was her rival. However, Bernardez was vindicated by re-acquiring rights to the lot. The relative formality of leasehold was actually sacrificed on the altar of jealousy between two women. The happy ending was that Bernardez was able to re-affirm the lot's place within his family.

Changes over Time

We asked what changes in succession we could identify during the 107 years of our study period that would throw light on customary practice. We calculated the total number of transactions starting from the 1893 to 1899 period and subsequently by decades up to 1999 and divided them by gender of donor and recipient.

Figure 5.7 shows the transactions per decade, which are reflected in the total height of each bar. Those with female donors sit in front of those with male donors. There are fewer lot transactions in the 1940s, the 1960s and the 1990s. Since 1950 the numbers of lot transactions in Barranco have declined dramatically. A more definitive study of the village socio-economy would help explain such a pronounced decline. The destructive impact of the 1945 hurricane accelerated out-migration from the village and started the precipitous outflow that intensified afterwards.

The back row represents male donors, which show the highest number in most decades. The men's donations remained predominant throughout except for the 1970s and the 1990s, when female donors amounted to more than half of the total transactions. This evidence of new primary gender roles within lot tenure needs further analysis, especially as the village has entered the uncharted socioeconomic times of the early 21st century.

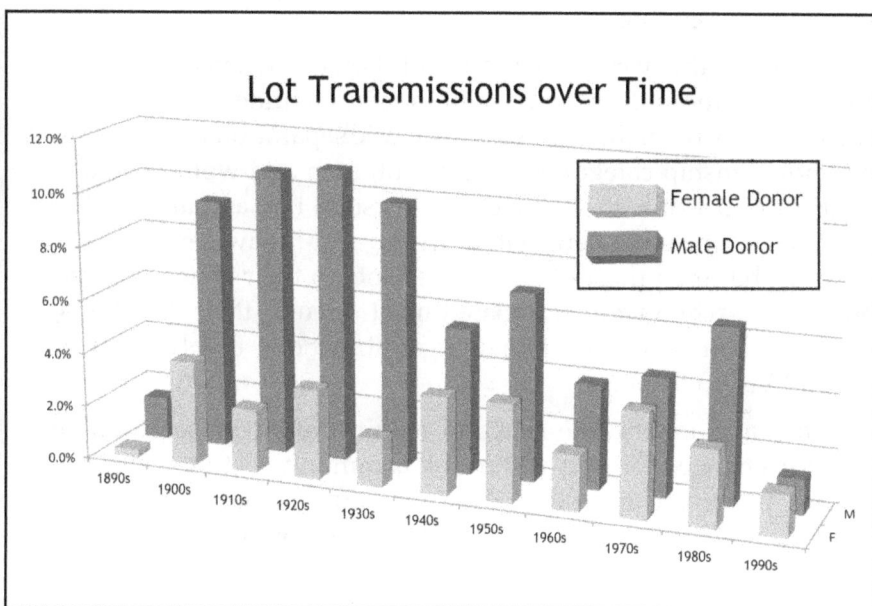

Figure 5.7. Lot Transmissions over Time

Summary and Conclusions

The theme of the overlap of the customary and formal practices in land tenure found in the rest of this volume initiates the narrative in this chapter. The customary practices fit into a structure that the community has worked for several generations, which allows the community to disregard such conditions as the expiry of leasehold at the death of the lessee. The officers in the formal land administration system are expected to show consideration for customary practices, if only to lighten their heavy workload. In this way the two systems have co-existed in their distinct sociopolitical spaces.

Another significant contribution of this study was the contrast of the settlement pattern in the Anglophone Caribbean with that found in Barranco. While house lots are the units of residence in Barranco, in the Caribbean it is the homestead. Freehold possession predominates in the Caribbean while in Barranco it is leasehold.

Within a field of study in the social sciences of the Anglophone Caribbean where bilateral kinship has been assumed to be a predominant medium of land inheritance, this study breaks new ground. It starts by isolating kinship ties underlying relations of lot succession into consanguineal and affinal, both of which total 184 from a total of 394 records. Two-thirds of the 184 transactions show consanguineal succession, and the remaining affinal succession. The latter is a significant minority which should be included within the context of lot succession.

To analyze the various patterns of house lot succession, we established degrees of distance within consanguineal and affinal relations using as basis the Garifuna idiomatic separation of closer and more remote kinship categories. As a result, men and women donors and recipients become stratified based on such ties as parent-child, husband-wife, uncle-nephew, father-in-law-son-in-law, and so on. We showed that men most often donated lots to their sons, followed by their wives; while women donated most often to their daughters, followed by their sons. The remaining transactions involved lower degrees of kinship distance.

Kinship and inheritance function within the larger social value system of exchange relations within the community. At one level the obligations to donate to one's offsprings and spouses is built into expectations, and aberrations from this norm meet communal acrimony. Sanctions against donating to relatives found at more remote degrees of kinship are less severe. The upshot is that donors and recipients have a wide range of options to engage in lot inheritance, which is helpful within a prevailing context of ever fewer lots that are available.

Our ability to supersede the limited scope of bilateral kinship and to highlight the gendered changes in lot transmissions over time came from our longitudinal study covering more than 100 years and a universal sample for the whole village of 394 records. Another contribution of this study is the prolonged time depth that we have covered, which contrasts with the limited time scope of most studies within the Caribbean region. As a result, the specificities of prolonged ownership have become clearer.[96]

This study has shown that over decades the frequency of lot succession started to decline in the 1950s and accelerated during the 1990 decade. We have also shown that during the last three decades the predominance of men as lot transmitters has declined in favour of women. These new trends demand scrutiny to know better what triggered them and how the community responded.

While lot succession functioned at the level of kinship, farmland tenure, the topic of the next chapter in this volume, covers a different dimension where geographical space within the extended periphery of the village becomes more significant.

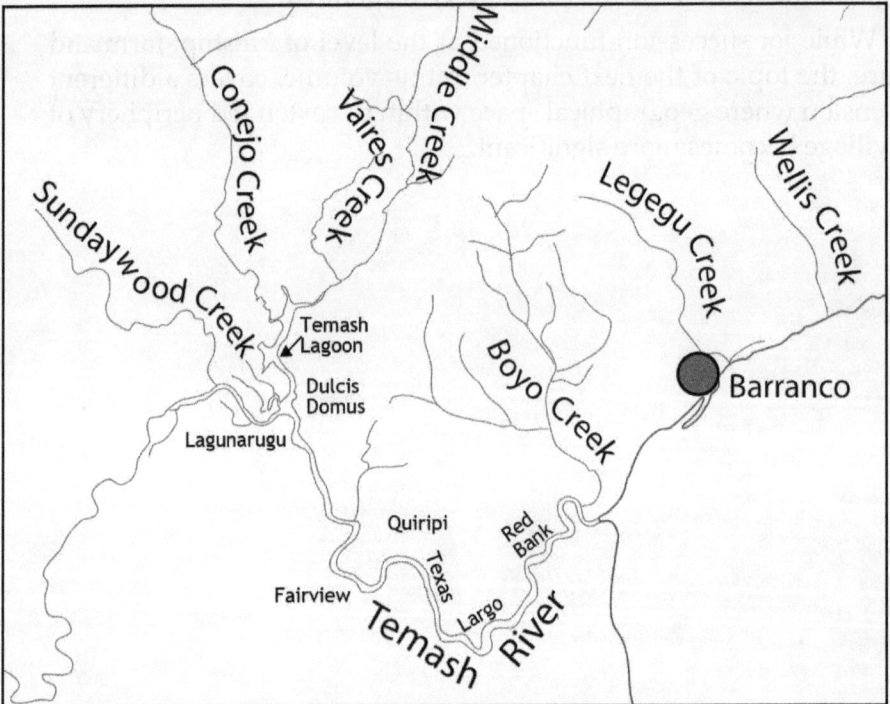

Figure 6.1. Map of Barranco Farm Area Names

Chapter Six
Farmland Tenure in Barranco

This chapter shows that the colonial government allocated hundreds of farmlands on leasehold for the Garifuna people in the Barranco area from the 1890s to 2000; promoted the export trade of banana as well as cash cropping for the local market; and did cadastral surveys of farmlands while maintaining an administrative system for their distribution. The people, on the other hand, responded within the limitations of their slash-and-burn agricultural practices, taking advantage of opportunities to work the land, as it became available. This chapter considers how the residents of the village of Barranco and others acquired their farmlands, where they were located, and how they moved across locations over time. Furthermore, it analyses the unfolding social relations they crystallized in land tenure in terms of gender, ethnicity, and local community identity. Finally, it introduces a typology of land ownership within the rural community.

The structure that we use to stratify the farmlands is borrowed from the study of habitat in cultural geography, where a community becomes a focal point to analyse relations with its corresponding parts spread out in space. Davidson applied this concept in his study of macro-habitat, meso-habitat, and micro-habitat among Garifuna villages.[97] Lundberg followed with a detail study of the habitat around Barranco, focusing not only on the physical environment but also on land use from the early beginnings of the village settlement in the 1850s to the 1970s.[98] We retain Lundberg's basic outline of farmland locations, but elaborate on overlaps in use over time within a structure which we term "core-periphery". It refers to a core, which is the focal point that impacts on farmlands extending far and wide. In turn the core is transformed by changes taking place within its several outlying peripheries.

The oral tradition on early land tenure among Baranguna refers to the efforts of their leaders to initiate a communal land lease in the early 1900s and the predominance of Boyo Creek, a distance of about five kilometers west, as the preferred farming location around the same time. Both of these point to the villagers overcoming obstacles in the use of land—the former resorting to communal leadership under the threat of prosecution for the illegal use of Crown Land and the latter walking a long distance to access good farmlands. After several unsuccessful efforts to probe for more examples of early oral tradition on land use, we concluded that part of the reason for this lapse is the excessive control by the colonial government, which forced the villagers, according to an elder to be "squatters on the lands of their ancestors", and did not provide them with any assistance in the marketing of their crops. History has now confirmed that government control consisted at first of alienating large blocks into the hands of non-Garifuna people and subsequently leasing smaller parcels to the Garifuna averaging twenty acres, as we shall see throughout this chapter. From early the villagers learned that owning land was not their legal right but a privilege more at the disposal of non-villagers and the non-Garifuna.

The period 1891 to 1911 is a watershed in the history of farmland tenure in the Barranco subregion. While beforehand the colonial government had provided surveys for large landowners, the government allocated lands for small farmers without formal surveys, using descriptive marks of location. This we term the pre-survey period. In 1913 the colonial authorities drew a map (Plan 541) indicating the parcels that had been allocated in the *lumua Barangu* before that time.

During the pre-survey period the *Honduras Gazette* gives several examples of large parcels that were available within the vicinity of the village as late as the 1890s. One example is a block along the Temash River for which the Surveyor General was inviting applications in 1894,

"St. Cross – Surveyor General to receive applications, stating the amount offered – 12 miles as the crow flies, and about 30 miles by river, from the bar – 1,470 acres – a mile and a half river frontage with 30-foot square house, 35 acres cleared land and planted with 2,000 banana shoots, rubber, cacao, lime, Annata, Alligator pear, granadilla vines, mame apple, vanilla vines, pineapple."[99]

Another entry shows an applicant for a block, also along the Temash, "11April, 1889 Fielding, S.T.E 1,370 acres right bank Temash River N by river and land of B Cramer, S. by land of B. Cramer and W. by land of H.J. Cramer being remaining part of land formerly leased by H. A. Wickham."[100]

Repeatedly the lands of the Cramers were used as boundaries for parcels being leased between the 1890s and 1910. Indeed, Minute Paper 1305, beginning in 1905 confirms that Cramer properties included half of all the lands found between the Moho and Temash Rivers. From the information on boundaries of parcels being leased, we observed that Sundaywood Creek, located within *lumua Barangu*, was adjoining a part of the Cramer lands. Another contemporaneous large landholder within the same area was Steinbrugger.

If the non-Garifuna were not engaged in estate agriculture along the Temash, they were using government-awarded concessions for logging and rubber bleeding. A review of several concessions during the pre-survey period showed that not one was given to a Garifuna. In 1901 Robert Henry Grant, for example, got a concession "to bleed rubber" on the north side of the Temash River. Oral information we received is that William N. Bourne, who got a 125-acre lease along the Sundaywood Creek in 1913, was involved in logging and later joined with his son-in-law Samuel B. Vernon in sawmilling. Vernon himself received his own 125-acre lease in Red Bank in 1916. Figure 6.1 is a map of the Barranco farming areas with their local names.

Decades before the Baranguna took up leases within the time of our study, their livelihood consisted of exploiting their adjoining land and sea resources for consumption, as well as surplus sales. From the sea they captured turtles and sold the shells for export. From the land they grew banana, root crops and several fruits, among them pineapple and coconuts. For transportation they built large dories to take their commodities to Belize City. They could also do wage labour on estate farms and logging concessions along the Moho and Temash Rivers, where some would have reached higher level positions, such as Eusebio Polonio.[101] Earning cash on their own or otherwise was relatively easy within their immediate surroundings during the latter 1800s and up to the early decades of the 1900s.[102]

Bananas and the Entry of the United Fruit Company

The involvement of villagers in banana cash-cropping, however, would have probably started with the Avilezes and Martinezes, who farmed on the Guatemalan side of the Sarstoon River.[103] Banana cash cropping by small farmers was taking place in the Livingston area from the early 1880s.[104] It would have taken little time for Baranguna to also get into the trade using lands behind their own village. The first 1890s land leases in the Boyo Creek North area were probably for banana fields.

Figure 6.2. Banana boat picking up bananas on the Temash River
(photo courtesy of James Curry and the Belize Maritime Museum Collection)

Non-Garifuna men, who were agents of foreign multinational corporations or lower level own-account farmers, were attracted by the economic gain that could accrue from the lands around Barranco. Locations along the Sundaywood Creek, Lagunurugu, and the Temash River bar were among those that received early attention. The Garifuna Baranguna, on the other hand, worked nearer to the village for their food supply as well as cash-cropping. They extended to lands further away on exhausting their nearby supply, noticeably during the large scale push toward banana production in the 1930s.

A deep traditional knowledge of the rainforest around the village was another by-product of early trekking among farms and logging camps. Men and women became aware of the savannahs, wetlands, the numerous streams—in general the overall micro-environments appropriate for growing particular crops. They learned where the trees were that were good for logging or for carving dories; as well as those producing leaves for thatching and vines for use to make utensils. They also became proficient in the seasonality of game animals and where they came to feed. To Baranguna cultivation was one among the several benefits that the land yielded for home use as well as cash. To them the village proper was a hub extending to locations within an integrated subregion where they worked and earned their livelihood.

Farmlands—Core/Periphery Distinction

No matter how far away within the subregion that there were works, be they estate farming, small farming, logging, or rubber bleeding; the village of Barranco, as the nearest coastal settlement, remained a node for the supply of goods and services, and overall communication and transportation. When the villagers reminisce in great delight about the "good ol' banana days", they are referring to the socioeconomic impact that redounded in their midst from the sale of their crops, the wages they earned as owners of dugouts ferrying bananas or as carriers of the fruit, (*Fig. 6.2*) as well as the flow of cash within the larger community. It was during that period that some built wooden houses modeled from those found in towns, one of which remains at this time (*Fig. 6.3*). The strength of the village as a regional core relied on its surrounding parts, and with the decline within the periphery so also came the depression that settled over the village since the 1940s.

For purposes of analyzing the subgrouping of applications we use the concept of core-periphery following the structural linkages that historically Barranco has retained with farmlands both closer as well as further away. While initially we had grouped farmlands into locations based on proximity to each other, as we proceeded deeper into the analysis of patterns across locations, we joined them into four basic areas—Core, South Periphery, West Periphery, and East Periphery. Figure 6.4 displays an overview of these four areas and Table 6.1 has a breakdown of their constituent locations, and the number of applications in each.

Figure 6.3. Home and shop of Jerome Alvarez, built in Barranco with lumber from the Temash area and still remaining in 2011

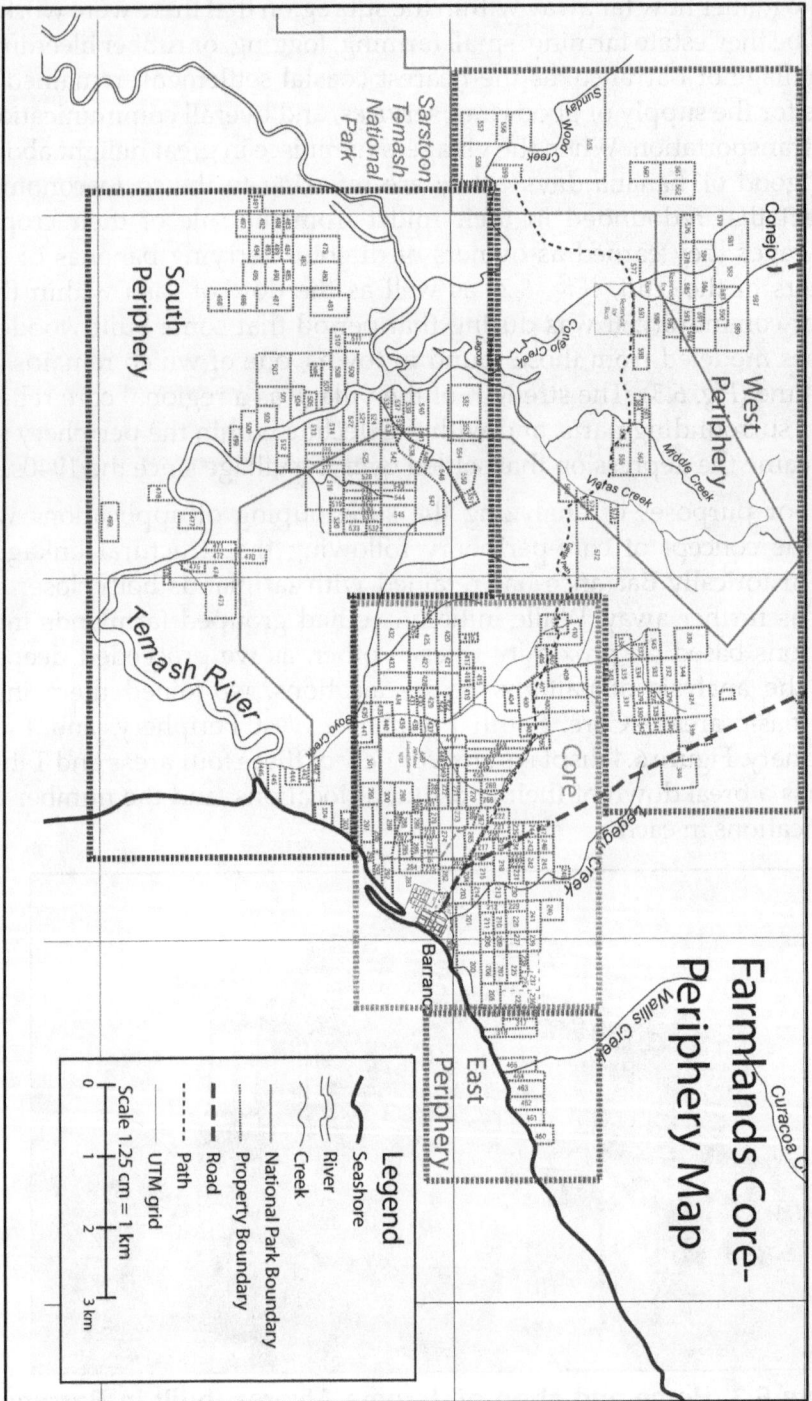

Figure 6.4. Farmlands Core-Periphery Areas Map

Table 6.1. Areas, Locations, and Applications

Area	Location	Number of Applications
Core	Barranco East	6
	Barranco Northwest	33
	Barranco South	77
	Barranco West	25
	Boyo Creek Cattle Path	6
	Boyo Creek Middle & Mouth	44
	Boyo Creek North	21
	Northeast of lots 33-38 & NW of Creek	5
	Lidise	22
	Unknown	4
	Subtotal	243
South Periphery	Big Bend	18
	Dulcis	33
	Fairview	11
	Lagunurugu	15
	Largo	27
	Red Bank	17
	Temash Bar	2
	Sea Southwest	2
	Subtotal	125
West Periphery	Conejo	25
	Middle Creek	8
	Sundaywood Creek	12
	Vairez Creek	11
	Subtotal	56
East Periphery	Wellis Creek	18
	Sea Northeast	5
	Subtotal	25
Total		**449**

As the name implies, the Core area includes locations closer to the village extending from the sea going west to the Boyo Creek and bending eastward to the coast a few meters south of the village. At roughly 60 square kilometers, it is the largest area. The South Periphery follows the Temash River from the bar to the Big Bend. The West Periphery covers parcels along the Sundaywood, Conejo, Middle, and Vairez Creeks—all tributaries of the Temash River. The smallest area, the East Periphery, covers locations running northeast of the village along the coast.

Our database included a total of 449 records, each representing an application, analysed to arrive at patterns based on locations as well as on gender, ethnicity, and local community identity. The complete spreadsheet of these records are included in Appendix D Table D6.1. Because the chronology is a key variable, we first looked at the number of farmland parcel transactions by decade (*Fig. 6.5*). There is a slow but marked beginning in the 1890s, two peaks in the 1930s and 1950s, and a final decline in the 1960s. Not shown in the chart is that while there were five applications in the 1960s, there was only one in the 1970s, none in either the 1980s and 1990s, and two in 2000.

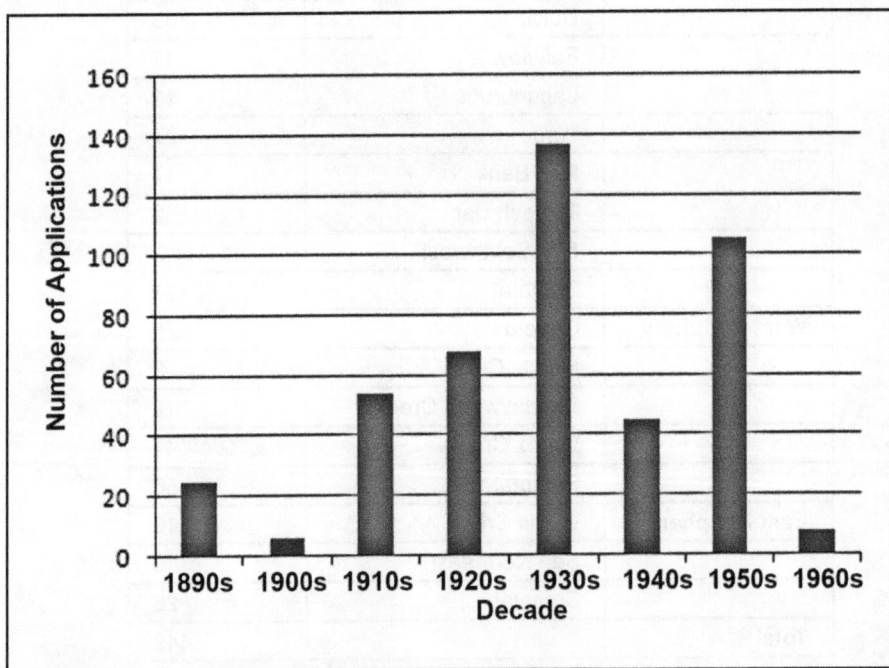

Figure 6.5. Farmland applications by decade

The dip between 1900 and 1909 probably resulted from administrative setbacks in approving applications that were resolved in 1913. The other dip in the 1940s came from the overall depression in the colonial economy as a result of WWII, when several men were recruited to join the British Honduras Defense Force and to participate otherwise in the war effort in the United Kingdom and United States. Besides, there were recurring shortages in consumer goods as ships bringing imports encountered delays. Villagers recount suffering not only from lack of imported foodstuff but also much needed implements, such as axes, machetes, and sharpening files. To add to these difficulties in 1945, the village and surrounding farmlands were devastated by a severe hurricane flattening houses and crops. Men and women were forced to leave on migratory wage labour in other parts of the country or to port towns in Guatemala and Honduras. With all the agricultural produce destroyed, they had to go to Crique Sarco to bake cassava bread.

The 1940 downturn took place between two decades with the sharpest surges in applications. The 1930s was the climax of the export of banana from southern Belize to the United States, resulting in a demand for plots west of the village and along the Temash River, especially from 1935 to 1939. The second surge in applications came as an effort of the Survey Department to re-align previous survey lines and add new parcels. Surveyor Carl Gibson stayed in the village in 1954 to do this task and generated much good will, talk of which still remains among villagers. One of his crowning achievements was doing the survey for a new agricultural subdivision located northwest of the village, called Lidise, which in Garifuna translates as "it is so far away." During that survey Gibson worked on 202 acres, where 14 agricultural blocks were demarcated. Eleven miles of boundary lines were cleared; five miles of traverse (compass) and 37 concrete pillars laid.[105]

Lidise marked the last concentrated effort to engage in small farming in village history. While there have been a handful of applications since then, the momentum generated in previous years dissipated after the 1950s. For a graphic illustration of the change in land use between 1939 and 1975 we include a map of farmland spread from Lundberg's thesis in Figure 6.6. He compiled the information using aerial survey maps available from the Lands Department in Belmopan. From a time when farmlands stretched for approximately 22 square miles (57 square kilometers) in 1939, they were reduced to a few spots immediately west of the village by 1975.[106]

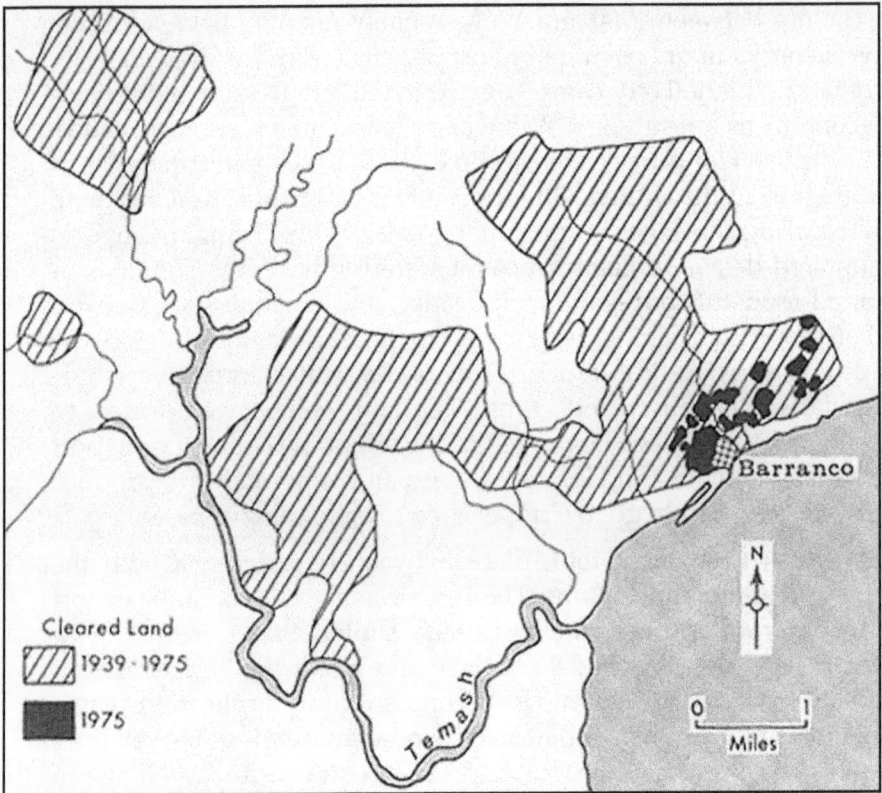

Figure 6.6. Lundberg's Map 4 comparing cleared areas in 1975 to those cleared in the period 1939–75 *(map courtesy Paul Lundberg)*

Farmland Core Area

With 243 applications the Core is the largest in space and numbers of parcels; it also shows the most consistent rise in decades (*Fig. 6.7*). As a microcosm, it captures many of the diagnostics that Davidson listed as typical of Garifuna village locations, such as a protected bay, a shoreline dissected by streams, and surrounding lands fit for cultivation.[107] There are several creeks marking the shoreline immediately in front of the village and along the northern and southern ends. Small crustaceans and fingerlings inhabit them, useful for food as well as bait. The largest creek, called "Legegu", provides a safe haven for boats during rough weather. Running along the extreme west of the farmlands, about seven kilometers in a straight line from the village there is another creek, called "Boyo", that forms from several tributaries draining lands that have been extensively farmed from the time of the village's first settlement in the 1850s. Boyo Creek was navigable up to the 1960s, facilitating the downstream transport of produce. Together with the Boyo and Legegu Creeks there are pockets of wetlands leaving a surrounding

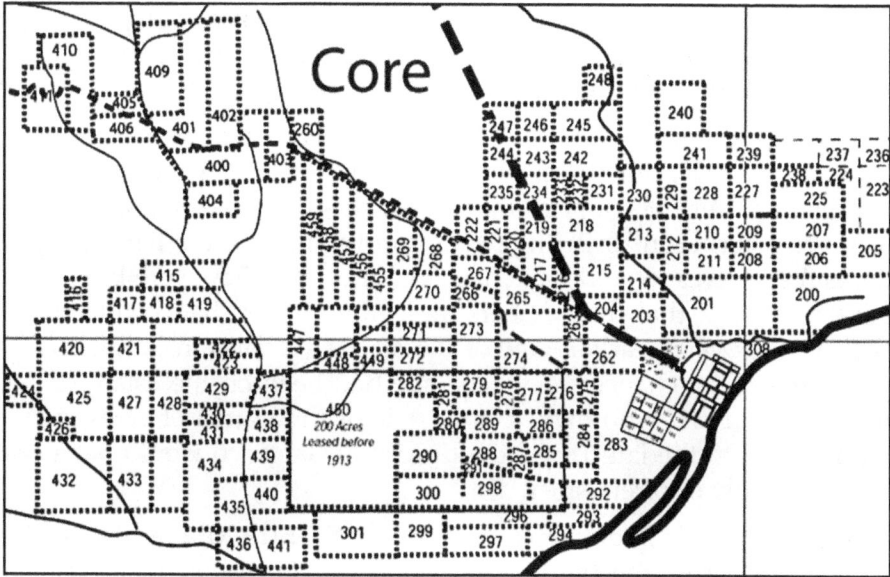

Figure 6.7. Map of the Core Area

landscape that is mostly flat, fairly well drained, and ideal for farming. Throughout the village history all Baranguna have been fed with crops grown in the Core. Besides, it continues to provide several kinds of plant medicines, game animals, hardwoods, leaves, and other building materials.

These basic needs are not the only bounty of the Core to the community. Historically its significance is that most of the earliest parcels were surveyed there—11 from 1892 to 1910 in the Boyo Creek North location. Among those receiving lands were Marcelo Cayetano, Augustin Paulino, Anastacio Palacio, and Pio Nolberto at 20 acres each. The shift to a much larger scale of farmland allocation took place a few years later, between 1905 and 1911, within another Core location, Barranco South. The irony leading to an historic turning point in local land tenure comes from the convergence of circumstances that could take place only once in the history of any community, as elaborated below.

1905 Minute Paper

Even as the settlement grew in numbers, as well as its articulation among neigbouring communities, the issue of the ownership of land for farms did not come to the attention of the government as a problem until 1905. After some correspondence between the governor and his chief surveyor, it was clarified that contrary to previous beliefs the land surrounding Barranco was not a Carib Reserve. The next question raised was whether it was on a part of Cramer's vast estates or on public lands. The governor dispatched surveyors to the area who confirmed in 1911 that Barranco was actually on public lands.

If the government did not know whether Barranco was on public lands in 1905, they must not have known whether the village residential lots were on public lands when they did the first survey thirteen years earlier in 1892. The persons most affected, the Barranco residents themselves, would have had no doubt that they were living on their own land that their fathers and grandfathers had civilized more than forty years earlier. One of the striking ironies in Barranco history is that if by chance the village site had been on the estate of Cramer, a *latifundista* who owned hundreds of thousands of acres in southern Belize in the late 1800s, the history of Barranco would have been a completely different story.[108]

This controversy is documented in the 1905-1912 Minute Paper, which are notes from meetings, discussions, and decisions arising at the level of the Executive Council and interactions among the Governor of the colony of British Honduras, Colonial Secretary, and Surveyor General (*Appendix D*).[109]

The flow of notes started in 1905 when Governor Brigham Sweet-Escot noted after a visit to Barranco that villagers had to go "considerable distance before they could find land fit for cultivation. ... Is that so?" he asked his senior advisors in the Executive Council. On learning that it was not certain whether the village and its farmlands were a Carib Reserve, the private lands of Cramer, or Crown land, the Governor instructed the Surveyor General to find the answer by doing a cadastral survey and to inform Cramer, but indicated that the survey was at no cost to Cramer. Six years afterwards in 1909 the survey showed that the village was on Crown land.

The next decision was to have the villagers, who had long been using these lands, apply for their leases to avoid being prosecuted in court for trespassing. A threatening sign was printed in 50 copies, which were erected in the area (*Fig. 6.8*).

As in the 1892 imposition of house lot gridline in the village, a customary practice of ownership, which had been entrenched for at least two generations, was abruptly broken in the face of colonial state imposition. The response of the villagers to this intrusion was to mobilize a group to lease a 200 acre block under the leadership of Macario Blas, Eulalio Loredo, and Norberto Palacio. The villagers delayed in amassing the necessary accession fees, placing the leaders

---

Surveyor General's Office

Belize, 10th July, 1911

Notice is hereby given that all persons trespassing on Crown lands West of the Village of Barranco will be prosecuted, unless, before the expiration of six weeks from the date hereof, they have made application to lease or purchase, to the District Commissioner, Toledo.

By Order

W.H. Carlin

Acting Surveyor General

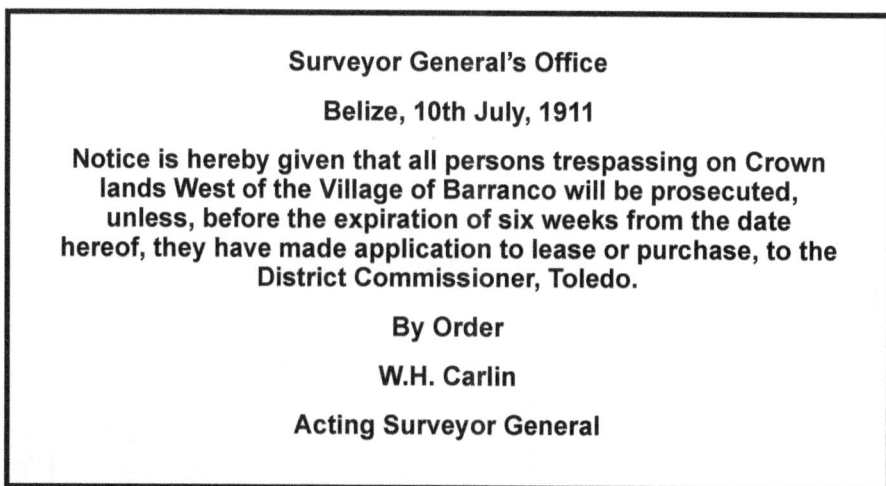

Figure 6.8. Signs posted in the Barranco area.

on the verge of being prosecuted. At the last moment the fees were collected, the leaders were vindicated, and the community members could continue their cultivation. Our reading of these procedures coincided with the oral account from Candido Arzu.[110]

According to Mr. Arzu, the block of land was known as Section 10.[111] He took pride in that two of the leaders included his own grandfather and his wife's grandfather. In standing up to the authorities, the Barranco leaders demonstrated the indomitable spirit of Jose Maria Nuñez, who on his death in 1886 bequeathed 960 acres of grant land west of Punta Gorda for the use of the Garifuna people of that community and their descendants. Nuñez had spearheaded the collection of funds from community members to pay for the land.

With the final clarification of Crown land status, the government proceeded to make farmlands available during the period before 1913. The result was a gradual surge in applications throughout all locations within the Core and spilling over into the other areas. Among those making applications included the corporate body of Walbank and Forslund for 50 acres in 1910 in Barranco South; also in Barranco South Philip Santino in 1913 for two parcels totaling 45 acres, and in Barranco Northwest Santiago Benguche for 40 acres, Jeronimo Alvarez for 20 acres, and Cecilio Polonio for 50 acres, all before 1913.[112] The largest Core location is Barranco South, which is important for including a subdivision of seventeen one and two-acre homesteads. A breakdown of Core locations is found in Table 6.1.

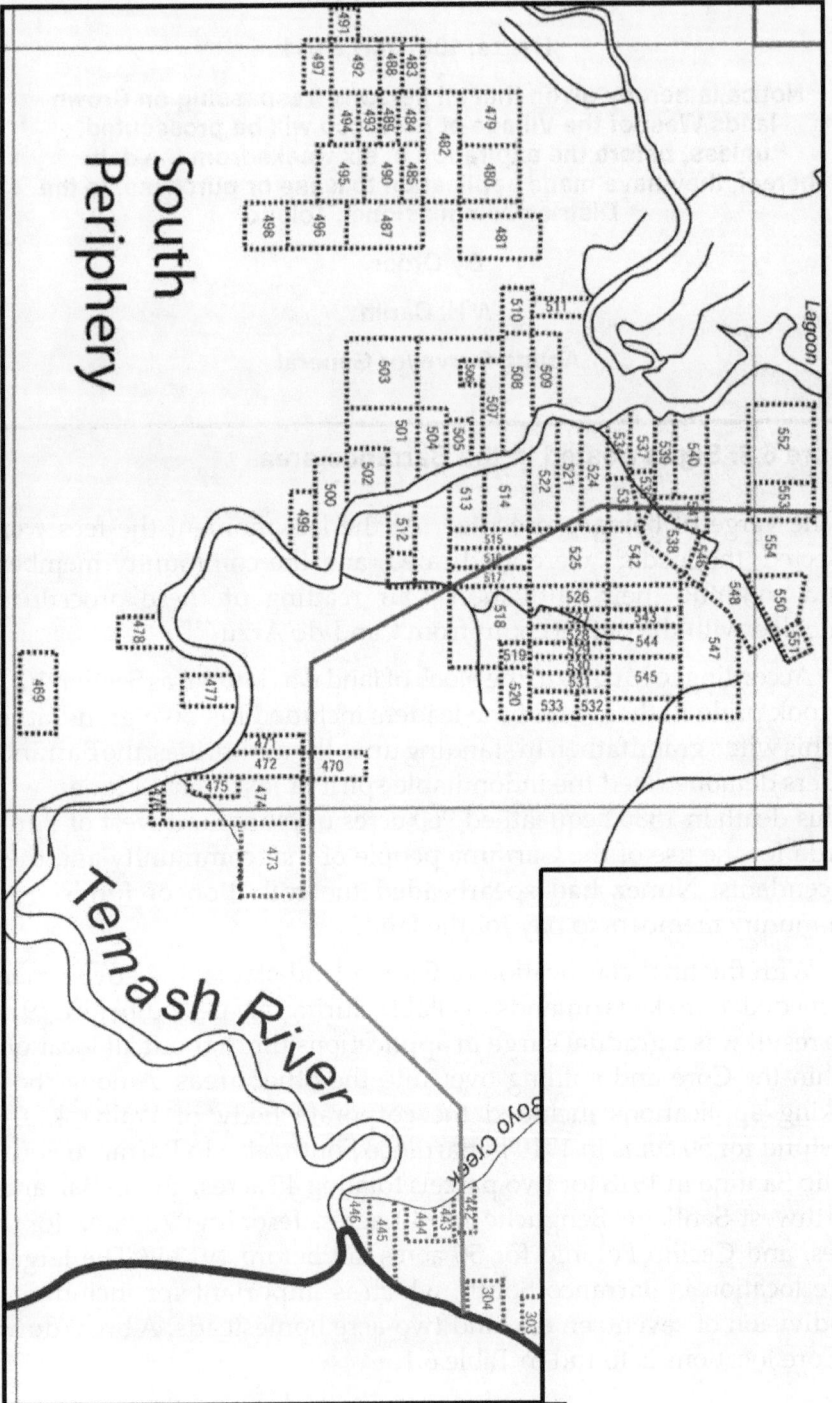

Figure 6.9. Map of the South Periphery Area

South Periphery

Next to the Core, the South Periphery area had the largest number of applications at 125. In describing the locations within this area we start on the sea southeast of Barranco and then ascend the Temash River alternating from the left to the right banks (*Fig. 6.9*). They include land for rice cash cropping done on the southeast coast. At the Temash bar there were two parcels on the left bank. Their significance is in being among the first to be surveyed along the entire river in 1892. The first substantive set of parcels on both banks is at Red Bank (*Fig. 6.10*), together numbering 17, where logging and sawmilling were the main activities. Houses built in the 1930s in Barranco used lumber from these operations. Further upstream one reaches the Fairview location on the left bank numbering 11 parcels. Opposite on the right bank there is the Largo location, numbering 27. Next on the left there is Lagunurugu, which has 15 parcels; and further on the right bank Dulcis Domus, which has the largest number of plots along the river at 33. A short distance along a curve on the left bank there is a group of 18 parcels, a location that we referred to as "Big Bend", the only name that is not a traditional one.

Access from east and west determined the early choice of plots along the Temash, going west from the sea and coming east through the Temash Lagoon. The mouth of the Temash is the location of two parcels

Figure 6.10. Ruben Palacio points out Red Bank on the Temash River

taken in 1892 by H.A. Wickham and James Crawford. The other main access to the part of the river flowing downstream toward the mouth is a body of brackish water called the Temash Lagoon. From this name comes the Garifuna word *Lagunurugu,* meaning "within the lagoon". The Temash Lagoon drains three tributaries of the larger Temash, the banks of which have seen agricultural and logging exploitation from the 19th century. They are Sundaywood Creek the furthest west, the Conejo Creek, and the meeting of the Middle and Vairez Creeks. Given the location of the Lagoon as a strategic access point, it is not surprising that parcels in Lagunurugu were taken from as early as 1894. During the first two decades of the twentieth century parcels immediately along the banks at Dulcis Domus, Big Bend, and Red Bank were also being taken. The surge in applications in the South Periphery was quite dramatic in the latter half of the 1930s, surpassing even that taking place in the Core. Similarly dramatic was the drop in applications during the post-banana period of the 1940s, going from 12% of all the applications to less than 5%.

Socially the Temash locations were best known for the gathering of extended families for social activities such as visits and lightening the workload by children, especially during the banana cultivation period of the 1930s. Memories of these events are often repeated by villagers, showing the accessibility of the farmlands. The names of owners included Sotero Nicholas, who had 15 acres at Red Bank; S.B. Daniels had a total of 85 acres at Dulcis Domus (*Fig. 6.10*), Red Bank, and Fairview; Saturnino Palacio had 40 acres at Fairview and Dulcis Domus; and Clarence Marin had five acres, Victor Nicholas ten acres, and Peter Palacio ten acres at Largo.

West Periphery Area

If the South Periphery area of applicants was dominated by locations scattered along the main Temash River from the Big Bend to the estuary, the West Periphery was subdivided into four creeks flowing from west to converge into the Temash Lagoon and continue downstream, as shown in Figure 6.11. The earliest parcels from 1892 to 1913 were four found along the Sundaywood Creek, reflecting the importance of this tributary in the pre-survey period. Middle Creek and Vairez Creek were next in time with parcels leased before 1920. Conejo Creek was the largest group in the West Periphery with 25 parcels leasaed beginning in 1921. Another significant feature of this area is a greater proportion of ethnic groups than in the others. Sundaywood, Middle, and Vairez Creeks had owners who were Creole, Mestizo, and Garifuna; on the other hand, Conejo Creek had owners who were Q'eqchi'. In the West

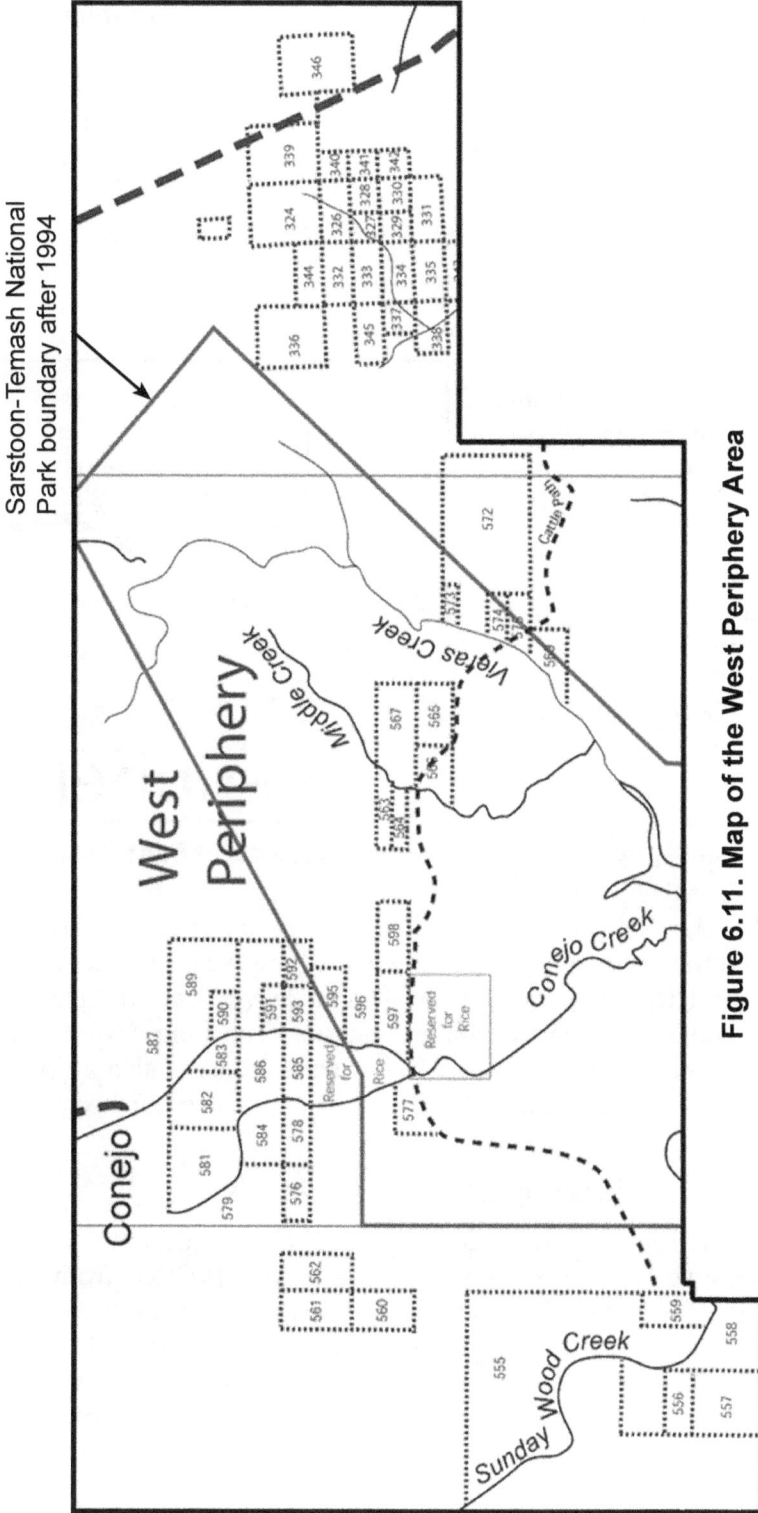

Figure 6.11. Map of the West Periphery Area

Periphery, more than in the other areas, Baranguna were interacting with neigbouring parcel owners, representing the cross-section of inter-ethnicity within their subregion. In the West Periphery Eusebio Polonio had 60 acres in the Sundaywood Creek area; James J. Avilez 90 acres and Simon Mejia 20 acres along Middle Creek; J.J. Zuniga 25 acres along Vairez Creek; and in the Conejo Creek area Augustine Palacio had ten acres, and Jose Maquin had 125 acres.

East Periphery

The East Periphery area brings us back to the immediate coastal zone, the habitat with which the Garifuna are most often identified (*Fig. 6.12*). Apart from being the area with the fewest number of parcels (25), this area is unusual in its limitation to the time period between 1912 and 1930. It was driven by the banana rush of the 1930s or the regularization taking place in the Core in the 1950s. The location with the most applicants is Wellis Creek (17). Mixed farming

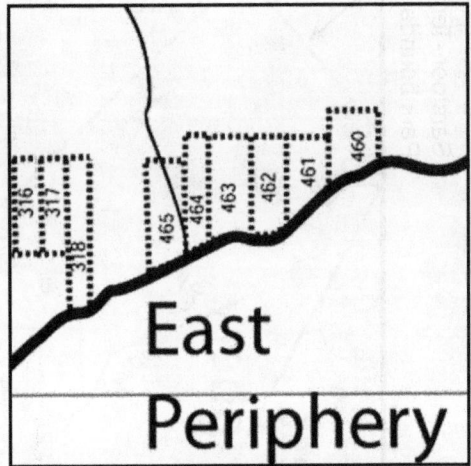

Figure 6.12. Map of East Periphery

was done in the Wellis Creek area. The other eight parcels are closer to Barranco on the northeast coast. Anywhere along the coast gave access for travel and transportation, as well as to leave boats for periodic repairs. Owners in the East Periphery included Feliciano Alvarez with 20 acres at Wellis Creek, John N. Lucas with 20 acres also at Wellis Creek, and Inocente Zuniga with five acres at Barranco northeast.

Moving among Farmlands

The narrative of areas together with their constituent locations should not give the impression of separate units isolated from each other. In 1939 farmlands flowed without interruption from Boyo Creek to the Temash, as shown in Figure 6.3. Through footpaths adults and children were able to reach from the village to Boyo Creek and Lidise, at distances in a straight line of 7.5 and 8.75 kilometers respectively. Earlier maps show a footpath extending even further, covering as long a distance as 19.4 kilometers in a straight line from Sundaywood Creek to the village. The several creeks within the larger subregion facilitated transportation, especially to farmers heavily laden with their produce. As the main river within the subregion, the Temash was a primary artery for dugout traffic. In some cases farmers walked part of the way and paddled the rest, as when accessing parcels in the West Periphery locations of Sundaywood Creek, Conejo Creek, Middle Creek, and Vairez Creek. Most households had at least one dugout that men, women, and children could navigate through the sea, river, and creeks.

The ebb and flow of movements within and across areas came from soil exhaustion and the availability of additional parcels, both of which form the backdrop for the analysis in this study. The call when to move and to where was the decision not only of the owner. The colonial government policy dictated the beginning of the banana export, as described by Moberg and Cal.[113] Government also created opportunities for rice cash cropping in the 1950s and was responsible for its unexpected demise. Villagers recall with shock the year 1959, when with little forewarning the government stopped buying their rice crop, forcing them to leave it to rot in the field. Finally, the government promoted mixed cropping through the survey of new lands in the Lidise location.

Kinship in Farmland Transmission

Despite the various efforts at promoting spurts of cultivation, the government did not proceed with the details of tenure and land husbandry. Though the small farmer was the centrepiece of rural community development, the location ticket system prevented him from remaining for extended periods on a given parcel.[114] In turn, he could not build lasting socioeconomic relations around his ownership. As a result, the prevalence of kinship, which was a significant medium for house-lot transmission, was barely present in farmlands, although both were held mainly under leasehold.

There were 63 parcels with repeated applications over time. We analyzed these to find out what ties existed between successive applicants (*Appendix D, Table D6.1*). While in most cases there were two applicants per parcel, in a few there were three and in two went as far as four. From the total of 149 records there were only ten that showed a kinship link underlying a transmission; 141 records showed neither kinship nor other links. Among the ten, one was by a man to a grandson; two by men to sons; one to a stepson; one to a wife and one by a woman to her brother (*Table 6.2*).

The overlapping of kinship ties among owners of contiguous parcels, often found among house lots, was rare in farmlands. A thorough review of the maps of locations shows that in only a few cases did adjoining owners share kinship. Examples include a man and wife sharing joint parcels, Margaret and James J. Avilez in parcels 297 and 294 in the Barranco South and Southeast locations, and Benita Ariola with her daughter Antonia Palacio in parcel 213 and 212 in Barranco Northwest.

The deliberate selection of close relatives and friends to initiate a new location took place in Lidise in 1956. As leader, Candido Arzu handpicked 16 men to start farms, all of whom were his friends or close relatives – uncles, cousins, a cousin-in-law, etc. Carl Gibson, the surveyor on the ground, approved Arzu's list and they received their land under the location ticket system, which allowed each one to purchase the land over the next few years. They were joined by several others, making a total of 22 parcels of bought land in Lidise. Notwithstanding this well knit group, the transmission to the next generation has not taken place for the abrupt disruption in all applications since the 1960s.

So far the narrative on farmland areas has focused on the distribution of locations over time and space. There are other aspects of social relations, however, that are implied in farmland ownership. In the following discussion we highlight gender, ethnicity, and local community identity.

Gender Considerations

The role of women in crop cultivation and processing has always been significant in Barranco, as in other Garifuna communities. On the other hand, discussion on the division of labour and responsibilities has rarely included the ownership of farmlands. Our data shows that the formal procedures in farmland applications have remained the domain of men. Globally, 87% of all applicants were men and the distribution across locations varied between 95% and 70%. Locations in the Core area, as shown in Table 6.3, had the most proportion of women. The case of Barranco South is worth highlighting for six out of the twelve parcels in women's names are homesteads, which measure only 2 acres or less and are adjoining the village. On deducting them from the number of parcels in Barranco South, the percentage of women's parcels in Barranco South reduces to 7%. This is the lowest for any location in the Core area, although it lies within the same radius as Barranco Northwest and Barranco West. The concentration in the nearby homesteads underscores the preference by women for parcels located closer to the village.

Table 6.3. Women Applicants

Location	#	Location Total	% of Location Total
Core			
Barranco - northwest	10	33	30%
Barranco - south	12	77	15%
Barranco - west	7	25	28%
Boyo Creek - middle	4	50	8%
West Periphery			
Lidise	1	22	5%
South Periphery			
Fairview	1	11	9%
Lagunurugu	4	12	26%
Big Bend	5	18	27%
Dulcis Domus	2	32	6%
Largo	4	27	14%
East Periphery	2	25	8%

Another location for specific mention is *Lagunurugu*. Although it shows the highest percentage for women owners in a non-Core location, one woman, Clara Enriquez, applied for three of the four parcels. Notwithstanding such anomalies, the following are summary statements that we can make about women applicants. Excluding the six homestead parcels in Barranco South, women's plots were generally the same size as men's. Even in remote locations along the Temash, some women were breaking the norms in the division of labour to apply for their own farmlands. The preference for women, however, was locations within the Core and closer to the village.

Ethnicity

There was a total of 92 non-Garifuna applicants out of the total of 449. It is difficult to say what were the distinct ethnic groups being represented. Our primary method of distinguishing was last names, which is certainly inadequate among persons in southern Belize. There were some Creoles who would have consisted of persons originating from further north in the country from Punta Gorda as far as Belize City. Included among them were Charles Bevans who applied for 20 acres and W.A. Bowen for 125 acres, both at Sundaywood Creek. George E. and Joseph Gray applied for 20 acres at Conejo Creek. The Creoles were distinguished by Baranguna from Jamaicans, who joined

Table 6.2. Kinship in Transmission of Farmlands

#	Size	Name	Year	Location	Relations
212		Palacio, Antonia		Barranco - NW	next to mother
213	10	Ariola, Benita	1955	Barranco - NW	
214	15	Ariola, Catarino	1928	Barranco - NW	next to husband
240	15	Cayetano, Eugenio	1936	Barranco - west	
240	15	McKenzie, George	1936		stepfather
273	25	Garcia, Maximiliano	1923	Barranco - south	
273	25	Castillo, Graciano	1929		sister's son
284	25	Loredo, Eulalio	1913	Barranco - south	
284	11	Nicholas, Cipriano	1951		wife's sister's son
410	20	Palacio, Anastacio	1891	Boyo Creek north	
410	5	Palacio, Liberato	1891		son
423	20	Castillo, Inez	1913	Boyo Creek middle, left	
423	20	Castillo, Nicodemus	1926		son
445	14	Cayetano, George	1948	Boyo Creek mouth, right	
445	14	McKenzie, Eugene	1951		stepson
452	20	Noralez, Venancio	1923	Boyo Creek cattle path - north	
452	10	Palacio, Gumercinda	1933		wife
534	20	Palacio, Saturnino	1931	Dulcis	
534	20	Valencio, Guillermo	1961		grandson
540	20	Arzu, Patrocina	1934	Dulcis	
540	20	Palacio, Joseph P.	1944		brother
595	10	Palacio, Peter	1937	Conejo Creek - right	
595	10	Marin, Clarence	1941		mother's mother's brother

in banana cultivation. Mestizos were another group; who are persons of mixed Hispanic and Maya ancestry coming from further south in Guatemala and Honduras. Finally, there were Q'eqchi', found in the Conejo area from the 1920s, where the surname Maquin was repeated. Altogether the non-Garifuna made up a significant minority of almost one out every five applicants.

A review of non-Garifuna applications reveals what choices they made on farmland locations, which differ from those of the majority Garifuna. From early the preference of the non-Garifuna was for the

South and West Periphery areas while the Garifuna choice was for the Core. Between 1890 and 1899 the locations for the non-Garifuna were Temash Bar, Dulcis Domus, and Lagunurugu (*Fig. 6.11*). After the dip in applications for both Garifuna and non-Garifuna in the 1900 to 1910 decade, the latter continued their preference toward the West Periphery locations of Sundaywood Creek, Middle Creek, Conejo Creek, and Vairez Creek. The South Periphery locations of Red Bank and Lagunurugu also received some attention. During the 1930s the non-Garifuna reached the climax of their applications, the majority going to widespread locations in the South Periphery followed by the West Periphery locations of Sundaywood, Vairez, and Middle Creeks. The only time when there was a slight shift among the non-Garifuna toward the Core area was during the 1950s. Even then they did not target the Core locations of Barranco South, Barranco Northwest, and Barranco West, which were filling up with the Garifuna during that time. They were more interested in parcels nearer to the village in the northeast. Two non-Garifuna also applied in Lidise (*Fig. 6.12*).

The non-Garifuna applications enable a closer understanding of land tenure practices in the Barranco subregion. Firstly, land tenure transcended ethnicity, as we had found out in house-lot tenure. Indeed, ten of the 64 non-Garifuna persons who applied for farmlands had close links within the Barranco community. But there is the possibility that these links grew after their arrival in search of farmlands. If the Garifuna came to join their kinfolk and subsequently found farmlands, for the non-Garifuna it was more often the reverse, of coming to find farmlands and then establishing close ties. Table 6.4 is a list of persons with links within Barranco.

Table 6.4. Links by non-Garifuna to Barranco

Name	Link
Samuel B. Vernon	Birth
Teodoro Andrade	Lot
Antonio Mejia	Lot
Rafael Clotter	Spouse
David Thousand	Lot
Simeona Mejia	Lot
James Bondswell	Spouse
Hylton Levy	Lot
Sam Conner	Spouse
Jack Watts	Lot

The concentration of non-Garifuna applications away from the Core and more towards the South and West Peripheries adds to the argument that the economic returns from land use to them was a greater motivation to come to the subregion. By and large their parcels were larger than those of the Garifuna. Furthermore, they exploited intensively parcels in the West Periphery and South Periphery during the 1920s and 1930s at the height of the banana boom. The Garifuna were doing likewise, but nearer to their homes within the Core. The overlap took place as the Garifuna spilled over to the West Periphery and South Periphery, on exhausting the soil closer to the village in the 1930s.

The overlap between non-Garifuna and Garifuna farming in the same location introduces the larger question of inter-ethnic relations taking place beyond land tenure. Oral history proved helpful in detailing examples of how the villagers interacted with the non-Garifuna. There was easy flow of cooperation on matters of marketing, such as informing each other about the imminence of buyers. Leisurely group activities took place, such as competing teams of cricket between Baranguna and Jamaicans. At social events men danced and played musical instruments across ethnic lines. The Jamaicans were known for clearing debris along the streams so that all could paddle their dories easily. Finally, the spirit of social interaction was shared among the children, who played with each other and grew up to be friends, even on meeting with each other years afterwards away from the village.

Baranguna—Local Community Identity

In a previous study on local community identity among the Garifuna the village of Barranco has taken centre stage. Out-migrants from the village were featured as they adjusted to urban life in Belize City.[115] The perspective was on Garifuna people simultaneously "juggling cultural spaces" as rural dwellers and inner city folk.[116] In this study the larger social context is small farm landowners within multiple locations and across multiple ethnicities. To what extent is being a Baranguna significant in the midst of this complexity? In what locations were Baranguna not showing a commanding lead? Finally, is there significance in being Garifuna but not Baranguna?

The answer to these questions start with how we defined being Baranguna at the outset. After testing responses from the villagers, the main criterion was having identifiable social and cultural roots within the village and consciously upholding them. Having been born there and/or building such strong ties over time, as keeping a lot and marrying within the community were often given as answers. A main qualifying test was the extent to which men and women built around themselves a strong social web, especially given the fact that multiple community identity is inherent in almost all Garifuna families. One's siblings may be born in another place and grow up there, not building lasting ties within the village. Alternatively, one can leave one's home community and fully adopt Barranco as a new permanent home. The example of Benita Ariola drives home this point. She was born in Punta Gorda but came to Barranco, married a Baranguna, and remained in the community until she died. There are many other examples, who did likewise, such as Jeronimo Alvarez, who came from Livingston.

Having received community consensus on local community identity, we went back to our data and asked in which farming locations were non-Baranguna predominating. In this exercise we deliberately excluded the Core where 95% of the applicants were Baranguna. Instead we selected locations in the West and South Peripheries, shown in Figure 6.13. Interestingly, we found out that in these locations the Baranguna exceeded the non-Baranguna by only three applications. Only in Largo and Dulcis Domus did the Baranguna show a significant lead by applications of 16 and 11 respectively. Earlier we saw that the Garifuna easily predominated in total applications, but we are now seeing that in locations removed from the immediate vicinity of the village, non-Baranguna, including Garifuna, were almost equally represented as the Baranguna.

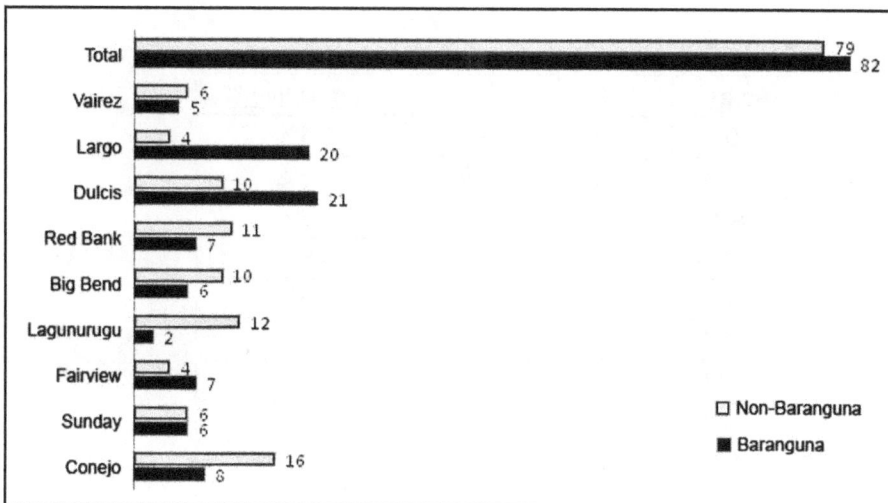

Figure 6.13. Baranguna and Non-Baranguna in Select Locations in the Periphery

We went a step further to ask what was the distribution between Baranguna and Garifuna who were not Baranguna. Here we were specifically referring to the Punta Gorda folks, called in Garifuna *Péinina*. We found out that Peinina exceeded Baranguna in Lagunurugu by six applications. In Big Bend the Garifuna were equally divided between Baranguna and Peinina. On the other hand, there were hardly any Peinina in Dulcis Domus and Largo, both strongholds of the Baranguna.

This brief analysis has shown that in focusing on land tenure surrounding Garifuna communities, there is a need to move away from a monolithic description of the Garifuna people without appreciating the significance of local community identity. In abiding by this distinction, its usefulness ultimately depends on each community. For Baranguna, there were over-arching ties between themselves and Peinina, which were not found between themselves and non-Garifuna. Peinina, for example, willingly received hospitality, including overnight stays, should they be delayed by storms to and from their farms along the Temash. During ancestral celebrations, they were, and currently are, invited to take their rightful place as common descendants of the spirits being honoured.

A Typology of Ownership

Earlier in discussing the chronology of farmlands we showed the progression of applications among locations. We now draw attention more to types of owners spotlighting at first acreage and then ownership of multiple parcels.

Table 6.5. Distribution of Parcels in Acres

Acres	#	%	Cumulative %
0–1	2	0.4%	0.4%
1–9	79	17.6%	18.0%
10–17	155	34.5%	52.6%
20–26	144	32.1%	84.6%
30–32	18	4.0%	88.6%
40	4	0.9%	89.5%
50	31	6.9%	96.4%
54–80	8	1.8%	98.2%
100+	8	1.8%	100.0%
Total		100.0%	

Some 85 percent of the total farmlands in our database consisted of parcels measuring less than 26 acres (*Table 6.5*). The predominance of small farms becomes clearer as slightly more than half (53%) measured between 10 and 17 acres. The remaining 47 percent are clusters around 20 acres (144), a smaller number around 30 acres (18), and 50 acres (31). In short, measurements in multiples of ten acres were most common at 10, 20, 30, and 50. The entire list with the names of owners is in Appendix D.

At twenty acres or less there was hardly any stratification among the owners. They were men and women working in all the locations. From 25 to 50 acres they were mainly men with increasing proportions of non-Garifuna. Parcels measuring 50 to 80 acres were divided equally between Garifuna and non-Garifuna. Some Garifuna included Pio Nolberto with 50 acres at Boyo Creek, John Justo Avilez with 50 acres at Middle Creek, Canuto Zuniga with 50 acres at Largo, and Martin Reyes with 80 acres at Dulcis Domus. Among the eight owners with one hundred or more acres there was only one owned by Garifuna, the Baranguna group spear-headed by Eulalio Loredo, Norberto Palacio and Macario Blas, who acquired 200 acres in 1913. Earlier we saw that this effort was done under duress from the colonial powers and on behalf of the larger village community.

While no single Garifuna had parcels of one hundred or more acres, it is noteworthy that there was a significant number owning parcels measuring between 50 and 80 acres. On the one hand, the vast majority of Garifuna owners remained with not more than three parcels; and, on the other hand, there were a few who accumulated four or more parcels (*Table 6.6*). While some were held simultaneously, others were held at different times, separated by decades.

Only 12 persons had four or more parcels. Of these eight were Garifuna, one a Q'eqchi', one a Mestizo, and another a Creole of Miskito descent. Perhaps the most important information forthcoming is the total number of acres that each one accumulated from his complement of parcels. The figures range from 43 to 147 acres, even though they were not amassing large acres in one spot. The larger questions are why did they change locations and why were they expending so much effort in disparate places. The answer may involve the limitations of their slash-and-burn type of cultivation or the sizes of the parcels as demarcated by the government surveyors. This form of widespread concentration demonstrates unequivocally the unusual capacity and dedication of a few persons toward their farming.

The typology of farm owners that we have sketched falls into three broad groups. The vast majority (85%) worked parcels that were less than 26 acres and not more than two areas at any one time. Most of them were Garifuna. A much smaller proportion (14%) worked parcels between 30 and 80 acres. Persons in this group include both Garifuna and non-Garifuna. At the other extreme there is a very small group of twelve men who worked multiple parcels scattered throughout the subregion.

Table 6.6. Applicants with more than one parcel

Name	Year	Location	Plot #	Acres	Total
Saturnino Palacio	1920	Boyo Creek	397	20	
	1923	Fairview	507	20	
	1928	Boyo Creek	451	20	
	1931	Dulcis	534	20	80
Jerome Alvarez	1913	Barranco - northwest	204	20	
	1920	Boyo Creek	418	10	
	1923	Boyo Creek	440	15	
	1924	Boyo Creek	418	10	
	1936	BarSouth	165	2	
	1941	Boyo Creek	419	10	67
John Chimilio	1916	Barranco - northwest	208	10	
	1923	Boyo Creek	437	15	
	1936	Boyo Creek	417	10	
	1952	Barranco - south	278	5	
	1957	Barranco - south	278	5	45
Joseph P. Palacio	1931	Barranco - northwest	205	10	
	1937	Dulcis	546	20	
	1944	Dulcis	540	20	
	1956	Lidise	326	20	70
John J. Zuniga	1927	Wallis Creek	460	20	
	1931	Barranco - southwest	318	10	
	1935	Dulcis	538	10	
	1941	Vairez Creek	569	25	
	1944	Middle Creek	564	10	75

Name	Year	Location	Plot #	Acres	Total
Thomas Fuentes	1928	Largo	525	50	
	1938	Dulcis	548	5	
	1938	Red Bank	472	15	
	1940	Red Bank	472	15	85
S.B. Daniels	1919	Wallis Creek	468	60	
	1928	Red Bank	473	20	
	1923	Fairview	504	40	
	1934	Dulcis	537	5	
	1935	Barranco - south	159	2	
	1934	Dulcis	553	20	147
Francois deBoire	1953	Barranco - east	307	10	
	1953	Barranco - south	289	10	
	1955	Barranco - east	308	6	
	1955	Lidise	339	50	
	1956	Boyo Creek	446	10	86
Jose Maquin	1917	Conejo	586	25	
	1941	Conejo	581	25	
	1941	Conejo	582	25	
	1941	Conejo	583	25	100
Clarence Marin	1937	Legegu	312	2	
	1934	Largo	512	5	
	1941	Conejo	595	10	
	1952	Barranco - south	277	10	
	1954	Barranco - south	275	6	
	1956	Lidise	328	10	43
Ignacio Nicholas	1929	Boyo Creek	428	30	
	1937	Boyo Creek	414	5	
	1944	Boyo Creek	430	5	
	1948	Boyo Creek	443	10	50
Walter Plummer	1931	Dulcis	542	50	
	1938	Sundaywood	560	20	
	1939	Dulcis	547	50	
	1953	Dulcis	537	3	
	1955	Barranco - east	308	6	129

Sarstoon-Temash National Park and Oil Exploration

A major influence upon Barranco's traditional farmlands was the declaration of the Sarstoon-Temash National Park (STNP) adjacent to Barranco in 1994.[117] A national survey of protected areas created a narrow window of opportunity to declare protected areas, so an effort was made to protect the impressive mangroves along the Temash River and the wetlands between the Temash and Sarstoon Rivers. Those involved realized they should consult the local communities, but because of time and financial constraints, they did not, so the national park was a big surprise to Baranguna.[118]

The boundaries of the National Park were drawn to include the headwaters of tributaries leading into the Temash Lagoon and exclude privately owned land, but without regard to the location of communities (*Fig. 6.14*). The result was that the National Park included much of the traditional farmlands of Baranguna and areas used for fishing, hunting, and gathering building materials by other villages such as Conejo, Sundaywood, Crique Sarco, and Midway. But none of these communities were even informed that the National Park had been declared.

On February 22, 1997, a workshop was held to consider co-management of the STNP by the local communities. The attendees included representatives from the villages of Barranco, Conejo, Crique Sarco, and Midway, Sundaywood, as well as resource persons from the government, environmental NGOs and funding agencies.[119]

The result of the workshop was the formation of the Sarstoon-Temash National Park Steering Committee which evolved into the Sarstoon-Temash Institute for Indigenous Management (SATIIM).[120]

In 2003, SATIIM, representing the five indigenous communities of the Sarstoon-Temash region, signed a co-management agreement with the Government of Belize, represented by the Forest Department, to manage the STNP and a management plan was developed in 2005.[121]

The management plan acknowledges that much of the STNP area has been and is still being used by the five communities. "From experience and through consultations with the communities, it has been established that the communities want rights to collect building materials such as thatch and poles, medicinal plants (which they have identified in several areas within the STNP), fish and game animals. Communities have also traditionally farmed inside the boundaries of the STNP but this can no longer be allowed in any area of the park since it is highly destructive to the ecosystems of the area and totally

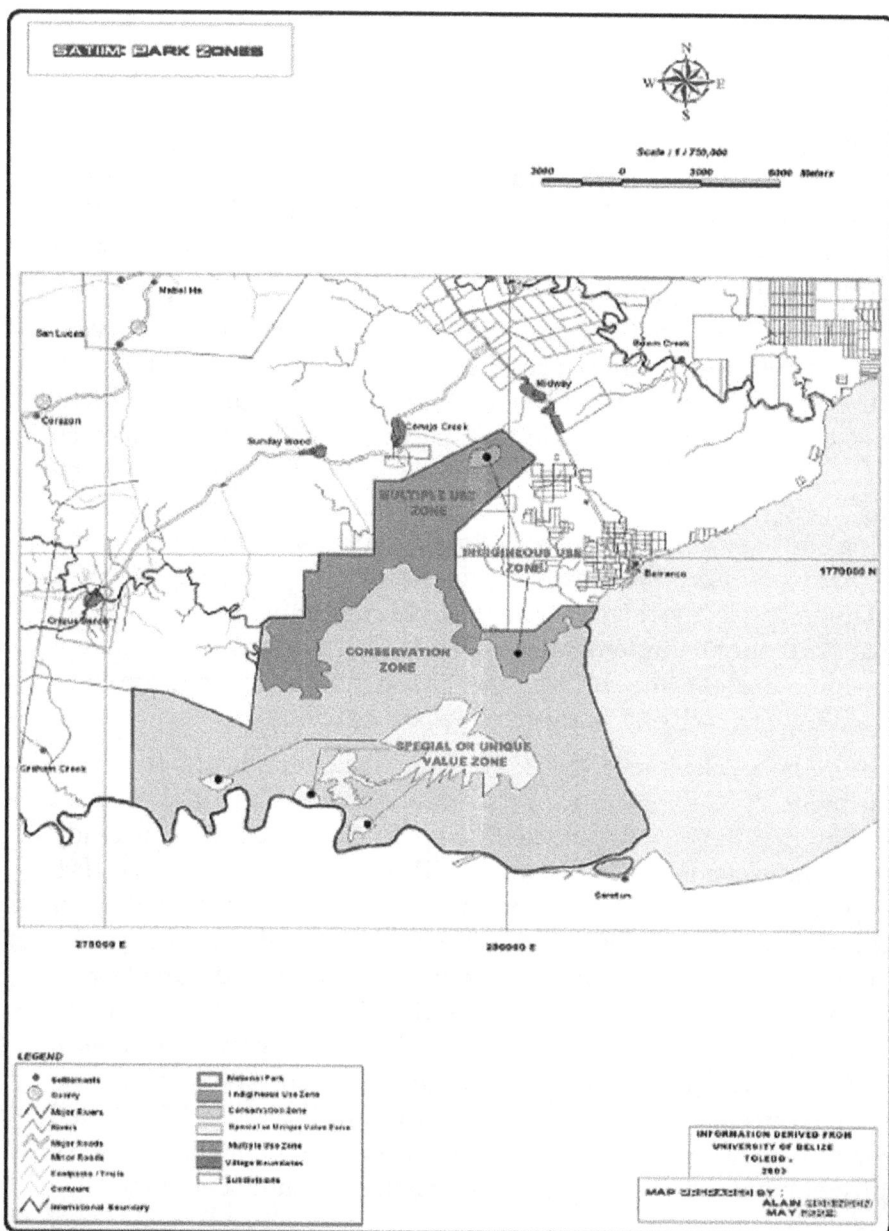

Figure 6.14. Sarstoon-Temash National Park (*map courtesy of SATIIM***)**

incompatible with the objectives of a national park except under the proviso given below under regulations."[122]

The management plan makes provisions for continued, though controlled, extraction of materials in two zones, the Multiple Use Zone and the Indigenous Use Zone (*Figure 6.12*). The regulations require that only residents of the buffer zone communities extract materials for their own use, not for profit or sale, and that a permit must be obtained from SATIIM and the Forest Department. The Indigenous Use Zone that covers the area north of the Temash River near the coast is designated for the extraction of comfrey palm.

Barranco has benefited from SATIIM's commitment to provide benefits to the buffer communities. Resource Centers were built in each of the villages, including Barranco (*Figure 6.11*). Rangers were hired from each of the villages, including Egbert Valencio from Barranco (*Figure 6.12*). Others have been hired for special projects, such as the Rapid Ecological Assessments, which also included ecological field training. But very little has been done to address lands now in the park that were used historically by the Barranco community. SATIIM facilitated a project funded by the Global Environment Facility Small Grants Programme implemented by the United Nations Development Programme to assess the shrimp nurseries in the waters along the coast adjacent to the STNP and Barranco (*Figure 6.14*).[123]

In 2005 SATIIM received a copy of a memorandum from the Department of Geology and Petroleum to the Forest Department indicating that the oil company, U.S. Capital Energy Belize, was ready to commence seismic testing in the STNP. As the co-manager, SATIIM, was opposed to any seismic testing or oil exploration in the STNP for several reasons. They believed that it would "significantly change the ecological character of the fragile wetlands, ... and could have lasting negative effects on the biodiversity ... and violated the spirit and intent of the National Parks System Act and the Geology and Petroleum Act."[124] They were most concerned about the unique sphagnum moss ecosystem through which the seismic lines would pass.[125] SATIIM filed suit against the Government of Belize and won an injunction because the proper environmental impact assessments had not been done.

Once the assessments were completed, the project was approved and in April and May of 2008 the first seismic testing was done by U.S. Capital. For those two months there was a flurry of activity in Barranco with increeased employment opportunity and much excitement. As this volume goes to press, U.S. Capital is planning more seismic tests.

Summary and Conclusions

The allocation of farmlands within the Barranco subregion accelerated after 1891, when the government surveyors made land available, until the last large scale effort in 1954. Before 1891 the colonial government gave large landowners (*latifundistas*) far greater access to surveyors and the lands themselves. To get a grip on the spread of farmlands over space and time we use the analogy of core-periphery, showing that the village itself was a focal point, not only as an intermediary for the rest of the country, but also in aggregating the largest concentration of farmland within its immediate vicinity. The success of the core, however, depended on the productivity of its peripheral areas. As they declined after the 1950s, so did the core.

The detailed narrative of the locations does not mean that they were discrete entities, separate from each other. Connecting them was a maze of footpaths, as well as the Temash and its several tributaries. Travel to the farms reinforced a knowledge of the micro-environments that the villagers had mastered earlier in travelling to work with loggers, as well on estate farms.

Periodic shifts in government policy on types of produce and markets forced corresponding movements among the farmers themselves. Such flexibility limited the social relations that they could form concerning the land, its ownership and its production among their close kin. As a result, there were only a few cases of transmitting one's farm to one's kinfolk.

An elaboration of the type of ownership revealed patterns in terms of gender, ethnicity, and community identity. Men took responsibility for applications at a much higher rate than women. Local community identity of being Baranguna was decisive in determining where one would farm. Finally, an analysis of the profile of applicants revealed three different types. The vast majority of applicants went for small farms of less than 26 acres. A smaller group worked parcels measuring between 30 and 80 acres. At the extreme end there is a very small group of twelve men who worked multiple parcels scattered throughout the region.

From as early as 1894 non-Garifuna men had received lands far west and south of the village. Starting with logging, they changed to farming as the opportunities became available. While a few got lots in the village, their main objective was less to enhance kinship ties with the villagers than to generate profit. However, the village became their main link to the rest of the colony, a place to purchase supplies and recruit labour and other services.

This chapter has filled a vacuum in the social history of rural land tenure during the 20th century in Belize, with specific reference to the Garifuna people. In demonstrating how men and women exercised their commitment to the land, it has shown how they fulfilled their customary rights, which pre-dated the government method of land allocation. Finally, the study shows some of the variables that are needed to understand the interplay between colonial government and the rural community on land tenure.

The story of the "discovery" of the Crown Land status of the Barranco farming area during the period 1905 to 1911, at least two generations after the arrival of its first settlers, is most revealing from the perspective of the colonial government and its *latifundistas*, as well as the reactions of the community itself. The government did not know whether the Barranco farms were on Crown land or land belonging to Cramer, who owned thousands of acres in the area. Faced with yet another threat of losing lands that they had already cultivated, the Garifuna community adopted a corporate response. Their leaders assumed responsibility to collect the rent that the authorities assessed; they paid the rent; and the villagers were allowed to continue with their farming. The alternative would have been to lose their lands and again be banished to look for other areas to farm and settle. The community acquired another major breakthrough toward its continuity.

Two other contributions of this chapter to Garifuna studies are within the topics of extensive use of geographical space and inter-ethnicity. While living along the coast the Garifuna have also used surrounding lands for farming, but there has been little understanding of the scope of such use. Baranguna exploited a large expanse, which they integrated within a framework of their communal lands, also called in Garifuna *lumua Barangu*, which covers several ecological zones that include the seacoast, lowlands, higher well-drained soils, together with the banks of main rivers and their tributaries. The flora and fauna added a great deal to their inventory of food items, as well as materials for construction and medicinal use.

Having focused on the physical land and its ownership, in the next chapter we turn to the cultural landscape, as expressed in art, poetry, and naming as linguistic art.

Chapter Seven
Cultural Imprints on the Village Landscape

While we have dedicated much narrative and analysis to the formal accession and transmission of house lots and farmlands, there is also a need to spotlight the cultural meanings and social values that villagers associate not only with occupied lands but also with the larger physical environment that constitutes their habitat. These intangibles are difficult to define, but men and women have integrated them into their interpretation of the landscape, contributing to the unique identity that over time has characterized the village community and its setting. s. First we review how students of the Garifuna have dealt with this broad topic. Secondly, we isolate four contexts for our discussion. Thirdly, we place within the four contexts ethnographic data. We present a case study that ties together the exercise of ownership not only to a lot but also to a tree within the lot, illustrating that iconic significance extends beyond the lot itself. Finally, we conclude the chapter with place names and their origins.

Earlier References to the Landscape

Cultural geographer Paul Lundberg has done the most complete biophysical analysis of Barranco and its environs.[126] The topic of traditional knowledge, also known as traditional ecological knowledge, has attracted a great deal of attention from anthropologists in arguing that what people have long known should not be easily dismissed in working with communities about their natural resources. The Sarstoon Temash Institute for Indigenous Management (SATIIM), the NGO co-managing the 42,000-acre Sarstoon Temash National Park, commissioned studies on the traditional knowledge of the physical environment among the Garifuna and Q'eqchi' buffer communities, documenting several flora and fauna, using information from the elders and presenting much baseline data awaiting fine-tuning.[127]

As a medium of popularizing traditional knowledge, folklore is most appropriate. Palacio has documented folklore among the Garifuna in southern Belize, especially in the use of coastal resources. The topics he covers include the behaviour of fish, birds, and mammals, which fisherfolk can interpret with messages as diverse as where to collect bait and possibilities of infidelity among their wives. Fisherfolk are able to locate fishing sites, predict the weather, and share an ethic of conservation with each other and across generations. The wastefulness of shrimp trawlers, according to them, is worsened when they throw overboard large amounts of rejects, which in turn attract predators like shark that scare away the fish. Closely related to folklore is mythology in spirituality, another topic where the physical environment looms large. The sea is used in rituals marking the end of the yearlong period of mourning for a deceased close relative, as well as the *adugahani*, the catching of seafood to be consumed during the *dügü* ceremony.[128]

Written studies limit full description of the physical environment as it impacts on human behaviour. On the other hand, the artist—song writer, poet, playwright, and painter—uses a wider mix of media, enabling him to better integrate the nuances of his message. Byron Foster recorded one of the dügü songs he heard in Hopkins about the spirit of an ancestor, having found himself in St. Vincent, anxiously awaits the spirit of a descendant traveling from Hopkins. The song has many references to the landscape bundled around the following themes—crossing the deep ocean from Central America to St. Vincent, in St. Vincent standing on the high cliff anxiously awaiting the new descendant from Central America, and beaming with joy on seeing him.[129]

Victor Nicholas eloquently describes moving, this time from one farmland to another, in his poem entitled *"Ka Tima Funa Wanibei –* What exactly say you are we doing?" *(p. 181)*[130] Using his own family beginnings in Boyo Creek, he traces how often they moved, leaving behind fruit trees to grow wild just at the point when they would start to bear. The repetition he makes listing the names of several crops planted in different places poetically accentuates the resultant waste of time and energy by not remaining permanently in one area.

Pen Cayetano *(p. 18)* is a world renowned Garifuna painter who uses the broad sweep of the landscape as a backdrop in his meticulous attention to fine detail. In their poetry E. Roy Cayetano, another Baranguna, and Marcela Lewis do likewise. On the page 182 are the first two stanzas of Marcella Lewis' poem, "Lubuidu láfuaru weyu binafi, How beautiful the sunrise"[131] and the last stanza of E. Roy Cayetano's poem, *"Hagarawoun Nagübürigu,* Drums of our Fathers."[132]

"Ka Timá Funa Wanibei
What exactly say you are we doing?"

—Victor Nicholas

My earliest memory
saw me
together.
Mother father sisters and brothers
Altogether
At our farm-Nicksville, Boyo Creek
The way-
We expended our energy
In agriculture!
I thought
we would emerge wealthy.

But-
When the palms, or coconuts, drop
(no more dire need to pull)
Cashew and other plants and trees
Bend branches- their twigs- in yield
'Mid miles of sugar loaf
Pineapples sweet-

When poultry, our stock-
Chicken, turkey, and duck
Increase!
We abandoned the farm
We moved to Barranco
- The town.

At majority age,
David
My parent's first born
Made his farm. The love
It carried …
That piece of land
For David- and his family,
I thought- they were
on the way to fortune.

When their trees and plants,
Myriad varieties!-
Bend branches – the twigs in yield
When pigs increase,
Vegetable crops
Tomato, ochre, pepper …
As you please!
They abandoned the farm.
They moved to Punta Gorda Town.

Since my family
Is somewhat strange
And- my father
Quiet – so very quiet …

Despite big surprise
In my heart, the bulge
Mine eyes - I too,
Remained silent.

But – it unsettled my mine
To such an extent,
I gave it a good look!
My mother's father
Had done this thing.
My father's father
Did the same-
Abandoning this produce
Leaving his labour - to rot
in the fields.

This thing is older
Than my brother David
Older than my father
This thing
Is older than my grandfather!

Incredible:
But listen and look!
Saturino did the same thing
And so did
Denis, Pasi, Jimu
Eusebio, Catá, Coüne
Clo, Clarence, Condes
Chico, Lallo…
They sacrifice
Years of tough labour
Leaving miles –
Of their own sweat and blood
To perish in the bush.

This thing, apparently,
Is as old as *Gañbü* –
Santiago Avilez the first,
The Father of Barranco.

When, therefore,
Angie and I venture
To expend –
Our feeble energy
In agriculture, Barranco
Who, Beside ourselves,
Do you think, are we fooling.

Ka funa tíma wanibei.

Lubuidu Láfuaru Weyu Binafi

Lubuidu láfuaru weyu binafi
Íchiga arugoungani lun ubóu
Chahinha lari barana le lugunda
Óurabahówa tubana wewe le lugunda
Laríenhe abürühati lau
    "Ladimurehañala."
Kasa lererubei? Ka lererubei?

Wariha luagu wübü
Ma tiluma wewe
    Hau sun hawíeri dunuru
        Ámuñeguéinarügü hayu
    Hau sun hawíeri íliru
        Ámuñeguéinarügü hagaburi
        Lun wawiwandu hawagu.

How Beautiful the Sunrise

How beautiful the sunrise
Giving light to the earth
The sea grins, happily showing its teeth
The leaves on the trees happily frolic
The writer says
    "They are all speaking"
What do they say? What do they say?

We look at the mountains
Such healthy trees
    With all kinds of birds
        With different types of feathers
    With all kinds of game animals
        Each with its own manner
        For us to live on [123]

Hagarawoun Nagübürigu

Mémegi, subudi huméi tia,
Ya ñadina lubaragien sun lira;
Ya ñadina lubaragien -
    lubaragien hayabin
    ha galatimábaña igibu;
An ni me túyanute ágani
Ni tagimedi rokola
Ni úyanu tun maría
Ni me tan tuguya tura ingleisi
    mámanichagüdü lubéi
Hagarawoun Nagübürigu
Adürüha lidan niruhure,
Hagarawoun Nagübürigu
Aburuchaguéi nisamina,
Hagarawoun Nagübürigu
Ásiraguóun ya nuáni, o
Hererun Nagübürigu
Átuluha niúmulugugien.
Hagarawoun Nagübürigu
    hama Nárugutinu
    hama Niúnagu
Áürüha lidan nisasa
Háhari Nagübürigu
Háfara! Háürüha!
        Háürüha Meme! Háfara Meme!
        AGANBA NAÜ MEME!!!

Drums of Our Fathers

Yet, you must know,
I was here before all that,
I was here before -
    before
    the paler faces came;
And organ music
Jukebox blaring
Hymns sung to mary
and the quean's english
        shall not quiet the
Drums of my Fathers
Rumbling in my bones,
Drums of my Fathers
Capturing my mind,
Drums of my Fathers
Recapturing my soul, or the
Words of my Fathers
Tumbling from my mouth.
Drums of my Fathers
    of my Grandfathers
    of my Ancestors
Drumming in my psyche
Souls of my Fathers
Drum! Beat!
        Beat On! Drum On!
        AND ON!!!

Cataclysmic events, such as the passage of hurricanes, bring to a head the very possibility of the demise of the community itself as known within its immediate surroundings. On October 4, 1945, a hurricane destroyed the village leaving behind badly damaged houses, fields without crops, and uprooted trees that could not be used to make badly needed house repairs. There has been no written account of the destruction and its aftermath. Oral information, however, adds that shortly afterwards the government suggested to the villagers that they relocate to Punta Gorda. The steadfast refusal eventually forced the government to assist with the rehabilitation efforts *in situ*. Subsequently the dwindling population has led the government at various times to question the viability of Barranco as a community and to suggest alternatives. The precariousness of village continuity has been a fact of life that its sons and daughters have had to live with since 1945.

These examples introduce the infinite scope available to the Garifuna to impute cultural meanings onto their surrounding environment. The examples also indicate the selectivity available to the ethnographer to initiate the analysis from his field data. For us the process in this chapter starts with identifying three social contexts of the human-environment interface and the details within each one:

- the significance of being adjacent to an international border,

- the social values originating from the source of land ownership, and

- a review of place names as indicators of the cultural significance of the landscape.

Adjacency to the International Border

As a community Barranco has benefitted from its strategic position near to the Sarstoon River, which is the international border between Belize and Guatemala. Because Guatemala's Caribbean coast is only 100 kilometers long, Honduras, a country with a far larger Garifuna population than Guatemala, is easy to reach by sea.

Having pioneered the initial settlement of Barranco, among others, families from both Honduras and Guatemala continued to attract their relatives to join them, augmenting the village population. In his exceptional recall as the consummate village historian, Candido Arzu shared the following information with Palacio in 1980. The first mass migration of mainly men from Livingston, Guatemala, arrived in 1910. A smaller group came between 1932 and 1935. In the 1930s between 20 and 25 Jamaican men came, many proceeding to Monkey River and Punta Gorda.

The flow was reciprocal. In the 1880s men and women from Punta Gorda and Barranco started small agricultural settlements on the Guatemalan side of the Sarstoon River.[133] Men, and later women, on migratory wage labour started going to Puerto Barrios in the 1920s as the United Fruit Company consolidated its port facilities in Guatemala and Honduras. While the two-way flow was not always driven by economic reasons, many also came from Guatemala as refugees escaping political persecution.

The most high profile person in this category was Fr. Salvatore di Pietro, who, according to oral history, was smuggled by Garifuna sailors from Livingston to Barranco when Guatemala expelled all Jesuits in 1871. Oral tradition elaborates that on arriving in the village, in gratitude Fr. di Pietro took off his shoes, washed them, and threw the water offshore. He then blessed the village, beseeching God that he keep it safe and as a home only for Garifuna people.[134] Villagers often repeat the story of Fr. di Pietro when something good has happened to their community. Fr. di Pietro later became the first Vicar General in Belize, a position a little lower than the bishop of a diocese.

We shift from the experiences of individuals like Fr. di Pietro to the larger process of the changes that arrivals underwent, especially in reference to the landscape. Here the currently growing diasporic literature on the Garifuna can be helpful in providing some parallels. Studies have shown how Garifuna immigrants and their home societies have been transformed by migration in terms of the political socio-economy[135] and religious rituals.[136] These poignant indications of social and cultural change bring fresh perspective to revisit the adjacency position of Barranco, where we can discern the convergence of two opposing influences.

On the one hand, being near to the United Fruit Company port towns of Puerto Barrios and Puerto Cortes dragged Barranco, probably more than any other Garifuna community in Belize, into the periphery of the metropolitan world. On the other hand, some of the arrivals reinforced aspects of the larger Garifuna culture that they brought along. This two-edged blade of the diasporic experience, the economic and the cultural, had long been felt as they moved from one community to another within their Central American homeland. The corollary is that exposure to contrasting localities together with their social and physical environment had long been integrated into Garifuna communities, including Barranco, before the large scale migration to North America.

Assad Shoman has shed some light on the significance of Barranco's adjacency to the southern border in the unresolved Belize-Guatemala territorial dispute. Shoman was involved in these negotiations from the 1970s onwards. He said, "From 1978 to 1981, both the UK and US put severe pressure on the Belizean government to cede land south of the Moho River to Guatemala as the price for independence, but George Price repelled that by saying, among other things, that the land included the Garifuna village of Barranco."[137]

Permanence and Security in Land Tenure

Having crossed the border to arrive in Barranco how did the newcomers become full-fledged Baranguna? Reciprocal exchanges through consanguineal and affinal ties helped at the personal level. Some men and women found blood relatives while others found spouses. At the informal group level, being Garifuna entitled them to find residential space, probably sharing a house with relatives until being able to build one within the same lot or in another. Similarly, they could share farmlands and acquire their own. The question, therefore, revolves around permanence and security in land tenure for all community members, notwithstanding the length of time they have been in the village.

We have already seen that early Mestizo arrivals acquired these same privileges, but they left the village permanently by 1920. Although some of these early settlers were buried in a cemetery that is now a residential area, their descendants have not come to pay their respects, thereby breaking their continuity with their ancestors. Such lack of concern would be unusual for the Garifuna who show regard, not only to the physical burial sites of their ancestors, but also to the wishes of the spirits of their dead. Similarly, former residents of a Cornish community visit the cemetery and derelict parts ot the community as a way of recharging their sense of cultural identity.[138] Further below we will note that ancestral spirits have insisted on celebrating their dügü in Barranco, although their descendants have migrated to other places.

The source of rights to village house lots stems from the traditional claims by the ancestors as first settlers, which preceded the first survey of the British colonial administrators in 1892. Through blood and marriage ties, the ancestors passed these rights down through the generations. Furthermore, traditional rights to land as against ownership through cash purchase came along with the pioneers and has remained as far as the beginning of the 21st century. Besides, the government pre- and post-colonial administration has sanctioned traditional rights by honouring transmission of leases to designated family members and not prosecuting breaches of lease provisions. The result, therefore, is security in land held traditionally, not only in spirit but also in actuality.

One of the most common lapses in leasehold administration is living in a lot registered in another person's name. The patterns are wide ranging. Juan may allow a niece single mother to live in a lot, as a favour for an absent son, with the understanding that she is responsible to pay the annual rent. Alternatively Juan might build a house in a lot he inherited from his father to shelter his sister, who does not have her own house. In both of these examples, Juan's obligation is far greater to provide for his needy women kinfolk than to stick to the rules of leasehold. This kind of sharing is also common in farmlands. Residents of lots know in whose name it is leased and to whom they should be grateful.

The importance of a lot is to serve as setting for a house but the two have different social and monetary values. Accommodating a relative in need, as we have already seen, is a priceless social value. On the other hand, the house, if it is durable timber, can be sold for cash. There are at least three houses that have been sold and moved from one lot to another in the village or from there to Punta Gorda. Older and unoccupied timber houses have been dismantled to be sold in pieces as much needed lumber within the village or in another locality. Permanence in tenure is directed more to the lot than to the house.

Although there may be little regard for the administrative formality of leasehold, the villagers have high regard for surveyors and the demarcation of lots and farmlands. The immediate benefit is the wage labour for several months. Secondly, a quick review of lot and farmland applications shows coincidence with the presence of surveyors within the immediate area. At such times villagers seek to formalize the boundaries of lands that they have been using or try to access more new lands. Having formally acquired it, they proceed to use it, following only some specifications of leasehold.

In a more transcendental form of validation, ancestral spirits insist that their dügü celebrations be held in their birth place, where they lived, farmed, and fished. Descendants, who have migrated to faraway places, are forced to come back to Barranco to attend the ceremonies to mark the transition to Seri, the final resting place. In this way, the permanence and security of tenure receive their ultimate validation together with renewing the intimate familiarity with the living habitat.

The relatively non-confrontational picture that we have painted about land tenure between the community and state contrasts with the claims of the Garifuna in Honduras,[139] or, even closer home, that the Maya have kept up against the Government of Belize. Although jurist Sue Noe has argued that the Belizean Garifuna have land claims justifiable in international law,[140] there is lacking political dimension and grassroots mobilization in Barranco as well as in other Garifuna communities in Belize to propel the case forward. Because daily livelihood is seen less from the use of land, there is hardly any demand for the formalization of land claims. Baranguna, however, are aware of their ancestors' problems with land, growing appetite by speculators for lands around their own village, and demand for lands in other Garifuna communities.

The most famous Baranguna, Andy Palacio, included a song on land claims in Honduras in his world acclaimed "Watina" compact disk. The introduction to the song "Miami" in the booklet accompanying the compact disk says, "This song reflects the increasing concern over land rights and land ownership in the Garifuna coastal communities of Honduras. Backed by a festive paranda beat, the singer finds that the area near the river in the village of Miami is now restricted territory."[141] Andy's inspiration was what is taking place among fellow Garifuna

Miami

— Andy Palacio

Gaweiyasúntina	I took a trip
Liumou Miami ma	to the river near Miami
Narihin ei aruruwa	When I looked,
Súdara nau	I was surrounded by soldiers
Háluguñóu nege	They were asking me
Nigáradan numa	for my papers
Bugarügüladina	Consul Feliz
Consul Feliz ei	just drove me away
Dánbeigu nachülürün	When I got
Liumou Miami ma	to the river near Miami
Náluguñei yebe nísebe owa	I was searching for my comfort
Náluguñei yebe louba kolonia	I was looking for the neighborhood
Nigu Miami ei mabaratina	Even in Miami, I have no place
Ówenbu mábuigaü	A special greeting
Houn sun gürigie	to all the people
Ha yabaña Hopkins	here in Hopkins
Haritaguágüle me hárigie	This will help you to remember
Gürigie ha adügübalin paranda	the people who made paranda

in one country becomes a rallying cry for others, wherever they are. Similarly, the successes achieved in Honduras should also be shared with the others, as they try to find solutions to parallel problems.

The Good Old Cedar Tree

Ultimately it is around the rights to a given space, such as a house lot, that the values of ownership are proclaimed loud and clear by the owner for the rest of the world to know. Mrs. Paulina Reyes McKenzie wrote two letters to the Surveyor General in August 20th and September 9th, 1947 (*p. 186*). Using the measured tone appropriate to a letter directed to officialdom, she complained that Feliciano Zuniga, who was the Village Alcalde, had cut to pieces a cedar tree in her lot. That tree had been a landmark in the village because it towered over the village and could have been seen from far out at sea, even before the cliff or anything else could be identified.

She was asking for redress as compensation for her tree as well as for the collateral damage caused to plants in her lot when the tree was being cut. The content of the letters were salvageable from deterioration in government files.[142] The following issues were among those that Mrs. McKenzie raised about ownership rights on a lease lot together with the cedar tree itself.

Ownership of lot precedes first government survey in 1892

Mrs. McKenzie states that her father had been in possession of the lot for over sixty years. Our research confirms that her father Martin Reyes was the owner of the lot when British colonial authorities did their first survey of village lots in 1892.

Recall of timeline

According to Mrs. McKenzie, her sister planted the cedar tree in 1901. At that time Mrs. McKenzie herself was nine years old, having been born in 1892. The other episode that precipitated Mrs. McKenzie's letter writing was the disastrous 1945 hurricane that uprooted the cedar tree.

Awareness of the official chain of command

From her comments Mrs. McKenzie knew that the steps in the bureaucratic hierarchy went from the Village Alcalde to the District Commissioner in Punta Gorda, who was a Mr. Meighan, or the Justice of Peace also in Punta Gorda, and then the Surveyor General in Belize City. She also knew that although the tree was in her lot, she needed to get government permission to dispose of it. Her main point of contention was that a villager had usurped his authority to dispose of the tree without informing her.

Letters of Mrs. Paulina McKensie to the Surveyor General

Barranco
August 20th 1947
Honourable Surveyor General

This is my complain to you asking you kindly to consider me in this matter. From the year 1901 my sister plant a cedar tree on lot no. 77 which my father rent on we are on that lot till now the cedar tree rooted up in the Hurricane, this lot is rent by my son and given to me. I told my husband to ask the DC for the tree being in the lot he did so. The reply was that Eugenio Cayetano who is my son is the lawful person to get such concession. (page 2). The alcalde came and told me he want the tree I ask him who want the tree he say I. I told him he cant get (it) for it is in this lot 77. He said he must get it my husband say well we will see about that. Someone went and told the JP that the lot is seven feet from the tree, the JP say that the tree is not in the lot so I have no claim on it none of the official came to see the tree. From thence the tree is sawed to in pieces and sold to all who want them they damage the lot by rooting up my plants and crushing some to death also trim my coffee with young ones (page 3) it is over 60 years since my father rent this up to now and I do not owe 1 year rent is it right Surveyor General that this alcade to damage my lot saw and carry away all the lumber and did not give me a piece even to make a chair. Please sir is that right. Not to forget me but to consider me.

I remain your obedient Serv. Paulina Reyes married name Paulina McKenzie

Please tell me what to do in the matter. The cedar tree was planted by my sister. I have witness to the fact. They begin to saw the tree on the 31st July.
Official stamp saying, "Registered D.S.O. August 30 1947"

Barranco
Sept. 9, 1947
Surveyor General

Honourable Sir:
I had posted an important letter to you asking your help and council for my cedar tree on lot No. 77 which my sister plant it is thrown down by hurricane 4th October 1945 I apply to use same. Through my husband from 1945. I apply to use same through my husband from 1945 November D.C. Meighan told me the lawful concession belongs to my son Eugenio Cayetano. My son rent that lot No. 77 and give it to me.
Feless Zuniga went to the D.C. behind me and take over the said tree leaving all dirt (next page) in my lot J.P. Bernard Avilez say they told him that the tree is 7 feet from said lot No. 77 which is not true. I am living on that lot. That said tree brak down my house and none of the officers even came to see the tree. I have that mind your letter do not reach you. I posted it from the 21st August. I am not chasing you for the reply my Worship, for I know when it reach you you will give me council. But if it don't reach you please give me permission to recall it from Barranco and Punta Gorda office.
(Following page)
My Worship, I am living on that (lot). My father Martin Reyes died leaving his families on that lot No. 77 till now over 65 years now and we dont owe no rent, Please consider me and help me
I am your servant
Paulina Reyes X Eugenio Cayetano's mother
Official Stamp saying "Registered D.S.O Sept. 16, 1947"

Awareness of demarcation line

Mrs. McKenzie knew the border of her lot. When Mr. Bernard Avilez, J.P. alleged that the tree was not in her lot, she was able to dispute that.

Plants grown in lot

Mrs. McKenzie alleged that among the plants destroyed in her lot when the tree was being cut to pieces were her coffee plants.

Lease payment obligation

The strength of her plea for redress, according to Mrs. McKenzie, came from the fact that all annual rents for the lot had been paid on time. For official purposes her primary proof of rights to ownership came from regularly paying the annual rent.

In those two letters Mrs. McKenzie demonstrated what was common knowledge about ownership rights among the villagers in 1947. She knew the hierarchy to whom she should write for redress; she knew that her familial right to the land extended back, even before the colonial government exerted control in 1892; she knew the exact boundaries of her lot; and she knew that payment of lease fees on time each year secured her claim to the land.

Place Names

For such a small place the wide proliferation of names for given locations is so large that it deserves a study on its own. Our objective is to review some of the names—their meaning, the actual locations, and do a brief statement on their cultural significance. The names are for parts of the village; wells, creeks, and ponds; non-Temash River farmlands, and Temash River farmlands. Table 7.1 (*pp. 214-6*) shows a list of the names, the literal meaning in Garifuna, and the contextual meaning specific to the geographic location. The Garifuna suffix "... *rugu*" at the end of a word signifies a place or location. *Lagunurugu* means "within the lagoon" and *Budeinrugu* means "where many bottles are found".

Parts of the Village

Up to 1880 the name of the village was Red Cliff or *Baranco Colorado* in Spanish, which comes from the cliff of red clay, that rises from the beach, giving the settlement a platform three meters high. Subsequently, *Barranco Colorado* was abbreviated to Barranco. From north to south the main areas are *Louba*, the central village, and *Pañaton. Colorado* is the name of one of the homesteads south of Barranco.

Ponds, Wells, and Creeks

Set within the District that receives the most precipitation in the whole country of Belize, the location of Barranco allows for runoff of its heavy showers through a network of creeks and ponds that circumscribe its perimeter. Surface water forms natural ponds or is captured in wells with live springs.

In the Table 7.1 there is a list of four creeks, four wells, and five ponds. The list of wells is incomplete for many that have been dug for private use did not have names. One well with a specific name *Miligirugu* would have received its name probably from the owner to describe its special milk-like colour. There is no explanation for the name *Calentura*, a Spanish word meaning "fever".

There was an annual cycle in the use of wells, with some used only during long dry spells when others became dry. At such times, the supply would be very low, forcing women and children to walk farther, wait hours, and wake early in the morning when the live spring would have collected. The creeks were an earlier favourite meeting point for women while washing clothes or for children to bathe.

Two pictures taken in 1979 depict the importance of a well. In Figure 7.1 the Public Well was being cleaned by bailing out the mud settled at the bottom to clear the live spring. This kind of servicing had to be done for some wells to ascertain the steady flow of water during long dry spells. In 1979 this well was no longer used for drinking purposes. Potable water came either from rain-fed vats or wells located in the village outskirts.

Salumerugu is an extension of Legegu Creek that some women and children had to cross to fetch firewood. Heavily laden with firewood, the women in the picture were doing the very precarious crossing by holding onto tree branches and walking on rolling logs (*Fig. 7.2*). By 2009 firewood had been mostly replaced by bottled butane gas, eliminating the need to do the Salumerugu crossing again. And the collective memory for ponds, wells, and creeks is quickly diminishing as they have been displaced by the running water system that was installed in 2003. The availability of good quality water year round has effectively taken over all the home water needs. The creeks have become blocked with debris, flowing only after heavy showers.

Farmlands

The list of farmland names goes back to the pre- and post- banana boom periods, but by 2009 there were only two families still growing crops. As in the case of creeks, ponds, and wells, modernity has

Figure 7.1. Cleaning the well

ignacia Reyes (*above*) and Alfonso Cayetano (*below*) (photos by Joseph O. Palacio)

overtaken the use of farmlands but some haunting reminders are left in the collective memory through physical presence as well as an abiding sense of humour.

When villagers started their farms at the "Miles" subdivision northwest of the village during the mid-1980s, there were already rumours that the roadway would be bulldozed from the Moho River providing access to the Punta Gorda – San Antonio Road for Barranco. By starting their farms along the proposed alignment, a few hardy villagers thought that they would be the first to reap the benefits of road access, even using the name "Miles" for their farming area. Twenty years afterwards the road indeed was built, becoming usable year round in 1998 when the bridge over the Moho River was completed. On the other hand, the farming efforts of the villagers at "Miles" have dissipated, leaving their coconut trees on lands that have been taken over by non-Baranguna. On seeing these trees, while driving to and from the village, many a Baranguna points to them and begins the litany of their forefathers having planted trees in several places while others are now reaping the fruits.

Figure 7.2 Lucille Zuniga Valencio (*in front*) and her daughter-in-law Jennifer Martinez carrying firewood from Salumerugu
(photos by Joseph O. Palacio)

If the coconut trees unfold a sentiment of regret for unrewarded hard labour, there are several other memories that evoke a sense of humour about the idiosyncratic behaviour of farming ancestors. Nicanora Garcia Palacio, or "Nikí", as she was called in the village, is well known in Barranco lore for being a restless farmer. Even during her time on migratory wage labour in Puerto Barrios during the 1930s and 1940s, she maintained a farm in a surrounding area, called "Pichilingo". Many Baranguna men also did farming while working in Puerto Barrios but the reports talk not about Niki's spouse as heading the farming but she herself.

After she returned to Barranco, she started another farm in the outskirts of the village, which she called "Yukuruku Farm". For her visitors to know whether she was at the farm, Niki established a coding system. The visitors were to holler "Yukuruku" a few times extending it out like a rooster's crow. If she was available, her response was "Cante el gallo", which in Spanish translates as, "let the rooster crow". This was the code for "Yes, I am here and you can come in."

Another claim to fame for Nikí, was her song-composing skill, many about her farming prowess. One of her songs became a village theme song, after it helped a queen's candidate representing the village to win the contest. During the first Queen of the South contest for candidates from Garifuna villages, the Barranco candidate sang the song, capturing the first prize with the catchy refrain, *"bunatina gien nehu ñei"*. It translates as, "Yes, I also planted okra there". Even after her death, Niki's sense of humour about her work in her farm brought glory to the village.

Summary and Conclusions

While the previous chapters have focused on the material side of lot and farmland tenure, this chapter is reflective in showing how Baranguna have placed their indelible stamp on their landscape.

The Garifuna nation is blessed with several artists—poets, playwrights, novelists, singers, song writers, painters, sculptors, folklorists, and so on. Many of them have incorporated the landscape into their art. Our function in this chapter has been to bring forward the ethnography and join it with folklore to illustrate how villagers have demonstrated their deep appreciation for their community.

The poetry of Marcela Lewis praises the Almighty for the beauty and bounty of nature. The fact that Marcela is not from Barranco is insignificant as her descriptions encapsulate a global quality of the relationship between humankind and its surrounding environment, which poetry can best express. Similarly there is a pan-Garifuna

Table 7.1 The Cultural Significance of Place Names

Garifuna Name	Literal Meaning	Contextual Meaning
Parts of the Village		
Pañatón	Creole word meaning "Spanish Town"	Extreme southern part earlier dominated by Mestizos
Louba	The other side	Extreme northern part of the village
Colorado	Abbreviation for Barranco Colorado	One of the homesteads in the southwest area
Kehelarugu	Among the sour orange trees	Benches used for relaxation northeast church building
Guana Church	Creole for "where iguanas meet"	Benches used for relaxation near Bartolo Polonio's lot
Ponds, Wells, and Creeks		
Trial Farm	Name given by owner to his farm in the Legegu area	There was a well in the farm used mainly during the dry by villagers
Legegu	Name for creek north of village	Creek draining the northern part of the village
Gumagarugu	Place of Cotton Tree	Pond use for bathing and washing during long dry in the extreme north
Salumerugu	Not known	A pond/creek draining western portion of village
Budeinrugu	Where bottles are found	Pond in the southwest where a man placed broken bottles to prevent children from bathing in it
Calentura	Spanish word for "fever"	A well near the entrance to Colorado
Miligirugu	Looks like milk	Well in Colorado probably named for its special taste
Sabudirugu	Where avocado trees are found	Well near Alfredo Rash's house
Duguyurugu	In a place of birds with the call "tukuyu"	Swampy spot located southwest of the village
Domairugu	Not known	Pond where the current village dump is located
Romerugu	Well in Romero's lot	Public well located east of Ray Valencio's lot

Public Well		Well located in a lot for public use
Magüsineru	Place for moccasins	Small stream near Cayetano's front lot. It is the creek where the village founder Santiago Avilez arrived
		Creek behind the temple
Rub mi belly bridge		Name for the bridge crossing the above creek
Live spring (no names)	Found in Marty Arana's lot	Becomes active and flows in heavy rains
Non-Temash Farmlands		
Bengorugu	Bengo's Place	Farm plot of Santiago Benguche located at village entrance
Vinland		Victor Nicholas gave this name to the above plot on acquiring it
Yukuruku Farm		Name given by Nicanora Palacio to her farm near Bengorugu
Trial Farm		Farm belonging to Catarino Ariola in Legegu
Lóubawagu	On the far side	Farmland belonging to Inocente Zuniga in the northeast
Cowpen		Farmland with pasture west of the village belonging to Felipe Santino
Polo Farm		Polo is abbreviation for Crispulo, who had a farm on his father's land, John Chimilio
Castilan Farm		Farmland belonging to Cornelio Castillo
Madagarugu	The bottom is unreachable	Farming area east of Tim Lorenzo's farm
Lidise	So far away	Farmland area northwest of village surveyed by Gibson in 1954-55
Miles		Farmlands northeast of Lidise located in the outskirts of Midway village

Dándeirugu	In the place of tapirs	
Falumágeirugu	In the place of coconuts	Farmland belonging to Eusebio Santino near Temash Bar
Temash Farmlands		
Red Bank		An area of 17 parcels on both banks of the Temash
Fairview		An area of 11 parcels on the left bank of the Temash
Lárugu (Garifuna)	Not known	Further upstream from Fairview on right bank 22 parcels
Quiripi	"Crooked"	Small section of Largo called from a bend in a tributary of the Temash
Lagunurugu	Within the lagoon	The Temash Lagoon; further upstream from Largo on the left bank, 15 parcels
Dulcis Domus	From Latin "Sweet Home"	On the right bank on the Temash Lagoon 15 parcels

resonance to Victor Nicholas' lament on the experience repeated too often for farmers on their need to move from one area to another in search of fertile soils. A prerequisite of slash-and-burn agriculture, it has led many to discouragement and to abandon farming altogether.

The community not only knows the breach of norms on behaviour related to the environment, it also knows that there are sanctions against such behaviour. Mrs. Paulina Reyes MacKenzie's written complaint on the appropriation of her cedar tree and asking for redress at the highest level of the government bureaucracy is a poignant reminder.

On the other hand, the cultural element within the landscape is not meant to portray only serious lapses in human behaviour. Folklore is especially important in introducing the lighter moments of life. A good example is Niki's method of communicating to her visitors that she is available by giving the response in Spanish to their pre-arranged way of calling her.

Assigning names to a multiplicity of geographical features by itself can be regarded as a form of linguistic art. The persons giving the names are expressing their individualism as unique members of the community. The names become their signature, an indelible stamp that can outlast them, rolling into the repertoire of village lore.

Chapter Eight
Conclusions and Future Perspectives

We start this chapter with the synergy of nationhood and the community by a brief perspective on Juan Pedro Cayetano and some of his descendants as they have lived through these two concepts over the past 214 years. The son of two arriving St. Vincent exiles, Juan Pedro Cayetano lived in San Pedro, one of the several Garifuna communities surrounding Trujillo. At the age of seventeen he had already taken the family responsibility of having a spouse Maria Dorotea. For the next twenty years between 1843 to the 1860s we see him in Guatemala as the father of sons and daughters being baptized first in Santo Tomas near Puerto Barrios and afterwards in Livingston. While tracing his parental obligations in church sacraments provides a glance on Juan Pedro's involvement within the larger community, we have to look further among his descendants to see the impact of his extended family on Garifuna nationhood, particularly in terms of spirituality and knowledge enhancement. Marcelo Cayetano, a grandson of Juan Pedro Cayetano, became a primary influence for the building of the village dabuyaba in 1996. The inauguration of the dabuyaba and the first dugu ceremony held there remain transfixed as historic moments in village memory. Every year the dabuyaba, known as the Marcelo Cayetano Dabuyaba Complex, has been the venue for dügü ceremonies. Besides, Juan Pedro's great-great-grandsons—Calistus, Fabian, Sebastian, and Joseph—have remained among those most dedicated to expanding awareness of Garifuna spirituality and culture throughout the country of Belize within the contemporary period.

From a spotlight on an illustrious family, grounded within the epic of the Garifuna people, we return to the social relations that Baranguna have built around land tenure. The following analysis builds on land tenure, while providing a framework to make projections about land and overall development in the village. Two main structural features, nationhood and community, have circumscribed the social relations of land tenure as the Barranco story has unfolded. The analysis portrays a logic that explains the basis of land tenure, while providing a framework to make projections about land and overall development in the village.

Nationhood

Nationhood as an idealized concept grew from the Garifuna territory in St. Vincent, which instigated a most covetous response from the Europeans that came to a climax during the latter part of the 18th century.[143] Nationhood in St. Vincent had provided the Garifuna with an economic infrastructure, a political power base, and a strong cultural identity. The violent decimation of the population prior to the exile inevitably neutralized land as an economic infrastructure, together with its usefulness as their political base. Their cultural identity took a wide ranging flux, especially as they became exposed to several groups in Central America.

The concerted effort to reduce them to squatters and cheap wage labour broke the resolve of many to retain their cultural identity, forcing them to join the majority mixed population, either Mestizo in Central America or Creole in Belize. For others, it strengthened their resolve to reconstitute their nationhood. This is the group that receives primary focus in this study. The relative isolation of Barranco provided the opportunity to build a settlement and cultivate farmlands for at least two generations before the British took official notice, indicating that the village had considerable scope to re-invigorate their nationhood.

Our use of the term "nation" as against "ethnic group" is deliberate and follows the terminology often used by indigenous people about themselves.[135] Nation provides an historic depth that gives justice to the transformations that a people undergo as a group. It introduces a concept of integrity for a people, while "ethnic group" is usually a subset as defined by others within the nation-state.

"Nation" counters the concept of hybridity by focusing on cultural integrity as against the parts that go into making a people. The British had accused the Garifuna as black people usurping the lands of the Caribs and gave this as a reason for their forceful extirpation from St. Vincent.[144] The response of the Garifuna was that they got their lands from their ancestors, which included the Caribs.[145] Altogether the term "nation" lends itself to the kind of analysis that we have incorporated into this study.

Community

The other structural feature in this analysis that is pivotal in making Barranco land tenure a unique study is the concept of community, which is subdivided into four components:

- kinship,
- gender,
- ethnicity, and
- social/cultural values.

Together they bring a degree of wholism to a community where land is the guide for analysis. Furthermore, a community study, such as this, facilitates the interplay of factors, which cannot be so easily appreciated otherwise.

Kinship (*iduheguaü*)

The significance of kinship as guide for land tenure became heightened after the individualization of lot and farmland ownership in the aftermath of bringing village tenure into the framework of colonial governance. What had been group ownership in customary practice, such as, the clustering of lots in the hands of extended families, became the property of individuals, albeit on leasehold. In the customary practice, transmission had not been necessary, as the family itself became extended over time. But individualization brought a need to identify who would be the designated successor. While the rural Caribbean family land remained perpetually inalienable and indivisible, the Garifuna have been forced to select who the successor would be. Thus, kinship became the framework for decision making, a primary intermediary of allocating residential space, both in the case of the very early settlers as well as afterwards in selecting succession of ownership.

A main contribution of this study is to by-pass the previous limitations of bilateral kinship in Caribbean studies and, instead, to include affinal kinship. Another elaboration important to lot succession is to arrive at analytic degrees of distance for consanguineal and affinal kin, placing lot recipients in an order of relative importance.

Gender

The inclusivity of kinship introduces the concept of gender, where men and women engage in land tenure activities within a spirit of mutuality—not one gender attempting to compete with the other. In the Caribbean literature the consanguineal household and matrifocality have tended to spotlight the relative strength and role durability of women as against men. Our study shows that in both lots and farmlands land tenure is too important to remain in the domain of one gender. Men and women have their own choices of who to become the recipient of their lands. And taken together the roster of recipients covers both men and women, signifying that overall there is minimal exclusion of one gender over the other.

There are external factors, of course, such as the availability of cash through the larger economy, that affect the capacity of one gender over the other. There are indications that since the 1960s women have been able to engage in lot transmissions because they have had more access to cash than beforehand. But earlier during the 1920s and 1930s men were engaging much more often than women. It was the time of extensive peasant cash-cropping when men took the initiative of acquiring farmlands to cultivate. The conclusion remains that men and women have opportunities which they exploit depending on their access to cash at any given time.

Ethnicity, Colour, and Class

Interethnic relations are important to understand the history of land tenure in coastal Central America. While there has been ample information about the co-existence of different "races" within communities in southern coastal Belize, this is one of the first studies to fine-tune how it actually happened. During its first few years Barranco was populated mostly by Garifuna, but Mestizo, non-Garifuna names gradually increased in the genealogical records, and by 1887 one-third of the confirmation class was non-Garifuna. By 1920, however, they had left the village permanently. While they lived in the village, they occupied the southern part (Pañatón). The Garifuna, on the other hand, occupied the mid-portion, the part of the village where they first landed, and then spread to the outer areas.

To what extent was colour discrimination important in the relations between the Garifuna and the Mestizos? Oral information from one person who remembers them reveals that the Mestizos discriminated against the Garifuna. While we do not have more information about discrimination between the Mestizo and the Garifuna, there is documented proof of discrimination by the colonial authorities against Garifuna lot owners during the immediate 1892 post-survey period. The attribute of class distinction was also operational in this case. Front lots previously owned by the Garifuna were taken away from them and given to Creoles, who were associates of *latifundistas* within the subregion.

Baranguna came in contact with greater proportion of other groups, who were working farmlands. They include Mestizos, Creole, Miskito, and Q'eqchi'. Like the Mestizos, who came and owned lots in the village, the owners of farmlands came more for economic gain than to engage in interethnic relations with the Garifuna. As the economic opportunities dwindled, they uprooted themselves from the subregion. Davidson gives the account of some Honduras villages, that were previously Garifuna but had been taken over completely by the Mestizos.[146] It was the reverse in Barranco, from where Mestizos relocated, leaving their lots for the Garifuna.

In short, the ebb and flow of Mestizos, Creoles, and others to and from Barranco around the turn of the twentieth century place in sharp profile the dedication of the Garifuna to the village as their community. They have also had to participate in their own ebb and flow movements but the difference remains in the continuity that they have retained within the community, where kinship and ethnicity have been primary intermediaries.

Social and Cultural Values

Social and cultural values highlight human behavior as it relates to the landscape. In this regard artistic expression becomes a medium between the behaviour and the landscape. At one level folklore as a form of art becomes a way of singing the praises of the village, reminding everyone how fortunate they are to be Baranguna. One example is Fr. di Pietro blessing the village in gratitude for being his *múñasu* when he was expelled from Guatemala. He ended by imploring God that the village remain only for the Garifuna people. Through the priest's invocation the village cultural landscape received spiritual validation.

The Garifuna nation is blessed with several artists—poets, playwrights, novelists, singers, song writers, painters, sculptors, folklorists, and so on. Many values become alive in their work. They include permanence and security of tenure, assigning names to geographical and other features, and reveling in the iconography of a cedar tree. The values by themselves are primarily cultural, but there is also a humanist component that comes through in a series of humorous incidents. As we have so often shown in this volume, land tenure can be a painful experience, but people also laugh and make fun of themselves during lighter moments.

Status of lots in Barranco 2000 and 2011

Carlson Tuttle and Alvin Loredo made an assessment of the status of lots and houses in 2000. For comparison, Carlson Tuttle and Egbert Valencio made a similar assessment in 2011 using the same criteria for their judgements. The complete assessment is found in Appendix E. Table 8.1 summarizes these data.

The 27% increase in houses in the last ten years is impressive for a village that is economoically depressed. People are investing in what they know best—houses. Besides the increase in the number of houses, there is an upgrade in materials, introducing vinyl and plycem as siding. There are fewer unfinished houses, but the same number of abandoned ones.

There is a definite improvement in the overall conditions of the lots. The number that were judged high bush 2000 was reduced nearly to half and a quarter more than were maintained in 2011.

Table 8.1. Status of Lots in Barranco 2000 and 2011

	Type	2000	2011	% change
Houses	Wasein[a]	14	4	-72%
	Board	22	32	+45%
	Wainscot[b]	6	4	-33%
	Cement	14	14	+71%
	Vinyl[c]	0	4	+100%
	Plycem[d]	0	3	+100%
	Total Houses	**56**	**71**	**+27%**
	unfinished	10	8	-20%
	abandoned	4	4	0
	Condition			
Lot	maintained	94	116	+23%
	medium bush	38	35	-8%
	high bush	44	25	-43%

[a] Wasein = traditional construction of houses using cabbage palm stick for walls and comfrey palm leaf for thatched roofs.
[b] Wainscot = walls made of a combination of cement blocks partly up and board above.
[c] Vinyl = vinyl metal siding
[d] Plycem = a cement-fiber siding material

Community Development

Village lore among other aspects of artistic expression is always a delightful diversion from the disappointment that Baranguna vent about what they regard as its lack of development. There is a great contrast in Barranco at the beginning of the 21st century from what had been at the beginning of the 20th in terms of the significance of land to overall community well-being. There is now hardly any use of the scores of agricultural plots that had been surveyed before 1913. There are more lots that are empty and allowed to become overgrown with grass than those that have houses. More than ever before it is appropriate to ask the question, "how can the village population overcome this malaise, which is bothersome to most men and women?"

Local community development in Barranco has had a chequered history, arising from the direction of government policy. During the 20th century probably the most effective intrusion into the village socio-economy was laying surveys for lots and farmlands that took place in 1928 for the former and for the latter before 1913 and in the 1950s. By providing access to additional lots and farm areas, the colonial government was investing in the villagers to enable them to further consolidate their community. Stories about the results in farm income from cash cropping, together with the availability of more space for housing have become legendary in village talk, most often contrasted with the bad times that subsequently have enveloped the village. Indeed, between 1960 and 1990 there was hardly any input by government into primary production within the village.

Starting in the 1990s government began investing in infrastructure within the village in such projects as providing electricity, road connection, water, refurbishing the comunity centre and the health centre, bussing students to secondary schools, and building a new school building. Later in the 1990s, monthly non-contributor pensions became available to elderly persons and there has been free health care provided for all, complete with doctor's consultation and medication. As highly commendable as these services are, there remained little consistent focus on generating cash income within the village economy. The result has been continued and more accelerated outflow for men and women from the village with minimal in-migration.

During the 1990s the Toledo District was targeted for several projects by bilateral aid agencies toward the sustainable use of the environment in agriculture, forest management, ecotourism, and related fields. However, Barranco was minimally impacted.

Prospects for the Future

There is an urgent need to confirm the boundaries for *lumua Barangu* and to insist that such lands be made available for the sole use of the villagers. The Ministry of Local Government can give more information on what steps to take to achieve this objective.

Substantive involvement in land survey and management by government in the past leads to the suggestion that future development will again have to be spearheaded by well articulated public policy. The arm of local government, the Village Council has to be the primary intermediary receiving information about government plans and bringing up suggestions for government programmes that would be suitable for Barranco to enhance their community development.

Barranco needs a development plan with defined objectives and a timeframe for implementation. Such a plan should receive the full participation of all members of the village community. It should also incorporate well conceived economic projects that interested individuals may want to undertake.

In that context, Barranco residents are encouraged to undertake their own income generating activities. From time to time opportunities for subsidized soft loans are made available through the Development Finance Corporation and Credit Unions. If the cash value of land can be used as collateral for loans to start personal income generating projects, then villagers will have to pay closer attention to their lots and farmlands.

As a means of generating greater commitment to lot maintenance, there is a need for a general review of village leasehold, using as precedent a programme implemented a few years ago to fast-track leases to become freehold. Using the information about the wide-ranging history of ownership of lots and farmlands in this volume, villagers have an unusual opportunity to undertake measures to finalize ownership from leasehold to freehold. But we do reiterate that all land information in this volume needs to be confirmed with the Lands Department before any decisive action.

Along with loans for capital investment, there are increasingly available opportunities to the villagers, even adults, to take skills development courses in technical secondary schools that are serviced by buses daily from the village.

Barranco has a willing resource in the Baranguna in the diaspora and others who have shown interest in the village welfare, to assist in all matters related to community development. There are many persons with technical skills, grounded in years of service in public policy, who would be willing to help in fine-tuning development plans and suggest sources of financial and technical assistance for individuals as well as for the community.

This volume presents the history of land tenure in Barranco and analyzes how it fits within the village social structure. We show that land tenure, enriched by the strong bonds of kinship, gender, ethnicity, and socio-cultural values, had at an earlier time been the basis of the overall well-being of Barranco. A re-vitalized approach to land tenure can continue to add value to these essential traits while spearheading economic growth for the next decades and into the future.

Endnotes

Chapter 2—Exile from St. Vincent and Settlement in Belize

2-1   Haviland (2002: 630)

2-2   Bolland (2006), Clay (1996), Corntassel (2003), Forte (2006), and Merlan (2009)

2-3   Gonzalez (1988: 48)

2-4   The two Carib Wars in Saint Vincent have been discussed in great detail by Fabel (2000), Gullick (1976, 1984 and 1985), and Kirby and Martin (1972).

2-5   In the context of the 18th and 19th centuries, we use Central America to refer to the Spanish-speaking countries as against Belize.

2-6   Jacobs (2003: 2)

2-7   Jacobs (2003)

2-8   Fabel (2000)

2-9   Gonzalez (1988: 21)

2-10   This use of the word "dory" refers to a canoe made from a single tree trunk, a dugout. It is derived from a Miskito word.

2-11   Juan Pedro Cayetano was listed as 17 years old in the Trujillo, Honduras 1821 census (Payne, 2008).

2-12   Gonzalez (1959b), Taylor (1951)

2-13   Gonzalez (1988)

2-14   Bilby (1996)

2-15   Barth (1956)

2-16   Crawford (1984), Taylor (1951), Kerns (1983)

2-17   Palacio (2006: 215-234)

2-18   Anderson (2009) and Brondo (2010)

2-19   Gullick (1984, 1985)

2-20   Gonzalez (1988: 48)

2-21   Payne (2008)

2-22   Woodward (1976)

2-23   Bolland (1987b)

2-24   Robinson (2006), Woodward (1976)

2-25   Simmons (2001)

2-26   Gullick (1984, 1985)

2-27   Gonzalez and Cheek (1986)

2-28   Gonzalez (1987: 151)

2-29   Bolland and Shoman (1977: 68)

2-30   Dobson (1973), Bolland (1977), Bolland and Shoman (1977), Barnett (1991), Shoman (1994)

2-31   Bolland and Shoman (1977: 93)

2-32   Bolland (1987b)

2-33   "Rules for Carib and Indian Reserves," *Supplement to the Honduras Gazette*. Belize, Saturday, 29 March, 1890, p. 15

2-34   Cal (1991: 240)

2-35   Wilk (1991: 65-6)

2-36   Villalobos (2006)

2-37   Cal (1991)

2-38   Wilk (1991: 54-71)

2-39   Our information comes from Kerns' analysis (1984) and from the report on the 1861 census in the Belize Archives.

2-40   Kerns (1984)

2-41   Cal (1991: 318)

2-42   Cal (1991)

2-43   Gonzalez (1988)

2-44   CarlsonTuttle, personal communication

2-45   Palacio (2005)

2-46   Ramos (2000) The Carib Development Society was a voluntary organization among several that were found in Garifuna communities. Their aim was to generate solidarity, especially in time of need.

2-47   Ramos (2000: 9)

2-48   Ramos (2000: 10-11)

2-49   The nationalist movement has never been able to reconcile the well-being of indigenous peoples within the larger purview of the nation-state, which applies to both the Maya as well as Garifuna peoples. A further analysis is beyond the scope of this volume.

2-50   Ramos (2000)

2-51   Hoffmann (2007), Hooker (2005), Ng'weno (2007), and Wade (1995)

2-52   Sambola (2007: 26)

2-53   Rey (2010)

2-54   Anderson (2007)

2-55   Forte (2005, 2006) and Palacio (1995)

2-56   Noe (2001: 1)

Chapter 3—The Founding of Barranco

3-57   Speech of His Excellency Sir Alfred Moloney at Punta Gorda, 24th March, 1896; *Supplement to the Honduras Gazette*, Belize, Saturday, 18 April, 1896, p. 91. H.E. had visited Barranco school on 30th February 1896, and was received by S. Ogaldez, Luis Palacio, Coronado Palacio, Manuel Castillo, Santiago Labriel and 45 others.

3-58   Craig (1966)

3-59   Letters and Notices (Vol. XII, 1879) p. 229

3-60   The coincidence of Genon's letter with the drafting of the Punta Gorda Carib Reserve plan also in the same year by C. S. Dwight underlines the severity of this concern.

3-61   While the other names in this heading are surnames, we are using "Desideria" to refer to the first woman in Barranco because her surname is quite variable in the records and oral tradition.

3-62   Palacio (1997)

3-63   Nicholas (2004: x)

3-64   Payne (2008)

3-65   di Pietro (1880)

3-66   Lundberg (1978)

3-67   Shoman (1994)

3-68   The documentation that is our primary source of information does not often include the next of kin—parent, spouse, and offsprings —making it difficult to place persons within the kinship network that we are using for this exercise. The more information we were able to accumulate from various events for one person, the easier it was to identify him/her as a source for kinship connections. However, in the end our focus was on direct ancestral ties, which are only one of several blood ties the Garifuna use.

3-69   Garifuna may not have received these sacraments earlier because the presence of church buildings and priests had been far more irregular in Central America (Gonzalez, 1988). Belize did not undergo state-led periods of anti-clericalism when ministers of the church were banned from practicing their ministry as happened especially during the initial years of republican rule in Central America (Woodward, 1976).

3-70   A more detailed study is necessary for some analysis. It is possible that the Garifuna at that time were adapting formal Christian marriage as part of their own ceremonial system of joining man and woman as husband and wife. They had their own ceremonies whether or not they were validated by the church. There came a time when it was convenient for the Garifuna to legitimize their unions under the church. There would have been a transitional time when both ceremonies were used and then the other goes into atrophy.

3-71   Difficulties in deciphering linkages come from the young age of the participants and the cryptic way the names were entered, many without last names. As we found out in the case of baptisms and births, it is possible that there were links that could not be identified. The other possibility is that the participants came with parents, who did not have direct ancestral ties with the pioneers but were still blood relatives. With the inflow of more persons into the village during the latter 1880s, a wider range of relatives as well as non-relatives were arriving. The confirmation lists for 1866 and 1880 indicate personal differences of the writers with varying degrees of usefulness to the researcher. The 1866 list was originally in Spanish. The persons being confirmed only had their first name but immediately adjoining was the name of the parent, making the child's identification easy. Besides, with only ten candidates for confirmation, doing the deciphering was easy unlike 1880 when the list had increased to 33 and the writer still retained the familiarity of a smaller community, dropping altogether last names.

3-72   In some of the registry entries there were notations about ethnic origin. However, we found them inaccurate and did not bother to rely on them afterwards.

Chapter 4—The 1892 Village Lot Survey

4-73   In the essay by Jean Besson "The appropriation of lands of law by lands of myth in the Caribbean region" (2000: 116-135) she describes squatters in Jamaica overtaking public lands as resistance to their claims of being historically deprived from rights to land.

4-74   Letter from Brother Reynolds Dec. 3, 1887. A.M.D.G. Letters and Notices XIX, 289-290, St. Louis University Jesuit Records.

4-75   Tzul (1993)

4-76   The misspellings of the names are corrected as indicated in Appendix A.

4-77   Kirby and Martin (1972: 23-39). We have observed an identical orientation among the houses currently in Hopkins, Belize, and Starnes (1976: 81-94) made similar observations for the village of Tornabe, Honduras, during a survey she made in the early 1970s.

4-78   Forte (2005)

4-79   Using secondary information for the 1870-1890 period Gullick (1976: 37) notes, "These [villages] were inhabited by a mixture of Creole, Black Caribs, and Spaniards. Each race had its own district in the settlement, and kept to it."

4-80   Letter from Brother Reynolds Dec. 3, 1887. *A.M.D.G. Letters and Notices XIX*, 289-290, St. Louis University Jesuit Records.

4-81   Bolland and Shoman (1977:90) give a point of reference for 1859, with the rent charged for each lot in Dangriga being $1.00 (Bolland 1977: 90), while the average (Indian) labourer earned only $7.00 to $8.00 per month.

Chapter 5—The Village Lots 1893–2000

5-82   Besson (2002)

5-83   Greenfield (1960)

5-84   Besson (2002) and Rubenstein (1987)

5-85   Smith (1965)

5-86   Besson (2002)

5-87   Gonzalez (1968:12)

5-88   Helms and Loveland (1976:151)

5-89   This analysis follows from Marshall Sahlins' discussion on generalized, balanced, and negative reciprocity (Sahlins, 1972).

5-90   Belize Archives

5-91   In 1857 a Crown Surveyor referred to the Dangriga Caribs calling lease documents "their" papers (Bolland and Shoman 1977:91).

5-92   We are grateful to Marty Arana for sharing her family's land documents.

5-93   *Honduras Gazette,* No. 320, 28 April 1924.

5-94   The distinction between lineal and collateral kinship systems together with their influence on behaviour is discussed in Schusky (1983: 14-15).

5-95   This analysis follows from Marshall Sahlins' discussion on generalized, balanced, and negative reciprocity (Sahlins 1972).

5-96   Apart from the studies by Besson (2002) and Smith (1965), due to their synchronic scope, most studies within region need to make conjectures on what it could have been over time (Rubenstein, 1987).

Chapter 6 Farmlands

6-97   Davidson (1976: 85-94)

6-98   Lundberg (1978)

6-99   *Honduras Gazette* (1894)

6-100 *Honduras Gazette* (11 April, 1899)

6-101 The inferences for this suggestion come from house lot and farmland tenure records. D.S. Wells had close business relations with Cramer. In 1894 he bought three seafront lots in Barranco, Nos. 62, 63, and 64, all of which he passed onto Eusebio Polonio. Between 1908 and 1923 Polonio got on lease 60 acres in the Sundaywood area, bordering lands owned by Cramer.

6-102 Lundberg (1978) and oral tradition

6-103 Lundberg (1978)

6-104 Gonzalez (1976: 32)

6-105 G. A. Elliott., 1954 Anual Report, Department of Surveys.

6-106 Lundberg (1978)

6-107 Davidson (1976)

6-108 Herman J. Cramer, the son of T.J. Bernard Cramer, died in 1947 and left behind over 70,000 acres of land in the Toledo District subdivided as follows–28,700 acres along the Temash, 10,500 along the Sarstoon, and 34,000 along the Moho (Belize Archives Department Probate Box No. 34, 1948, #11).

6-109 Minute Paper No. 1350/1905, which extends from 1905 to 1912, Belize National Archives. The entire Minute Paper is transcribed in Appendix D.

6-110 Candido H.Arzu was interviewed by Joseph O. Palacio in November, 1978.

6-111 On Plan 541 there was no number indicated. We had assigned 540 to this parcel before learning that it was called "Section 10".

6-112 These parcles are given the 1913 date because they were approved before 1913 and appeared on the 1913 map in ink. We don't know the actual date of appproval.

6-113 Moberg (1996) and Cal (1991)

6-114 For a critique of the location ticket system together with recommendations for its improvement see Wright, *et al* (1959: 262-279).

6-115 Palacio (2006: 177-196)

6-116 Palacio (2005: 230-250).

8-117 Statutory Instrument 42 of 1994. This declaration was a follow-up to a national survey of the mangroves of Belize that was carried out in 1991 by the Department of Geography, University of Edinburgh, Scotland, and the Forest Department, Ministry of Natural Resources. (Zisman 1992)

6-118 Zisman, personal communication

6-119 Lumb and Horwich (1998)

6-120 SATIIM registered as a not-for-profit corporation in 1999. The Board of Directors includes Representatives from the five villages, Barranco, Conejo, Crique Sarco, Midway, and Sundaywood, as well as Representatives from the National Garifuna Council, Q'eqchi' Council of Belize, Toledo Alcalde Association and the Forest Department. The Chairman of the SATIIM Board of Directors has always been a Baranguna, Marian Cayetano for two terms, Alvin Loredo for two terms and now Alejandro Rodriguez.

6-121 Herrera (2004)

6-122 Herrera (2004: 53-54)

6-123 SATIIM (2010)

6-124 SATIIM (2006: 13)

6-125 Meerman (2006: 15)

Chapter 7—Cultural Imprints on the Village Landscape
7-126 Lundberg (1978)

7-127 Richard Stepp and Santiago Ruiz (2005) did the assessment for Barranco.

7-128 Palacio (2001, 2004) and Palacio, *et al,* 2006: 78-104). Further afield in the Atlantic Ocean between Venezuela and the Lesser Antilles, Honychurch (2002) has reconstructed what adjustments the first Arawakans from South America would have had to undergo in Pre-Columbian times on establishing their early settlements in the islands, which had completely different rock forms, flora and fauna, and overall physical environments. In his study Honychurch focused on figurines and other artefacts used by the settlers as reference markers in their cultural transformation from mainlanders to islanders.

7-129 Foster (2005)

7-130 Nicholas (2004: 33-34)

7-131 This is the beginning of a poem by Marcella Lewis from her book, *Walagante Marcella: Marcella Our Legacy*, published in 1994.

7-132 "Drums of our Fathers" by E. Roy Cayetano is a well known poem that is often performed in Belize. The last stanza is shown here.

7-133 Lundberg (1978: 59)

7-134 Lundberg (1978: 155) quotes a similar version of this lore.

7-135 England (2006)

7-136 Johnson (2007)

7-137 Assad Shoman, personal communication

7-138 Laviolette (2003: 215-240)

7-139 Anderson (2007:384-413) and Thorne (2004:21-25)

7-140 Noe (2001)

7-141 "Miami" is on the compact disc *Watina* by Andy Palacio and the Garifuna Collective, produced by Stone Tree Records, 2008Chapter 8—Conclusions and Future Perspectives

7-142 Belize Archives

Chapter 8—Cultural Imprints on the Village Landscape

8-143 "Nation" as an imaginary concept has been used in the literature mainly during 19th century Europe.

8-144 Merlan (2009), Bolland (2006), Clay (1996: 188-189), Corntassel (2003: 75-100), Forte (2006), Anderson (2007)

8-145 Kirby and Martin (1972) Note that some modern day Garifuna have emphasized their African roots while neglecting mention of the Amerindian Izard (2005).

8-146 Davidson (1984)

Bibliography

Anderson, Mark, 1997. The significance of blackness: representations of Garifuna in St. Vincent and Central America 1700–1900. *Transforming Anthropology* 6 (1–2): 22–35.

Anderson, Mark, 2007. Where Afro becomes (like) indigenous: Garifuna and Afro–Indigenous politics in Honduras. *Journal of Latin America and the Caribbean 12* (2): 384–413.

Anderson, Mark, 2009. *Black and Indigenous: Garifuna Activism and consumer Culture in Honduras.* Minneapolis MN: University of Minnesota Press

Arrivillaga, Alfonso, 2005. Marcos Sanchez Diaz: from hero to híuraha–200 years of Garifuna settlement in Central America. In J.O. Palacio, ed., *The Garifuna: A Nation across Borders*, pp. 64–84. Belize: Cubola Books.

Ashcraft, Norman, 1973. *Colonialism and underdevelopment: processes of political economic change in British Honduras.* New York: Teachers College Press, Columbia University.

Ashdown, Peter, 1978. Antonio Soberanis and the disturbances in Belize 1935–37. *Caribbean Quarterly* 24 (No.1 & 2, March–June): 61–74.

Barnett, Carla Natalie, 1991. *The Political economy of land in Belize: "Machete Must fly".* Doctoral Dissertation. Jamaica: University of the West Indies.

Barth , Fredrik, 1956. Ecological relationship of ethnic groups in Swat, North Pakistan. *American Anthropologist* 58: 1079-1089.

Beckles, Hilary McD, 1992. Kalinago (Carib) resistance to colonization. *CARICOM Perspective,* 54 & 5: 15–18.

Beckles, Hilary and Verene Shepherd, Eds., 1996. *Caribbean Freedom: Economy and society from emancipation to the present.* Princeton: Markus Weiner Publishers

Besson, Jean, 2000. The appropriation of lands of law by lands of myth in the Caribbean Region. In *Land, law, and environment–mythical land, legal boundaries*, A. Abramson and D. Theodossopoulos, Eds., pp. 116–135). London: Pluto Press.

Besson, Jean, 2002. *Martha Brae's Two Histories: European expansion and Caribbean culture building in Jamaica.* Jamaica: Ian Randle Publishers Ltd.

Bilby, Ken, 1996. Ethnogenesis in the Guianas and Jamaica: two maroon cases. In Jonathan D. Hill, ed., *History, Power, and identity: ethnogenesis in the Americas 1492-1992*. Iowa City: University of Iowa Press, pp. 119–141.

Bishop, Andrew, 2003. Presentation to the Committee on Trade and Economic Development (COTED). In Allan N. Williams, ed. *Land in the Caribbean: Issues of policy, administration and management in the English–speaking Caribbean.* (pp. 1–4). University of Wisconsin–Madison: Land Tenure Center.

Bolland, O. Nigel, 1977. *The formation of a colonial society: Belize from conquest to crown colony.* Baltimore and London: Johns Hopkins University Press.

Bolland, O. Nigel, 1987a. African Continuities and Creole Culture in Belize Town in the Nineteenth Century. *African-Caribbean Institute of Jamaica Res. Rev.* 2: 63–82.

Bolland, O. Nigel, 1987b. Alcaldes and reservations: British policy toward the Maya in the late 19th century, Belize. *America Indigena XLVII*, 33–76.

Bolland, O. Nigel, 1987c. Race ethnicity and national integration in Belize. *Belize ethnicity and development,* First Annual Studies on Belize Conference. Belize: Society for the Promotion of Education and Research.

Bolland, O. Nigel, 1988. *Colonialism and resistance: Essays in historical sociology,* Institute for Social and Economic Research, University of the West Indies, Jamaica; Society for the Promotion of Education and Research, Belize. Belize: Cubola Productions.

Bolland, O. Nigel, 2006. Caribbean culture and identities: Interpreting Garifuna Stories. The Elsa Goveia Memorial Lecture, Department of History and Archaeology, University of the West Indies, Jamaica.

Bolland, O. Nigel, and Assad Shoman, 1977. *Land in Belize 1765–1871.* Institute of Social and Economic Research, University of West Indies.

Bonfil, Antonio Higuera, 2002. *Quintana Roo entre tiempos: Politica, poblamiento y explotacion, forestal, 1872–1925.* Chetumal, Mexico: Instituto Quintanarroense de la Cultura, Universidad de Quntana Roo.

Bristowe, Lindsay and Philip B. Wright, 1888. *Handbook of British Honduras, 1888–1889.* London: H.M. Stationery Office.

Brondo, Keri V., 2010. When Mestizo becomes (like) Indio ... or is it Garifuna? Multicultural rights and "making space" on Honduras north coast. *Journal of Latin American and Caribbean Anthropology* 15 (1): 170–194.

Burdon, J.A., ed., 1933–35. *Archives of British Honduras 1–3*. London: Sifton Praed and Co.

Burton, R., 1685. *The English Empire in America*. London: Nathan Crouch.

Caiger, S. L., 1951. *British Honduras past and present*. London: Allen and Unwin.

Cal, Angel Eduardo, 1991. *Rural society and economic development: British Mercantile capital in nineteenth-century Belize*. Ph.D dissertation. Tempe, Arizona: University of Arizona.

Camille, Michael A., 1986. Historical geography of the U.S. Confederate settlement at Toledo, Belize: 1868–1930. *Belcast Journal of Belizean Affairs* 3 (Nos. 1 and 2): 39–44.

Canningham, A., 1802. Letter to the Magistrates of British Honduras, 17 December, 1802. in Burdon, J.A., ed. 1933–35. *Archives of British Honduras II*, p. 60. London: Sifton Praed and Co.

Carnegie, Charles V., 1987. Is family land an institution? In *Afro-Caribbean villages in perspective* (pp. 83–99). African-Caribbean Institute of Jamaica.

Carey, Beverly, 1997. *The Maroon Story: The authentic and original history of the Maroons in the History of Jamaica 1490–1880*. Jamaica: Agouti Press.

Cayetano, Eldrid Roy, 1977. Garifuna songs of mourning. *Belizean Studies 5* (2): 17–26.

Cayetano, Marion and Roy Cayetano, 2005. Garifuna language, dance, and music–a masterpiece of oral and intangible heritage of humanity. How did it happen? In J.O. Palacio, ed., *The Garifuna: A Nation across Borders*, (pp. 64–84). Belize: Cubola Books.

Cayetano, Sebastian, no date. *Garifuna history, language, and culture of Belize, Central America, & the Caribbean.*

Cayetano, Sebastian, and Fabian Cayetano, 1997. *Garifuna history, language, and culture of Belize, Central America, & the Caribbean.*

Clay, J. W., 1996. What's a nation? In W.A. Haviland and R.J. Gordon Eds. *Talking about People* (2nd Ed.), Mountain View, CA: Mayfield

Clegern, Wayne M., 1967. *British Honduras: colonial dead end, 1859–1900.* Lousiana State University Press: Baton Rouge.

Clegern, Wayne, 1968. Maudslay's Central America: A strategic view in 1887. *Studies in Middle American Economics 29.* New Orleans, Louisiana: Tulane University Middle American Research Institute.

Conteh, Abdulai, 2007. Judgment in the Supreme Court of Belize Claim No. 171 of 2007 and Claim 172 of 2007.

Corntassel, J., 2003. Who is Indigenous? "peoplehood" and ethno-nationalist approaches to rearticulating indigenous identity, *Nationalism and Ethnic Politics* 9 (1): 75–100.

Craig, Alan K, 1966. *Geography of fishing in British Honduras and adjacent c.oastal waters.* Baton Rouge: Louisiana State University Press.

Craton, Michael (1984. *Testing the chains: Resistance to slavery in the British West Indies.* Ithaca: Cornell University Press.

Crawford, Michael H., ed., 1984. Black Carib: a case study in beiocultural adaption. *Current Developments in Anthropological Genetics 3,* New York: Plenum Press.

Crichlow, Michaelene A., 2004. Book review of *Martha Brae's two histories, New West Indian Guide* 78 (3/4): 318–320.

Davidson, William V., 1976. Black Carib (Garifuna) habitats in Central America. In M. Helms and F. Loveland, Eds. *Frontier Adaptation in Lower Central America.* Philadelphia: Institute for the Study of Human Issues, pp. 85–94.

Davidson, William V., 1979. Dispersal of the Garifuna in the western Caribbean. *International Congress of Americanists* 6: 467–74.

Davidson, William V., 1980. The Garifuna of Pearl Lagoon: Ethnohistory of an Afro-American enclave in Nicaragua. *Ethnohistory* 27(1): 31–63.

Davidson, William V., 1984. The Garifuna in Central America: ethnohistorical and geographical foundations. In Crawford, M.H. (ed.) *Black Caribs: A Study in Biocultural Adaption. Current Developments in Anthropological Genetics 3*: 13–36.

Dobson, Narda, 1973. *A history of Belize.* Trinidad and Jamaica: Longman Caribbean Ltd.

Downie, Jack, 1959. *An economic policy for British Honduras, 1959.* Archives of Belize.

Dreyfus, Simone, 1982. The relationship between political systems, history, linguistic affiliation, and ethnic identity as exemplified by the XVI to XVIIIth Centuries social organization of the so–called "Island Caribs" (Arawak-speaking) and "True-Speaking Caribs" of the mainland coast. 44th International Congress of Americanists.

Ellis, Godsman, 1999. Garifuna lands in Belize. Presented to the Land Alliance for National Development Workshop, 29 April–1 May, 1999, at the Cockscomb Basin Wildlife Sanctuary, Belize.

England, Sarah, 2006. *Afro Central Americans in New York City: Garifuna tales of transnational movements in racialized space.* Gainesville: University Press of Florida.

Euraque, Dario A., 1998. The banana enclave, nationalism, and Mestizaje in Honduras, 1910s–1930s. In *Identity and struggle at the margins of the nation–state,* Aviva Chomsky and Aldo Lauria–Santiago, ed. Duke University Press: Durham, North Carolina.

Fabel, Robin F.A., 2000. *Colonial challenges: Britons, Native Americans, and Caribs, 1759–1775.* Gainesville, Florida: University Press of Florida.

Finnamore, Daniel R., 1994. *Sailors and slaves on the wood–cutting frontier–archeology of the British Bay Settlement, Belize.* Ph.D. Dissertation. Boston, Massachusetts, USA: Boston University.

Forte, Maximilian C., 2005. *Ruins of absence, presence of Caribs– (post) colonial representations of aboriginality in Trinidad and Tobago.* Gainesville: University Press of Florida.

Forte, Maximilian C., 2006. The dual absences of extinction and marginality—what difference does an indigenous presence make. In *Indigenous Resurgence in the Contemporary Caribbean— Amerindian survival and revival,* Maximilian C. Forte, ed, pp.1–18.

Foster, Byron, 1981. Body, soul and social structure at the Garifuna dügü. *Belizean Studies 9* (4): 1–11.

Foster, Byron, 1982. An interpretation of spirit possession in southern coastal Belize. *Belizean Studies 10* (2): 18–23.

Foster, Byron, 1994. *Heart Drum: Spirit Possession in the Garifuna.* Benque Viejo, Belize: Cubola Productions.

Foster, Byron, 2005. Heart drum: spirit possession in the Garifuna communities of Belize. J.O. Palacio, ed., *The Garifuna: A Nation across Borders,* (pp. 159–175). Belize: Cubola Books.

Gibbs, Archibald Robertson, 1883. *British Honduras: An historical and descriptive account of the colony from its settlement, 1670.* London: Sampson Low.

Gonzalez, Candace, 2000. *Survey of land–related laws of Belize.* Belize: Land Alliance for National Development.

Gonzalez, D., 1961. Memoiras sobre el Departamento del Peten. *Guatemala indigena* 1: 75–102.

Gonzalez, Nancie L., 1959a. The non–unilineal descent group in Central America and the Caribbean. *American Anthropologist* 61: 578–83.

Gonzalez, Nancie L., 1959b. West Indian Characteristics of the Black Carib. *Southwestern Journal of Anthropology* 15:300-7.

Gonzalez, Nancie L., 1969. *Black Carib household organization.* Seattle: University of Washington Press.

Gonzalez, Nancie L., 1976. From Black Carib to Garifuna: The Coming of Age of an Ethnic Group. *Actes* of the Forty-second ICA 6: 57–88.

Gonzalez, Nancie L., 1984. Garifuna (Black Carib) social organization. In Crawford, M.H, ed. *Black Caribs: a study in biocultural adaption. Current Developments in Anthropological Genetics* 3: 51–65.

Gonzalez, Nancie L., 1987. Una mayor recompense en el cielo: actividades de misioneros metodistas entre los amerindios de Belice. America Indígena Vol XLVII, pp. 139–168. Mexico City: Instituto Indigenista Interaméricano.

Gonzalez, Nancie L., 1988. *Sojourners of the Caribbean: ethnogenesis and ethnohistory of the Garifuna.* Urbana and Chicago: University of Illinois Press.

Gonzalez, Nancie L. and Charles D. Cheek, 1986. Garifuna traditions in historical perspective. *Belizean Studies* 14 (2): 11–24.

Greene, Oliver, 2005. Music behind the Mask: men, social commentary and identity in Wanáragua. In J.O. Palacio, ed., *The Garifuna: A Nation across Borders*, pp. 196-229. Belize: Cubola Books.

Greenfield, Sidney M., 1960. Land tenure and transmission in rural Barbados. *Anthropological Quarterly 33* (4): 165–176.

Gullick, Charles, J.M.R.C., 1976. *Exiled from St. Vincent: The development of Black Carib Culture in Central America up to 1945.* Malta: Progress Press.

Gullick, Charles, J.M.R.C., 1984. The changing Vincentian Carib population. In *Current Developments in Anthropological Genetics 3*, Crawford, Michael H., ed., New York: Plenum Press.

Gullick, Charles, J.M.R.C., 1985. *Myths of a minority: The changing traditions of the Vincentian Caribs.* Assen, Netherlands: Royal Van Gorcum.

Hadel, Richard E., 1972. *Carib folk songs and Carib culture.* Ph.D. Dissertation. University of Texas, Austin.

Hadel, Richard E., 1975. Male and female speech in Carib. *National Studies* 3 (4): 32–36.

Hall, Stuart, 1992. New ethnicities. In J. Donald and A. Rattansi, Eds. *Race, culture and difference.* London: Sage.

Handler, Richard and Jocelyn Linnekin, 1984. Tradition, genuine or spurious. *Journal of American Folklore.* 97 (385): 273–90.

Harper, Laurie Greene, 1987. Language and ethnicity in Belize. Caribbean Studies Association XII International Congress, Belize City.

Haviland, William A., 2002. *Cultural Anthropology* (10th ed.). Glendale CA: Thomson Learning, Inc., pp. 192–4.

Helms, Mary W., 1981. Black Carib domestic organization in historical perspective: Traditional origins of contemporary patterns. *Ethnology* 20: 77–86.

Helms, Mary W. and Franklin O. Loveland, 1976. Introduction to James Howe's "Communal land tenure and the origin of descent groups among the San Blas Cuna," pp. 151–152. In Mary W. Helms and Franklin O. Loveland (Eds.). *Frontier Adaptations in Lower Central America.* Philadelphia: Institute for the Study of Human Issues.

Herrera, Allan, 2004. *Sarstoon-Temash National Park Management Plan,* Punta Gorda, Belize

Hoffmann, Odile, 2007. *Comunidades negras en el pacific colombiano.* Mexico: Centre d'Etudes Mexicianes et Centre Americaines, Mexico (CEMCA).

Holm, John, 1978. Caribs in Central America. *Belizean Studies* 6 (6): 23-32.

Honychurch, Lennox, 2002. The leap at Sauters: the lost cosmology of indigenous Grenada. <http://www.uwichill.edu.bb/bncdde/grenada/conference/paperdex.html> (accessed January 2, 2010).

Hooker, Juliet, 2005. Indigenous Inclusion/Black Exclusion: Race, ethnicity and multicultural citizenship in Latin America. *Journal of Latin American Studies* 37:1–26.

Humphreys, R.A., 1961. *The Diplomatic history of British Honduras 1638–1901.* London: Oxford University Press.

Hutson, Sir E., 1925. *The handbook of British Honduras.* London.

Hunter-Krohn, Lita, ed. 1987. *Readings in Belizean History* (2nd Ed.). Belize City: Belizean Studies, St. John's College.

Iyo, Joe, *et al*, 2002. Belize: Land policy, administration and management in Belize. In Allan N. Williams, ed. *Land in the Caribbean: Issues of policy, administration and management in the English–speaking Caribbean,* pp. 141–174. University of Wisconsin–Madison: Land Tenure Center.

Izard, Gabriel, 2005. Patrimonal Activation and Construction of Garifuna Identity in Contemporary Belize. In J.O. Palacio, ed., *The Garifuna: A Nation across Borders*, pp. 176-195. Belize: Cubola Books.

Jacobs, Curtis, 2003. The Brigands's War in St. Vincent: The View from the French Records, 1794-1796. Paper presented at the St.Vincent and the Grenadines Country Conference.

Johnson, Melissa A, 2005. Racing nature and naturalizing race–rethinking of the nature of Creole and Garifuna identities. *Belizean Studies* 27 (2): 43–56.

Johnson, Paul Christopher, 2007. *Diaspora conversion: Black Carib religion and the recovery of Africa.* Berkeley: University of California Press.

Jones, Carey N.J., 1953. *The Patterns of a Dependent Economy: The national income of British Honduras.* Cambridge: Cambridge University Press.

Kerns, Virginia, 1983. *Women and the ancestors: Black Carib kinship and ritual.* Chicago: University of Illinois Press.

Kerns, Virginia, 1984. Past and present evidence of interethnic mating. In Crawford, M.H., ed. *Black Caribs: a study in biocultural adaption. Current Developments in Anthropological Genetics 3*: 95–114.

Kirby, E.I. and C.I. Martin, 1972. *The rise and fall of the Black Caribs of St. Vincent.* St. Vincent.

Laviolette, P, 2003. Landscaping death: Resting places for Cornish identity. *Journal of Material Culture* 8 (2): 215–240.

Lewis, Marcella, 1994. *Walgante Marcela: Marcella our legacy.* Caye Caulker, Belize: *Producciones de la Hamaca.*

Lumb and Horwich, 1998. *Sarstoon-Temash National Park: Transcript of Stakeholders' Workshop.* Caye Caulker, Belize: *Producciones de la Hamaca.*

Lundberg, Paul Arthur, 1978. Barranco: A sketch of a Belizean Garifuna (Black Carib) habitat. MS thesis, University of California at Riverside.

Marshall, Bernard, 1973. The Black Caribs: Resistance to British penetration in the windward side of St. Vincent. *Caribbean Quarterly* 19 (4): 4–19.

Meerman, Jan, 2006. A New Ecosystem for Belize. *BAS Newsletter* 38 (2): 10-14

Merlan, Francesca, 2009. Indigeneity: Global and Local with Current Anthropology comments, *Current Anthropology* 50 (3): 303-334.

Merzgen, Monrad Sigfrid, and Henry Edney Conrad Cain, 1925. *Handbook of British Honduras.* London: The West India Committee

Miller, David L, 1979. *The European impact on St. Vincent, 1600– 1763: Suppression and displacement of the native populations and landscapes.* MS Thesis, University of Wisconsin, Milwaukee.

Mintz, Sidney, 1974. *Caribbean transformations.* Baltimore: The Johns Hopkins University Press.

Mintz, Sidney W., 1984. *Sweetness and power.* New York: Viking Press.

Mintz, Sidney W., 1987. 1–19

Mintz, Sidney W., 1989. *Caribbean transformations.* Morningside Edition. New York: Columbia University Press.

Mintz, Sidney, W., 1996. Enduring substances, trying theories– the Caribbean region as *Oikoumenê. Journal of the Royal Anthropological Institute* 2 (2): 289–311.

Moberg, Mark, 1996. Crown colony as banana republic: The United Fruit Company in British Honduras, 1900–1920. *J. Latin American Studies* 28: 357–81.

Moberg, Mark, 2005. Continuity Under Colonial Rule: The Alcalde System. In J.O. Palacio, ed., *The Garifuna: A Nation across Borders,* pp. 196–229. Belize: Cubola Books.

Morris, Daniel, 1883. *The colony of British Honduras, Its resources and prospects.* London: Edward Stanford.

Ng'weno, Bettina, 2007. Can ethnicity replace race? Afro-Colombians, Indigeneity and the Colombian multicultural state. *Journal of Latin American and Caribbean Studies* 12 (2): 414–440.

Nicholas, Victor J., 2004. *The Poems: Vinland, Barranco*. Belmopan: University of Belize.

Noe, Sue Y, 2001. *Land rights of the Garifuna of Belize: a preliminary analysis under domestic and international law*. International Human Rights Advocacy Center, University of Denver, Denver, Colorado.

Palacio, Joseph O., 1983. Food and body in Garifuna belief systems. *Cajanus* 16 (3): 148–60.

Palacio, Joseph O., 1984. Food and social relations in a Belizean Garifuna village. *Belizean Studies* 12 (3), 1–35.

Palacio, Joseph O., 1986. *Report on a study of the 1984 amnesty–"illegal aliens" in Belize*. Hemispheric Migration Project, Centre for Immigration Policy and Refugee Assistance. Washington, D.C.: Georgetown University.

Palacio, Joseph O., 1995. Aboriginal peoples—their struggle with cultural identity in the CARICOM region. *Bulletin of Eastern Caribbean Affairs* 20 (4): 25-40.

Palacio, Joseph O., 1997. Gulisi, a daughter of the Paramount Chief Joseph Chatoyer. *Belize Historical Society Newsletter* May/June issue.

Palacio, Joseph O., 2001. Coastal Traditional Knowledge and Cultural Values: their significance to the Garifuna and the rest of the Caribbean region. <cavehil.uwi.edu/bnccde/belize/conference/papers /palacio.html> accessed January 2, 2010.

Palacio, Joseph O., 2004. Exploring Spirituality, Income Generation, and the use of Coastal Resources among the Garifuna in Southern Belize. Final Project Report to the IDRC–CBRM Programme for the Caribbean.

Palacio, Joseph O., 2005. Reconstructing Garifuna oral history–techniques and methods in the history of a Caribbean people. In J.O. Palacio, ed., *The Garifuna: A Nation across Borders*, (pp. 64–84). Belize: Cubola Books.

Palacio, Joseph O., 2006. Cultural Identity among Rural Garifuna Migrants in Belize City, Belize. In Maximilian C. Forte, ed. *Indigenous Resurgence in the contemporary Caribbean: Amerindian survival and revival*. New York: Peter Lang Publishing.

Palacio Joseph O., 2010. House lot tenure in Barranco, southern Belize—Opening the family chest. *Garifunas y problemas emergentes en Mesoamerica* 5 (8): 5–29, Revista Pueblo y Fronteras Digital <pueblosyfronteras.unam.mx/a09n8/art_01.html>

Palacio, Joseph, Camilo Coral, and Hugo Hidalgo, 2006. Territoriality, technical revitalization, and symbolism in indigenous communities. In Y. Breton, D. Brown, B. Davy, M. Haughton, and L. Ovares. (Eds). *Coastal Resource Management in the Wider Caribbean – resilience, adaptation and community diversity.* Kingston: Ian Randle Publishers for the IDRC, Ottawa, pp. 78–104.

Palacio Joseph, Judith Rae Lumb, and Carlson Tuttle, 2008. The power of the survey line, the first lot survey in Barranco, southern Belize.

Payne Iglesias, 2008. Presentación del Padrón de Truxillo de 1821. <afehc-historia-centroamericana.org/index.php?action=fi_aff&id=2046>

di Pietro , S., 1880. Letter from Father S. di Pietro to Father Provincial dated July 30, 1880. *A. M. D. G. Letters and Notices XIII*

Ramos, Adele, 2000. *Thomas Vincent Ramos: The Man and His Writings.* Dangriga, Belize: National Garifuna Council.

Report of enquiry of Board of Public Offices on the Survey Department, 31 January 1884, R. 118, pp 159–71 Archives of Belize.

Rey, Nicolás, 2010. La movilización de los Garífuna para preservar sus tierras "ancestrales" en Guatemala. *Revista Pueblos y Fronteras digital* 5 (8): 30-59.

Reynolds, Brother, 1887. *A. M. D. G. Letters and Notices XIX*, 289 –90, Jesuit Archives, St. Louis (December 3, 1887).

Robinson, St. John, 2006. *Peopling Belize: Chapters in migration.* Belize City: Institute of Social and Cultural Research (ISCR)

Rosenberger, D.G, 1958. An examiniation of the perpetuity of southern US institutions in British Honduras by a colony of ex–confederates. D.Ed. dissertation, School of Education. New York: New York University.

Rouse, Irving, 1956. Settlement patterns in the Caribbean area. In Gordon Wiley, ed.) *Pre-historic settlement patterns in the New World.* (pp. 165–72). New York: Viking Fund Publications in Anthropology, No. 23.

Rubinstein, Hymie, 1983. Remittances and rural underdevelopment in the English–speaking Caribbean. *Human Organization 42* (4): 295–306.

Rubenstein, Hymie, 1987. *Coping with poverty: Adaptive strategies in a Caribbean village.* Boulder: Westview Press.

Sahlins, Marshall, 1972. *Stone Age Economics.* Chicago: Aldine-Atherton.

Sambola, Kensy, 2007. *Territorialidad de la comunidad de Orinoco desde la cosmovisión Garífuna.* M.A. thesis in Social Anthropology, Universidad de las Regiones Autonomas de la Costa Nicaragüense, URACAN.

SATIIM, 2006. Statement of the Sarstoon Temash Institute for Indigenous Management to the General Public on the Issue of Oil Exploration in the Sarstoon Temash National Park. *BAS Newsletter* 38 (2): 10–14.

SATIIM, 2010. *Community Management of Shrimp Nurseries: Enhancing the Sustainable Use of Resources in the Marine Area Adjacent to the Sarstoon Temash National Park in the Gulf of Honduras.* Caye Caulker, Belize: *Producciones de la Hamaca*

Saunt, Claudio, 2005. *Black, White, and Indian: Race and the unmaking of an American family.* Oxford: Oxford University Press.

Schlesinger, Stephen, and Stephen Kinzer, 1982. *Bitter Fruit.* Garden City, New York: Anchor Books.

Schusky, Ernest L., 1983. *Manual for Kinship Analysis, 2nd Ed.* Lanham MD: University Press of America, Inc. p. 14–15).

Shoman, Assad, 1994. *Thirteen chapters of a history of Belize.* Belize: The Angelus Press.

Simmons, Donald C., Jr, 2001. *Confederate settlements in British Honduras.* North Carolina, USA: McFarland and Co.

Smith, M.G., 1965. The transformation of land rights by transmission in Carriacou. In M.G. Smith, ed. *The Plural Society in the British West Indies.* (pp. 221–261). Berkeley: University of California Press.

Solien, Nancie L., 1959. The nonunilineal descent group in the Caribbean and Central America. *American Anthropologist* 61: 578–583.

Starnes, Sylvia K., 1976. House styles and other settlement features of Tornabe, Honduras. In *Field Studies in Central America–Tela and vicinity, Honduras,* pp. 81–94. Baton Rouge, Louisiana, Dept of Geography and Anthropology.

Stephens, John L., 1841. *Incidents of Travel in Central America, Chiapas Yucatan* Vol. I. New York: Dover Publications (reprinted 1969).

Stepp, Richard and Santiago Ruiz, 2005. Garifuna traditional knowledge and natural resource management in the Sarstoon–Temash Region. *SATIIM Reports.*

Sullivan, Paul, 2000. John Carmichael–life and design on the frontier in Central America. *Revista Mexicana del Caribe* 10: 6–88.

Taylor, Douglas, 1946. Kinship and social structure of the Island Carib. Southwestern Journal of Anthopology 2:180–212.

Taylor, Douglas, 1951. The Black Caribs of British Honduras. New York: Viking Fund Publications in Anthropology, No. 17, p. 27–31.

Taylor, Douglas, and Irving Rouse, 1955. Linguistic and archeological time depth in the West Indies. *International Journal of American Linguistics* 21:105–15.

du Tertre, Jean–Baptiste, 1667–71. *Histoire générale des Antilles habitués par les François 2*. Paris: T. Jolly.

Thorne, Eva, 2004. Land rights and Garifuna identity. *NACLA Report on the Americas* 38 (2): 21–25.

Thomson, P.A.B., 2004. *Belize: A Concise History.* Oxford: Macmillan Publishers, Ltd.

Topsey, Harriot, 1987. The ethnic war in Belize. *Belize ethnicity and development,* First Annual Studies on Belize Conference. Belize: Society for the Promotion of Education and Research.

Tzul, Alfonso Ambrosio, 1993. *After 100 years of isolation, determination, and industry—the oral history and traditions of San Antonio, Cayo District, Belize.* Belize: U Kustal Masewal, Maya Institute of Belize.

Villalobos, Martha Herminia Gonzalez, 2006. *El Bosque Sitiado: Asaltos armados, concesiones forestaes y estratgias de resistencia durante la Guerra de Castra.* Mexico City: Conaculta-INAH.

Wade, Peter, 1995. The cultural politics of blackness in Colombia. *American Ethnologist* 22(2): 341–357.

Whipple, Emory, 1971. The Music of the Black Caribs of British Honduras. M.A. thesis, University of Texas, Austin.

Wilk, Richard R, 1991. *Household ecology: Economic change and domestic life among the Kekchi Maya in Belize.* Tucson, Arizona: University of Arizona Press.

Williams (2003)

Woodward, Ralph Lee, Jr, 1976. *Central America: A nation divided.* New York: Oxford University Press.

Wright, Charles, D.H. Romney, R.H. Arbuckle, and V.E. Vial, 1959. *Land in British Honduras, report of the British Honduras Land Use*

Survey Team. D.H. Romney, ed. London: Her Majesty's Stationery Office.

Young, Thomas, 1847. *Narrative of a residence on the Mosquito Shore.* London: Smith, Elder and Co.

Young, William, 1764. *Consideration which may tend to promote the settlement of our new West-India Colonies by encouragement of individuals to embark on the undertaking.* London: James Robson.

Young, William, 1795. *An account of Black Charaibs in the island of St. Vincent.* Reprinted in 1971. London: Frank Cass.

Zisman, Simon, 1992. *Mangroves in Belize: Forest Planning and Management Project for the Belize Forest Department*, Belmopan, Belize. Belize: Belize Government Printery.

Appendices

To avoid confusion with the designations for tables in the chapters, the tables in the Appendices are labeled with the Appendix letter, the chapter number, and then sequential numbers. For example, Table C3.2. Garifua Marriages in Barranco, is in Appendix B, from Chapter 3, and is the second table from that chapter.

Appendix A
Name Index

Table A1.1. Name Misspelling Index

Given Name	Surame	Misspellings / Other names
Serapia	Alvarez	Serapia de Jesus, Serapia de Jesus Nolberto, Serapia Teus, Serapia Flores, Serafina Garcia, Serapia Nolberto, and Josefa Secundino
Blasisia	Apolonio	Blacuina Apolonio
Patricio	Ariola	Patriocio Hariola
Rufino	Ariola	Rapino Reolo
Ambrocio	Avilez	Narciano Vivilas
Santiago	Avilez	Santiago Avelez
Florencia	Blas	Florencia Blass
Balbino	Burgos	Balbino Borgos
Inez	Castillo	Enis Castillo
Luis	Castillo	Luis Caleso
Maria Baltazar	Castillo	Maria Baretha Carleuz
Vivciona	Cayetano	Vivciona, Venderana, Beltrana
Eugenio	Cayetano	Eugenio McKenzie
Tiburcio	Fernandez	Tibrucio Fernando
Ciriaco	Francisco	Sariaco Francisco
Jose Apolinario	Garcia	Paulino Regarcia
Maximiliano	Garcia	Maximiliana Garcia, Smith Garcia, Esmith Garcia
Basilio	Gutierrez	Basilio Gutierez
Fermin	Jimenez	Fermin Jiminez
Eugenio	Kuylen	Eujenio Kuylen
Antonio	Lambey	Antonio Lamby
Desideria	Lambey	Martina Francisca Desideria, Desideria Alvarez, Francisca Isideria, Quiteria, Francisca Desideria
Jane	Lambey	Jane Lamby
John	Lambey	John Lamby, Lambi
Rosa Mistica	Lambey	Rafaelo Rosa, Rosa Lamby, Rafaela La Rosa, Rosa Miguel
Leocardio	Lopez	Leocadio Lopez

Given Name	Surame	Misspellings / Other names
Manuel	Lorenzo	Manuel Livindo
Eduardo	Luis	Luis Lamby
Lenadro	Luis	Leonardo Luis
Simon	Mejia	Simon Magill, Simon Miguel
Nicolasa	Moralez	Nicolaso Morallis, Nicholasa Noralez
Alexander	Nicholas	Alejandro Casimiro, Joseph Alexander Nicholas
Andrea	Nicholas	Arihenia Nicolas
Casimira	Nicholas	Casimira Leandro
Leoncio	Nicholas	Ygnacio Nicholas
Ciriaco	Nolberto	Cirrio Alberto
Macario	Nolberto	Nasario Nolberto
Pio	Nolberto	Peon Alberto
Cristino	Ortiz	Christillo Ortez
Anastacio	Palacio	Anistacio Palacio
Martires Coronados	Palacio	Marcello Palacio
Norberto	Palacio	Alberto Palacio
Ruben	Palacio	Gregorio Ruben Palacio
Theodoro	Palacio	Teodoro, Theodora Palacio
Vivana	Palacio	Bibiana Palacio
Ascenciona	Paulino	Ausencion Paulino
Narciso	Paulino	Narcisso Vispo, Obispo Lino, or Narciso Obispo, or Bishop Lino
Victoria	Peña	Victoria Paria
Mauricio	Polonio	Mauritio, Nauritio Polonio
Antolino	Requeña	Anbeleno Ricano, Anteleno Recano
Philip	Santino	Phillipio Santino
Norberto	Santos	Alberto Santios
Louisa	Santos	Santos Louisa
Eleuteria	Satuye	Lauteria Satuye
Juan Bautista	Teo	Juano Bropliola Reno
Procopio	Torres	Procopio Tones
Augustino	Vairez	Augustino Berez
Francisco	Vairez	Francisco Vera
Serapio	Vairez	Serapio Viras, Virez, Bairez, Bayrez
Tomas	Vairez	Tomas Viera

Appendix B—The Founding of Barranco

Table B3.1. Garifuna Birth and Baptism in Barranco

Before 1884 birth dates were gleaned from baptism records that also state the birth date. After 1884 there are also government records when births were registered. There are gaps in the records where the information was not available or could not be deciphered.

Given Name	Surname	Birth	Baptism
Maria Loretta	Palacio	1862-12-10	1862-12-31
Andrea	Cayetano	1863-02-04	1863-02-21
Dominga	Marin	1863-08-03	1863-08-28
Eustachio*	Paulino	1863-08-20	
Macario	Nolberto	1864-03-08	1864-05-27
Alexandra	Nicholas	1864-05-03	1864-06-11
Justina	Cayetano	1865-09-25	1865-09-27
Francisco Xavier	Sanchez	1865-12-06	1866-01-03
Delfina	Paulino	1865-12-24	1866-02-21
Gregoria	Nolberto	1866-05-25	1866-05-03
Casimira	Nicholas	1868-03-04	1868-03-31
Petrona**	Cayetano	1868-04-03	1868-06-07
Eleuteria	Cayetano	1868-04-18	1868-05-30
Nolberto	Palacio	1868-06-06	1868-06-20
John Baptist	Palacio	1868-08-18	1868-09-21
Josefa	Paulino	1868-08-27	1868-09-02
Philip Neri Henry	Sanchez	1870-05	1870-06-10
Jose Apolinario	Garcia	1870-05-29	1870-06-10
Lucia	Nicholas	1871	1871-03-03
Augustin	Castillo	1871-02-21	1871-02-22
Eustaquia	Palacio	1871-11-01	1871-11-26
Alberta	Nolberto	1872-03-28	1872-04-27
Policarpio	Paulino	1873-01-20	1873-02-18
Hilario	Sanchez	1878-03	1878-03
Vincenta	Castillo	1878-07-22	1879-02-07
Stephen	Trigueno		1879-06

*Birth or baptism in Punta Gorda, but involves Baranguna.
**Birth and baptism in Livingston, but involves Baranguna.

Given Name	Surname	Birth	Baptism
Juan	Garcia		1879-06-26
Sebastian	Garcia	1879-12-05	1880-01-27
Santita	Reyes	1880-01-04	1880-01-27
Martires Coronado	Palacio	1881-12-02	1882-02-11
Juliana	Garcia	1882-02-16	1882-05-22
Marcelina	Gamboa	1884-01-16	
Gabian Sebastian	Palacio	1884-01-20	1884-02-07
Romalda	Zuniga	1884-02-07	1884-02-08
John de Malha	Palacio	1884-02-08	1884-02-08
Philippa	Garcia	1884-05-01	1884-06-09
Juana	Nolberto	1884-05-24	1884-06-09
Gregorio	Cayetano	1884-11-28	1885-02-7
Eusabio	Paulino	1884-12-16	
Felicita	Bermudez	1885-02-21	1885-04-25
Anaseto	Nicholas	1885-04-17	1885-04-30
Bernardina	Santino	1885-05-20	1885-07-11
Bruno	Nolberto	1885-10-6	1885-07-11
Felicita	Reyes	1886-07-12	1886-08-03
Nicolasa	Zuniga	1887-02-03	1887-03-27
Josepha	Paulino	1887-03-19	1887-03-27
Isidora	Bermudez	1887-04-04	1887-04-19
Marcelino*	Castillo	1887-04-26	
Brigida	Paulino	1887-10-08	1887-12-09
Felicia	Diaz	1887-10-23	
Barcamia	Gamboa	1888-01-02	
Scholactica	Santino	1888-02-10	1888-03-20
Gabina	Zuniga	1888-02-19	1888-03-01
Juana (Jane)	Palacio	1888-03-08	1888-06-13
Benita	Andrade	1888-03-21	
Pablo	Jimenez	1888-06-07	1888-07-01
Romana*	Nolberto	1888-08-03	
Maxima	Ariola	1888-11-16	1888-12-28
Leonarda	Nicholas	1888-11-21	

*Birth or baptism in Punta Gorda, but involves Baranguna

Given Name	Surname	Birth	Baptism
Telesfora	Bermudez	1889-01-01	
Policarpio	Zuniga	1889-01-26	
Roberto	Sanchez	1889-03-27	1889-06-26
Stanislao	Reyes	1889-06-27	1889-06-27
Elena	Paulino	1889-08-19	1889-09-08
Nicanora	Garcia	1890-01	1890-02-11
Romana*	Nolberto	1890-01	1890-02
Feliciano*	Garcia	1890-01-09	
Jeronima	Garcia	1890-01-10	
Vincenta	Palacio	1890-04-06	1890-05-03
Fiburcio	Zuniga	1890-04-14	1890-07-11
Francisco	Gamboa	1890-05	
Augustine*	Santino	1890-05-05	
Pasquala	Ramirez	1890-06-14	1890-07-07
Claudio	Ariola	1890-10-30	1891-01-01
Pascacio	Cayetano	1891-02-22	1891-03-30
Basilio	Palacio	1891-05	
Pablo	Nicholas	1891-06-07	1891-08-02
Vela	Nolberto	1891-06-15	1891-08-02
Apolinaria	Meija	1891-07-21	1891-08-02
Polinario	Mejia	1891-07-21	
Sixto	Avilez	1891-08-06	1891-08-02
Manuel (Nicholas)	Lambi	1891-09-15	1891-11-01
Rafael*	Zuniga	1891-10-26	
Juana	Sanchez	1891-12-12	

*Birth or baptism in Punta Gorda, but involves Baranguna

Table B3.2. Garifuna Marriages in Barranco

Date	Groom	Bride	Groom Link[a]	Bride Link[b]
1865-02-24[c]	Sebastian Sanchez	Vivciona Cayetano		d Juan Pedro Cayetano
1869-07	Justo James Avilez	Cornelia Luis	s Santiago Avilez	
1870-05-03	Eduardo Nunez	Rosa Mistica Lambey		
1871-11	Martin Garcia	Gregoria Avilez		d Santiago Avilez
1871-11-01	Gregorio Maximo	Sabia Santiaga Nolberto		
1875-01-14	Claro Zuniga	Mauricia Cayetano		d Anacleto Cayetano
1877-06-02[d]	Leoncio Nicholas	Cristina Garcia	s Alejandro Nicholas	
1877-11-29	Alejandro Castillo	Victoriana Cayetano		d Anacleto Cayetano
1878-08-03	Jose Andrade	Juliana Fuentes		
1880-01-28	Teodoro Palacio	Petrona Cayetano	s Desideria	d Juan Pedro Cayetano
1880-01-28	Narcisco Bermudez	Dominga Marin		d Luisa Cayetano
1880-03-30	Augustin Paulino	Juana Luis	s Dominga Cayetano	
1882-05-18	Pedro Luis	Clara Martinez		
1883	Aloysius (Luis) Gamboa	Juana		
1883-02-05	Marcello Cayetano	Maria Loretta Palacio	s Anacleto Cayetano	d Teodoro Palacio
1883-03-30	Martin Reyes	Luisa V. Roches		step-d Anastacio Palacio
1883-03-30	Augustin Paulino	Juana Nazarena	s Dominga Cayetano	
1883-04-01	Philip Santino	Justina Cayetano		
1883-06-14	Valentino Ramirez	Marcelina Jimenez		d Rafaela Cayetano

Date	Groom	Bride	Groom Link[a]	Bride Link[b]
1883-06-15	Pio Nolberto	Casimira Nicholas	s Francisco Nolberto	d Alejandro Nicholas
1884-02-09	Policarpio Cayetano	Maria Gregorio	s Juan Pedro Cayetano	
1886-06-07[d]	Celestino Paulino	Mercedes Palacio	s Dominga Cayetano	d Anastacio Palacio
1887-12-20[d]	Fermin Jimenez	Petrona Cayetano		d Anacleto Cayetano
1888-01-03[d]	John Lambey	Gregoria Nolberto		d Francisco Nolberto
1888-01-12[d]	Clement Satuye	Eleuteria Cayetano		d Vivciona Cayetano
1888-05-08[d]	Rufino Ariola	Ascenciona Paulino		d Dominga Cayetano
1889-01-31	Carmen Ramirez	Eustaquia Palacio		d Teodoro Palacio
1890-01-07[d]	Maximiliano Garcia	Blacuina Apolonio		
1890-02-04	Nolberto Palacio	Ignacia Arana	s Teodoro Palacio	
1890-02-17	Pedro Martinez	Regina Virgen Luis		
1890-10-17	Simon Mejia	Andrea Nicholas		d Alejandro Nicholas

[a]Links to founding families: s = son of.
[b]Links to founding families: d = daughter of; step d = stepdaughter of.
[c]This wedding took place in Punta Gorda, but all of their children were born in Barranco, so it is included here.
[d]This wedding took place in Punta Gorda, but most of their children were born in Barranco, so it is included here.

Appendix C—Village Lots

Table C5.1. Village Lot Transmission Data

Lot#	Name of Owner	Map	L/G	L/G #
1	Government Reserve	1892		
	Martinez, Pasqual		L	337/1923
	Martinez, Francisco		L	65/1937
	Carr, Alanza		L	67/1937
	Carr, Alanza		L	134/55
	Casimiro, Fermin		L	1815/82
1A	Henry E. Loredo		L	656/22
	Arzu, Gregorio		L	546/27
	Arzu, Gregorio		L	
2	Government Reserve	1892		
	Loredo, Henry		L	366/23
	Loredo, Henry		L	430/33
	Loredo, Henry	1928		
3	Escartinas, Santos	1892		
	Palacio, Catarino		L	app 14 Aug 1899
	Palacio, Catarino		L	62/00
	Palacio, Catarino			15/1916
	Arzu, Francisco		L	app 27 Dec 1915
	Arzu, Francisco		L	41/17
	Arzu, Francisco		L	
	Palacio, Augustine		L	725/27
	Palacio, Augustine		L	0805
	Palacio, Augustine	1928	L	192/60
4	Palacio ? 23/4/99			
	Viris, Serapio		L	86/96
	Palacio, Hipolito		L	54/00
	Palacio, Hipolito		L	10/07
	Palacio, Hipolito		L	app 13 Sept 1915
	Palacio, Hipolito		L	
	Palacio, Hipolito		L	0090
	Palacio, Reuben		L	818/64
5	Colesa, Luis	1892		
	Nicholas, Philip		L	app 12 Jun 1909
	Nicholas, Philip		L	57/10
	Nicholas, Philip		L	600/1926
	Nicholas, Fabiana		L	5074
6	blank	1892		
	Palacio, Luis		L	app 22 Dec 1903
	Noralez, Venancio		L	app 4 Aug 1913

app = date applied
DS = Director of Surveys
Fol =Folio
L/G = Lease or Grant, L = lease, G = grant
L/G # = Number assigned by Lands Department, date, or other source of information
MP = Minute Paper
SG = Surveyor General
vol = volume/number

Lot#	Name of Owner	Map	L/G	L/G #
	Noralez, Venancio		L	55/14
	Norelez, Martin B		L	162/1933
	Avilez, James		L	0305
	Avilez, Margarita		L	276/78
7	Government Reserve	1892		
	Corp Body RC Church		L	app 4 Sept 1913
	Corp Body RC Church		L	27/1914
	Corp Body RC Church		G	10/41
7A	Government Reserve	1892		
	Corp Body RC Church		L	app 4 Sept 1913
	Corp Body RC Church		L	27/1914
	Corp Body RC Church		G	10/1941
8	Hernandez, Dolores	1892		
	Hernandez, Dolores		L	79/1898
	Hernandez, Dolores		L	39/1906
	Satuya, Romana		L	app 25 Mar 1914
	Satuya, Romana		L	76/1915
	Behe, Francisco		L	513/23
	Avilez, John Justo		G	543/1928
	Corp Body RC Church			
9	Martinez, Luis	1892		
	Martinez, Luis		L	app 6 Apr 1899
	Martinez, Luis		L	56/00
	Avilez, John Justo		L	app 1 Mar 1906
	Avilez, John Justo		G	app to purchase 13.06.06
	Avilez, John Justo		G	1/1907
	Corp Body RC Church		G	
10	Reyes, Natividad	1892		
	Anguana, John		L	app 31 Aug 1899
	Anguana, John		L	55/00
	Avilez, John Justo		L	app 24 Jul 1906
	Avilez, John Justo		L	56/07
	Avilez, John Justo		G	app to purchase 16 Jan 1913
	Avilez, John Justo		G	14/1913
	Corp Body RC Church			
11	Vargas, Malvino	1892		
	Reyes, Natividad		L	app 5 Dec 1898
	Reyes, Natividad		L	57/1900
	Nolberto, Teresa		L	545/1922
	Reyes, Natividad		L	55/23
	Avilez, John Justo	1928	G	309/1926
	St.Joseph Credit Union			vol.2/62 Fol 480-483
12	Teo, Juana Baptista	1892		
	Ortega, Cristino		L	54/1896
	Ortega, Cristino		L	13/9/07
	Toro, Vicente		L	app 14 Mar 1907
	Toro, Vicente		L	59/07
	Andrade, Teodoro		L	app 28 Sept 1911
	Andrade, Teodoro		L	54/13

Lot#	Name of Owner	Map	L/G	L/G #
	Ariola, Petrona		L	233/1923
	Arzu, Estanislao		L	5200
	Arzu, Estanislao	1928		
13	Ortiz, Cristino	1892		
	Lopez, Pedro		L	app 23 Feb 1901
	Ortiz, Cristino		L	72/02
	Lopez, Pedro		L	202/14
	Arzu, Luciano		L	app 11 May 1914
	Arzu, Luciano		L	
	Palacio, Roman		L	SG320/27
	Bondswell, Balbina		L	SG0219
	Levy, Hylton	1928		
	Arzu, Benito		L	594/65
13A	Darthel, Felicia	1892	L	
	Strange, H.P.		L	app 24 Feb 1893
	Mendozo, Cruz		L	app. 21 Dec 1900
	Mendozo, Cruz		L	76/02
	Arzu, Luciano		L	app 11 May 1914
	Arzu, Luciano		L	202/14
	Serana, Antonio			SG553/1928
	Castro, Michaela		L	app. 29.9.3? SG1045
	Castro, Michaela		L	819/63
	Castro, Michaela			104/80
14	Requeña, Antonio	1892	L	
	Ponce, Tiburcio		L	app 5 Dec 1898
	Ponce, Tiburcio		L	50/00
	Martinez, D.C.		L	app 20 Oct 1903
	Paulino, Eugenio		L	app 13 Dec 1906
	Paulino, Eugenio		L	12/08
	Paulino, Eugenio		L	SG48/1930
	Nixon, Julia		L	202/36
	Nixon, Julia	1928		
	Porter, James & Elwith		L	914/76
	Palacio, Joseph O.			236/89
15	Para, Toliarosa	1892		
	Rodas, Dolores		L	app 1 Nov 1900
	Sanchez, C.		L	20/11/01
	Rodas, Dolores		L	28/02
	Sanchez, Cayetana		L	app 20 Oct 1903
	Lorenzo, Timoteo		L	app 9 Jul 1906
	Lorenzo, Timoteo		L	55/07
	Lorenzo, Timoteo		L	SG1296/1921
	Lorenzo, Victor			5761
	Lorenzo, Victor	1928		
16	Vairez, Francisco	1892	L	
	Vairez, Nicolasa		L	15 April 1899
	Vairez, Nicolasa		L	67/00
	Arzu, Isidro		L	app 2 Sept 1907
	Arzu, Isidro		L	10/09
	Arzu, Isidro		L	app 19 Dec 1918
	Arzu, Isidro		L	69/20

Lot#	Name of Owner	Map	L/G	L/G #
	Arzu, Maxima			app. 12.9.38 SG0933
	Arzu, Maxima	1928	L	
	Loredo, Hector			895/63
17	Vairez, Serapio	1892		
	Arzu, Luciano		L	app 24 Mar 1913
	Arzu, Luciano		L	100/1913
	Betancourt, Porfirio		L	app 15 Sept 1919
	Betancourt, Porfirio		L	SG571/1919
	Betancourt, Porfirio		L	SG597/1923
	Corp Body RC Church		G	SG414/1936
	Corp Body RC Church	1928	G	
18	R. Catholic Church	1892		
	R.C. Church		G*	MP3685/1913
	R.C. Church	1928	G	
19	Torres, Procopio	1892		
	Torres, Procopio		L	app 24 jul 1899
	Torres, Procopio		L	68/00
	Chimilio, John		L	app 21 Feb 1907
	Chimilio, John		L	57/07
	Chimilio, John		L	SG501/27
	Chimilio, John		L	?.10.37 SG0313
	Chimilio, John	1928		
	Chimilio, Timoteo		L	1601/64
	Chimilio, Crispulo		L	1619/84
	Hijinio, Anita			282/95
	Hijinio, Anita			
20	Ariola, Patricio	1892		
	Ariola, Patricio		L	app 13 Dec 1900
	Ariola, Patricio		L	73/02
	Ariola, Catrino			SG1326/22
	Ariola, Petrona		L	5328
	Ariola, Petrona		L	144/67
	Ariola, Petrona		L	2573/87
21	Garcia, Maximiliano	1892		
	Garcia, Smith		L	app 8 Apr 1899
	Garcia, Smith		L	70/00
	Garcia, Smith			824/20
	Garcia, Victor			259/1931
	Garcia, Victor			app. 13.5.52
	Garcia, Placida	oral		
	Palacio, Jacinto		L	1242/75
22	Martinez, Francisco	1892		
	Martinez, Francisco		L	app 12 Apr 1900
	Martinez, Francisco		L	97/00
	Arzu, Marcelino		L	12 Jan 1917
	Arzu, Marcelino		L	126/17
	Arzu, Marcelino		G	app to purchase 1 Aug 1921
	Arzu, Marcelino		G	16/1926
	Arzu, Marcelino	1928		
23	Zuniga, Claro	1892		

Lot#	Name of Owner	Map	L/G	L/G #
	Zuniga, Claro		L	app 8 Apr 1899
	Zuniga, Claro		L	58/1900
	Zuniga, Claro		L	82/1906
	Zuniga, Rafael C.		L	app 12 Oct 1918
	Zuniga, Rafael C.		L	207/1922
	Martinez, Hipolito		L	app. DS1493
	Martinez, Hipolito		L	80/61
	Martinez, Hipolito		L	86/83
	Martinez, Eliot		L	86/83
24	Polonio, Mauricio	1892		
	Velasquez, Gabriel		L	app 4 Apr 1899
	Velasquez, Gabriel		L	63/00
	Velasquez, Gabriel		L	24/1904
	Velasquez, Gabriel		L	app 4 Sept 1915
	Velasquez, Gabriel		L	192/16
	Marin, Emelda		L	400/1936
	Marin, Clarence	1928	L	57/53
	Martinez, Evilia		L	1100/78
25	Clemencia, Maria	1892		
	Zuniga, Claro		L	58/00
	Blas, Florencia		L	app 30 Sept 1901
	Blas, Florencia		L	19/02
	Polonio, Petrona		L	app 29 Sept 1916
	Polonio, Petrona		L	64/17
	Polonio, Petrona	1928	G	11/1927
26	Nolberto, Ciriaco	1892		
	Nolberto, Ciriaco		L	3 April 1899
	Nolberto, Ciriaco		L	91/00
	Nolberto, Ciriaco			11/07
	Nolberto, Teresa			
	Casimiro, Amos C.			DS5330
	Casimiro, Amos C.	1928		
	Nicholas, Justin		L	
	Gonzalez, Marcario		L	
27	Paulino, Augustin	1892		
	Paulino, Augustin		L	app 8 Apr 1899
	Paulino, Augustin		L	82/00
	Paulino, Augustin		L	18/08
	Paulino, William		L	app 2 Nov 1918
	Paulino, William		L	733/1921
	Lucas, Josefa		L	1458
	Community Centre		L	283/78
28	Martinez, Clara	1892		
	Martinez, Clara		L	app 13 Dec 1900
	Martinez, Clara		L	71/02
	Malla, Josefa		L	app 11 Oct 1913
	Malla, Josefa		L	
	Martinez, Albina		L	app 28 Aug 1920
	Martinez, Albina		L	

Lot#	Name of Owner	Map	L/G	L/G #
	Bermadez, M., Vincente, M., & Martinez, R.	1928		
	Community Centre			
29	Nolberto, Pio	1892		
	Nolberto, Pio		L	app 9 Sept 1903
	Nolberto, Pio		L	64/03
	Nolberto, Dionisio			MPSG11/1922
	Nolberto, Dionisio		L	5489(5481?)
	Nolberto, Dionisio	1928	L	
	Nolberto, Paula		L	619/81
30	Lambey, Rosa	1892		
	Mejia, Matildo		L	app 1 Nov 1900
	Mejia, Matildo		L	79/02
	Palacio, Lewis		L	app 26 Mar 1908
	Palacio, Lewis		L	106/08 MP1234/1908
	Gibbons, Stephen		L	app 2 Sept 1918
	Gibbons, Stephen		L	SG45/1918
	Gibbons, Stephen		L	SG720/1927
	Arzu, Petrona	1928	L	8964
	Roches, Wilfred		L	81/88
31	blank	1892		
	Rodriguez, Andres		L	5 April 1900
	Rodriguez, Andres		L	96/00
	Garcia, Nicanora		L	app 30 Apr 1914
	Garcia, Nicanora		L	122/1914 MP2441/1914
	Santino, Augustine		L	MP783/1922
	Lucas, Felix		L	315/34
	Lucas, Felix	1928	L	
32	blank	1892		
	Santino, Augustine		L	app 22 May 1915
	Santino, Augustine		L	2557/1915
	Palacio, Nicanora		L	app 25 Jun 1917
	Palacio, Nicanora		L	166/1918 MP2955/1917
	Palacio, Nicanora		L	1.3.34
	Arzu, Angel		L	07.06.44 DS5395
	Palacio, Nicanora		L	
	Avilez, Euphemio		L	331/51
33	Fernandez, Francisco	1892		
	Fernandez, Francisco		L	app 1 Nov 1900
	Fernandez, Francisco		L	29/02
	Santino, Augustine		L	app 20 Jun 1916
	Santino, Augustine		L	78/18
	Santino, Augustine		L	SG0306
	Santino, Augustine	1928		
	Santino, Frank G.		L	477/62
	Hibbard, Avelina		L	477
	Hibbard, Avelina		G	appd for
34	Pitts, James	1892		
	Pitts, James		L	app 29 Mar 1899

Lot#	Name of Owner	Map	L/G	L/G #
	Pitts, James		L	66/00
	Mejia, Antonio		L	app 12 Jul 1917
	Mejia, Antonio		L	89/18
	Jimenez, Angel		L	transfered appd MP53/1922
	Enriquez, Nazaria		L	3.12.37 SG0437
	Enriquez, Nazaria	1928	L	
	Chimilio, Nazaria		L	1610/64
35	Santios, Alberto	1892		
	Gutierrez, Basilio		L	app 26 Dec1899
	Gutierrez, Basilio		L	app 10 Dec 1900
	Gutierrez, Basilio		L	90/02
	Mejia, Simeona		L	app 17 Jun 1918
	Mejia, Simeona		L	108/19
	Roberteau, Henrietta		L	SG425/1933
	Rose, William		L	SG24/1936
	Duncan, Alvin		L	04.07.1949
	Zuniga, Clotildo		L	30.06.1952
	Zuniga, Clotildo		L	1240/75
36	Acosta, Blacina	1892	L	
	Acosta, Blacuina		L	27 Apr 1903
	Acosta, Blacuina		L	66/03
	Benguche, Santiago		L	187/14
	Benguche, Santiago		L	app 29 May 1916
	Paulino, Stephen		L	SG0776
	Nicholas, David W.	1928	L	9441
	Colon, Naomi		L	1620/84
37	Fernandez, Tiburcio	1892		
	Ramirez, Santos		L	app 29 June 1915
	Ramirez, Santos		L	45/16
	Benguche, Santiago		L	SG117/1926
	Benguche, Santiago		L	SG666/1926
	Benguche, Santiago		L	DS5768
	Martinez, Escolastica	1928	L	9910
	Nolberto, Isabel		L	1210/79
38	Government Reserve	1892		
39	Lambey, Luis	1892		
	Gutierrez, C.M.		L	app 20 Mar 1906
	Gutierrez, C.M.		L	45/06
	Gutierrez, C.M.		L	SG497/1926
	Zuniga, Catarina		L	.5.38
	Zuniga, Felix			6.5.40 DS1834
	Zuniga, Felix	1928		
	Santino, Dionicia		L	484/61
40	Santino, Philip	1892		
	Santino, Philip		L	app 14 Apr 1899
	Santino, Philip		L	59/00
	Santino, Eusabio		L	SG387/27
	Santino, Eusabio		L	10.12.48
	Santino, Eusabio		L	LC466/70
	Santino, Eusabio		L	6802

Lot#	Name of Owner	Map	L/G	L/G #
41	Avila, Narciano	1892		
	Zuniga, Viviano		L	app 30 June 1913
	Zuniga, Viviano		L	56/14
	Zuniga, Viviano		L	
	Zuniga, Viviano	1928		
	Irene Gibbons		L	188/59
	Irene Gibbons		L	987/87
	Casimiro, Felicia		G	1501/86
42	Carleuz, Maria Baretha	1892		
	Castillo, Victoriano		L	app 20 Mar 1906
	Castillo, Victoriano		L	61/06
	Castillo, Victoriano			SG472
	Zuniga, Clotildo		L	25.4.49
	Zuniga, Clotildo		L	1241/75
	Zuniga, Clotildo			
43	Lambey, John	1892		
	Lambey, John		L	app 8 Apr 1899
	Lambey, John		L	100/00
	Lambey, John		L	16/06
	Flores, Candido		L	app 2 Nov 1918
	Flores, Candido		L	130/19
	Flores, Candido & Isidora		L	
	Flores, Candido & Isidora	L	L	11.1.52
	Joseph, Ambrocio		L	26.9.52
	Joseph, Ambrocio		L	9694
44	Paulino, Regarcia	1892		
	Garcia, Sebastian J. A.		L	52/00
	Garcia, Margarito		L	164/09
	Garcia, Margarito		L	app 14 Oct 1919
	Garcia, Margarito		L	79/22
	Castillo, Casimiro W.		L	SG117/1942
	Garcia, Margarito		L	SG468/1934
	Garcia, Margarito	1928		
	Garcia, Jeronimia		L	12.4.60
	Zuniga, Carmen		L	1243/75
	Nunez, Leonard		L	1243/75
45	Santos Louisa	1892		
	Garcia, Smith		L	app 29 Mar 1901
	Garcia, Smith		L	app 21 Sept 1901
	Garcia, Smith		L	63/02
	Vargas, Nicasio		L	app 19 Apr 1915
	Vargas, Nicasio		L	139/16
	Vargas, Nicasio		L	3.10.25
	Vargas, Nicasio		L	6263
	Vargas, Nicasio	1928		
	Cayetano, Lucy		L	1149/80
46		1892		
	Velasquez, Gabriel		L	app 4 Apr 1899
	Lambey, Jane		L	64/00
	Sevilla,Marcelina		L	app 23 Dec 1916
	Sevilla,Marcelina		L	81/18

Lot#	Name of Owner	Map	L/G	L/G #
	Sevilla,Marcelina		L	SG26/1928
	Castillo, Eustacio R		L	.4.37 SG0102
	Gamboa, Luciano		L	25.1.49 DS6837
	Cayetano, Silas C.		L	9406
	Cayetano, Silas C.	1928		
	Alvarez, Fabiana		L	1282/80
47	Palacio, Marcelo	1892		
	Sebastian, Andres		L	app 21 Jul 1908
	Sebastian, Andres		L	11/09
	Lucas, Sebastian		L	app 26 Feb 1917
	Lucas, Sebastian		L	34/19
	Lucas, Sebastian		L	SG1028/24
	Lucas, Sebastian		L	SG47/1925
	Martinez, Andres		L	1304
	Martinez, Andres	1928	L	
	Martinez, Melvinia		L	1056/77
48	Avilia, Pedro	1892	L	
	Jimenez, Fermin		L	app 30 April 1895
	Avila, Pedro		L	30/02
	Avilia, Pedro		L	MP1180/1912
	Avilia, Pedro		L	SG1217/1921
	Avilia, Viviana		L	30.5.45
	Avila, Viviana	1928	L	
	Avila, Nicolasca		L	1135/66
49	Polonio, Mauricio	1892	L	
	Blas, Macario		L	app 22 Apr 1899
	Blas, Macario		L	57/00
	Santino, Eusebio		L	SG426/1923
	Garcia, Tanis R.		L	6801
	Garcia, Tanis R.	1928	L	
	Martinez, Martin		L	165/78
50	Castillo, Rafael	1892		
	Castillo, Rafael		L	app 22 Aug 1899
	Castillo, Rafael		L	77/00
	Castillo, Simeona		L	app 16 Jan 1910
	Castillo, Simeona		L	78/10
	Ariola, Patricio		L	app 23 Dec 1920
	Ariola, Patricio		L	SG1375/1920
	Ariola, Patricio		L	app 27 Sept 1921
	Ariola, Patricio		L	SG1050/1921
	Ariola, Patricio		L	SG763/1922
	Ariola, Patricio		L	SG298/1935
	Colon, Francisca		L	8153
	Colon, Francisca	1928	L	
	Diaz, Elvin		L	2392/77
	Gutierrez, Valentina			
51	blank	1892		
	Nicholas, Pablo		L	app 2 Nov 1914
	Nicholas, Pablo		L	77/15
	Nicholas, Pablo		G	29/1927
	Nicholas, Pablo	1928	G	

Lot#	Name of Owner	Map	L/G	L/G #
52	Nicholas, Ignacio	1892	L	
	Nicholas, Philip		L	99/00
	Santino, Philip		L	app 28 Jan 1910
	Santino, Philip		L	63/10
	Santino, Philip		L	SG1311/1921
	Palacio, Joseph P.		L	SG274/1936
	Palacio, Joseph P.	1928	L	
	Palacio, Olivia		L	DS472/61
	Palacio, Joseph		L	1609/64
	Palacio, Olivia		L	116/89
53	Lambey, Antonio	1892	L	
	Lambey, Antonio		L	app 8 Apr 1899
	Lambey, Antonio		L	74/00
	Lambey, Antonio		L	17/06
	Nicholas, Pablo		L	SG368/27
	Nicholas, Pablo		L	5841
	Nicholas, Pablo	1928	L	
	Zuniga, Isaac		L	369/77
	Zuniga, Kevin		L	
54	Ramirez, Carmen	1892	L	
	Ramirez, Carmen		L	app 5 Apr 1899
	Ramirez, Carmen		L	49/00
	Ramirez, Carmen		L	21/06
	Paulino, Telefora		L	79/18
	Ramirez, Carmen		L	SG452/1926
	Ramirez, Eustaquia		L	SG1044
	Ramirez, Eustaquia	1928		
	Ramirez, Bonifacio		L	813/63
55	blank	1892		
	Paulino, Domingo		L	app 14 Jan 1914
	Paulino, Domingo		L	MP1203/1914
	Satuye, Eleuteria		L	app 13 Sept 1921
	Satuye, Eleuteria		L	SG1028/1921
	Satuye, Eleuteria		L	SG665/1922
	Satuya, Enriqueta		L	SG261/1936
	Arzu, Conrad		L	1227/79
56	Jimenez, Fermin	1892		
	Kuylen, Eujenia		L	27/1896
	Alvarez, Jeronimo		L	SG1334/1921
	Alvarez, Jeronimo		L	6727
	Alvarez, Jeronimo	1928		
	Alvarez, Zita		L	98/83
57	Avilez, John	1892		
	Avilez, John			app 24 Dec 1900
	Avilez, John		L	69/02
	Paulino, Telefora		L	app 13 Oct 1916
	Paulino, Telefora		L	79/1918
	Jimenez, Dominica		L	29.02.44 DS5287
	Trapp, Julian		L	792/73
	Martinez, Gloria		L	
	Nunez, Joseph		L	1239/75

Lot#	Name of Owner	Map	L/G	L/G #
	Nunez, Joseph		L	114/85
58	Castillo, Orlando	1892		
	Nicholas, Sotero		L	app 5 Sept 1899
	Nicholas, Sotero		L	78/00
	Nicholas, Sotero		L	12/06
	Nicholas, Sotero		L	app to purchase 24.Dec 11 1910
	Nicholas, Sotero		G	24/1911
	Nicholas, Sotero	1928	G	
59	Obispo, Narcisco	1892		
	Lino, Bishop		L	app 8 Apr 1899
	Lino, Bishop		L	80/00
	Lino, Bishop		L	93/1906
	Zuniga, Marcos		L	app 30 Oct 1916
	Zuniga, Marcos		L	80/18
	Castillo, Graciano S.		G	91/1929
	Castillo, Graciano S.	1928	G	
60	Nicholas, Arihenia	1892		
	Mejia, Simon		L	app 8 Apr 1899
	Mejia, Simon		L	53/00
	Mejia, Simon		L	23/06
	Cayetano, Pascasio		L	MP786/1906
	Cayetano, Pascasio		L	app 30 Nov 1917
	Cayetano, Pascasio		L	MP1115/18
	Cayetano, Pascasio		L	SG716/1927
	Cayetano, Pascasio		L	Sg477/1928
	Cayetano, Pascasio		L	05.05.50
	Cayetano, Pascasio	1928	L	
	Palacio, Sarah		L	8317
	Palacio, Sarah		L	40/92
61	Cayetano, ? (crossed out)	1892		
	Arnold, William H.		G	66/1894
	Arnold, William H.			
62	Wells, D.S.	1892	G	67/1894
	Polonio, Eusebio	1928		
	Smith, Horace		L	1034/77
63	Cayetano, Anacleto	1892		
	Wells, D.S.		G	67/1894
	Polonio, Eusebio	1928		
64	Moralez, Nicolasa	1892		
	Wells, D.S.**		G	58/1894
	Polonio, Eusebio	1928		
65	Lopez, Lecardio	1892	L	
	Melhado C.		G	58/1894
	Whitman, Irving B.		L	2.4.43 DS5036
	Marketing Board			6.12.54
	Marketing Board	1928		
	Electric Plant			
	Cayetano, Nathaniel and Reuben Palacio		L	1229/84
66	Haughn,William	1892		

Lot#	Name of Owner	Map	L/G	L/G #
	Palacio, Liberata		L	87/98
	Polonio, Eusebio		L	app 25 Apr 1910
	Polonio, Eusebio		L	MP3277/10
	Polonio, Eusebio		L	SG737/1922
	Marin, Clarence		L	SG212/1936
	Marin, Clarence	1928		
	Marin, Clarence		L	128/61
	Marin, Charles		L	996/86
67	,Francisco	1892		
	Beatty, Leonidas		L	12/1896
	Palacio, Liberato		L	app 15 Sept 1899
	Palacio, Liberato		L	65/00
	Polonio, Eusebio		L	app 25 Apr 1910
	Polonio, Eusebio		L	61/14
	Polonio, Eusebio		L	SG737/1922
	Garcia, Estanislao R		L	SG175/1936
	Garcia, E	1928		
	Nicholas, Ignacio L.		L	348/58
	Cayetano, Beatrice		L	53/89
68	Palacio, Theodore	1892		
	Palacio, Theodore		L	app 3 Mar 1899
	Palacio, Theodore		L	61/00
	Palacio, Theodore		L	28/1906
	Palacio, Louis		L	app 8 Mar 1913
	Palacio, Louis		L	208/14
	Martinez, Augustina		L	app 17 Jan 1919
	Martinez, Augustina		L	75/22
	Martinez, Melvinia		L	5.12.40 DS3063
	Dispensary	1928		
69	Avilez, Santiago	1892		
	Palacio, Saturnino		L	app 12 Sept 1912
	Palacio, Saturnino		L	67/13
	Palacio, Saturnino		L	SG278/1923
	Palacio, Saturnino		L	26.7.44 DS5459
	Dispensary	1928		
70	Beatty, Leonidas	1892		
	Palacio, Mercedes			app 13 Dec 1900
	Palacio, Mercedes		L	52/02
	Marin, Brigida		L	app 6 Sept 1915
	Marin, Brigida		L	129/17
	Velasquez, Mercedes		L	SG155/1924
	Velasquez, Mercedes		L	SG286/1934
	Marin, Brigida		L	21.8.36 SG0170
	Marin, Brigida	1928		
	Palacio, Theodore J.		L	1s/61
	Palacio, Theodore J.		L	216/90
71	Paulino, Diego	1892		
	Paulino, Dominga		L	app 4 Apr 1899
	Paulino, Dominga		L	46/1900
	Paulino, Dominga		L	27/1906
	Ariola, Ascenciona		L	SG721/1927

Lot#	Name of Owner	Map	L/G	L/G #
	Diego, Virginia		L	SG721/1927
	Ariola, Petrona		L	22.1.48 DS6515
	Diego, Virginia		L	8.3.48 DS6588
	Diego, Virginia	1928		
	Enriquez, Bertram		L	451/77
	Casimiro, Petrona		L	327/79
	Casimiro, Felicia		L	221/90
72	Rosa, Rafael	1892	L	
	Francisco, Jeronimo		L	app 16 Nov 1901
	Francisco, Jeronimo		L	46/02
	Paulino, Dominga		L	46/00
	Mejia, Simon		L	app 3 feb 1913
	Mejia, Simon		L	128/13
	Castillo, Cornelio R.		L	SG52/1923
	Castillo, Cornelio R.		L	SG419/1935
	Castillo, Cornelio R.		L	6/61
	Martinez, Melvinia		L	259/96
73	Magill, Simon	1892	L	
	Nicholas, Leoncio		L	73/00
	Nicholas, Leoncio		L	app 12 Feb 1905
	Nicholas, Leoncio		L	62/06
	Nicholas, Leoncio		G	app to purchase 16 Nov 1908
	Nicholas, Leoncio		G	5/09
	Nicholas, Leoncio	1928	G	
74	Castillo, Inez	1892	L	
	Castillo, Inez		L	app 5 Apr 1899
	Castillo, Inez		L	74/00
	Castillo, Inez		L	25/1906
	Castillo, Cornelio R.		L	SG190/1931
	Castillo, Cornelio R.		L	9404
	Castillo, Cornelio R.	1928	L	
75	Ariola, Rufino	1892	L	
	Martinez, Liborio		L	9 Feb 1900
	Martinez, Liborio		L	125/00
	Arana, Alejandro		L	SG110(770?)-20
	Arana, Narcisco		L	30.9.40 DS2042
	Arana, Narcisco	1928	L	500/61
	Arana, Eulalia		L	99/83
76	Livindo, Manuel	1892		
	Jimenez, Fermin		L	app 11 Mar 1902
	Jimenez, Fermin		L	65/03
	Jimenez, Angel		L	app 22 Sept 1913
	Jimenez, Angel		L	152/14
	Jimenez, Angel		L	10.3.23 DS_/23
	Martinez, Bernadina		L	25.11.39 DS1604
	Martinez, Bernadina		L	131/61
	Nolberto, Vickie		L	442/91
77	Reyes, Martin	1892	L	
	Reyes, Martin		L	app 15 April 1899
	Reyes, Martin		L	App 6 Dec 1900

Lot#	Name of Owner	Map	L/G	L/G #
	Reyes, Martin		L	89/02
	Reyes, Joseph		L	app 4 Apr 1916
	Reyes, Joseph		L	19/1917
	Cayetano, Eugenio		L	Sg 264/1936
	Cayetano, Eugenio		L	252/56
78	Palacio, Norberto	1892		
	Palacio, Norberto		L	app 6 Dec 1900
	Palacio, Norberto		L	27/02
	Palacio, Norberto		L	app 27 Nov 1920
	Palacio, Norberto		L	SG237/20
	Palacio, Norberto		L	27.5,22 SG_ /1922
	Palacio, Norberto		L	SG 329/2_
	Palacio, Paul		L	8.7.44 DS5455
	Palacio, Paul		L	1159/73
	Palacio, Paul		G	112/86
79	Palacio, Teodoro	1892		
	Andrade, Teodoro		L	app 24 Sept 1901
	Andrade, Teodoro		L	67/02
	Martinez, Liborio		L	SG212/1922
	Martinez, Teofilo	oral	L	
	Gabriel, Diega	oral	L	
	Ariola, Benita		L	_7.37 SG0142
	Ariola, Benita		L	5. 9.38 SG0920
	Ariola, Benita		L	1322/63
80	Cayetano, Marcelo	1892	L	
	Cayetano, Marcelo		L	app 9 May 1898
	Cayetano, Marcelo		L	96/98
	Cayetano, Gregorio		L	app 30 June 1913
	Cayetano, Gregorio		L	53/14
	Chimilio, Marcial		L	SG_ /24
	Chimilio, Marcial		L	SG122/30
	Chimilio, Innocente		L	12.12.50
	Chimilio, Innocente	1928	L	
	Arana, Lauriano		L	1661/74
81	Cayetano, Marcelo	1892	L	
	Cayetano, Marcelo		L	96/1898
	Cayetano, Marcelo		L	app 15 Apr 1899
	Cayetano, Marcelo		L	71/00
	Cayetano, Pascasio		L	12/07
	Cayetano, Pascasio		L	SG477/1928
	Cayetano, Pascasio		L	5.5.50
	Cayetano, Pascasio	1928		
	Petillo, Mary		L	239/66
	Petillo, Mary		G	527/78
	Petillo, Sheridan			vol. Rol.696-703
82	Government Reserve	1928		
83	Palacio, Liberato	1892	L	
	Loredo, Eulalio		L	86/98
	Loredo, Henry		L	SG1226/21
	Loredo, Henry		L	SG202/1933
	Velasquez, Christobel		L	17.10.49

Lot#	Name of Owner	Map	L/G	L/G #
	Velasquez, Christobel		L	320/81
	Blanco, Elvira		L	8023A
84	blank	1892		
	Nolberto, Macario		L	app 8 Apr 1899
	Nolberto, Macario		L	69/00
	Nolberto, Macario		L	10/08
	Zuniga, Inocente		L	app 20 Jun 1917
	Zuniga, Inocente		L	91/18
	Zuniga, Inocente		L	106/37
	Zuniga, Inocente	1928	L	
	Zuniga, Lucille		L	204/82
	Zuniga, Alvin		L	204/82
85	Nolberto, Macario	1892	L	
	Nolberto, Macario		L	app 2 Nov 1914
	Nolberto, Macario		L	49/16 MP4282
	Nolberto, Ireno		L	app 20 Mar 1920
	Nolberto, Ireno		L	SG869/1921
	Nolberto, Ireno		L	SG949/23
	Nolberto, Ireno		L	SG821/1925
	Ariola, Patricio		L	SG264/1930
	Ariola, Patricio		L	SG0218
	Ariola, Patricio	1928	L	
	Ariola, Francisco		L	00.12.61
	Ariola, Francisco		L	2059/77
86	Zuniga, Natividad	1892	L	
	Zuniga, Natividad		I	app 30 Sept 1901
	Zuniga, Natividad		L	74/02
	Zuniga, Natividad		L	app 31 May 1915
	Zuniga, Natividad		L	MP2553/1915
	Zuniga, Natividad		L	SG471/1926
	Zuniga, Canuto		L	SG379/1936
	Zuniga, Canuto		L	812/63
	Zuniga, Lazarus		L	LC703/1973
87	Palacio, Anasticio	1892		
	Gutierrez, Soltera		L	app10 Dec 1900
	Gutierrez, Soltera		L	91/02
	Palacio, Anasticio		L	app 21 Jun 1912
	Palacio, Anasticio		L	20/13
	Palacio, Anasticio		L	SG232/23
	Loredo, Gregoria		L	SG351/1934
	Nunez, Evaristo F.		L	SG351/1934
	Nunez, Evaristo F.		L	353/60
88	Luis, Leonardo	1892		
	Lucas, Joseph R.		L	app 14 May 1901
	Lucas, Joseph R.		L	75/02
	Lucas, Joseph R.		L	
	Barrera, Prudencio		L	app 4 Nov 1918
	Barrera, Prudencio		L	107/19
	Martinez, George		L	SG784/1922
	Lucas, John		L	SG836/26
	Cayetano, Francis		L`	25.4.3_ SG0677

Lot#	Name of Owner	Map	L/G	L/G #
	Cayetano, Francis		L	133/61
	Cayetano, Nathaniel		L	
89	Serapia, Francisco	1892	L	
	Serapia, Francisco		L	app 2 Nov 1901
	Serapia, Francisco		L	20/02
	Nolberto, Macario		L	app 23 Sept 1913
	Nolberto, Macario		L	206/14 DS9855
	Baltazar, William			SG172/1923
	Nolberto, Venancia		L	SG496/1924
	Marketing Board	1928		
	Marketing Board			8.11.53
	Zuniga, Abraham		L	124/74
	Zuniga, Abraham		G	
90	Government Reserve	1892		
	Police Station	1939		
	Police Station	1928		
91	Palacio, Anastacio	1892	L	
	Palacio, Anastacio		L	app 8 Apr 1899
	Palacio, Anastacio		L	75/00
	Palacio, Anastacio		L	26/06
	Reyes, Paulina		L	app 14 May 1921
	Reyes, Paulina		L	SG617/1921
	Reyes, Paulina		L	SG322/1933
	Reyes, Paulina		L	5767
	Reyes, Paulina	1928	L	
	Cayetano, Eugene		L	1110/72
	Sanchez, Vicenta		L	1211/87
92	blank	1892		
	Casimiro, Pablo		L	app 12 Jun 1909
	Casimiro, Pablo		L	4/10
	Casimiro, Pablo		L	SG226/1924
	Casimiro, Bernadina		L	SG297/1935
	Casimiro, Paul		L	13.5.52
	Casimiro, Paul	1928	L	103/73
93	Martinez, Anacleto	1892	L	
	Fuentes, Antonio		L	app 29 Aug 1902
	Fuentes, Antonio		L	63/03
	Martinez, Anacleto		L	app 24 Nov 1908
	Martinez, Anacleto		L	48/11
	Martinez, Anacleto		L	
	Ariola, Manuela		L	SG120/1923
	Lucas, Daniel		L	SG257/36
	Lino, Gladys		L	14.7.52
	Lino, Gladys	1928	L	9490
	Lino, Gladys		L	441/79
	Lino, Gladys		G	425/92
94	blank	1892		
	Jimenez, Fermin		L	app 26 Dec 1899
	Jimenez, Fermin		L	88/00
	Polonio, Pantaleon		L	app 14 Mar 1917
	Polonio, Pantaleon		L	88/18

Lot#	Name of Owner	Map	L/G	L/G #
	Palacio, Thomasa P.		L	SG154/1937
	Avila, Viviana		L	
	Avila, Reginaldo		L	9992
	Avila, Reginaldo	1928	L	
95	blank	1892		
	Ramirez, Sebastian		L	app 27 Nov 1911
	Ramirez, Sebastian		L	MP327/1912
	Ramirez, Sebastian		L	app 10 Jun 1912
	Ramirez, Sebastian		L	MP118/1913
	Ramirez, Manuela		L	app 15 Sept 1913
	Ramirez, Manuela		L	83/14
	Palacio, Jacob		L	SG466/27
	Martinez, Bernadina		L	SG0141
	Baltazar, Bernadina		L	SG0141
	Baltazar, Bernadina	1928		
	Sandoval, Felicita		L	36/90
96	blank	1892		
	Gregorio, Vivian		L	app 19 Dec 1911
	Gregorio, Vivian		L	82/12
	Martinez, Bernadina		L	SG688/1922
	Martinez, Bernadina		L	SG598/1923
	Martinez, Bernadina		L	SG539/1926
	Martinez, Bernadina		L	27.8.49
	Martinez, Bernadina	1928		
	Martinez, Vickie		L	779/75
	Martinez, Vickie		L	139/99
97	Blank	1892		
	Castillo, William		L	app 1 Apr 1912
	Castillo, William		L	69/13
	Castillo, Nicomedes R.		L	SG370/1926
	Castillo, Nicomedes R.		L	SG0860
	Bernardez, John		L	14.8.42 DS4751
	Bernardez, John	1928	L	
	Nolberto, Trinidad		L	
	Nolberto, Paula		L	LC640/69
	Nolberto, Paula		L	80/81
	Tuttle, Valerie Delcy		L	13/90
98	Blank	1892		
	Norales, Felix		L	app 14 May 1912
	Norales, Felix		L	120/12
	Norales, Felix		L	SG2421923
	Norales, Felix		L	14.5.45
	Norales, Juana		L	407/69
	Norales, Leonarda		L	1186/77
	Norales, Terese		L	
	Norales, Terese			
99	Blank	1892		
	Bernardez, John		L	app 31 May 1912
	Bernardez, John		L	12/14
	Bernardez, John		L	
	Paulino, Eusebio		L	app 13 Jul 1917

Lot#	Name of Owner	Map	L/G	L/G #
	Paulino, Eusebio		L	90/18
	Paulino, Eusebio		L	SG719/27
	Paulino, Eusebio		L	1.2.38 SG0570
	Paulino, Eusebio	1928	L	
	Loredo, Hector		L	1474/63
	Nolberto, Anacleta		G	348/1999
100	Bermudez, Isidora		L	app11 May 1914
	Bermudez, Isidora		L	157/14
	Nolberto, Ireno		L	app 30 Oct 1916
	Nolberto, Ireno		L	MP4001/1916
	Gabriel, Rosendo		L	app 30 Sept 1918
	Gabriel, Rosendo		L	SG?/1918
	Gabriel, Rosendo		L	5.2.4? DS4031
	Alvarez, Eustacio		L	28.5.52
	Chimilio, Sylvin	1928	L	9423
	Chimilio, Sylvin		L	101/88
101	Santino, Victoriana		L	app 3 Sept 1914
	Santino, Victoriana		L	73/15
	Mejia, Victoriana Santino		L	SG151/1937
	Mejia, V.S.	1928		
	Castillo, Eleutina M.			
	Augustine, Hazel		L	1621/84
102	Colindres, Victor		L	app 31 July 1909
	Colindres, Victor		L	23/10
	Colindres, Victor		L	
	Gonzalez, Daniel		L	app 18 Sept 1919
	Gonzalez, Daniel		L	66/22
	Lopez, Feliciano		L	SG681/1923
	Avilez, Lucio		L	SG451/1927
	Santino, Vincenta		L	8543
	Santino, Vincenta		L	1236/75
103	Ramirez, E		L	SG370/1929
	Martinez, Nicholas		L	?.11.50
	Martinez, Nicholas	1928		
	Casimiro, Adriana		L	247/96
104	Lopez, Feliciano		L	SG41/1948
	Lopez, Feliciano		L	15.11.41 DS4484
	Arana, Frank		L	6958
	Arana, Frank		L	
105	Martinez, Anacleto	wri	L	
	Martinez, Anacleto		L	SG982/23
	Colindrez, Victor		L	?.1.42 DS4544
	Colindrez, Victor		L	13.7.42 DS4719
	Arzu, Catarino		L	16/53
106	Benguche, Diega	wri	L	
	Benguche, Diega		L	SG68/1928
	McKenzie, George		L	SG369/1928
	Lino, Jane		L	
	Lino, Jane		L	28/37
	Mejia, Santiaga		L	5.9.45
	Mejia, Santiaga	1928	L	

Lot#	Name of Owner	Map	L/G	L/G #
107	Thousand, David		L	SG41/1933
	Sambula, Magdelana		L	DS4482
	Palacio, Reuben	1928	L	9991
108	Thousand, David		L	SG41/1933
	Sambula, Magdelana		L	DS4482
	Castillo, Casimiro V.		L	6.5.53
	Castillo, Casimiro V.		L	1543
109	Sinall, Uriah		L	SG220/1933
	Medina, Loreto		L	11.9.40 DS2015
	Nolberto, Hilma		L	194/88
110	Garcia, Virgin		L	SG723/1927
	Garcia, Virgin		L	
	Arana, Cipriano		L	287/56
	Arana, Saturino V.		L	LD545/79
	Ogaldez, Anthony		L	LC498/91
111	Paulino, Paula		L	SG718/1927
	Paulino, Paula		L	
	Paulino, Paula	1928	L	
	Palacio, Victoria		L	7071
	Ogaldez, Anthony		L	LC60/82
112	Benguche, Santiago	wri	L	
	Benguche, Santiago			app 5 June 1919
	Chimilio, Timoteo		L	9516
	Chimilio, Timoteo	1928	L	
	Arana, Pia		L	1260/77
113	Arzu, Petrona	wri	L	
	Arzu, Petrona		L	app 17.03.19
	Arzu, Petrona		L	SG656/1924
	Palacio, Peter		L	
	Palacio, Peter		L	SG825/1926
	Palacio, Peter		L	3.6.38 DS0757
	Palacio, Peter	1928		
	Paulino, Paula		L	458/62
114	Cunningham, James	wri		
	Cunningham, James		L	app 5 Dec 1918
	Cunningham, James		L	SG270/23
	Paulino, Teleflora		L	SG245/1923
	Paulino, Teleflora		L	286/1935
	Palacio, Fred		L	24.3.52
	Palacio, Fred			448/65
	Palacio, Fred	1928	L	23/92
	Cayetano, John		L	
115	Velasquez, Solomon		L	MPSG387/1924
	Hernandez, Serapio		L	17.11.41 DS4494
	Hernandez, Serapio	1928	L	
	Gabriel, Diega		L	
116	Martinez, Julio F		L	SG722/1927
	Nolberto, Fabiana		L	44/53
	Alvarez, Jovita		L	1340/81
117				
118				

Lot#	Name of Owner	Map	L/G	L/G #
119				
120	Ramirez, Bonifacio		L	app 17 Sept 1921
	Ramirez, Bonifacio		L	SG1026/1928
	Green, Ida		L	SG334/33
121	Palacio, Joe		L	SG130/1922
	Palacio, Felipa		L	SG174/32
	Palacio, Felipa	1928	L	
122	Palacio, Felipa		L	SG448/1931
	Palacio, Felipa		L	SG174/1932
	Velasquez, Jose		L	SG336/33
123	Arzu, Patrocina		L	SG571/1938
	Arana, Eulalia		L	23.1.4? DS4565
	Arana, Eulalia		L	SG894/63
124	Nicholas, Victor		L	SG731930
	Nicholas, Victor		L	4509
	Nicholas, Victor	1928	L	
	Lopez, Raymond		L	839/82
125	Nicholas, V.		L	SG255/1929
	Nicholas, V.		L	23.1.4? DS4565
126	Ariola, Manuela		L	7.12.39 DS1686
	Zuniga, John Jacob		L	SG225/29
	Zuniga, John Jacob		L	14.5.45 DS5766
	Zuniga, John Jacob	1928	L	
	Zuniga, Derick		L	LC89/83
127	Zuniga, John Jacob		L	SG225/29
	Zuniga, John Jacob		L	14.5.45 DS5766
	Zuniga, John Jacob	1928	L	
	Valencio, Daisy Mae		L	LC71/88
128	Zuniga, John Jacob		L	SG225/29
	Zuniga, John Jacob		L	14.5.45 DS5766
	Zuniga, John Jacob	1928	L	
129	Palacio, F.	1928	L	
	Zuniga, Rodney		L	16/88
130	Palacio, Felicta		L	SG53/1930
	Johnson, Beatrice		L	9492
	Johnson, Beatrice	1928	L	
	Valencio, Raymond		L	453/81
131	Velasquez, Solomon		L	SG84/1936
	Velasquez, Solomon	1928	L	
	Martinez, Ambrosine		L	1237/75
132	Velasquez, Solomon		L	SG312/30
	Velasquez, Solomon		L	DS231/54
	Velasquez, Solomon		G	DS8761 &4566
	Velasquez, Solomon	1928	G	
133	Romero, Emerterio		L	SG348/28
	Velasquez, Solomon		L	SG312/1930
	Romero, Emerterio		L	?.9.39 DS1537
	Velasquez, Solomon		L	?.1.4? DS4566
	Velasquez, Solomon		G	DS231/54
	Velasquez, Solomon	1928	G	
134	Romero, Emeterio		L	20/30 SG297/29

Lot#	Name of Owner	Map	L/G	L/G #
	Romero, Emeterio		L	DS2065
	Romero, Emeterio	1928	L	
	used as public well			
135	swampy never any lessee			
136	Baltazar, Angel		L	SG286/1930
	Baltazar, Angel	1928	L	
	Mejia, Isabella		L	471/63
137	Chimilo, Marcial	1928	L	
	Alvarez, Feliciano		L	SG286/1930
	Alvarez, Feliciano		L	2.12.? DS3069
	Alvarez, Feliciano		L	24.2.62
	Alvarez, Feliciano		L	1237/75
	Alvarez, Viviano		L	LC648/81
138	Nicholas, Ignacio L.		L	SG389/29
	Casimiro, Gonzales		L	DS1652
	Casimiro, Gonzales		L	SG896/63
	Casimiro, Mary		L	190/85
139	Nicholas, Cipriano C.		L	SG669/28
	Nicholas, Ursula		L	27.8.49
	Nicholas, Ursula		L	61/70
	Arzu, Julian		L	61/70
140	Nicholas, Cipriano C.		L	SG482/1929
	Givera, Joseph	1928	L	8343/50
141	Pasqual, John		L	27/1930 SG668/1928
	Martinez, Ambrocia	1928	L	8287
	Martinez, Ambrocia	1928	L	
142	Arzu, Patrocina		L	SG451/1929
	Arzu, Candido H.		L	384/50
	Arzu, Candido H.		G	154/83
143	Arzu, Patrocina		L	SG451/1929
	Arzu, Candido H.		L	384/50
	Arzu, Candido H.		G	154/83
144	Ramirez, Bonifacio	wri	L	SG1026/1921
	Noralez, Philip		L	SG290/1930
	Palacio, Gumercinda		L	SG497/1930
	Ramirez, Bonifacio			6353
	Ramirez, Bonifacio	1928		
145	Palacio, Joe	wri	L	SG1306/1922
	Palacio, Ethel		L	24.9.51
	Palacio, Ethel	1928	L	
	Ramirez, Dorothy		L	LC105/85
146	Norelez, Martin B.		L	SG176/1932
	Avilez, James		L	0305
	Avilez, James	1928		
	Avilez, Margarita		L	277/78
	Patnett, Leonie		G	12/96
	Patnett, Leonie			/98
	Watts, Jack, Roger M. Brown, John S. Briggs and Theresa Fairweather		G	
147	Avila, Benigno		L	SG763/1927
	Frazer, Francisco		L	SG418/1930

Lot#	Name of Owner	Map	L/G	L/G #
	Frazer, Francisco		L	SG75/1931
	Palacio, Theodore J.		L	9791
	Palacio, Theodore J.	1928	L	
148	Avila, Benigno		L	SG763/1927
	Noralez, Valentin		L	SG377/1930
	Noralez, Dominica		L	SG335/1933
	Noralez, Dominica	1928	L	
	Martinez, Eulalia		L	1352/63
	Arzu, Nolbert J.		L	441/81
149	Avila, Benigno		L	SG763/1927
	Noralez, Valentin		L	SG377/1930
	Palacio, Gumercinda		L	SG311/1930
	Lopez, Jeffrey		L	13.3.41 DS4106
	Cayetano, Inez		L	8762
	Cayetano, Inez		L	179/78
151	Alvarez, Jerome		L	SG513/28
	Alvarez, Jerome		L	SG97/1929
	Alvarez, Jerome		L	8250
	Alvarez, Jerome	1928		
	Cayetano, Inez		L	167/78
	Mirada(sic), Rhoda			
152	Lorenzo, Victoriano		L	245/56
	Martinez, Elliot		L	195/80
153	Lorenzo, Victoriano		L	245/56
	Martinez, Elliot		L	195/80
154	Arzu, Benito		L	3/57
155	Thomas, Estefana		L	
	Arana, Benedicta		L	2380/77
156	Lino, Jane		L	157/58
157	Lino, Jane		L	588/67
158				
159	Arana, Frank		L	475/66
160				
161				
162	Wells, W.S.		G	
163	Wells, W.S.		G	
164	Wells, W.S.		G	
165	Nicholas, Victor Joseph		L	1105/64
	Arzu, Alfred		L	962/86
166	Nicholas, Victor Joseph		L	1103/64
	Arzu, Alfred		L	963/86
167	Nicholas, Andres		L	116/64
	Martinez, Tolentina		L	530/79
168	Nicholas, Andres		L	2/57
	Nicholas, Andres		L	
169				
170				
171				
172				
173				

Table C5.2. Relationships in House Lot Transmissions

Lot#	Name	Relationship
3	Palacio, Catarino	
3	Arzu, Francisco	Francisco's wife niece of Catarino
3	Palacio, Augustine	brother of Francisco's wife, nephew of Catarino
4	Palacio, Hipolito	
4	Palacio, Reuben	son
5	Nicholas, Philip	
5	Nicholas, Fabiana	wife of Philip
6	Noralez, Venancio	
6	Norelez, Martin B	son of Venancio
6	Avilez, James	1st cousin, nephew of Venancio
6	Avilez, Margarita	wife
9	Avilez, John Justo	
9	Corp Body RC Church	John Avilez's will—daughter Prefecta Nicholas nee Avilez.
10	Avilez, John Justo	
10	Corp Body RC Church	John Avilez's will—daughter Prefecta Nicholas nee Avilez.
12	Ariola, Petrona	
12	Arzu, Estanislao	son of Petrona
15	Lorenzo, Timoteo	
15	Lorenzo, Victor	son
16	Arzu, Isidro	
16	Arzu, Maxima	daughter
19	Chimilio, John	
19	Chimilio, Timoteo	son of John
19	Chimilio, Crispulo	brother, son of John
19	Hijinio, Anita	1C1R, 1C2R of John
20	Ariola, Patricio	
20	Ariola, Catrino	son of Patricio
20	Ariola, Petrona	aunt, sister of Patricio
23	Zuniga, Claro	
23	Zuniga, Rafael C.	son of Claro
23	Martinez, Hipolito	nephew, grandson of Claro
23	Martinez, Eliot	son of Hipolito, great-grandson of Claro
24	Marin, Emelda	
24	Marin, Clarence	brother of Emelda
24	Martinez, Evilia	3C1R, husband 3C
26	Nolberto, Ciriaco	
26	Nolberto, Teresa	daughter ?
29	Nolberto, Pio	
29	Nolberto, Dionisio	son of Pio
29	Nolberto, Paula	daughter, granddaughter of Pio
30	Gibbons, Stephen	
30	Arzu, Petrona	Half sister

1C = first cousin
2C = second cousin
3C = third cousin
1R = once removed
2R = twice removed
3R = thrice removed

Lot#	Name	Relationship
30	Roches, Wilfred	
33	Santino, Augustine	
33	Santino, Frank G.	son of Augustine
34	Jimenez, Angel	
34	Enriquez, Nazaria	common-law wife
34	Chimilio, Nazaria	Same person
36	Paulino, Stephen	
36	Nicholas, David W.	
36	Colon, Naomi	granddaughter of Stephen Paulino
37	Martinez, Escolastica	
37	Nolberto, Isabel	2C1R
39	Zuniga, Catarina	
39	Zuniga, Felix	son of Catarina
39	Santino, Dionicia	2nd cousin, 1C1R of Catarina's husband
40	Santino, Philip	
40	Santino, Eusabio	son of Philip
41	Zuniga, Viviano	
41	Irene Gibbons	2C1R of Viviano
41	Casimiro, Felicia	daughter, 2C2R of Viviano
42	Castillo, Victoriano	
42	Zuniga, Clotildo	grandson of Victoriano
43	Flores, Candido	
43	Flores, Candido and Isidora	wife added to lot
44	Zuniga, Carmen	
44	Nunez, Leonard	common law husband
46	Cayetano, Silas C.	
46	Alvarez, Fabiana	3C & 1C of Silas
47	Martinez, Andres	
47	Martinez, Melvinia	sister of Andres
48	Avila, Pedro	
48	Avila, Viviana	wife of Pedro
48	Avila, Nicholasca	daughter
49	Blas, Macario	
49	Santino, Eusebio	son-in-law of Macario
49	Garcia, Tanis R.	
49	Martinez, Martin	1C2R of Eusebio
50	Castillo, Rafael	
50	Castillo, Simeona	wife of Rafael
50	Ariola, Patricio	
50	Colon, Francisca	daughter of Patricio
52	Nicholas, Ignacio	
52	Nicholas, Philip	brother ?
52	Palacio, Joseph P.	
52	Palacio, Olivia	daughter of Joseph P.
52	Palacio, Joseph O.	brother, son of Joseph P.
52	Palacio, Olivia	sister, daughter of Joseph P.
53	Zuniga, Isaac	
53	Zuniga, Kevin	son of Isaac

Lot#	Name	Relationship
54	Ramirez, Carmen	
54	Paulino, Telesfora	
54	Ramirez, Carmen	
54	Ramirez, Eustaquia	wife of Carmen
54	Ramirez, Bonifacio	son
56	Alvarez, Jeronimo	
56	Alvarez, Zita	granddaughter of Jeronimo
59	Zuniga, Marcos	
59	Castillo, Graciano S.	brotherin-law- of Marcos
60	Nicholas, Andrea	
60	Mejia, Simon	husband
60	Cayetano, Pascasio	
60	Palacio, Sarah	daughter of Pascasio
66	Palacio, Liberato	
66	Polonio, Eusebio	
66	Marin, Clarence	none, grand-nephew of Liberato
66	Marin, Charles	son, great-grand-nephew of Liberato
67	Garcia, Estanislada R	
67	Nicholas, Ignacio L.	his mother is Christine Garcia-relation?
67	Cayetano, Beatrice	husband is the great-grand-nephew
68	Palacio, Theodore	
68	Palacio, Louis	son of Theodore
68	Martinez, Agustina	
68	Martinez, Melvina	daughter of Agustina
69	Avilez, Santiago	
69	Palacio, Saturnino	step-grandson
70	Palacio, Mercedes	
70	Marin, Brigida	daughter
70	Velasquez, Mercedes	mother (same person as Mercedes Palacio)
70	Marin, Brigida	daughter
70	Palacio, Theodore J.	husband
71	Paulino, Diego	
71	Paulino, Dominga	wife of Diego
71	Ariola, Ascenciona	daughter of Diego
71	Diego, Virginia	grand-daughter, great-granddaughter of Diego
71	Ariola, Petrona	daughter of Ascenciona, granddaughter of Diego
71	Diego, Virginia	niece, great-granddaughter of Diego
71	Enriquez, Bertram	
71	Casimiro, Petrona	daughter of Virginia, great-great-granddaughter of Diego
71	Casimiro, Felicia	2C, great-great-granddaughter of Diego
72	Castillo, Cornelio R.	
72	Martinez, Melvinia	Mother of Cornelio
74	Castillo, Inez	
74	Castillo, Cornelio R.	son of Inez
75	Arana, Alejandro	
75	Arana, Narciso	son of Alejandro
75	Arana, Eulalia	sister, daughter of Alejandro
76	Jimenez, Fermin	

Lot#	Name	Relationship
76	Jimenez, Angel	son of Fermin
76	Martinez, Bernadina	
76	Nolberto, Vickie	granddaughter of Bernadina
77	Reyes, Martin	
77	Reyes, Joseph	son of Martin
77	Cayetano, Eugenio	nephew, grandson of Martin
78	Palacio, Nolberto	
78	Palacio, Paul	grandson of Nolberto
80	Cayetano, Marcelo	
80	Cayetano, Gregorio	son of Marcelo
80	Chimilio, Marcial	2C
80	Chimilio, Innocenta	wife
81	Cayetano, Marcelo	
81	Cayetano, Pascasio	son of Marcelo
81	Petillo, Mary	daughter, granddaughter of Marcelo
81	Petillo, Sheridan	daughter, great-granddaughter Marcelo
83	Palacio, Liberato	
83	Loredo, Eulalio	brother-in-law of Liberato
83	Loredo, Henry	son, nephew of Liberato
83	Velasquez, Cristobel	sister, niece of Liberato
83	Blanco, Elvira	daughter, grandniece of Liberato
84	Nolberto, Macario	
84	Zuniga, Inocente	nephew-in-law, wife is niece
84	Zuniga, Lucille	daughter
84	Zuniga, Alvin	son
85	Nolberto, Macario	
85	Nolberto, Ireno	son of Macario
85	Ariola, Patricio	
85	Ariola, Francisco	grandson of Patricio
86	Zuniga, Natividad	
86	Zuniga, Canuto	son of Natividad
86	Zuniga, Lazarus	son, grandson of Natividad
87	Palacio, Anastacio	
87	Gutierrez, Soltera	2nd wife
87	Palacio, Anastacio	husband
87	Loredo, Gregoria	daughter
87	Nunez, Evaristo F.	husband
88	Lucas, Joseph R.	
88	Barrera, Prudencio	
88	Martinez, George	
88	Lucas, John	son of Joseph R.
88	Cayetano, Francis	son, grandson of Joseph R.
88	Cayetano, Nathaniel	son, great-grandson of Joseph R.
89	Nolberto, Francisco	
89	Nolberto, Macario	son of Francisco
89	Baltazar, William	
89	Nolberto, Venancia	sister of Macario, daughter of Francisco
89	Marketing Board	
89	Zuniga, Abraham	grand-nephew, great-grandson of Francisco

Lot#	Name	Relationship
91	Palacio, Anastacio	
91	Reyes, Paulina	daughter-in-law's sister
91	Cayetano, Eugene	son
91	Sanchez, Vicenta	great-grand-niece of Anastacio
92	Casimiro, Pablo	
92	Casimiro, Bernadina	wife of Pablo
92	Casimiro, Paul	son
93	Ariola, Manuela	
93	Lucas, Daniel	
93	Lino, Gladys	half-sister of Manuela
94	Polonio, Pantaleon	
94	Palacio, Tomasa P.	daughter of Pantaleon
94	Avila, Viviana	1C of Tomasa's husband
95	Palacio, Jacob	
95	Martinez, Bernadina	1C1R of Jacob
95	Baltazar, Bernadina	same person married name
95	Sandoval, Felicita	2C1R of Jacob
96	Gregorio, Vivian	
96	Martinez, Bernadina	common-law wife
96	Martinez, Vickie	daughter, step-granddaughter of Vivian
97	Nolberto, Paula	
97	Tuttle, Valerie Delcy	1C1R
98	Norales, Felix	
98	Norales, Juana	wife of Felix
98	Norales, Leonarda	daughter, granddaughter of Felix
98	Norales, Terese	daughter, great-granddaughter of Felix
99	Paulino, Eusebio	
99	Loredo, Hector	
99	Nolberto, Anacleta	common-law wife of Hector Loredo, 2C1R of Eusebio
101	Santino, Victoriana	
101	Mejia, Victoriana Santino	Same person
101	Castillo, Eleuteria M.	daughter
111	Paulino, Paula	
111	Palacio, Victoria	niece of Paula
111	Ogaldez, Anthony	1C1R, grandson of Paula
114	Palacio, Fred	
114	Cayetano, John	1C1R & 2C1R
121	Palacio, Joe	
121	Palacio, Felipa	father's first cousin's wife
124	Nicholas, Victor	
124	Lopez, Raymond	1C2R of Victor
126	Zuniga, John Jacob	
126	Zuniga, Derick	grandson of John
127	Zuniga, John Jacob	
127	Valencio, Daisy Mae	2C2R
130	Palacio, Felicita	
130	Johnson, Beatrice	daughter of Felicita

Lot#	Name	Relationship
130	Valencio, Raymond	son, grandson of Felicita
137	Alvarez, Feliciano	
137	Alvarez, Viviano	son
138	Nicholas, Ignacio L.	
138	Casimiro, Gonzales	1C1R
138	Casimiro, Mary	wife
142	Arzu, Patrocina	
142	Arzu, Candido H.	son of Patrocina
143	Arzu, Patrocina	
143	Arzu, Candido H.	son of Patrocina
144	Palacio, Gumercinda	
144	Ramirez, Bonifacio	2nd cousin
146	Avilez, James	
146	Avilez, Margarita	wife
146	Patnett, Leonie	stepdaughter & niece of husband
148	Avila, Benigno	
148	Noralez, Valentin	
148	Noralez, Dominica	1C1R of Benigno
149	Avila, Benigno	
149	Noralez, Valentin	1st cousin of Benigno
149	Palacio, Gumercinda	Dominica's mother, probably related to Valentin
149	Martinez, Hazel E.	2C2R & 1C2R of Benigno
151	Alvarez, Jerome	
151	Cayetano, Inez	common-law-wife
151	Mirada(sic), Rhoda	granddaughter
152	Lorenzo, Victoriano	
152	Martinez, Elliot	nephew
153	Lorenzo, Victoriano	
153	Martinez, Elliot	nephew
167	Nicholas, Andres	
167	Martinez, Tolentina	common-law-wife

Table C5.3. Degree of Distance of Relationships

Donor	Distance	Recipients			
		Male		Female	
Males	CD1	35	29%	10	8%
	CD2	5	4%	2	2%
	CD3	8	10%	8	10%
	Subtotal	48		20	
Males	AD1	0	0%	22	13%
	AD2	16	13%	4	4%
	AD3	4	3%	5	8%
	Subtotal	20		31	
	Total	68	57%	51	43%
Females	CD1	11	19%	14	26%
	CD2	1	2%	6	9%
	CD3	5	9%	10	18%
	Subtotal	17		30	
Females	AD1	2	4%	0	0%
	AD2	5	9%	1	2%
	AD3	1	2%	1	2%
	Subtotal	8		2	
	Total	25	44%	32	56%

AD1 = Affinal Distance, first degree
AD2 = Affinal Distance, second degree
AD3 = Affinal Distance, third degree
CD1 = Consanguineal Distance, first degree
CD2 = Consanguineal Distance, second degree
CD3 = Consanguineal Distance, third degree

Table C5.4. Male Donors—Consanguineal Recipient

Relationship of Recipient	Total	Male	Female
CD1			
Sons	33	33	
Daughters	8		8
1st Cousin	4	2	2
Subtotal	45	35	10
CD2			
Nephews	5	5	
Nieces	2		2
Subtotal	7	5	2
CD3			
2nd Cousin	5	3	2
1st Cousin once removed	4	2	2
Grandson	3	3	
2nd Cousin once removed	2		2
2nd Cousin twice removed	1		1
Granddaughter	1		1
Subtotal	16	8	8
Total	68	48	20

CD1 = Consanguineal Distance, first degree
CD2 = Consanguineal Distance, second degree
CD3 = Consanguineal Distance, third degree

Table C5.5. Male Donors—Affinal Recipient

Relationship of Recipient	Total	Male	Female
AD1			
Wives	22		22
AD2			
Brother-in-law	6	6	
Son-in-law	4	4	
Nephew-in-law	2	2	
Stepdaughter	2		2
Stepson	1	1	
Wife's sister-in-law	1		1
Step-grandson	1	1	
Co-brother-in-law	1	1	
Co-spouse	1	1	
Niece-in-law	1		1
Subtotal	20	16	4
AD3			
1st Cousin-in-law	3	2	1
2nd Cousin-in-law	2		2
1st Cousin twice removed in-law	1	1	
Wife's brother-in-law	1	1	
Granddaughter-in-law	1		1
Daughter's co-spouse	1		1
Subtotal	9	4	5
Total	51	20	31

AD1 = Affinal Distance, first degree
AD2 = Affinal Distance, second degree
AD3 = Affinal Distance, third degree

Table C5.6. Female Donors—Consanguineal Recipient

Recipient Relationship	Total	Male	Female
CD1			
Daughter	13		13
Son	10	10	
1st Cousin	2	1	1
Subtotal	25	11	14
CD2			
Niece	6		6
Nephew	1	1	
Subtotal	7	1	6
CD3			
Granddaughter	4		4
1st Cousin once removed	4	1	3
2nd Cousin twice removed	2		2
2nd Cousin	2	1	1
1st Cousin twice removed	1	1	
2nd Cousin once removed	1	1	
Grandson	1	1	
Subtotal	15	5	10
Total	47	17	30

CD1 = Consanguineal Distance, first degree
CD2 = Consanguineal Distance, second degree
CD3 = Consanguineal Distance, third degree

Table C5.7. Female Donors—Affinal Recipient

Recipient Relationship	Total	Male	Female
AD1			
Husband	2	2	
Subtotal		2	
AD2			
Son-in-law	3	3	
Nephew-in-law	1	1	
Niece-in-law	1		1
Husband's brother-in-law	1	1	
Subtotal	6	5	1
AD3			
2nd Cousin-in-law	1		1
Father of co-spouse	1	1	
Total	10	8	2

AD1 = Affinal Distance, first degree
AD2 = Affinal Distance, second degree
AD3 = Affinal Distance, third degree

Appendix D—Farmlands

Minute Paper No. 1350/1905

From H. E. the Governor   Date   6 May, 1905

To Ag. Surveyor General

For the favour of your report …

Subject – Reserve at the back of Barranco

1. Please ask the Acting Surveyor General to report whether there is any Crown Land at the back and western of Barranco; if so, is it stated as a Reserve for the people of Barranco, and on what terms are they allowed to cultivate it?

2. I was impressed on the 9th ultimo, when I visited the settlement, that the people of Barranco had to go a considerable distance before they could find land fit for cultivation. Is this so?

(Signed) Brigham Sweet-Escott, Governor

(2) Ag Surveyor General

For the favour of your report

(3) Hon. Ag. Col. Sec.

1 There is no Carib Reserve at the back of Barranco

2. Half the land along the seacoast between the Moho River and the Temash River belongs to the Cramer Estate, the other half to the Crown.

3. Barranco, or Red Cliff village is situate between the above-mentioned rivers. It has not yet been ascertained whether it is on Crown, or private land. I have put up a tracing shewing lands in that vicinity. Please see dnPs 532/1904 and 796/1904, the first of which contains a report by the later Surveyor General.

W.H. Carlin, Ag. Surveyor General …

(5) Hon. Ag Colonial Secretary

This is another instance of the necessity of a systematic survey being undertaken of the Colony's Crown Lands.

Please circulate …

(6) Hon. Acting Colonial Secretary

These papers were laid before the Executive Council at its meeting held on the 23rd instant. It was mentioned that there were some previous papers on the subject showing that the town of Baranco was situated on Crown Lands.

His Excellency states that he would ask the Acting Colonial Secretary to have a search made and that the matter would be brought up again.

H.E. Phillips, Acting Clerk of Councils26 May, 1905

(7) Ag. Surveyor General

Can you trace from the records in your office the papers relating to the survey of Red Cliff or Baranco?

H.E. W. Grant, 13.6.05

(8) Hon. Ag. Col. Sec.

There are previous papers on the survey of Barranco. See R 400/998 of 1892

W. H. Carlin, Ag Surveyor General

(9) Hon. Colonial Secretary

I cannot find in the papers any report on the survey of Baranco. Please refer again to the Ag. Surveyor General. ....

(11) Hon. Ag. Col. Sec.

Please see R 474/2145 92 [of 1892]

I have reason to believe that they contain reports on Barranco.

W.H. Carlin,Ag Surveyor General,19.6.05

(12) Hon,. Colonial Secretary

Please ask the Ag. Surveyor General to justify the statements made in paragraph 3 of (3).

From the paper it would clear that Baranco is on Crown Land. I am not aware that Messrs Cramer

claim this stretch as their property. 22/21.6.05

(14) I herewith enclose a sketch to illustrate my statement of 3 of 3, this work was the first survey made by Mr. Bowen in this Colony, he made the survey from A to B to fix the starting point of the line from B to C, no survey was made from F to E, or E to A, not from E to D, so that Mr. Bowen's account as to the position of Barranco is only guesswork, as no survey was made to determine its position, about five years ago I was to go and make the survey from D to E, but other work stopped me, lands could have been leased near Baranco had this line been run. Please see Surveyor General's letter in R 400/998 dated 23.4.92. Messrs. Cramer, as far as I know have made no claim to Baranco, the line referred to may have to be opened in connection with the trespass in 532/1904.

W.H. Carlin, Ag Surveyor General, 23.6.05 ...

(16) Honourable Acting Colonial Secretary

Laid before the Executive Council at this meeting held in the 30th June last.

It was agreed that these papers be held over till the arrival of the new Surveyor General

A. Baum Dellow, Acting Clerk of Councils ...

B. On arrival of Mr. Perkins H.E.W. Grant

(17) Hon. C.S.

I am now able to send a surveyor to undertake this work and should be glad of an interview with you and explain the plans that are in the office.

(18) Tomorrow at 11

Signed W. Collet, C.S. 4.9.07

(19) Hon. C.S.

I saw you on 9/9/07 at 11:30. I AM SENDING Mr. Williams to make survey. Pease return papers.

Signed H. E. Perkins, S.G.9.9.07 ...

(22) Hon. Ag Col. Sec.

A survey of the sea coast from Moho to Temash River mouth has been made. I propose to run the line dividing the property of Mr. H.J. Cramer from that of the Crown and shall be glad of permission to write to him proposing that the line start from the middle point of the line between Moho River mouth and that of the Temash to the middle point of the boundary on the west.

Signed H.E. Perkins, S.G. 2.4.09 ...

(24) Col. Sec

At a meeting of the Executive Council on the 20th instant the Surveyor Generals suggestion that he should write to Mr. Cramer as proposed above was approved.

Signed H. Phillips, Clerk of Council

(25) For action

Signed C. Reid Davis, Ag C.S.

(26) Hon. Ag. C.S.

Letter from Mr. Cramer herewith. Please return papers.

Signed H.E. Perkins, S.G. 17.06.09 ...

(28) S.G.

It is impossible for the Government to know what proposal you made to Mr. Cramer as no copy of your letter is put up. Please put up a copy.

Signed C. Reid Davis, Ag. C.S., 3.7.09

(29) Hon. AG. C.S.

Copy of letter to Mr. Cramer attached.

Signed H.E. Perkins, S.G. 6.7.09 , ...

(31) Colonial Secretary

At a meeting of the Executive Council on the 13th instant it was decided that the Surveyor General should be directed to carry out the survey in due course without cost to Mr. Cramer.

Signed H. Phillips, Clerk of Council 16.7.09 ...

(33) 1191/1911 Hon.. Col. Sec.

The survey to the North of Barranco between Crown and private land has now been made. It is found that a good number of Caribs have plantations on Crown Lands. As Mr. Williams is about to proceed to Toledo District to make surveys, I would recommend that a notice be printed informing them that unless application is made to lease or purchase the land they occupy they will be prosecuted. Copy of Notice for approval herewith.

Signed W.H. Carlin, Ag S.G. 30.6.11

NOTICE

Surveyor General's Office
Belize, 10th July, 1911

Notice is hereby given that all persons trespassing on Crown lands West of the Village of Barranco will be prosecuted, unless, before the expiration of six weeks from the date hereof, they have made application to lease or purchase, to the District Commissioner, Toledo.

By Order
W.H. Carlin
Action Surveyor General

(35) C.S.

This may be done, but it will be necessary before sending Mr. Williams to the Toledo District to arrange for some surveyor to assist the Superintendent of Railway in his work. ...

(37) Hon. C.S.

I have instructed Mr. Williams to go to Stann Creek and report himself to the Supt. Railway next Monday the 10th instant in accordance with our conversation of the 5th instant.

I should be pleased to received approval of notice as asked for in 33.

Signed W. H. Carlin, Ag. S.G. 6.7.11

(38) Ch.Cl

Have copies of the notice printed, W.G. 7.7.11

Done

JRW

Gazetted on 15 Jul 1911

(39) S.G.

How many copies do you want?

Signed W. Collet, C.S. 7.7.11

(40) Fifty copies were forwarded to the S.G. on the 17th instant.

JRW 17.7.11

(41) 1375/1911

Hon. Col Sec.

Fifty copies of notice has been received and forwarded to D.C. Toledo

Signed W.H. Carlin, Ag S.G.18.7.11 ...

(44) Hon. Col. Sec.

Mr. Williams has not started to lay out lands at the back of Barranco yet, but the notice has had some effect as several Caribs have joined together and made application for a lease of 200 acres.

SignedW. H. Carlin, Asst S.G. 6.11.11 ...

(45) S.G.

How are things now?

Signed W. Collet, C.S. 12.3.12

(46) Hon. C.S.

Mr. Williams reports that the Caribs are continuing cultivating as formerly. The rent on this 200 acres has not yet been paid.

Signed H.E. Perkins, S.G. 15.3.12

(47) S.G.

Was the application for lease approved?

Signed W. Collet, C.S. 16.3.12

(48) 481/1912

Hon. C.S.

Yes

H.E. Perkins, S.G. 19.3.12

(49) S.G.

Better prosecute.

W. Collet, C.S. 19.4.12

(50) 708/1912

Hon. C.S.

Noted

H.E. Perkins, S.G. 19.4.12

(51) S.G.

What action has been taken?

W. Collet, 7.6.12

(52) 1108/1912

Hon. C.S.

The rent for 1912 has been paid on 8.5.12 without prosecution.

H.E. Perkins, S.G. 7.6.12

(53) Submitted, W.G. 8.6.12, File 10.6.12

Table D6.1. Farmland Parcel Applications

#*		Size	Name	Year	F/M	L/G	Location
153	*	1	Loredo, Wilhelmina	1936	F	L	Barranco - south
154		1	Lawrie, Florencio	1954	M	L	Barranco - south
155		2	Palacio, Carlota	1954	F	L	Barranco - south
156		1	Avila, Sotera N.	1937	F	L	Barranco - south
156		1	Apolonio, Vicente	1954	M	L	Barranco - south
156		1	Marin, Aparicio	1961	M	L	Barranco - south
157		2	Nolberto, Albert	1954	M	L	Barranco - south
158		2	Nicholas, Tiburcio	1954	M	L	Barranco - south
159	*	2	Daniels, S.B.	1935	M	L	Barranco - south
160		2	Nightingale, Jack	1980	M	L	Barranco - south
161		2	Nicholas, Cipriano	1954	M	L	Barranco - south
162		2	Noralez, Dominica	1940	F	L	Barranco - south
162		2	Zuniga, Amanda	1954	F	L	Barranco - south
163		2	Martinez, Matildo	1939	M	L	Barranco - south
163		2	Arzu, Dominica	1954	F	L	Barranco - south
164		1	Valencio, Guillermo	1954	M	L	Barranco - south
165		2	Alvarez, Jerome	1936	M	G	Barranco - south
180	*	10	Alvarez, Estanislao	1978	M	L	Barranco
180	*	10	Alvarez, Eustace Vr		M	L	Barranco
181	*	2	Aponcio, Maria		F	L	Barranco

*Parcel numbers were not assigned by GOB for many parcels. Where * appears, the parcel number for this parcel is one we assigned, not assigned by GOB.

**Parcel numbers from the 1954 map are approximate locations on Plan 541.

***A 200 acre parcel was leased by a group. All parcels marked *** are part of this parcel. Parcel 279 is the SW corner.

G = Grant; L = Lease; P = Location ticket purchase

#*		Size	Name	Year	F/M	L/G	Location
182	*	20	Arana, Cipriano	1958	M	L	Barranco
200		50	Polonio, Cecilio	1913	M	L	Barranco - northwest
201		54	Polonio, Cecilio	1954	M	L	Barranco - northwest
203		40	Benguche, Santiago	1913	M	L	Barranco - northwest
203		20	Benguche, Santiago	1918	M	G	Barranco - northwest
204		20	Alvarez, Jeronimo	1913	M	L	Barranco - northwest
205	**	10	Palacio, Joseph P.	1931	M	L	Barranco - northwest
206	**	25	Alvarez, Eustacio	1954	M	L	Barranco - northwest
207	**	20	Martinez, Matildo	1937	M	L	Barranco - northwest
208	**	10	Chimilio, John	1916	M	L	Barranco - northwest
210		10	Martinez, Julio	1931	M	L	Barranco - northwest
210		10	Zuniga, Abraham		M	L	Barranco - northwest
211	**	10	Zuniga, Catarina	1928	F	L	Barranco - northwest
211		12	Martinez, Wilhemina		F	L	Barranco - northwest
212		10	Martinez, Francisco	1928	M	L	Barranco - northwest
212		9	Palacio, Antonia		F	L	Barranco - northwest
213		10	Lopez, Feliciano	1928	M	L	Barranco - northwest
213		10	Ariola, Benita		F	L	Barranco - northwest
214		15	Ariola, Catarino	1928	M	L	Barranco - northwest
214	**	20	Nicholas, Victor	1955	M	L	Barranco - northwest
214	**	20	Gabriel, Diega	1955	F	L	Barranco - northwest

#*		Size	Name	Year	F/M	L/G	Location
215		15	Palacio, Nicorana	1923	F	L	Barranco - west
215		20	Avilez, Euphemio	1953	M	F.G.	Barranco - west (ex-serviceman)
218		20	Martinez, Pascual	1923	M	L	Barranco - west
218		20	Palacio, Nicodemus	1950	M	F.G.	Barranco - west (ex-serviceman)
218		20	Nicholas, Cipriano	1954	M	F.G.	Barranco - west (ex-serviceman)
220		10	Johnson, Beatrice	1954	F	L	Barranco - west
221	**	10	Loredo, H.E.	1922	M	L	Barranco - west
222		5	Chimilio, John	1936	M	L	Boyo Creek - cattle path -north
224	**	20	Velasquez, Soloman	1936	M	L	Barranco - northwest
225	**	10	Loredo, Henry	1936	M	L	Barranco - northwest
226		5	Martinez, Bernadina		F	L	Barranco - northwest
227		10	Ramirez, Justina	1958	F	L	Barranco - northwest
228		10	Ramirez, Bonifacio	1954	M	L	Barranco - northwest
229	**	15	Ariola, Benita		F	L	Barranco - northwest
230	**	15	Ariola, Catarino	1928	M	L	Barranco - west
231		10	Cayetano, Eugenio	1954	M	L	Barranco - west
232		5	Arana, Eulalia	1954	F	L	Barranco - west
234		10	Arana, Eulalia	1954	F	L	Barranco - west
235		10	Arana, Lauriano	1939	M	L	Barranco - west
238	*	5	Nicholas, Cipriano	1957	M	L	Barranco - northwest
238	*	5	Nicholas, I.C.	1930	M	L	Barranco - northwest
238		10	Zuniga, Filomena	1937	F	L	Barranco - northwest
239	**	10	Nicholas, Frederick	1953	M	L	Barranco - west

#*		Size	Name	Year	F/M	L/G	Location
240	*	15	McKenzie, George	1936	M	L	Barranco - west
240	*	15	Cayetano, Eugenio	1936	M	L	Barranco - west
241	**	15	Ariola, Catarino P.	1953	M	L	Barranco - west
245		20	Palacio, Nicodemus	1954	M	F.G.	Barranco - west (ex-serviceman)
248	*	10	Blanco, Elvira	1954	M	L	Barranco - west
249		30	Avilez, Santiago J.	1955	M	L	Barranco - west
251		10	Castro, Michaela	1955	F	L	Barranco - west
252	**	5	Palacio, Saturino	1928	M	L	Barranco - west
255	**	20	Noralez, Venancio	1923	M	L	Barranco - west
255	**	10	Palacio, Gumercinda	1933	F	L	Barranco - west
255	**	10	Castillo, Cornelio R.	1939	M	L	Barranco - west
258	**	5	Martinez, Bernadina	1930	F	L	Barranco - west
260	**	10	Lorenzo, Timoteo	1928	M	L	Barranco - south
262	**	20	Polonio, Pantaleon	1913	M	L	Barranco - south
262	**	20	Polonio, Pantaleon	1917	M	G	Barranco - south
263		20	Martinez, Domingo C.	1919	M	L	Barranco - south
263	**	10	Arzu, Domingo	1955	M	L	Barranco - south
265		20	Nicholas, Merehildo	1950	M	F.G.	Barranco - south (ex-serviceman)
266	**	5	Garcia, M.	1928	M	L	Barranco - south
267		11	Paulino, Telesfora	1954	F	L	Barranco - south
269	**	10	Castillo, Cornelio R.	1945	M	L	Barranco - south
270	**	10	Garcia, Margarito	1923	M	L	Barranco - south
270	**	10	Casimiro, Innocente	1939	M	L	Barranco - south

#*		Size	Name	Year	F/M	L/G	Location
270		10	Nicholas, Victor	1954	M	L	Barranco - south
270	**	10	Nicholas, Cipriano		M	L	Barranco - south
271	**	20	Arana, Atanacio	1939	M	L	Barranco - south
271		20	Casimiro, Gonzalez	1954	M	F.G.	Barranco - south (ex-serviceman)
272	**	25	Guevarra, Joseph	1939	M	L	Barranco - south
272		25	Casimiro, Paul	1954	M	L	Barranco - south
273	**	25	Garcia, Esmith	1913	M	L	Barranco - south
273	**	25	Garcia, Esmith	1923	M	L	Barranco - south
273		25	Castillo, Graciano	1929	M	L	Barranco - south
274		20	Palacio, Paul	1950	M	F.G.	Barranco - south (ex-serviceman)
275		6	Marin, Clarence	1954	M	L	Barranco - south
276	**	5	Santino, Philip	1952	M	L	Barranco - south
276		12	Santino, Philip	1954	M	L	Barranco - south
277	**	10	Marin, Clarence	1952	M	L	Barranco - south
277		10	Marin, Clarence	1954	M	L	Barranco - south
278	**	5	Chimilio, John	1952	M	L	Barranco - south
278		5	Chimilio, John	1954	M	L	Barranco - south
278	**	5	Chimilio, John	1957	M	L	Barranco - south
279	***	10	Nicholas, Ursula	1928	F	L	Barranco - south
279		14	Nicholas, Ursula	1954	F	L	Barranco - south
281	***	5	Harvey, Louis	1953	M	L	Barranco - south
281		6	Harvey, Louis	1954	M	L	Barranco - south
282		10	Meijia, Abraham	1954	M	L	Barranco - south

*Parcel numbers were not assigned by GOB for many parcels. Where * appears, the parcel number for this parcel is one we assigned, not assigned by GOB.

**Parcel numbers from the 1954 map are approximate locations on Plan 541.

***A 200 acre parcel was leased by a group. All parcels marked *** are part of this parcel. Parcel 279 is the SW corner.

G = Grant; L = Lease; P = Location ticket purchase

#*		Size	Name	Year	F/M	L/G	Location
283		20	Fernandez, Francisco	1901	M	L	Barranco - south
283		50	Walbank & Forslund	1912	M	G	Barranco - south
283		50	Conner, Sam		M	L	Barranco - south
284	**	25	Loredo, Eulalio	1913	M	L	Barranco - south
284	**	11	Nicholas. Cipriano	1951	M	L	Barranco - south
285	***	10	Chimio, Simon	1953	M	L	Barranco - south
286	***	10	Cayetano, M.	1918	M	L	Barranco - south
288	***	14	Flowers, C.	1952	M	L	Barranco - south
289	***	10	de Boire, Francios	1953	M	L	Barranco - south
290		23	Boire, F.D.		M	L	Barranco - south
291	*	5	Chimilio, Simon		M	L	Barranco - south
292		20	Avilez, John, Justo	1912	M	G	Sea - SW of Barranco
293		10	Nicholas, Sotero	1922	M	L	Barranco - south
293	*	10	Nicholas, Sotero	1930	M	L	Sea - SW of Barranco
293		10	Watts, Jack	2000	M	L	Barranco - south
294	*	10	Avilez, James J.	1946	M	L	Sea - SW of Barranco
294	*	10	Avilez, James J.	1949	M	L	Sea - SW of Barranco
294		13	Watts, Jack	2000	M	L	Barranco - south
296	**	10	Palacio, Augustine	1952	M	L	Barranco - south
297	*	11	Velasquez, Saloma	1922	F	L	Barranco - south
297		11	Avilez, Margarita	1955	F	L	Barranco - south
299		25	Santino, Philip	1913	M	L	Barranco - south
301		10	Juarez, Timoteo	1919	M	L	Barranco - south
302	*	20	Wickham, H.A.	1892	M	L	Temash Bar - left
303	*	20	Enriquez, Nazaria	1957	F	L	Barranco - south
304		20	Santino, Philip		M	G	Barranco - south

#*		Size	Name	Year	F/M	L/G	Location
305	*	20	Polonio, Pantaleon		M	L	Barranco - south
306	*	60	Crawford, James	1892	M	L	Temash Bar - left
307	*	10	Arzu, Luciano	1917	M	L	Barranco - south
307	*	10	de Boire, Francios	1953	M	L	Barranco - northeast
308	*	6	Clark, John A.	1932	M	L	Barranco - northeast
308	*	6	Clark, John A.	1942	M	L	Barranco - northeast
308	*	6	Clark, John A.	1944	M	L	Barranco - northeast
308	*	6	Plummer, Walter	1955	M	L	Barranco - northeast
308	*	6	de Boire, Francios	1955	M	L	Barranco - northeast
310	*	2	Magdelano, Joseph	1931	M	L	Legegu
311	*	2	Magdelano, Bernardo	1932	M	L	Legegu
312	*	2	Marin, Clarence	1937	M	L	Legegu
313	*	0.5	St. Clair, John	1929	M	L	Barranco - northeast
314	*	0.5	Palacio, Nicanora	1930	F	L	Barranco - northeast
315	*		Salome, Vicente	1927	M	L	Sea - NE of Barranco
316	*	15	Zuniga, Innocente	1920	M	L	Sea - NE of Barranco
317	*	5	Zuniga, Innocente	1938	M	L	Sea - NE of Barranco
318	*	10	Zuniga, John Joseph	1931	M	L	Sea - NE of Barranco
324		50	Arzu, C. H.	1954	M	L	Lidise
326		20	Palacio, J.	1956	M	L	Lidise

*Parcel numbers were not assigned by GOB for many parcels. Where * appears, the parcel number for this parcel is one we assigned, not assigned by GOB.

**Parcel numbers from the 1954 map are approximate locations on Plan 541.

***A 200 acre parcel was leased by a group. All parcels marked *** are part of this parcel. Parcel 279 is the SW corner.

G = Grant; L = Lease; P = Location ticket purchase

#*		Size	Name	Year	F/M	L/G	Location
327		10	Palacio, A.	1956	M	P	Lidise
328		10	Marin, C.	1956	M	P	Lidise
329		10	Palacio, P.	1956	M	P	Lidise
330		10	Zuniga, C.	1956	M	P	Lidise
331		20	Garcia, Secondino	1956	M	P	Lidise
332		20	Avila, R. P.	1956	M	P	Lidise
333		20	Nolberto, L.	1956	M	P	Lidise
334		20	Castillo, C.	1956	M	P	Lidise
335		20	Castillo, F. B.	1956	M	P	Lidise
336		50	Heyer, Irving A.	1956	M	P	Lidise
337		10	Nicholas, Adriano	1956	M	P	Lidise
338		15	Gonzales, Felicita	1960	F	P	Lidise
339	*	50	de Boire, Francois	1955	M	P	Lidise
340	*	10	Martinez, Clinton	1964	M	P	Lidise
341	*	10	Nicholas, Andres	1958	M	P	Lidise
342	*	10	Augustine, Timothy	1959	M	P	Lidise
343	*	20	Arana, Cipriano	1956	M	P	Lidise
344	*	20	Chimilio, Sylvan	1956	M	P	Lidise
345	*	20	Palacio, Inez	1958	M	P	Lidise
346	*	50	Barranco Farmers Coop	1956	M	P	Lidise
396	*	10	Sanchez, Juan	1894	M	L	Boyo Creek - north
397	*	20	Palacio, Saturnino	1920	M	L	Boyo Creek - north
398	*	50	Ramirez, Bonifacio	1917	M	L	Boyo Creek - north
399	*	20	Garcia, Smith	1922	M	L	Boyo Creek - north
400	*	32	Paulino, Diego	1892	M	L	Boyo Creek - north

#*		Size	Name	Year	F/M	L/G	Location
401	*	20	Fernandez, F.	1892	M	L	Boyo Creek - north
402	*	20	Paulino, Augustin	1892	M	L	Boyo Creek - north
403	*	8	Requena, Antolino	1892	M	L	Boyo Creek - north
404	*	20	Lambey, John	1893	M	L	Boyo Creek - north
405	*	8	Blas, Macario	1891	M	L	Boyo Creek - north
406	*	8	Palacio, Nolberto	1891	M	L	Boyo Creek - north
407	*	5	Lino,Obispo	1891	M	L	Boyo Creek - north
408	*	16	Gutierrez, Basilio	1904	M	L	Boyo Creek - north
409	*	10	Palacio, Hipolito	1912	M	G	Boyo Creek - north
410	*	5	Palacio, Liberato	1891	M	L	Boyo Creek - north
410	*	20	Palacio, Anastacio	1891	M	L	Boyo Creek - north
411	*	30	Cayetano, Marcelo	1891	M	G	Boyo Creek - north
411	*	30	Cayetano, Marcelo	1898	M	G	Boyo Creek - north
412	*	20	Nolberto, Pio	1894	M	L	Boyo Creek - north
413	*	25	Lambey, Santiago	1893	M	L	Boyo Creek - north
414	*	5	Nicholas, Ignacio	1937	M	L	Boyo Creek - north
415	*	20	Cayetano, John	1936	M	L	Boyo Creek - middle, left
416	*	5	Avilez, Margarita	1942	F	L	Boyo Creek - middle, left
417	*	10	Chimilio, John	1936	M	L	Boyo Creek - middle, left
418	*	10	Alvarez, J.	1920	M	L	Boyo Creek - middle, left
418	*	10	Alvarez, J.	1924	M	L	Boyo Creek - middle, left
419	*	10	Alvarez, J.	1941	M	L	Boyo Creek - middle, left

#*		Size	Name	Year	F/M	L/G	Location
420	*	50	Garrett, William	1929	M	L	Boyo Creek - middle, left
421	*	30	Clotter, Rafael	1925	M	L	Boyo Creek - middle, left
422	*	20	Velasquez, Gabriel	1917	M	L	Boyo Creek - middle, left
422	*	20	Velasquez, Gabriel	1923	M	L	Boyo Creek - middle, left
423	*	20	Castillo, Inez	1913	M	L	Boyo Creek - middle, left
423	*	20	Castillo, Nicodemus R.	1926	M	L	Boyo Creek - middle, left
424	*	10	Nicholas, Leonicio	1908	M	L	Boyo Creek - middle, left
425	*	10	Nicholas, Philip	1923	M	L	Boyo Creek - middle, left
425	*	50	Palma, David	1933	M	L	Boyo Creek - middle, left
426	*	5	Robateau, Henrietta	1941	F	L	Boyo Creek - middle, left
426	*	5	Palma, David	1943	M	L	Boyo Creek - middle, left
427	*	30	Ariola, Patricio	1913	M	L	Boyo Creek - middle, left
428	*	30	Nicholas, Ignacio L.	1929	M	L	Boyo Creek - middle, left
429	*	20	Nicholas, Leoncio	1893	M	L	Boyo Creek - middle, left
429	*	20	Nicholas, Leoncio	1910	M	G	Boyo Creek - middle, left
429	*	20	Nicholas, Leoncio	1913	M	L	Boyo Creek - middle, left
430	*	5	Nicholas, Ignacio Leoson	1944	M	L	Boyo Creek - middle, left
431	*	10	Jimenez, Angel F.	1920	M	L	Boyo Creek - middle, left
432	*	25	Johnson, Henry	1932	M	L	Boyo Creek - middle, left
433	*	10	Arzu, Petrona	1923	F	L	Boyo Creek - middle, left
433	*	10	Nicholas, Joaquin	1930	M	G	Boyo Creek - middle, left
434	*	50	Alvarez, Pio	1923	M	L	Boyo Creek - middle, left

#*		Size	Name	Year	F/M	L/G	Location
435	*	10	Norales, Felix	1935	M	L	Boyo Creek - middle, left
436	*	10	Francisco, Fernando	1939	M	L	Boyo Creek - middle, left
437	*	15	Chimilio, John	1923	M	L	Boyo Creek - middle, right
438	*	10	Zuniga, Rafael	1917	M	L	Boyo Creek - middle, right
438	*	10	Zuniga, Rafael	1923	M	L	Boyo Creek - middle, right
439	*	10	Zuniga, Innocente	1922	M	L	Boyo Creek - middle, right
440	*	15	Alvarez, Jeronimo	1923	M	L	Boyo Creek - middle, right
440	*	15	Timoteo Lorenzo	1950	M	G	Boyo Creek - middle, right
441	*	15	Cayetano, John	1946	M	L	Boyo Creek - middle, right
442	*	10	Hill, Julio	1952	M	L	Boyo Creek - mouth, right
443	*	10	Nicholas, Ignatius	1948	M	L	Boyo Creek - mouth, right
444	*	10	Arzu, Petrona	1947	F	L	Boyo Creek - mouth, right
445	*	20	Jimenez, Angel F.	1908	M	L	Boyo Creek - mouth, right
445	*	14	McKenzie, George	1948	M	L	Boyo Creek - mouth, right
445	*	14	Cayetano, Eugene	1951	M	L	Boyo Creek - mouth, right
446	*	10	de Boire, Francios	1956	M	L	Boyo Creek - mouth, right
447		20	Arzu, Domingo	1951	M	F.G.	Barranco - south
448	**	10	Arzu, Domingo	1951	M	L	Barranco - south
450	***	200	Loredo, Blas, Palacio	1913	M	L	Barranco - south

*Parcel numbers were not assigned by GOB for many parcels. Where * appears, the parcel number for this parcel is one we assigned, not assigned by GOB.

**Parcel numbers from the 1954 map are approximate locations on Plan 541.

***A 200 acre parcel was leased by a group. All parcels marked *** are part of this parcel. Parcel 279 is the SW corner.

G = Grant; L = Lease; P = Location ticket purchase

#*		Size	Name	Year	F/M	L/G	Location
450		300	Gray, George E.	1929	M	L	Barranco - south
455	*	20	Palacio, Paul	1950	M	F.G.	Boyo Creek - cattle path -south
456	*	20	Casimiro, Gonzales	1950	M	F.G.	Boyo Creek - cattle path -south
457	*	20	Casimiro, Peter	1950	M	F.G.	Boyo Creek - cattle path -south
458	*	20	Nolberto, Lorenzo	1950	M	F.G.	Boyo Creek - cattle path -south
459	*	20	Nicholas, Cipriano	1950	M	F.G.	Boyo Creek - cattle path -south
460	*	20	Zuniga, John J.	1927	M	L	Wallis Creek on Sea
461	*	20	Suazo, M.	1913	U	L	Wallis Creek on Sea
461	*	20	Nuñez, Francisco	1926	M	L	Wallis Creek on Sea
462	*	20	Simms, James	1913	M	L	Wallis Creek on Sea
462	*	20	Avilez, Antonio	1919	M	L	Wallis Creek on Sea
462	*	20	Arana, John	1929	M	L	Wallis Creek on Sea
462	*	20	Avilez, Antonio	1930	M	L	Wallis Creek on Sea
462	*	20	Alvarez, Feliciano	1946	M	L	Wallis Creek on Sea
463	*	26	Nuñez, Thomas	1913	M	L	Wallis Creek on Sea
463	*	26	Nuñez, Thomas	1922	M	L	Wallis Creek on Sea
463	*	26	Nuñez, Thomas	1929	M	L	Wallis Creek on Sea
464	*	17	Avilez, Antonio	1913	M	L	Wallis Creek on Sea
464	*	17	Colin?, Frank	1931	M	L	Wallis Creek on Sea
465	*	20	Lucas, John N.	1913	M	L	Wallis Creek on Sea
465	*	20	Enriquez, Anaceta	1925	F	L	Wallis Creek on Sea

#*		Size	Name	Year	F/M	L/G	Location
466	*	20	Lucas, Victor B.	1919	M	L	Wallis Creek on Sea
467	*	20	Lambey, Severiano	1919	M	L	Wallis Creek on Sea
468	*	60	Daniels, Salvador B.	1919	M	L	Wallis Creek on Sea
469	*	25	Bailey, Jeremiah	1943	M	L	Temash - left X from Red Bank
470	*	125	Vernon, Samuel B	1916	M	L	Temash - Red Bank - right -Quiripi
470	*	15	Garvin, A. and H. E. Baily	1942	M	L	Temash - Red Bank - right -Quiripi
471	*	15	Nicholas, Sotero	1937	M	L	Temash - Red Bank - right
472	*	30	Arzu, Isidoro	1913	M	L	Temash - Red Bank - right
472	*	15	Fuentes, Thomas	1938	M	L	Temash - Red Bank - right
472	*	15	Fuentes, Thomas	1940	M	L	Temash - Red Bank - right
472	*	15	Garvin, A. and E.S. Baily	1941	M	L	Temash - Red Bank - right
472	*	30	Pearce, Levi	1930	M	L	Temash - Red Bank - right
473	*	20	Daniels, S. B.	1928	M	L	Temash - Red Bank - right
474	*	20	Bermudez, Martin	1942	M	L	Temash - Red Bank - right
475	*	6	Avilez, Lucio	1931	M	L	Temash - Red Bank - right - Texas
475	*	6	Cayetano, John	1939	M	L	Temash - Red Bank - right - Texas
476	*	6	Canelo, Leonicio	1938	M	L	Temash - Red Bank - right
477	*	20	Avila, Reginald	1949	M	L	Temash - left X from Red Bank
478	*	20	Pollard, Ernesto	1939	M	L	Temash - left X from Red Bank
479	*	30	Roches, Secundo	1913	M	L	Temash - left - W (big bend)

#*		Size	Name	Year	F/M	L/G	Location
480	*	30	Paulino, Augustin	1913	M	L	Temash - left - W (big bend)
481	*	25	Garcia, Mrs.	1964	F	L	Temash - left - W (big bend)
482	*	40	Colon, Angela	1913	F	L	Temash - left - W (big bend)
484	*	20	Daniels, S. B.	1934	M	L	Temash - left - W (big bend)
485	*	8	Nicholas, Candida C.	1937	F	L	Temash - left - W (big bend)
487	*	50	Roches, Petrona	1930	F	L	Temash - left - W (big bend)
488	*	12	King, Enemecio A.	1930	M	L	Temash - left - W (big bend)
489	*	10	Ariola, Benita	1930	F	L	Temash - left - W (big bend)
490	*	20	Bailey, Octavio L.	1935	M	L	Temash - left - W (big bend)
491	*	10	Nicholas, Cipriano	1938	M	L	Temash - left - W (big bend)
492	*	20	Ruiz, Justo	1935	M	L	Temash - left - W (big bend)
493	*	10	Fuentes, C	1949	U	L	Temash - left - W (big bend)
494	*	10	Fuentes, C	1949	U	L	Temash - left - W (big bend)
495	*	20	Martinez, F.B.	1930	M	L	Temash - left - W (big bend)
496	*	30	Martinez, Secundino	1934	M	L	Temash - left - W (big bend)
497	*	13	Zuniga, T. (Tom or Toya)	1949	U	L	Temash - left - W (big bend)
498	*	20	Roches, Nolberto	1945	M	L	Temash - left - W (big bend)
499	*	2	Martinez, Pedro	1937	M	L	Temash - left - Fairview
500	*	10	Jimenz, Angel	1929	M	L	Temash - left - Fairview
500	*	10	Casimiro, Pablo	1930	M	L	Temash - left - Fairview
501	*	50	Duncan, Bartimeus	1933	M	L	Temash - left - Fairview

#*		Size	Name	Year	F/M	L/G	Location
502	*	10	Duncan, Bartimeus	1933	M	L	Temash - left - Fairview
503	*	60	Martinez, Gregorio	1923	M	L	Temash - left - Fairview
504	*	40	Daniels, Michael B.	1923	M	L	Temash - left - Fairview
505	*	10	Paulino, Telesfora	1935	F	L	Temash - left - Fairview
506	*	10	Palacio, Nolberto	1936	M	L	Temash - left - Fairview
507	*	20	Palacio, Saturino	1923	M	L	Temash - left - Fairview
507	*	20	Martinez, Eulogio	1936	M	L	Temash - left - Fairview
508	*	20	Paulino, Martina	1937	F	L	Temash - left - Lagunurugu
508	*	20	Paulino, Martin	1937	M	L	Temash - left - Lagunurugu
508	*	20	Williams, Thomas A.	1937	M	L	Temash - left - Lagunurugu
509	*	30	Juarez, Timoteo	1919	M	L	Temash - left - Lagunurugu
509	*	25	Belizario, Isaac	1936	M	L	Temash - left - Lagunurugu
510	*	20	Pitts, James	1894	M	L	Temash - left - Lagunurugu
510	*	30	Pitts, James	1905	M	L	Temash - left - Lagunurugu
510	*	5	Enriquez, Clara	1928	F	L	Temash - left - Lagunurugu
510	*	5	Enriquez, Clara	1938	F	L	Temash - left - Lagunurugu
510	*	5	Enriquez, Clara	1951	F	L	Temash - left - Lagunurugu
511	*	5	Roches, S.	1951	M	L	Temash - left - Lagunurugu
512	*	5	Marin, Clarence	1934	M	L	Temash - right - Quiripi

*Parcel numbers were not assigned by GOB for many parcels. Where * appears, the parcel number for this parcel is one we assigned, not assigned by GOB.

**Parcel numbers from the 1954 map are approximate locations on Plan 541.

***A 200 acre parcel was leased by a group. All parcels marked *** are part of this parcel. Parcel 279 is the SW corner.

G = Grant; L = Lease; P = Location ticket purchase

#*		Size	Name	Year	F/M	L/G	Location
513	*	10	Nicholas, Victor	1944	M	L	Temash - right - Quiripi
514	*	16	Zuniga, Canuto	1933	M	L	Temash - right - Quiripi
515	*	5	Palacio, Pedro	1933	M	L	Temash - right - Largo
516	*	5	Arana, Eulalia	1941	M	L	Temash - right - Largo
517	*	10	Nicholas, F.	1933	M	L	Temash - right - Largo
518	*	30	Martinez, Ramon-CDS	1934	M	L	Temash - right - Largo
519	*	5	Nolberto, Trinidad	1947	F	L	Temash - right - Largo
520	*	15	Nolberto, Dominga	1936	F	L	Temash - right - Largo
521	*	50	Andrade, M.	1894	M	L	Temash - right - Largo
521	*	50	Mason, James Rogers	1928	M	L	Temash - right - Largo
521	*	10	Plummer, Guillermo	1955	M	L	Temash - right - Largo
522	*	15	Baily, Jeremiah	1936	M	L	Temash - right - Largo
523	*	20	Philip Santino	1892	M	L	Sundaywood Creek mouth - right
524	*	15	Reid, L.	1935	M	L	Temash - right - Largo
524	*	15	Plummer, Walter	1955	M	L	Temash - right - Largo
525	*	50	Fuentes, Thomas	1928	M	L	Temash - right - Largo
526	*	10	Nicholas, Fabriana	1937	F	L	Temash - right - Largo
527	*	10	Marin, Aparicio	1932	M	L	Temash - right - Largo
527	*	10	Marin, Aparicio	1947	M	L	Temash - right - Largo
528	*	20	Nicholas,Victor	1939	M	L	Temash - right - Largo
529	*	10	Nuñez, Evaristo	1936	M	G	Temash - right - Largo
530	*	10	Flores, Domingo	1936	M	G	Temash - right - Largo

#*		Size	Name	Year	F/M	L/G	Location
531	*	10	Mejia, Ambrocine	1936	M	L	Temash - right - Largo
532	*	5	Martinez	1942	M	L	Temash - right - Largo
533	*	5	Martinez, Eulalia	1944	F	L	Temash - right - Largo
533	*	5	Martinez, Ramon *et al* (CDS)	1933	M	L	Temash - right - Largo
534	*	20	Palacio, Saturino	1931	M	L	Temash - right A - Dulcis
534	*	20	Valencio, Guillermo	1961	M	L	Temash - right A - Dulcis
535	*	20	Clark, Juan A.	1934	M	L	Temash - right A - Dulcis
536	*	20	Avilez, J.J.	1934	M	L	Temash - right A - Dulcis
537	*	5	Daniels, S. B.	1934	M	L	Temash - right A - Dulcis
537	*	5	Casimiro	1934	M	L	Temash - right A - Dulcis
537	*	3	Bevans	1932	M	L	Temash - right A - Dulcis
537	*	3	Avilez, Euphemio	1949	M	L	Temash - right A - Dulcis
537	*	3	Plummer, Walter	1953	M	L	Temash - right A - Dulcis
538	*	10	Zuniga, John J.	1935	M	L	Temash - right A - Dulcis
538	*	10	Daniels, S.B.	1943	M	L	Temash - right A - Dulcis
539	*	5	Levy, Hylton	1937	M	L	Temash - right A - Dulcis
540	*	40	Crawford, James	1892	M	L	Temash - right A - Dulcis
540	*	20	Arzu, Patrocina	1934	F	L	Temash - right A - Dulcis
540	*	20	Palacio, Joseph P.	1944	M	L	Temash - right A - Dulcis
541	*	20	Bermudez, Eli	1933	M	L	Temash - right A - Dulcis
541	*	10	Bondswell, James	1937	M	L	Temash - right A - Dulcis

#*		Size	Name	Year	F/M	L/G	Location
542	*	50	Plummer, Walter	1931	M	L	Temash - right A - Dulcis
543	*	10	Noralez, Felix (Lucas, Felix)	1937	M	L	Temash - right A - Dulcis
544	*	50	Audinette, E.	1932	M	L	Temash - right A - Dulcis
545	*	50	Palacio, Carlos (Catarino)	1898	M	L	Temash - right A - Dulcis
545	*	50	Palacio, Carlos	1933	M	L	Temash - right A - Dulcis
546	*	20	Palacio, J.	1937	M	L	Temash - right A - Dulcis
547	*	50	Plummer, Walter	1939	M	L	Temash - right A - Dulcis
548	*	5	Fuentes, Thomas	1938	M	L	Temash - right A - Dulcis
548	*	5	Enriquez, Nazaria	1943	F	L	Temash - right A - Dulcis
550	*	50	Fowler, George	1929	M	L	Temash - right A - Dulcis
551	*	10	Bondswell, James	1937	M	L	Temash - right A - Dulcis
552	*	80	Reyes, Martin	1893	M	L	Temash - right A - Dulcis
552	*	50	Williams, Edward	1929	M	L	Temash - right A - Dulcis
553	*	20	Daniels, Salvatore	1934	M	L	Temash - right A - Dulcis
554	*	30	Duncan, Bartimeus	1935	M	L	Temash - right A - Dulcis
555	*	60	Arzu, Maximo	1894	M	L	Temash - right A - Dulcis
555	*	100	Moore, Zadock	1925	M	L	Sundaywood Creek
556	*	20	Baily, Jeremiah	1945	M	L	Sundaywood Creek
557	*	125	Bourne, William Norman	1913	M	L	Sundaywood Creek
557	*	125	Bowen, W. A.	1930	M	L	Sundaywood Creek
558	*	50	Polonio, Eusebio	1908	M	L	Sundaywood Creek

#*		Size	Name	Year	F/M	L/G	Location
558	*	50	Polonio, Eusebio	1915	M	L	Sundaywood Creek
558	*	60	Polonio, Eusebio	1926	M	L	Sundaywood Creek
559	*	10	Polonio, Eusebio	1913	M	L	Sundaywood Creek
560	*	20	Plummer, Walter	1938	M	L	Sundaywood - Conejo Creek
561	*	20	Enriquez, Basilio	1938	M	L	Sundaywood - Conejo Creek
562	*	20	Bevans, Charles	1940	M	L	Sundaywood - Conejo Creek
563	*	10	Moore, Zadock	1930	M	L	Middle Creek
563	*	10	Moore, Zadock	1931	M	L	Middle Creek
563	*	20	Mejia, Simon	1916	M	L	Middle Creek
564	*	10	Zuniga, J.J.	1944	M	L	Middle Creek
565	*	70	Avilez, James J.	1932	M	L	Middle Creek
566	*	20	Andrade, Teodoro	1916	M	L	Middle Creek
566	*	20	Avilez, James J.	1939	M	L	Middle Creek
567	*	50	Avilez, John, Justo	1916	M	L	Middle Creek
568	*	10	Posar, Basilio	1933	M	L	Vairez Creek
569	*	25	Moore, Zadook	1939	M	L	Vairez Creek
569	*	25	Zuniga, J.J.	1941	M	L	Vairez Creek
570	*	25	Mencias, Miguel	1931	M	L	Vairez Creek
570	*	25	Heyer, Irving	1957	M	L	Vairez Creek
572	*	200	Mejia, Antonio	1916	M	L	Vairez Creek
572		25	Mejia, Simeona	1919	M	L	Vairez Creek
573	*	6	Avilez, Cipriano	1937	M	L	Vairez Creek

*Parcel numbers were not assigned by GOB for many parcels. Where * appears, the parcel number for this parcel is one we assigned, not assigned by GOB.

**Parcel numbers from the 1954 map are approximate locations on Plan 541.

***A 200 acre parcel was leased by a group. All parcels marked *** are part of this parcel. Parcel 279 is the SW corner.

G = Grant; L = Lease; P = Location ticket purchase

#*		Size	Name	Year	F/M	L/G	Location
574	*	25	Harvey, Robert	1939	M	L	Vairez Creek
575	*	25	Mejia, Simon	1919	M	L	Vairez Creek
575	*	15	Mencias, Miguel	1931	M	L	Vairez Creek
576	*	20	Cruz, Gumercinda	1940	F	L	Conejo Creek - left
577	*	50	Barrara, P.	1916	U	L	Conejo Creek - left
578	*	20	Gray, E. & Joseph	1932	M	L	Conejo Creek - left
579	*	50	Lambey	1929	U	L	Conejo Creek - left
581	*	50	Maquin	1921	M	L	Conejo Creek - left
581	*	25	Maquin, Jose	1941	M	L	Conejo Creek - right
582	*	25	Smith, Joseph	1937	M	L	Conejo Creek - right
582	*	25	Maquin, Jose	1941	M	G	Conejo Creek - right
583	*	25	Maquin, Jose	1941	M	G	Conejo Creek - right
584	*	25	Coy, Andrew	1923	M	L	Conejo Creek - right
585	*	20	Lambey, Philip	1937	M	L	Conejo Creek - right
586	*	25	Maquin, Joseph	1917	M	L	Conejo Creek - right
587	*	25	Maquin	1921	M	L	Conejo Creek - right
587	*	25	Selgado, Casimiro	1937	M	L	Conejo Creek - right
589	*	100	Rash, Juan	1921	M	L	Conejo Creek - right
590	*	20	Selgado, Victoriana	1937	F	L	Conejo Creek - right
591	*	10	Palacio, Augustine	1938	M	L	Conejo Creek - right
592	*	10	Palacio, Carlos	1931	M	L	Conejo Creek - right
593	*	10	Babe, Francis	1927	M	L	Conejo Creek - right

#*		Size	Name	Year	F/M	L/G	Location
595	*	10	Palacio, Peter	1937	M	L	Conejo Creek - right
595	*	10	Marin, Clarence	1941	M	L	Conejo Creek - right
596	*	30	Garcia, William E.	1937	M	L	Conejo Creek - right
597	*	20	Gutierrez, Dionicio	1955	M	L	Conejo Creek - right
598	*	20	Arzu, Benito	1936	M	L	Conejo Creek - right
598	*	20	Lopez, Beatrice	1937	F	L	Conejo Creek - right
599	*	2	Alvarez, Jerome	1936	M	L	Sarstoon River right
600	*	100	Cayetano, Corinne	1998	M	L	Midway
601	*	100	Cayetano, Fabian	1998	F	L	Midway
602	*	100	Cayetano, Joseph	1998	M	L	Midway
603	*	100	Cayetano, Sebastian	1998	M	L	Midway
604	*	20	Padawadilla, John	1893	M	L	Conejo Creek - unknown location
605	*	20	Borgas, Balbino	1893	M	L	Conejo Creek - unknown location
605	*	20	Borgos, Balbino	1898	M	L	Conejo Creek - unknown location
606	*	30	Ciriaco, Francisco	1894	M	L	unknown location
607	*	1370	Fielding, S.T.E.	1899	M	L	Temash River -right - unknown
608	*	50	Lucas, Joseph	1899	M	L	Black Creek, Moho River
609	*	10	Martinez, Liburio	1900	M	L	Sarstoon River, right
609	*	10	Perret, Edwin	1923	M	L	Sarstoon River, right
610	*	40	Ponce, Tiburcio	1901	M	L	Conejo Creek - unknown location
611	*	20	Hamilton, Alexander	1910	M	L	Temash River -left -lagunurugu
612	*	20	Pitts, Louisa	1910	M	L	Temash River -left -lagunurugu

#*		Size	Name	Year	F/M	L/G	Location
613	*	20	Gentle, Behaviour	1910	M	L	Temash River -right - unknown
614	*	20	Polonio, Pantaleon	1916	M	L	Sarstoon River, right
615	*	20	Gentle, William R.	1918	M	L	Temash River -right - unknown
616	*	20	Lambey, Severiano	1918	M	L	Temash River -right - unknown
617	*	20	Gonzalez, Celedonio	1929	M	L	Temash River -right - unknown
618	*	25	Thousand, David	1929	M	L	Temash River -left -lagunurugu
618	*	30	Noralez, Pedro	1934	M	L	Temash River -left -lagunurugu
619	*	50	Curshen, Stephen	1929	M	L	Boyo Creek-left -unknown
620	*	50	Brewster, Haziel E.	1929	F	L	Boyo Creek-left -unknown
621	*	50	Rosales, Valentine	1929	M	L	Temash River -right -above Red Bank
623	*	10	Loredo, Gregoria	1930	F	L	Barranco - northwest
624	*	10	Cayetano, Pascasio	1930	M	L	Barranco - northwest
625	*	5	Pascual, Juan	1931	M	L	Barranco - northwest
626	*	10	Zuniga, Viviano	1931	M	L	Barranco - northwest
627	*	50	Zuniga, Canuto	1933	M	L	Temash River -right - Largo
628	*	10	Andrade, Teodoro	1904	M	L	Temash River - unknown
629	*	30	Palacio, Catarino	1906	M	L	Boyo Creek - unknown

*Parcel numbers were not assigned by GOB for many parcels. Where * appears, the parcel number for this parcel is one we assigned, not assigned by GOB.

**Parcel numbers from the 1954 map are approximate locations on Plan 541.

***A 200 acre parcel was leased by a group. All parcels marked *** are part of this parcel. Parcel 279 is the SW corner.

G = Grant; L = Lease; P = Location ticket purchase

Table E8.1. Status of Lots 2000

2000	Occupant	House	Type	Roof	Floor	Septic	Lot
1A		house	B	Z	D		B
1		none					B
2		none					M
3	Urban Avila	house	B	Z	B	O	M
4	Ruben Palacio	house	B	Z	C	O	M
5		abandoned					M
6		none					M
7	R.C. Church	building	B	Z	B		B
7A	R.C. Church	none					B
8	R.C. Church	none					B
9	R.C. Church	none					M
10	R.C. Church	none					M
11	Credit Union		B	Z	B		M
12	Procopio Flores	house	B	Z	B	O	M
13		none					B
13A		none					M
14		none					H
15	Virgilia Lorenzo	house	C	Z	C	S	M
16		none					M
17	park						B
18	park						B
19		house	C	Z	C	S	M
20		none					B
21	Jacinta Palacio	house	C/B	Z	C		M
22	Felicita Zuniga	house	B	Z	B	O	M
23	rental	house	C/B	Z	C	O	M
24		none					M

Abbreviations: B=board, B/C=two houses (one board, one cement), C=cement, C/B=wainscot with cement partway up the walls, C/U=unfinished cement house, D=dirt floor, M=Mennonite house with vinyl-covered zinc siding, O=outhouse P=plycem, P/B=two houses (one board, one plycem), P/C=plysom and cement, S=septic, T=thatch, V=vinyl-covered zinc, Z=zinc.

Table E8.2. Status of Lots 2011

2011	Occupant	House	Type	Roof	Floor	Septic	Lot
1A		none					B
1	rental	house	C	V	C	S	M
2	Fermin Casimiro	house	B/C	Z	D		M
3	rental	house	M	V	B	S	M
4		house	B	Z	C	O	M
5	Dawn Dean	house	B	Z	B	O	B
6		none					B
7	church	building	C	V	C		B
7A	church						B
8	R.C. Church	none					B
9	R.C. Church	none					M
10	R.C. Church	none					M
11	Credit Union		B	Z	B		M
12	Procopio Flores	house	B	Z	D	O	M
13		none					B
13A		none					M
14		house	P	Z	C		M
15	Dale Gutierrez	house	C	Z	C	S	M
16	rental	house	M	V	B	S	M
17	park						B
18	park						B
19		house	C	C	C	S	M
20		none					B
21	Jacinta Palacio	house	C/B	Z	C	S	M
22	Dercy Sandoval	house	P/B	Z	P/C	O	M
23	George Coc	house	C/B	Z	C	O	M
24		none					M

Abbreviations: B=board, B/C=two houses (one board, one cement), C=cement, C/B=wainscot with cement partway up the walls, C/U=unfinished cement house, D=dirt floor, M=Mennonite house with vinyl-covered zinc siding, O=outhouse P=plycem, P/B=two houses (one board, one plycem), P/C=plysom and cement, S=septic, T=thatch, V=vinyl-covered zinc, Z=zinc.

2000	Occupant	House	Type	Roof	Floor	Septic	Lot
25		none					M
26	Cassava Co-op	building	B	Z	C		M
27	Community Centre	building	C	Z	C		M
28		none					M
29	Paula Nolberto	house	B	Z	C	O	M
30		abandoned					M
31		unfinished	C/U				B
32		unfinished	C/U				B
33		unfinished	C/U				B
34		none					B
35		none					M
36		none					M
37		none					M
38		none					H
39	Dionicia Marin	house	C	Z	C	S	M
40	Kevan Zuniga	house	W	Z	C	O	M
41		house	B	Z	B		B
42	Clotildo Zuniga	house	C	Z	C		M
43		none					H
44		none					H
45	Irma Gonzalez	house	C/B	Z	C	O	M
46		none					B
47	Melvinia Martinez	house	W	Z	C	O	M
48		unfinished	C/U	C	C		B
49		house	B	Z	B		M
50		house	C	Z	C	S	B
51		none					H
52		house	C	Z	C		M
53		unfinished	C/U	Z	C		M
54	Eduviges Ramirez	house	W	Z	B	S	M
55		none					H
56		none					M

2011	Occupant	House	Type	Roof	Floor	Septic	Lot
25		none					M
26	Cassava Co-op	building	B	Z	C		M
27	Community Centre	building	B	Z	C		M
28	SATIIM Centre	building	B	V	B	O	M
29	Paula Nolberto	house	B	Z	C	O	M
30		none					M
31		house	C	C	C		M
32							M
33		house	B/C	Z	C	O	B
34		none					B
35		house	B	Z	D		M
36		none					M
37		house	B	Z	C	O	M
38		none					M
39		house	C	Z	C	S	M
40	Joseph Gay	house	W	Z	C	O	M
41		abandoned	B	Z	B		B
42	Jean Zuniga	house	C	Z	C	O	M
43		none					B
44		none					B
45	Irma Gonzalez	house	C/B	Z	C	O	M
46		none					M
47	Mevinia Martinez	house	C	Z	C	O	M
48		unfinished	C	C	C	S	M
49	Chub	house	B	Z	B		M
50		house	C	V	C	S	M
51		none					B
52		house	C	Z	C	S	M
53		house	C	Z	C	O	M
54	Claude Zuniga	house	B	Z	B	S	M
55		none					B
56		house	B	Z	C		M

2000	Occupant	House	Type	Roof	Floor	Septic	Lot
57		none					M
58	Dabuyaba	building	W	T	D	O	M
59		none					B
60	Dabuyaba	building	W	T	D	O	M
61		none					H
62		none					H
63		none					B
64	Bartolo Polinio	house	B	Z	B	O	M
65		none					M
66		none					M
67		unfinished	C/U	C	C		M
68	Dispensary	none					B
69	Dispensary	building	C	Z	C	S	B
70		house	C/B	V	C	S	M
71	Irene Gibbons	house	C	C	C	S	M
72		unfinished	C/U	Z	C		B
73		none					M
74		none					M
75		none					B
76	Vickie Nolberto	house	C	Z	C	O	M
77		house	B	Z	B		M
78	Paul Palacio	house	B	Z	B	O	M
79	Antonia Palacio	house	W	T	C	O	M
80	Alvin Loredo	house	W	T	C	O	M
81	Lenard Petillo	house	C/B	Z	C/B	S	M
82	Guest House	building	B	T	C	S	B
83		none					B
84		house	B	Z	B	O	M
85		unfinished	C/U				M
86		none					B
87	Elorine Nunez	house	B	Z	B	O	M
88		house	W	T	C		M

2011	Occupant	House	Type	Roof	Floor	Septic	Lot
57		none					M
58	Dabuyaba	building	W	T	D	O	M
59		none					B
60	Dabuyaba	building	W	T	C	O	M
61		none					M
62		none					H
63		none					M
64	Bartolo Polinio	house	RV	V	D	O	M
65	Judy Lumb	house	M	V	B	S	M
66		house	B	V	B	O	M
67		house	C	C	C		M
68	Dispensary	none					B
69	Dispensary	building	C	Z	C	S	B
70		house	C	V	C	S	M
71	Irene Gibbons	house	C	C	C	S	M
72		none					M
73		house	C	V	C	S	M
74		unfinished	C/U				B
75		house	B	Z	C		M
76	Jovita Casimiro	house	C	Z	C	O	B
77		house	C	C	C	S	M
78	Paul Palacio	house	B	Z	B	O	M
79	Jacinta Palacio	house	B	Z	B	O	M
80	Alvin Loredo	house	B	V	C	O	M
81	Sheridan Petillo	house	C	V	C	S	M
82	Guest House	building	B	T	C	S	B
83	Amanda Zuniga	bar bamboo		T	D		M
84		abandoned	B	Z	B		M
85		unfinshed	C/U				M
86	Abraham Zuniga	house	B	Z	C	O	M
87	Elorine Nunez	house	B	Z	B	O	M
88		car frame					M

2000	Occupant	House	Type	Roof	Floor	Septic	Lot
89	Abraham Zuniga	house	B	Z	C	O	M
90	Police Station		C	Z	C	S	M
91	Luisa Sanchez	house	B	Z	C	O	M
92		house	W	T	D		B
93	Gladys Lino	house	B	Z	C		M
94		none					B
95		none					M
96	P Gregorio	house	C/B	Z	C		M
97	Delcy Tuttle	house	W	Z	B	O	M
98		house	C	Z	C	S	B
99	Anacleta Nolberto	house	B	Z	C		M
100		house	W	Z	B		M
101		none					H
102	Mare Zuniga	house	W	Z	D	O	M
103		unfinished	C/U		C		H
104		none					H
105		none					H
106	C Martinez	house	W	T	D		H
107		none					H
108		none					H
109		none					B
110		none					M
111	Antonio Ogaldez	house	C	Z	C	S	M
112	Pia Magdalena	house	C	Z	C	S	M
113	LeslieColon	house	B	Z	C		M
114		none					H
115		none					H

2011	Occupant	House	Type	Roof	Floor	Septic	Lot
89		fence pillars					M
90	Police Station		C	Z	C	S	M
91	Luisa Sanchez	house	B	Z	C	O	M
92		none					B
93	Felicita Zuniga	house	B	Z	C	O	M
94		none					M
95		none					M
96	P Gregorio	house	C/B	Z	C		M
97	Carlson Tuttle	house	B	Z/V	B/P	O	M
98		house	C	Z	C	S	M
99		house	B	Z	C	S	M
100		house	B	Z	B		M
101		none					H
102		abandoned	W	Z	D		B
103		unfinished	C/U		C		B
104		shed					B
105		none					M
106	Lynn Nicholas	house	B	Z	D	O	B
107		none					M
108		none					M
109		none					H
110							M
111	Antonio Ogaldez	house	C	V	C	S	M
112	Pia Magdalena	house	C	Z	C	S	M
113	Leslie Colon	house	B	Z	C		M
114		none					M
115		none					H

Abbreviations: B=board, B/C=two houses (one board, one cement), C=cement, C/B=wainscot with cement partway up the walls, C/U=unfinished cement house, D=dirt floor, M=Mennonite house with vinyl-covered zinc siding, O=outhouse P=plysom, P/B=two houses (one board, one plyscem), P/C=plycem and cement, S=septic, T=thatch, V=vinyl-covered zinc, Z=zinc.

2000	Occupant	House	Type	Roof	Floor	Septic	Lot
116		none					H
117		none					H
118		none					H
119		none					H
120		none					M
121	Maria Rash	house	B	T	B	O	M
122		none					H
123		none					M
124	John Rodriguez	house	B	Z	B	O	M
125		none					B
126		none					B
127		none					M
128		none					H
129		none					H
130	Raymond Valencio	house	C	Z	C	S	M
131		unfinished	C/U				M
132		house	B	Z	B		B
133		none					B
134		none					H
135		none					H
136	L Norberto	house	W	T	D		M
137		none					H
138	Mary Casimiro	house	W	Z	B	O	M
139		none					B
140		none					M
141		none					M
142		house	B	Z	C	S	M
143		none					M
144	Leticia Ramirez	house	W	Z	D	O	M
145		none					B
146		none					M
147		none					M
148		none					M

2011	Occupant	House	Type	Roof	Floor	Septic	Lot
116		none					H
117		house	B	Z	B	S	M
118		none					M
119		none					H
120		none					M
121	Maria Rash	house	B	T	B	O	M
122		none					H
123		none					B
124	John Rodriguez	house	B	Z	B	O	M
125		none					M
126		house	B	Z	D	O	M
127		sheep shed		Z			M
128							H
129		house	C	Z	C	S	M
130	Raymond Valencio	house	C	Z	C	S	M
131		unfinished	C/U				H
132		unfinished	C/U				M
133							M
134		sheep shed	C				M
135		none					B
136		unfinished	C/U				M
137		none					B
138	Mary Casimiro	house	P/B	Z	B	O	M
139	Ignacia Reyes	house	P	Z	B	S	M
140		none					M
141		none					M
142		house	C	V	C	S	M
143		none					M
144	Ramirez	house	B	Z	D	O	M
145		house	B	T	D	O	M
146		house	B/C	V	C	S	M
147		none					M
148		none					M

2000	Occupant	House	Type	Roof	Floor	Septic	Lot
149		house	C	Z	C	S	M
150		none					M
151		none					M
152	Hipolito Martinez	house	C	Z	C	S	M
153		none					M
154		none					B
155		none					H
156		none					H
157		none					H
158		none					H
159		none					H
160		none					H
161		none					H
162		none					H
163		none					H
164		none					H
165		none					H
166		none					H
167		none					H
168	Alfred Arzu	house	B	Z	B		M
169		none					H
170		none					H
171		none					H
172		none					H
173		none					H

2011	Occupant	House	Type	Roof	Floor	Septic	Lot
149		house	C	V	C	S	M
150		unfinished	C/U				M
151		none					M
152	Viola Martinez	house	C	Z	C	S	M
153		none					M
154		none					B
155		none					H
156		none					H
157		none					H
158		none					H
159	Medina	house	B	T	B	O	M
160		none					H
161		none					H
162		none					H
163		none					H
164		none					H
165		none					H
166		none					H
167		none					H
168		abandoned	B	Z	B		M
169		none					H
170		none					H
171		none					H
172		none					H
173		none					H

Abbreviations: B=board, B/C=two houses (one board, one cement), C=cement, C/B=wainscot with cement partway up the walls, C/U=unfinished cement house, D=dirt floor, M=Mennonite house with vinyl-covered zinc siding, O=outhouse P=plysom, P/B=two houses (one board, one plycem), P/C=plycem and cement, S=septic, T=thatch, V=vinyl-covered zinc, Z=zinc.

2000	Occupant	House	Type	Roof	Floor	Septic	Lot
*							
*	Victor Nicholas	house					
*	Coc	house					
*	Teacher house	house					
*	School	building	B	Z	B	O	M
*							B
*	Amanda Zuniga	house	B	Z	B	OM	
*							
*		house	B	Z	B	O	
*	Victor Alvarez	house	B	Z	C	O	
*							
*							

*Lots that have no number.

2011	Occupant	House	Type	Roof	Floor	Septic	Lot
*	Ivors	house	B	Z	C		B
*	Colin Nicholas	house	C	C	C	S	M
*	Joseph Palacio	house	C	V	C	S	M
*	Allison	house	C	Z	C		M
*	School	abandoned	B	Z	B	O	M
*	New School	building	C	C/V	C	S	M
*	Amanda Zuniga	house	B	Z	B	O	M
*	Jason Sandoval	house	B	Z	B		M
*	Laselle	house	B	Z	D	O	M
*		house	B	Z	C	O	M
*	rental	house	C	C	C	S	M
*	Angie Nicholas	house	C	C	C	S	M

*Lots that have no number.

Index